THE DARKNESS®

ACCURSED
VOLUME 1

D1318783

WRITTEN BY:
PHIL HESTER

THE DARKNESS CREATED BY:
MARC SILVESTRI, GARTH ENNIS
AND DAVID WOHL

published by
Top Cow Productions, Inc.
Los Angeles

THE DARKNESS
ACCURSED VOLUME 1

writer: **Phil Hester**
penciler: **Michael Broussard**
inker: **Ryan Winn**
colors: **Matt Milla** issues #1-4
Sheldon Mitchell issues #5-6
letters: **Troy Peteri**

issue #3 flashback sequence: by: **Dale Keown**
and **Joe Weems**

Jackie's caption font by: **Dave Lanphear**

M **MATURE AUDIENCE**
GRAPHIC CONTENT
SOME MATERIAL MAY NOT
BE SUITABLE FOR CHILDREN

For Top Cow Productions, Inc.:
Marc Silvestri - Chief Executive Officer
Matt Hawkins - President and Chief Operating Officer
Filip Sablik - Publisher
Rob Levin - VP - Editorial
Mel Caylo - VP - Marketing & Sales
Chaz Riggs - Graphic Design
Phil Smith - Managing Editor
Alyssa Phung - Controller
Adrian Nicita - Webmaster
Scott Newman - Production Lead
Jennifer Chow - Production Assistant

for *image* comics
publisher:
Eric Stephenson

888-COMIC-BOOK
888-266-4266

to find the comic shop
nearest you call:
1-888-COMICBOOK

Want more info? check out:
www.topcow.com and *www.topcowstore.com*
for news and exclusive Top Cow merchandise!

For this edition Cover art by:
Michael Broussard,
Steve Firchow

For this edition
Book Design and Layout by:
Phil Smith

The Darkness: Accursed volume 1 Trade Paperback
January 2009. FIRST PRINTING. Book Market Edition. ISBN: 978-1-58240-958-0

TABLE OF CONTENTS

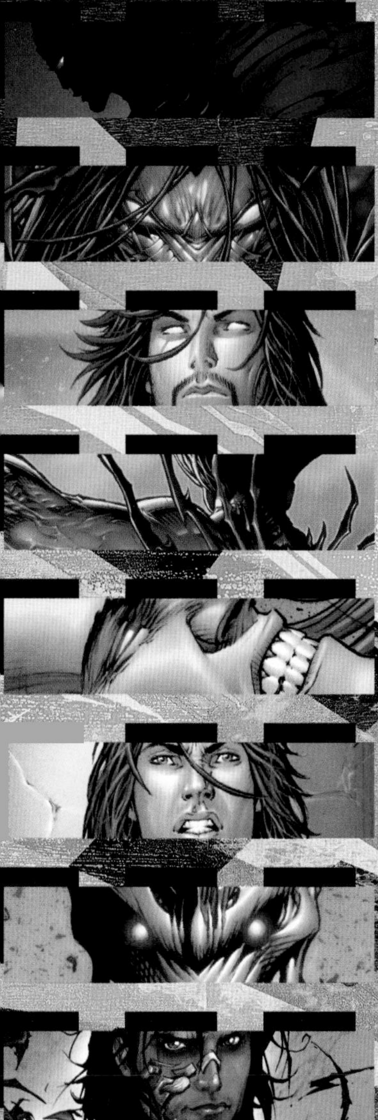

IN+R⊕DUC+I⊕N

Phil Hester has guts.

And balls. Don't forget his balls.

How do I know? It's not because I've ever seen them, thank God. It's because it takes a little of each to write a story as ruthless and brutally perverse as the one you're now holding in your hands.

Jackie Estacado has never been a particularly nice guy. In fact, he's long been one of the most wickedly remorseless mass murderers and joyfully perverse horndogs you'll find headlining a mainstream comic series. Call me crazy, but that's exactly what I've always liked about the guy. For a writer, those are the characters that are always the most fun to write. The kinds of guys you'd never want to meet in real life, but love being able to pal around with in the world of make-believe. The kind of dude who'd come to your house and turn you into a steaming pile of red mush with a head sticking out of it, then piss on the head, fuck your sister and roll out, all because you owed him twenty bucks. Later he might feel bad about it for a while, but that wouldn't stop him from doing it again if he had to.

Phil Hester obviously delights in writing about tortured bastards like Jackie Estacado, and judging from the six issues collected in this trade, he's quite adept at it, too. Within these pages, Hester answers the question, what does a superpowered hitman do when he has the chance to recreate a whole country any way he likes? Why, he turns the people into addicts and sets himself up as the mother of all kingpins, generating a drug from his own flesh that makes heroin look like Flintstones chewables, that's what he does. And on top of that, we also find out what a guy who can't get laid lest he die does to get his rocks off when he's really lonely. He creates the world's creepiest sex toy, a beautiful woman made entirely from the same eerie goop Estacado uses to kill people. And in the end, Estacado proves he's so manly and viral that he can even get a blow-up doll knocked up.

And just wait'll you meet the bouncing baby boy.

In addition to a particularly grisly childbirth scene (as if childbirth wasn't already grisly enough), artist Michael Broussard gives us some gorgeously rendered moments, like Estacado's colossal battle against a team of Apache helicopters and not one but two of my all-time favorite images featuring a legless, eviscerated torso. Being able to draw unspoiled intestines is undoubtedly a must if you're going to be penciller on THE DARKNESS, and Broussard handles it with great aplomb, securing a spot for himself among Top Cow's long list of dynamic artists.

So what more do you need to hear from me to get you to buy this book already? I already told you about the creepy love slave and the sex and drugs and spilled intestines, right? Well, if that doesn't whet your appetite, then maybe you'd be better suited seeking out one of those books where everybody wears neon spandex and nobody ever stays dead. Where the good guys are always good and the bad guys are always bad.

But if you're like me and enjoy your comics to have heaping helpings of moral ambiguity and your heroes to be tortured and flawed and a little bit dangerous, then look no further, friend. If you enjoy good old-fashioned ass-kicking action and a bit of evisceration now and then, then come on in and let Phil Hester and Michael Broussard show you their guts.

And their balls.

And probably a few other things as well.

--Jason Aaron
October 2008

Jason Aaron is the Eisner-nominated creator of *SCALPED* and *THE OTHER SIDE* for Vertigo Comics and writer on *WOLVERINE, GHOST RIDER* and *BLACK PANTHER* for Marvel. He lives in Kansas City and wants everyone to know he has never seen Phil Hester's balls.

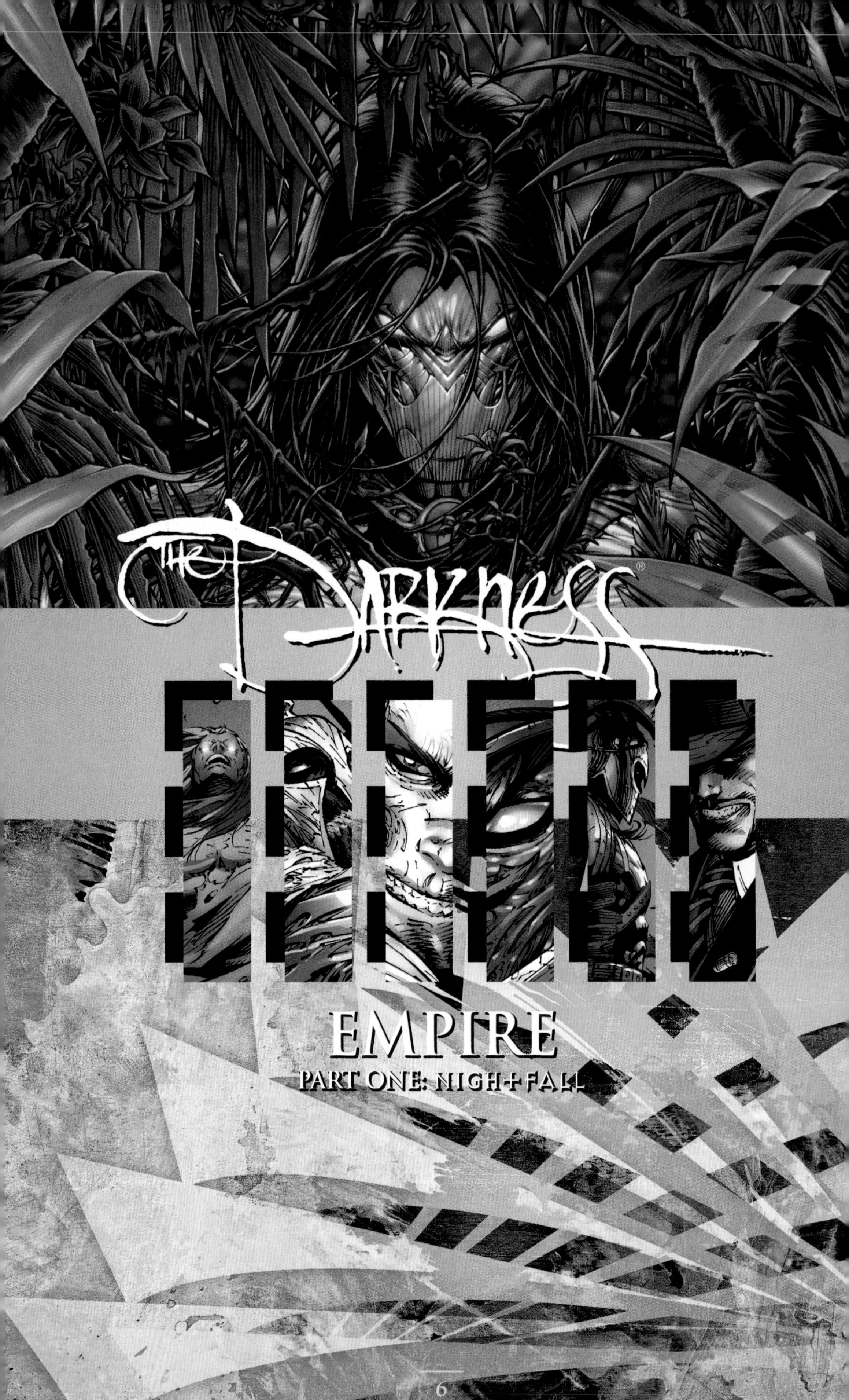
THE DARKNESS®
EMPIRE
PART ONE: NIGHTFALL

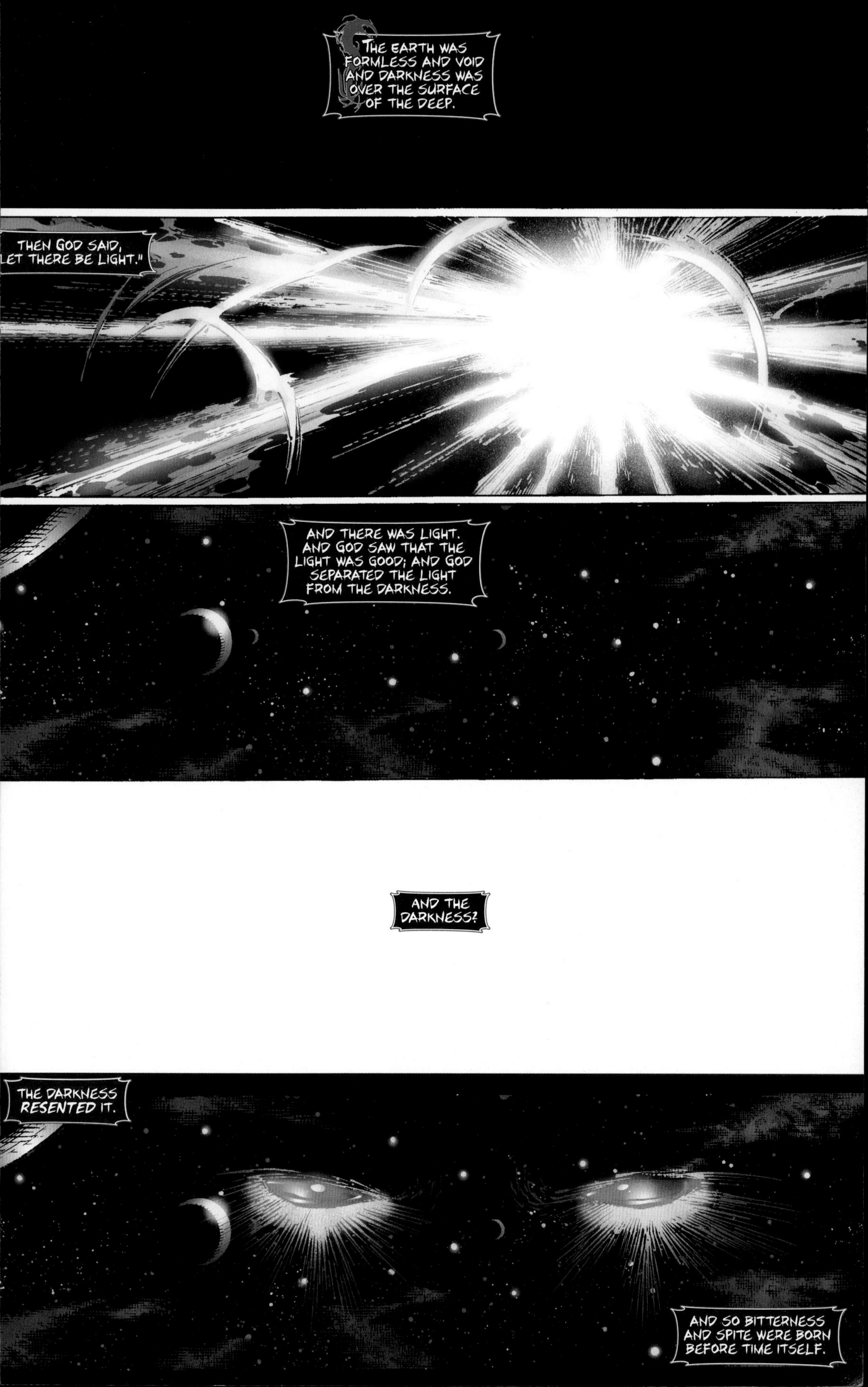
THE EARTH WAS FORMLESS AND VOID AND DARKNESS WAS OVER THE SURFACE OF THE DEEP.
THEN GOD SAID, "LET THERE BE LIGHT."
AND THERE WAS LIGHT. AND GOD SAW THAT THE LIGHT WAS GOOD; AND GOD SEPARATED THE LIGHT FROM THE DARKNESS.
AND THE DARKNESS?
THE DARKNESS RESENTED IT.
AND SO BITTERNESS AND SPITE WERE BORN BEFORE TIME ITSELF.

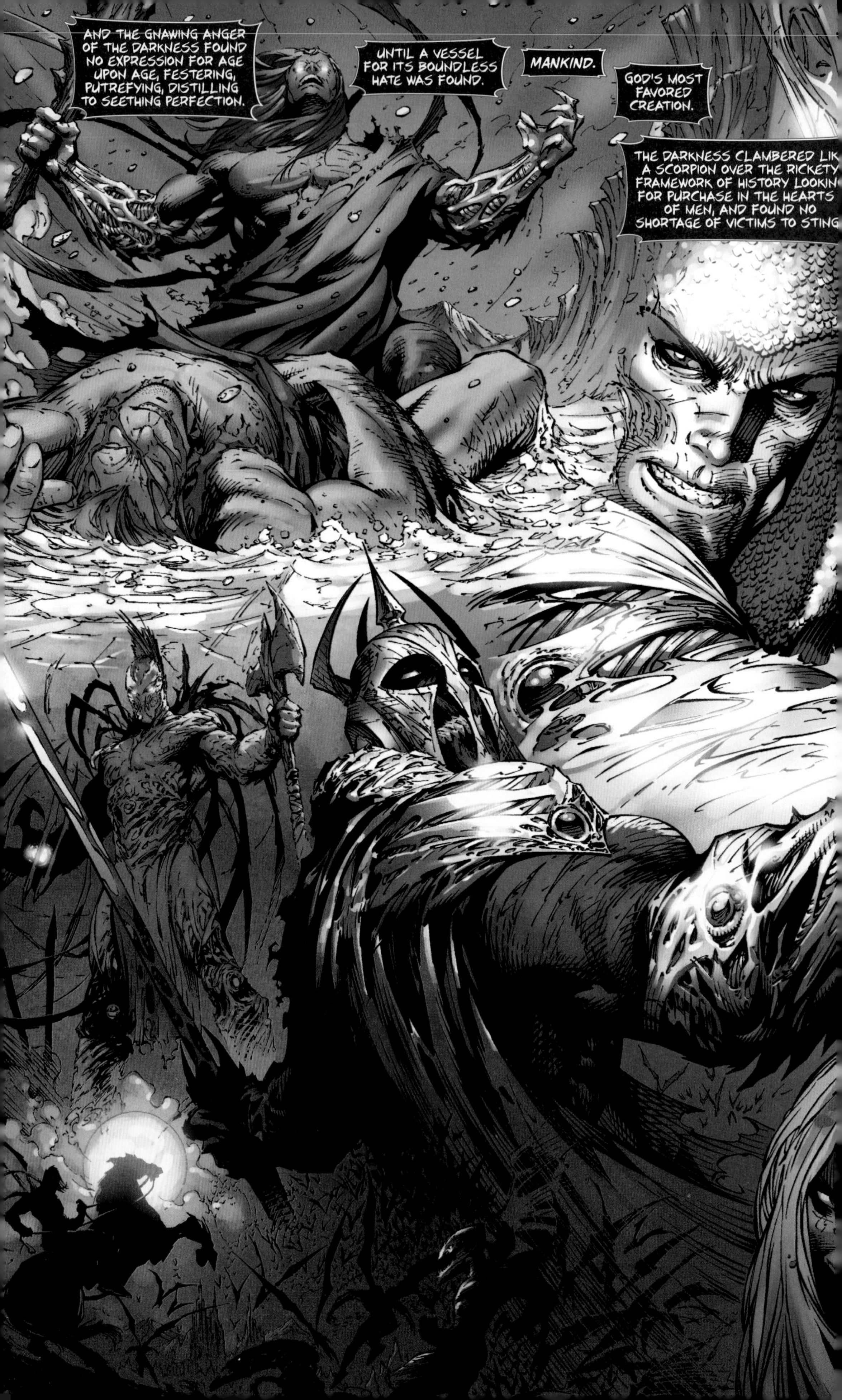
AND THE GNAWING ANGER OF THE DARKNESS FOUND NO EXPRESSION FOR AGE UPON AGE, FESTERING, PUTREFYING, DISTILLING TO SEETHING PERFECTION.
UNTIL A VESSEL FOR ITS BOUNDLESS HATE WAS FOUND.
MANKIND.
GOD'S MOST FAVORED CREATION.
THE DARKNESS CLAMBERED LIK A SCORPION OVER THE RICKETY FRAMEWORK OF HISTORY LOOKIN FOR PURCHASE IN THE HEARTS OF MEN, AND FOUND NO SHORTAGE OF VICTIMS TO STING

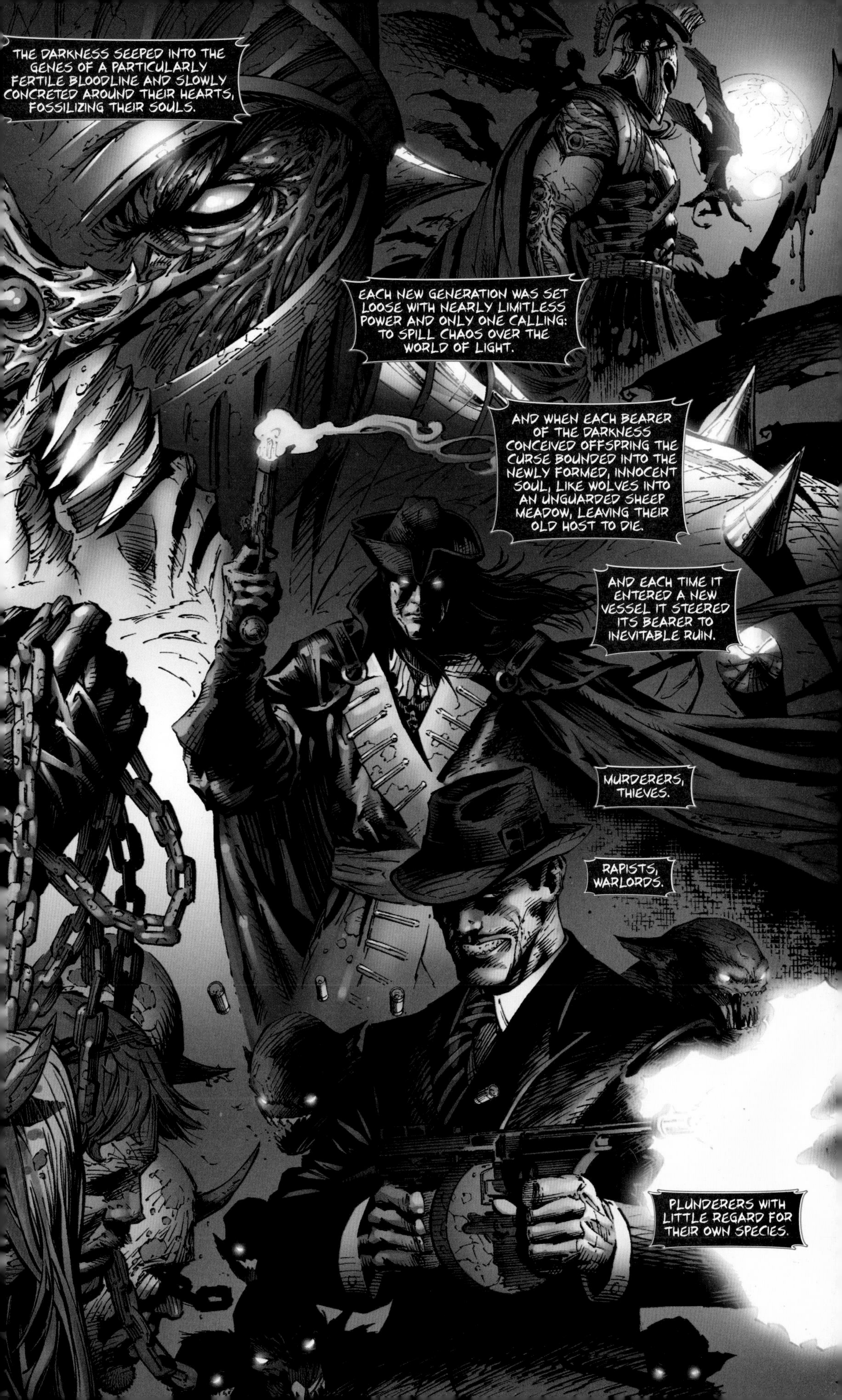
THE DARKNESS SEEPED INTO THE GENES OF A PARTICULARLY FERTILE BLOODLINE AND SLOWLY CONCRETED AROUND THEIR HEARTS, FOSSILIZING THEIR SOULS.
EACH NEW GENERATION WAS SET LOOSE WITH NEARLY LIMITLESS POWER AND ONLY ONE CALLING: TO SPILL CHAOS OVER THE WORLD OF LIGHT.
AND WHEN EACH BEARER OF THE DARKNESS CONCEIVED OFFSPRING THE CURSE BOUNDED INTO THE NEWLY FORMED, INNOCENT SOUL, LIKE WOLVES INTO AN UNGUARDED SHEEP MEADOW, LEAVING THEIR OLD HOST TO DIE.
AND EACH TIME IT ENTERED A NEW VESSEL IT STEERED ITS BEARER TO INEVITABLE RUIN.
MURDERERS, THIEVES.
RAPISTS, WARLORDS.
PLUNDERERS WITH LITTLE REGARD FOR THEIR OWN SPECIES.

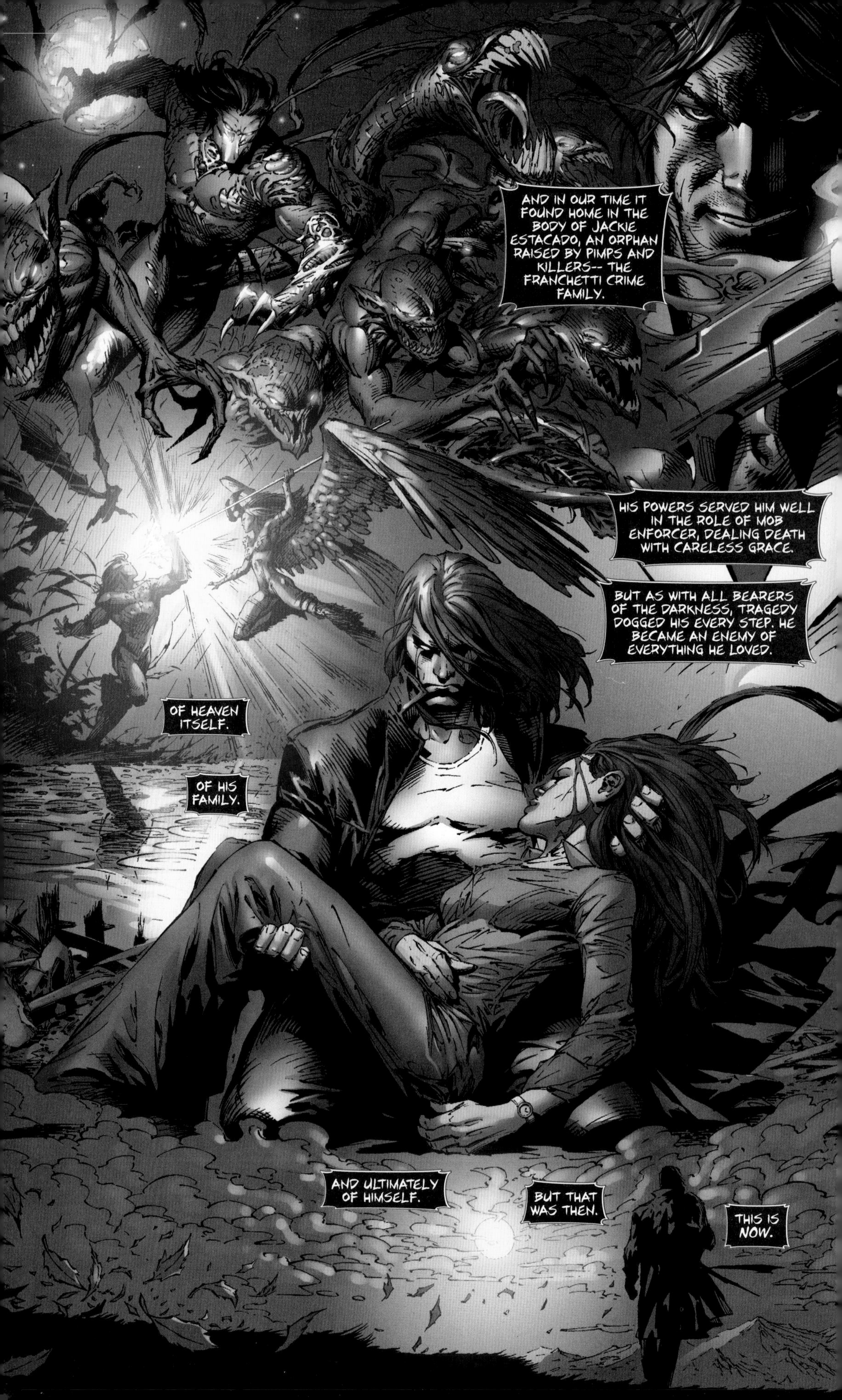
AND IN OUR TIME IT FOUND HOME IN THE BODY OF JACKIE ESTACADO, AN ORPHAN RAISED BY PIMPS AND KILLERS-- THE FRANCHETTI CRIME FAMILY.
HIS POWERS SERVED HIM WELL IN THE ROLE OF MOB ENFORCER, DEALING DEATH WITH CARELESS GRACE.
BUT AS WITH ALL BEARERS OF THE DARKNESS, TRAGEDY DOGGED HIS EVERY STEP. HE BECAME AN ENEMY OF EVERYTHING HE LOVED.
OF HEAVEN ITSELF.
OF HIS FAMILY.
AND ULTIMATELY OF HIMSELF.
BUT THAT WAS THEN.
THIS IS NOW.

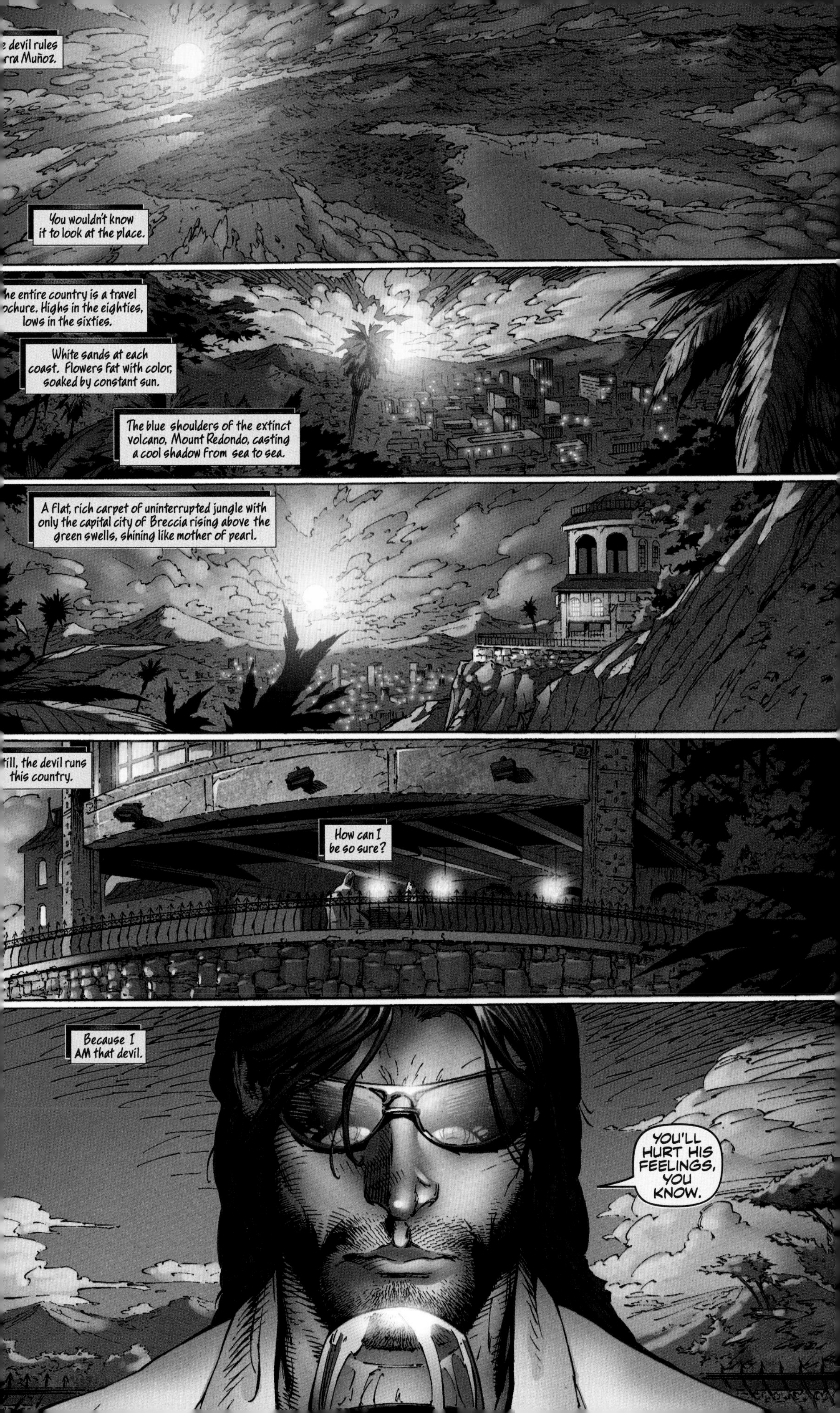
e devil rules
rra Muñoz.
You wouldn't know it to look at the place.
he entire country is a travel ochure. Highs in the eighties, lows in the sixties.
White sands at each coast. Flowers fat with color, soaked by constant sun.
The blue shoulders of the extinct volcano, Mount Redondo, casting a cool shadow from sea to sea.
A flat, rich carpet of uninterrupted jungle with only the capital city of Breccia rising above the green swells, shining like mother of pearl.
till, the devil runs this country.
How can I be so sure?
Because I AM that devil.
YOU'LL HURT HIS FEELINGS, YOU KNOW.

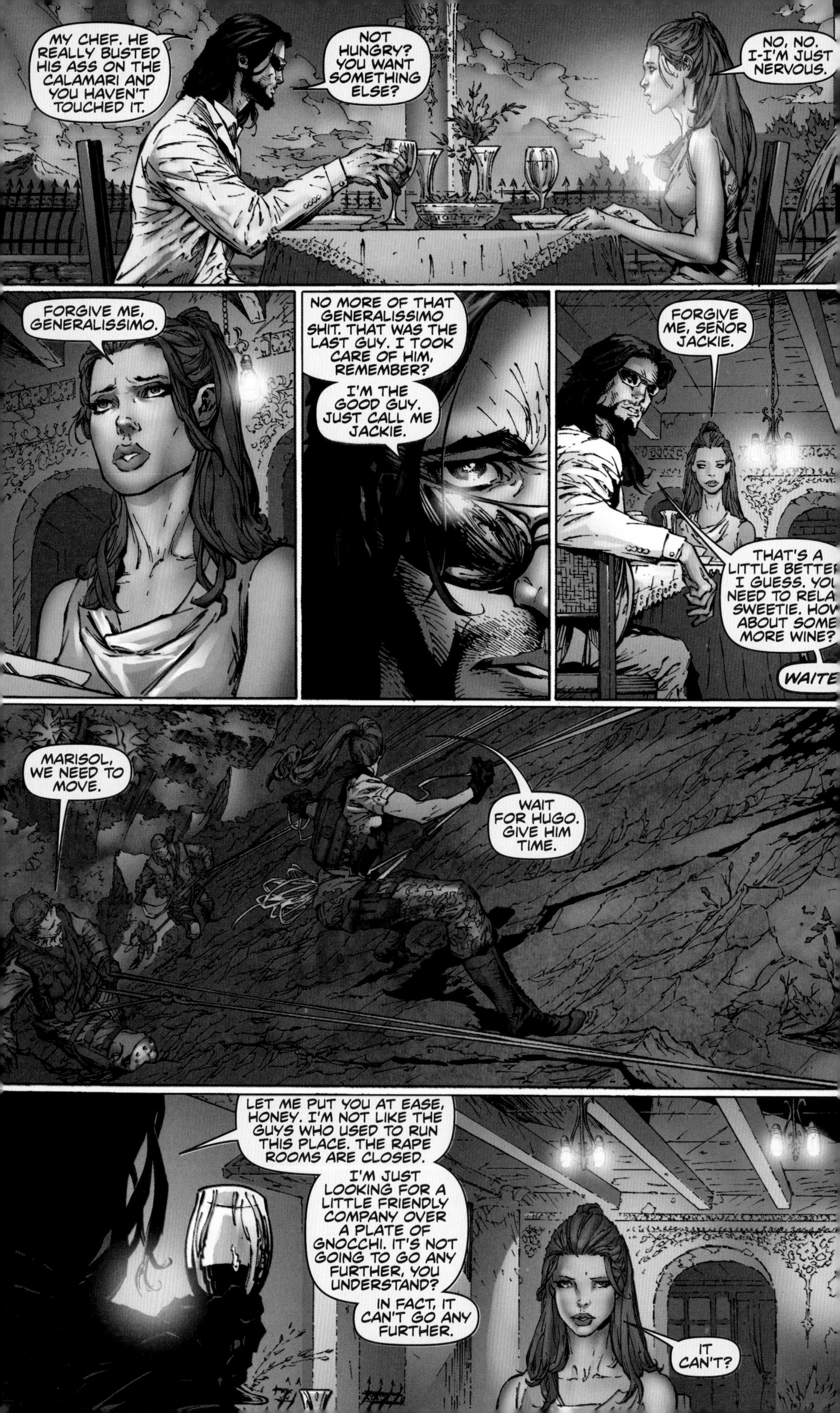
MY CHEF. HE REALLY BUSTED HIS ASS ON THE CALAMARI AND YOU HAVEN'T TOUCHED IT.
NOT HUNGRY? YOU WANT SOMETHING ELSE?
NO, NO. I-I'M JUST NERVOUS.
FORGIVE ME, GENERALISSIMO.
NO MORE OF THAT GENERALISSIMO SHIT. THAT WAS THE LAST GUY. I TOOK CARE OF HIM, REMEMBER?
I'M THE GOOD GUY. JUST CALL ME JACKIE.
FORGIVE ME, SEÑOR JACKIE.
THAT'S A LITTLE BETTER I GUESS. YOU NEED TO RELAX SWEETIE. HOW ABOUT SOME MORE WINE?
WAITE
MARISOL, WE NEED TO MOVE.
WAIT FOR HUGO. GIVE HIM TIME.
LET ME PUT YOU AT EASE, HONEY. I'M NOT LIKE THE GUYS WHO USED TO RUN THIS PLACE. THE RAPE ROOMS ARE CLOSED.
I'M JUST LOOKING FOR A LITTLE FRIENDLY COMPANY OVER A PLATE OF GNOCCHI. IT'S NOT GOING TO GO ANY FURTHER, YOU UNDERSTAND?
IN FACT, IT CAN'T GO ANY FURTHER.
IT CAN'T?

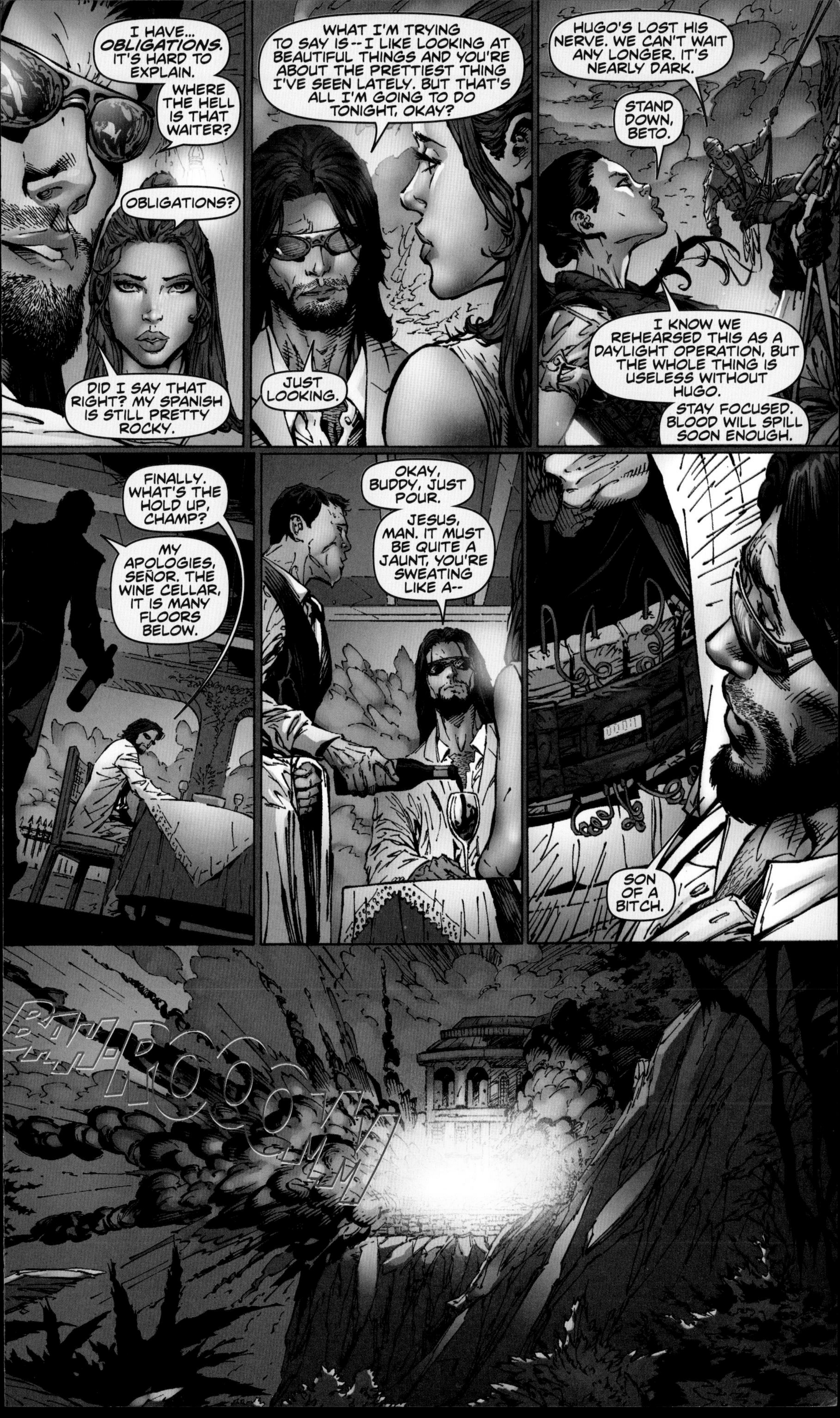
I HAVE... OBLIGATIONS. IT'S HARD TO EXPLAIN.
WHERE THE HELL IS THAT WAITER?
OBLIGATIONS?
DID I SAY THAT RIGHT? MY SPANISH IS STILL PRETTY ROCKY.
WHAT I'M TRYING TO SAY IS--I LIKE LOOKING AT BEAUTIFUL THINGS AND YOU'RE ABOUT THE PRETTIEST THING I'VE SEEN LATELY. BUT THAT'S ALL I'M GOING TO DO TONIGHT, OKAY?
JUST LOOKING.
HUGO'S LOST HIS NERVE. WE CAN'T WAIT ANY LONGER. IT'S NEARLY DARK.
STAND DOWN, BETO.
I KNOW WE REHEARSED THIS AS A DAYLIGHT OPERATION, BUT THE WHOLE THING IS USELESS WITHOUT HUGO.
STAY FOCUSED. BLOOD WILL SPILL SOON ENOUGH.
FINALLY. WHAT'S THE HOLD UP, CHAMP?
MY APOLOGIES, SEÑOR. THE WINE CELLAR, IT IS MANY FLOORS BELOW.
OKAY, BUDDY, JUST POUR.
JESUS, MAN. IT MUST BE QUITE A JAUNT, YOU'RE SWEATING LIKE A--
SON OF A BITCH.
BAHROOOOM

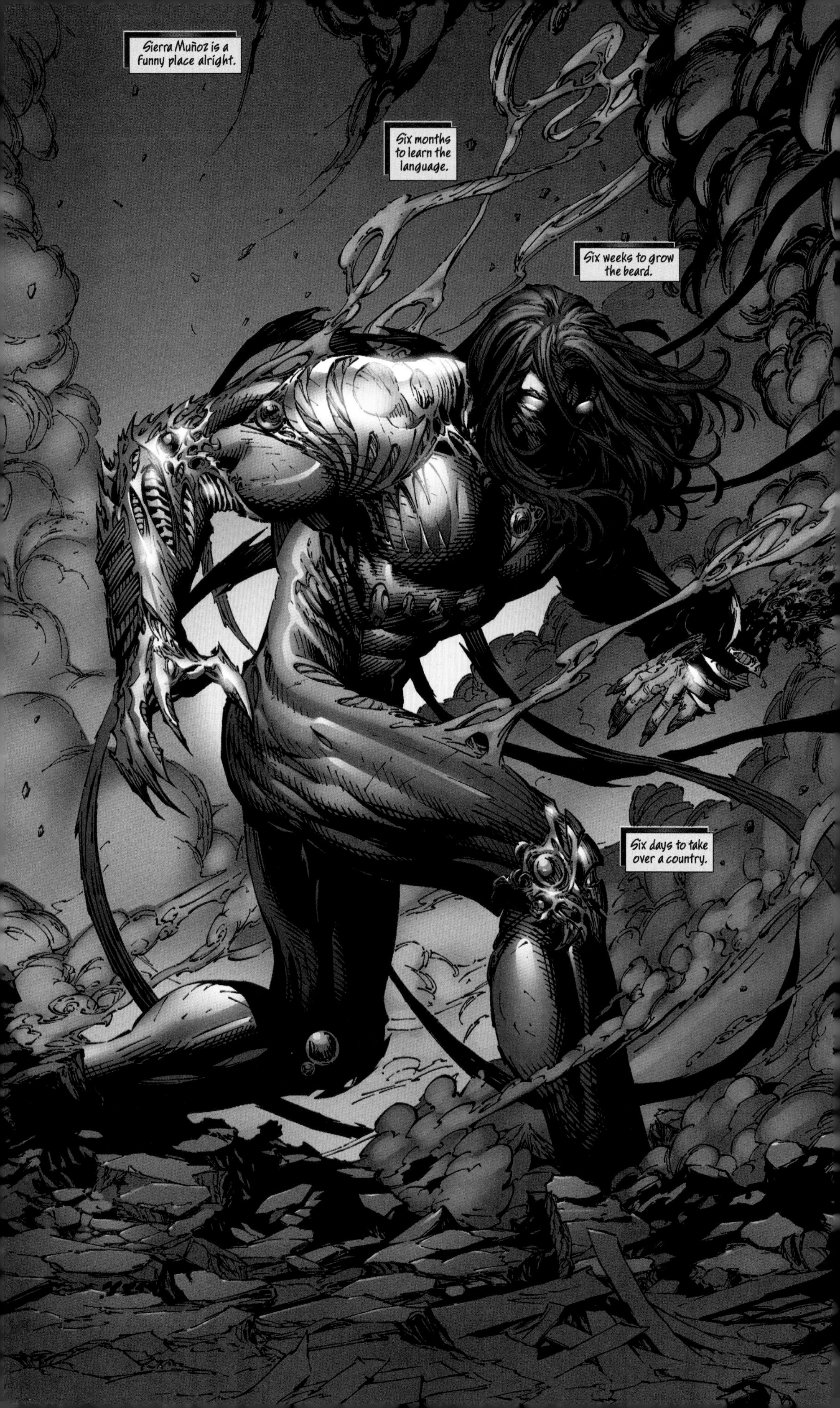

Sierra Muñoz is a funny place alright.
Six months to learn the language.
Six weeks to grow the beard.
Six days to take over a country.

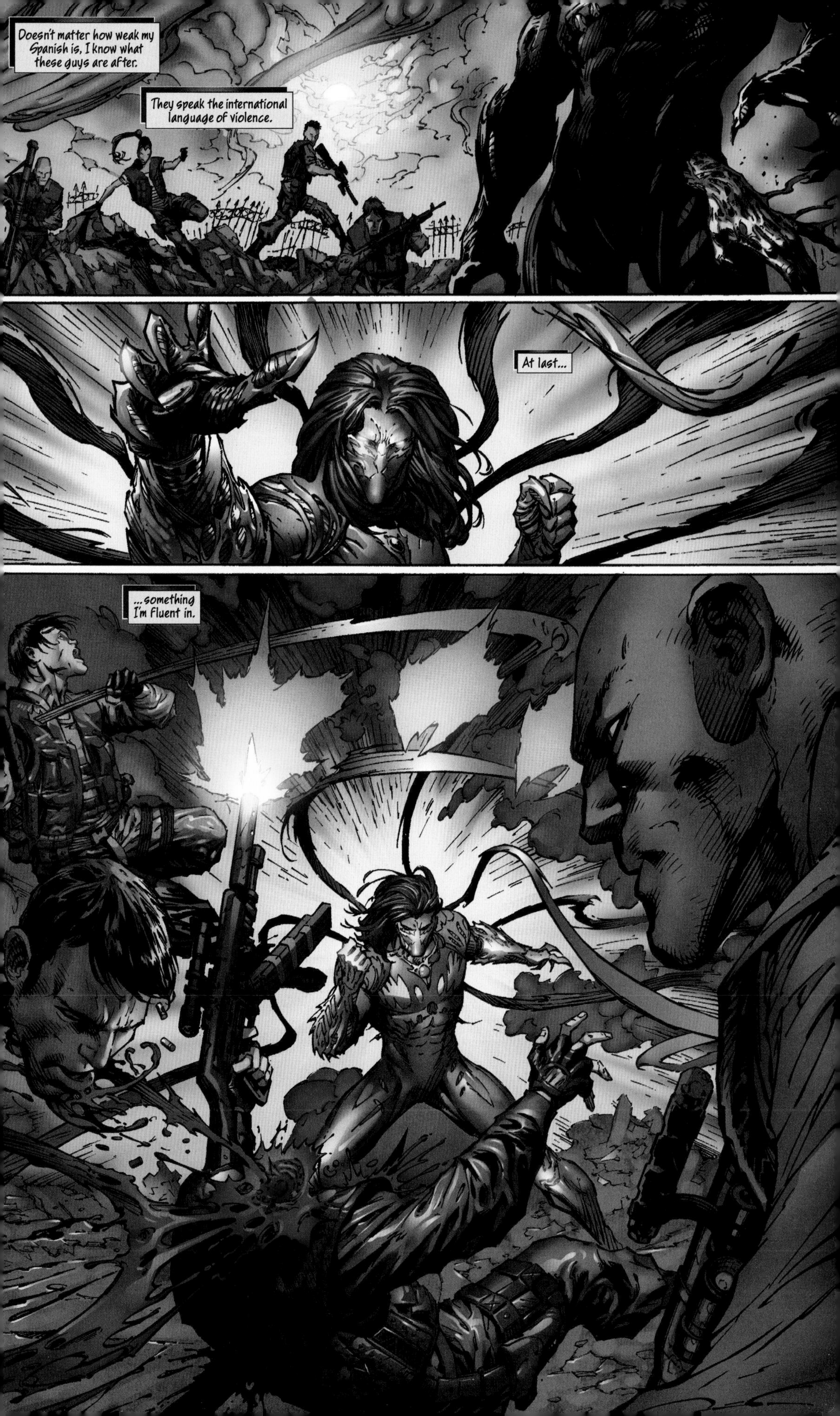
Doesn't matter how weak my Spanish is, I know what these guys are after.
They speak the international language of violence.
At last...
...something I'm fluent in.

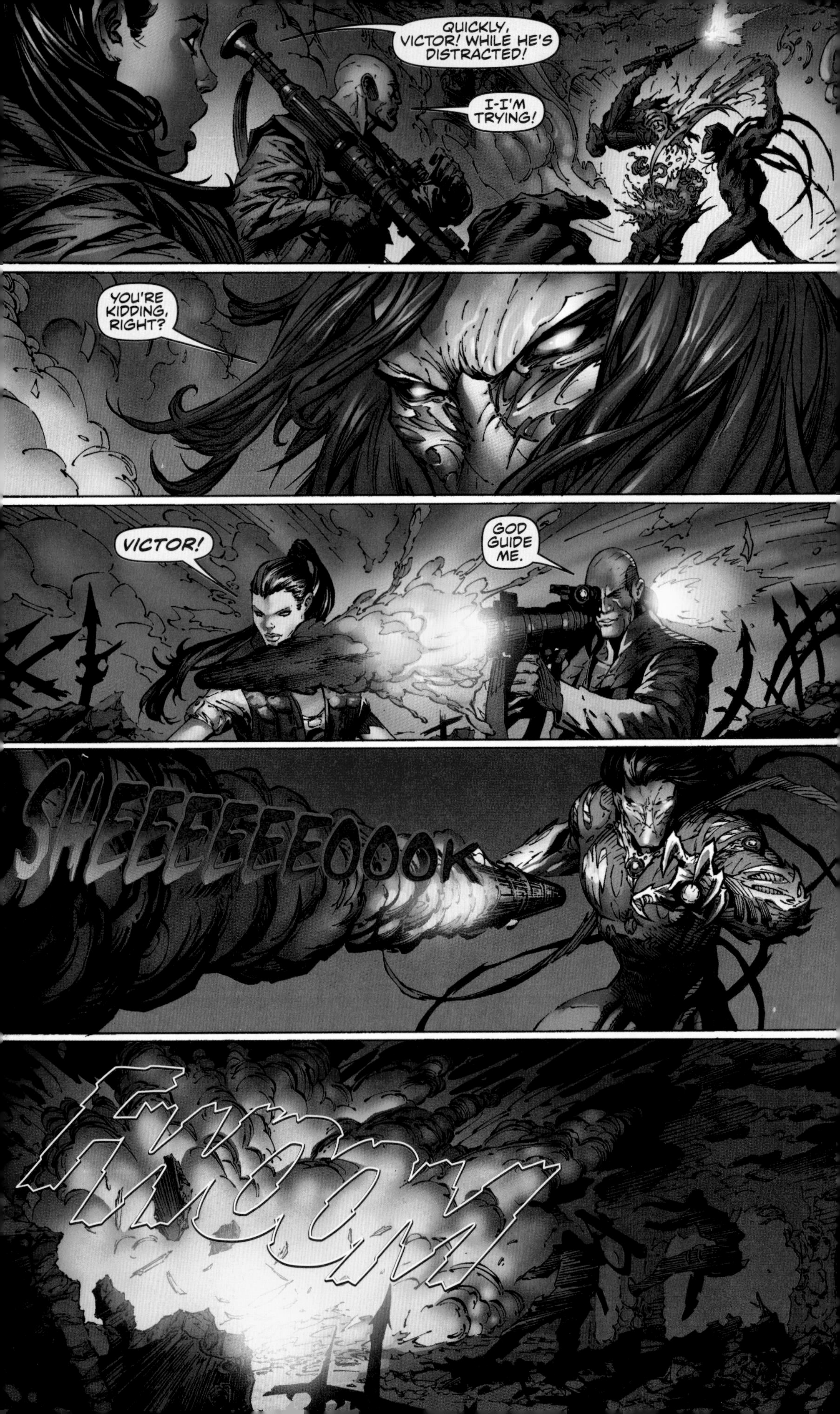
QUICKLY, VICTOR! WHILE HE'S DISTRACTED!
I-I'M TRYING!
YOU'RE KIDDING, RIGHT?
VICTOR!
GOD GUIDE ME.
SHEEEEEEEOOOOK

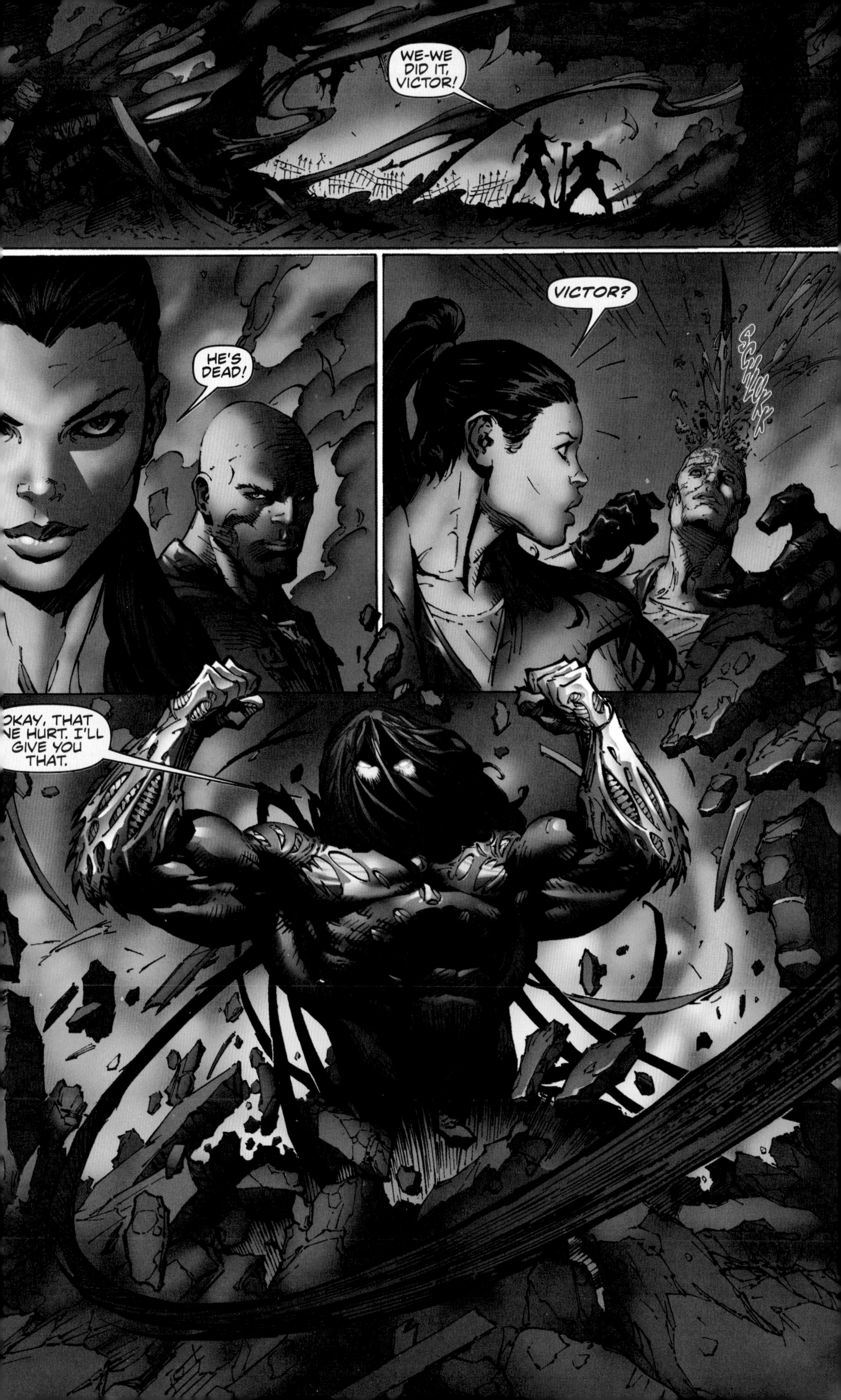
WE-WE DID IT, VICTOR!
HE'S DEAD!
VICTOR?
SCHLUKK
OKAY, THAT NE HURT. I'LL GIVE YOU THAT.

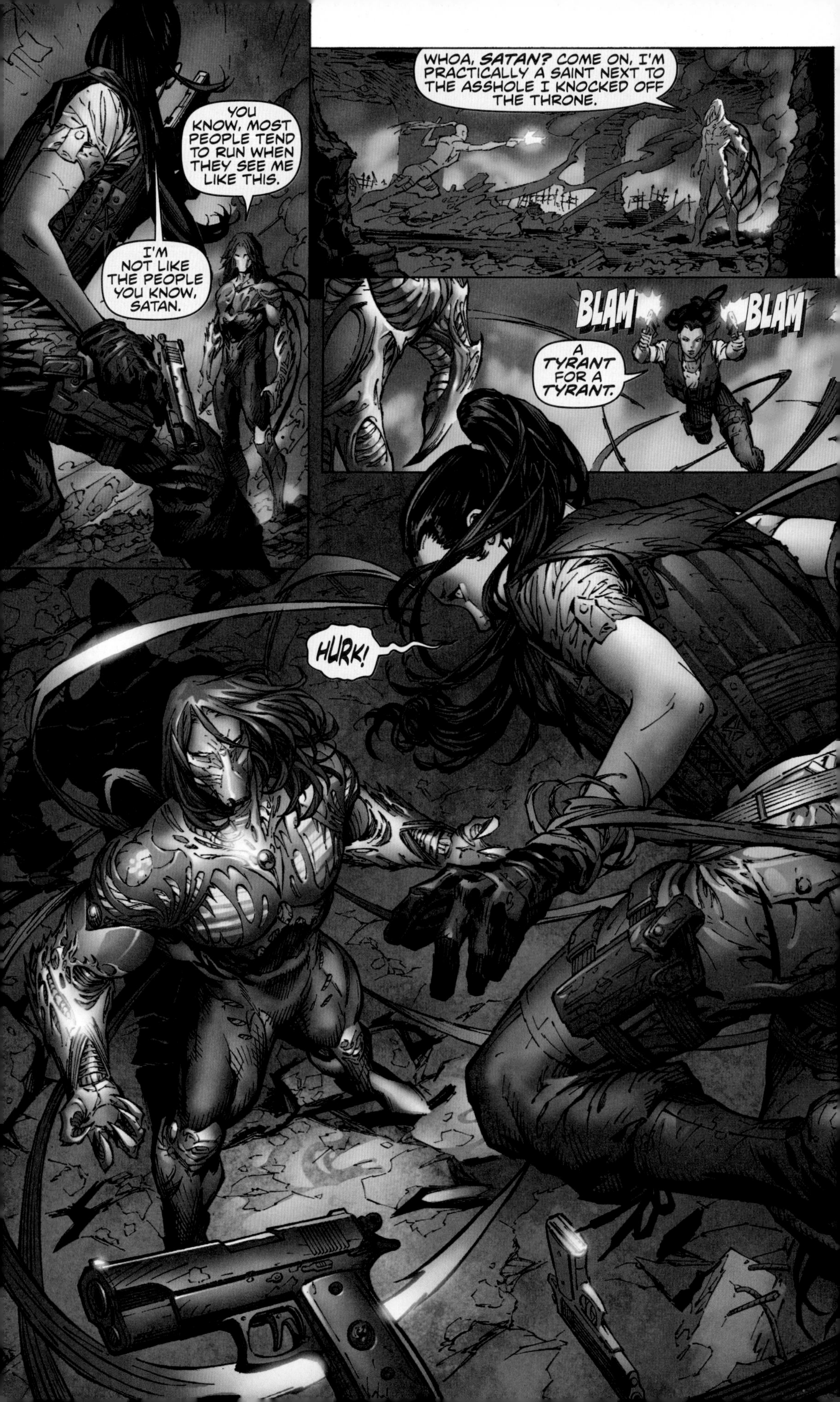
YOU KNOW, MOST PEOPLE TEND TO RUN WHEN THEY SEE ME LIKE THIS.
I'M NOT LIKE THE PEOPLE YOU KNOW, SATAN.
WHOA, SATAN? COME ON, I'M PRACTICALLY A SAINT NEXT TO THE ASSHOLE I KNOCKED OFF THE THRONE.
BLAM
BLAM
A TYRANT FOR A TYRANT.
HURK!

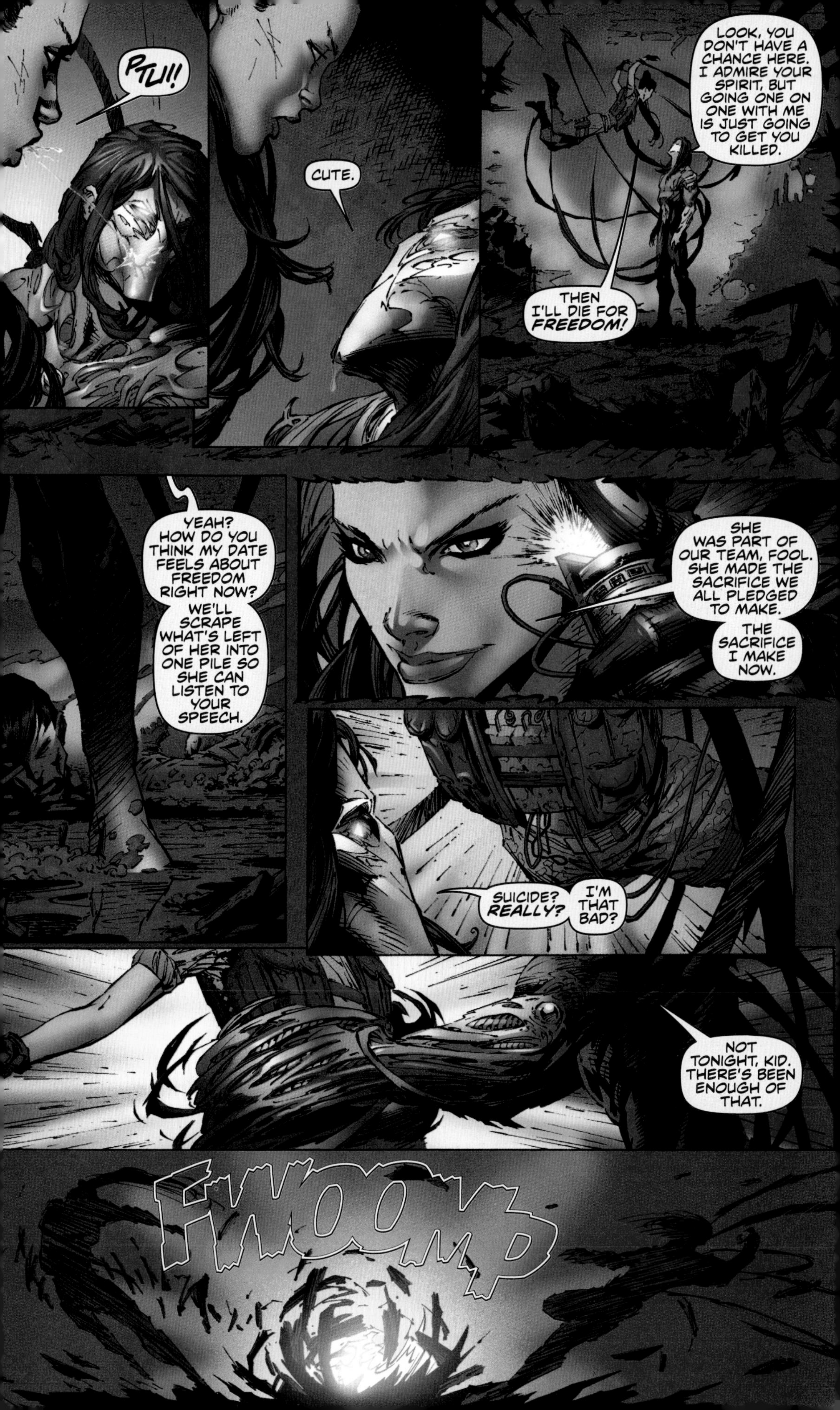
PTU!!
CUTE.
LOOK, YOU DON'T HAVE A CHANCE HERE. I ADMIRE YOUR SPIRIT, BUT GOING ONE ON ONE WITH ME IS JUST GOING TO GET YOU KILLED.
THEN I'LL DIE FOR FREEDOM!
YEAH? HOW DO YOU THINK MY DATE FEELS ABOUT FREEDOM RIGHT NOW?
WE'LL SCRAPE WHAT'S LEFT OF HER INTO ONE PILE SO SHE CAN LISTEN TO YOUR SPEECH.
SHE WAS PART OF OUR TEAM, FOOL. SHE MADE THE SACRIFICE WE ALL PLEDGED TO MAKE.
THE SACRIFICE I MAKE NOW.
SUICIDE? REALLY?
I'M THAT BAD?
NOT TONIGHT, KID. THERE'S BEEN ENOUGH OF THAT.
FWOOMP

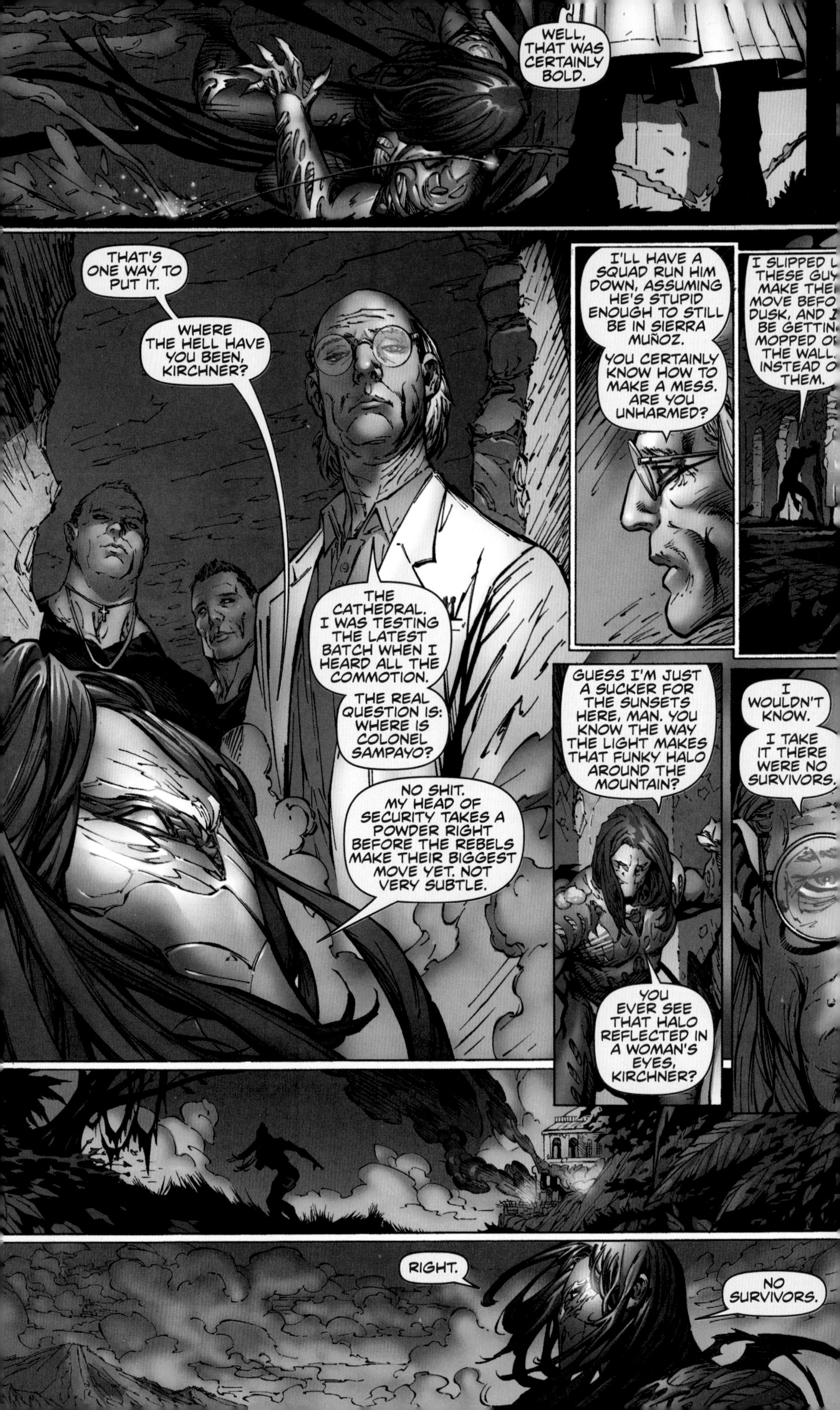
WELL, THAT WAS CERTAINLY BOLD.
THAT'S ONE WAY TO PUT IT.
WHERE THE HELL HAVE YOU BEEN, KIRCHNER?
THE CATHEDRAL. I WAS TESTING THE LATEST BATCH WHEN I HEARD ALL THE COMMOTION.
THE REAL QUESTION IS: WHERE IS COLONEL SAMPAYO?
NO SHIT. MY HEAD OF SECURITY TAKES A POWDER RIGHT BEFORE THE REBELS MAKE THEIR BIGGEST MOVE YET. NOT VERY SUBTLE.
I'LL HAVE A SQUAD RUN HIM DOWN, ASSUMING HE'S STUPID ENOUGH TO STILL BE IN SIERRA MUÑOZ.
YOU CERTAINLY KNOW HOW TO MAKE A MESS. ARE YOU UNHARMED?
GUESS I'M JUST A SUCKER FOR THE SUNSETS HERE, MAN. YOU KNOW THE WAY THE LIGHT MAKES THAT FUNKY HALO AROUND THE MOUNTAIN?
YOU EVER SEE THAT HALO REFLECTED IN A WOMAN'S EYES, KIRCHNER?
I WOULDN'T KNOW.
I TAKE IT THERE WERE NO SURVIVORS.
RIGHT.
NO SURVIVORS.

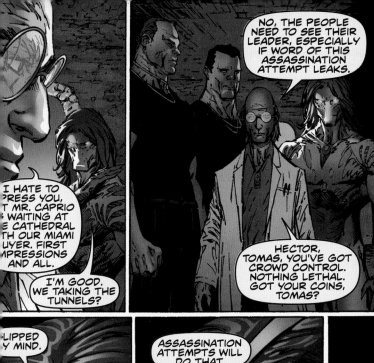

NO, THE PEOPLE NEED TO SEE THEIR LEADER, ESPECIALLY IF WORD OF THIS ASSASSINATION ATTEMPT LEAKS.

I HATE TO PRESS YOU, [B]UT MR. CAPRIO [I]S WAITING AT [THE] CATHEDRAL [WI]TH OUR MIAMI [B]UYER. FIRST [IM]PRESSIONS AND ALL.

I'M GOOD. WE TAKING THE TUNNELS?

HECTOR, TOMAS, YOU'VE GOT CROWD CONTROL. NOTHING LETHAL. GOT YOUR COINS, TOMAS?

ALWAYS, DOC.

THEN LET'S ROLL.

HOLD ON. YOU FORGETTING SOMETHING? THE MASSES CAN'T SEE YOU LIKE THIS.

[S]LIPPED [M]Y MIND.

ASSASSINATION ATTEMPTS WILL DO THAT.

HOW'S THIS?

BEAUTIFUL.

I'll never get used to this part.

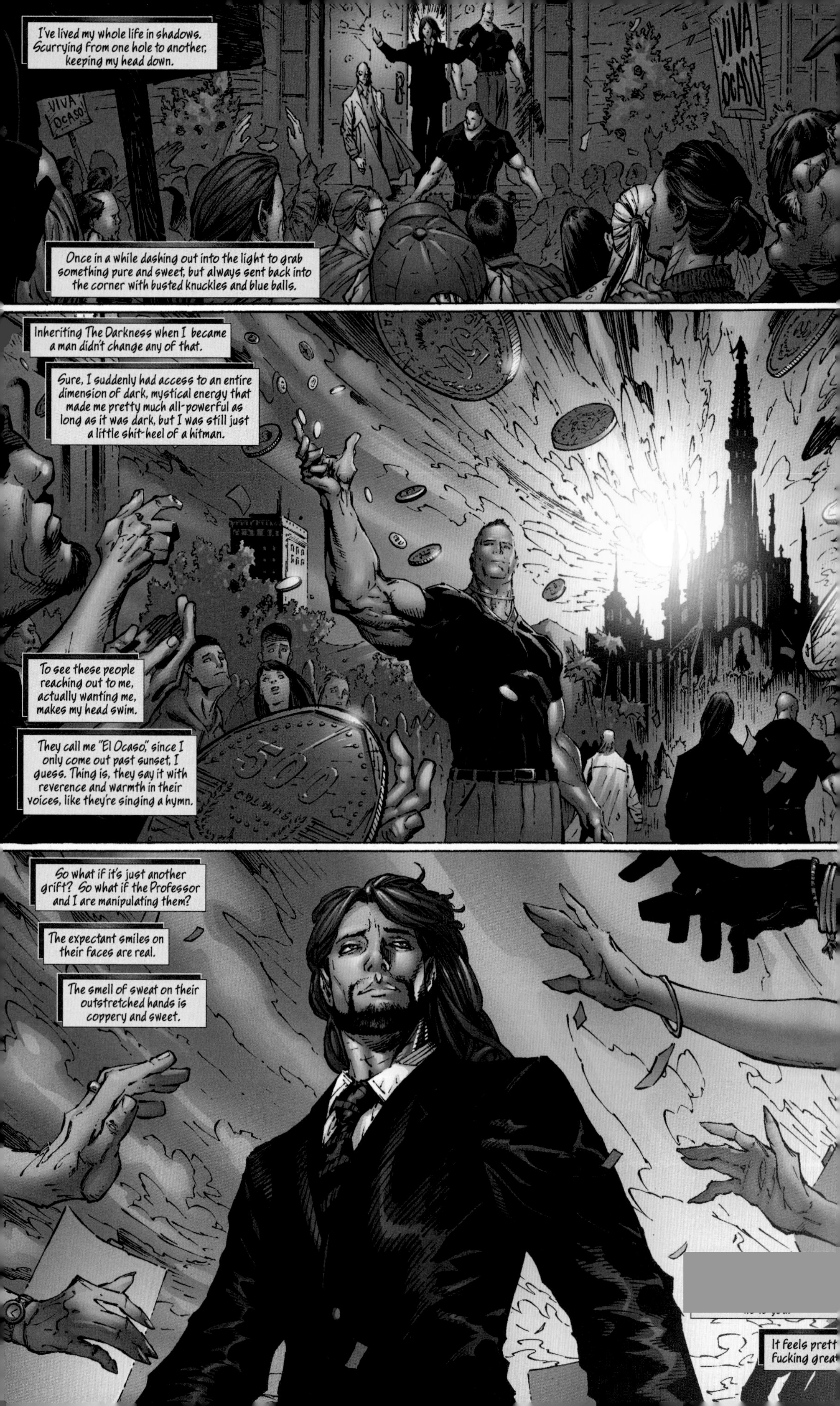
I've lived my whole life in shadows. Scurrying from one hole to another, keeping my head down.
VIVA OCASO!
VIVA OCASO
Once in a while dashing out into the light to grab something pure and sweet, but always sent back into the corner with busted knuckles and blue balls.
Inheriting The Darkness when I became a man didn't change any of that.
Sure, I suddenly had access to an entire dimension of dark, mystical energy that made me pretty much all-powerful as long as it was dark, but I was still just a little shit-heel of a hitman.
To see these people reaching out to me, actually wanting me, makes my head swim.
They call me "El Ocaso," since I only come out past sunset, I guess. Thing is, they say it with reverence and warmth in their voices, like they're singing a hymn.
So what if it's just another grift? So what if the Professor and I are manipulating them?
The expectant smiles on their faces are real.
The smell of sweat on their outstretched hands is coppery and sweet.
It feels prett
fucking grea

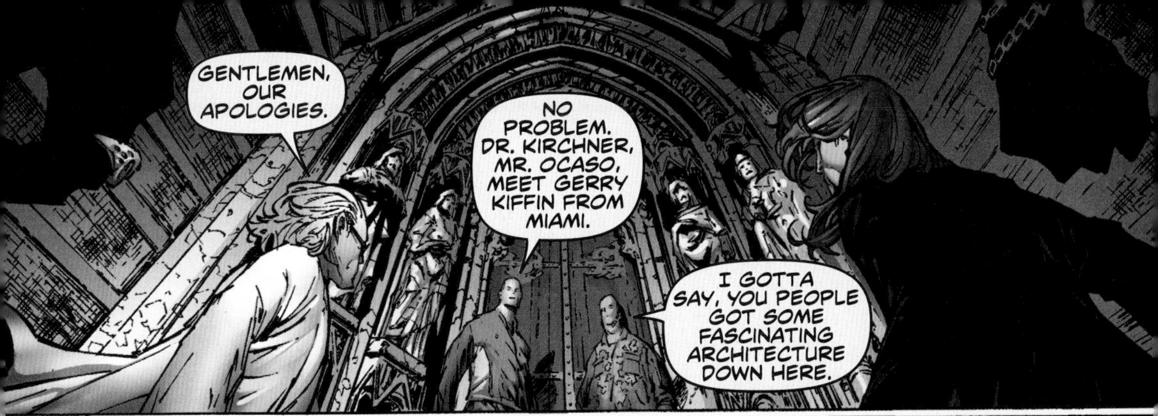
GENTLEMEN, OUR APOLOGIES.
NO PROBLEM. DR. KIRCHNER, MR. OCASO, MEET GERRY KIFFIN FROM MIAMI.
I GOTTA SAY, YOU PEOPLE GOT SOME FASCINATING ARCHITECTURE DOWN HERE.

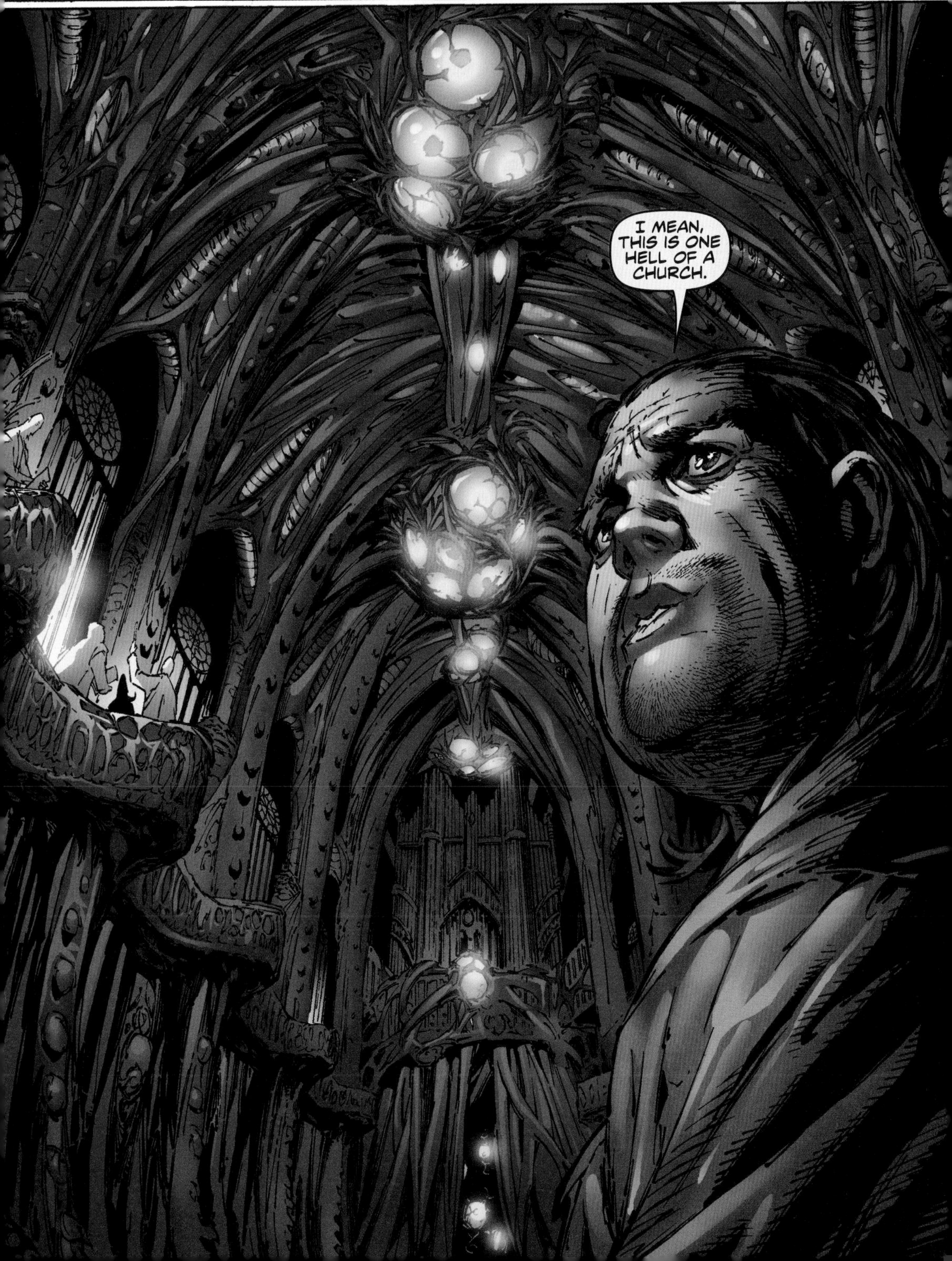
I MEAN, THIS IS ONE HELL OF A CHURCH.

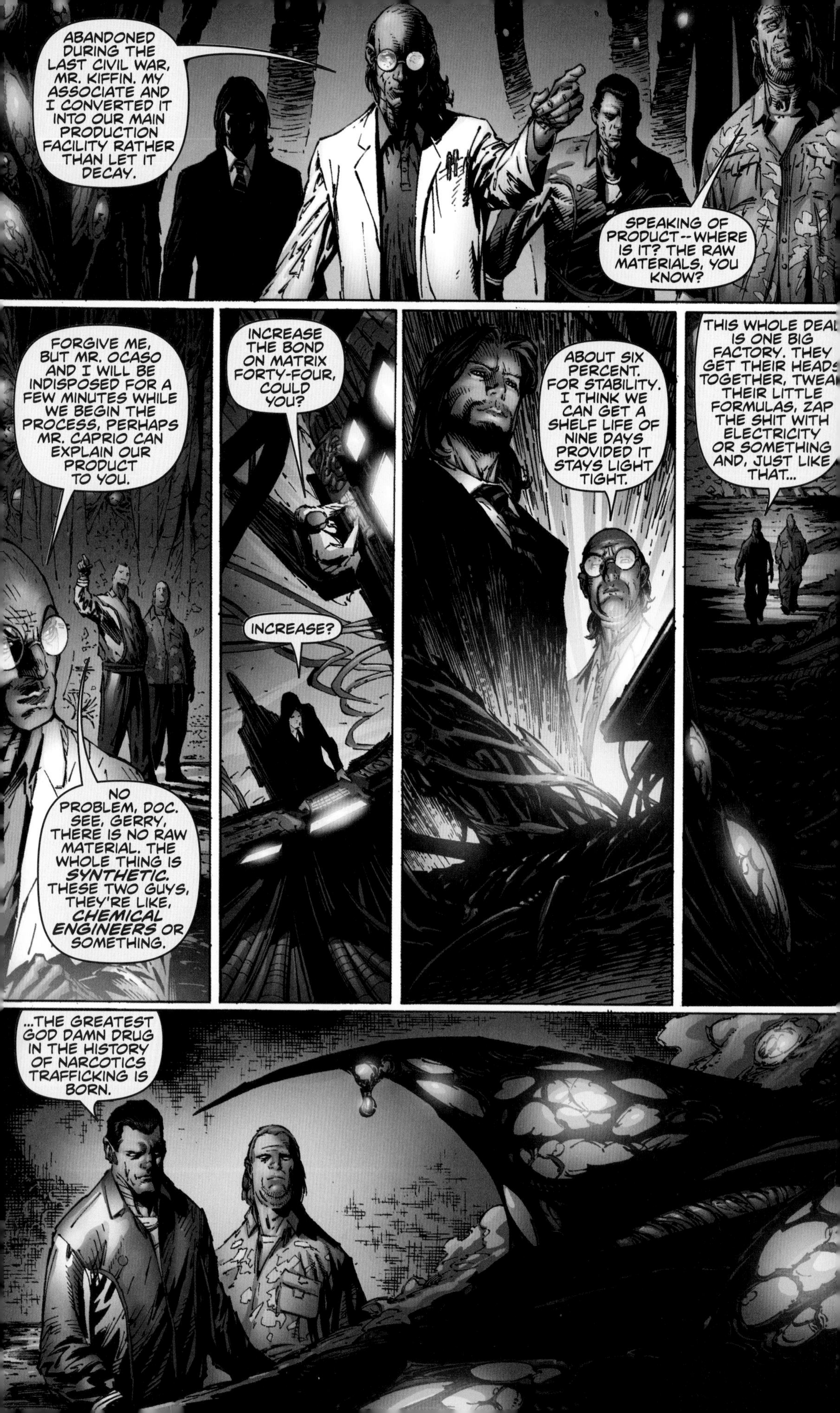
ABANDONED DURING THE LAST CIVIL WAR, MR. KIFFIN. MY ASSOCIATE AND I CONVERTED IT INTO OUR MAIN PRODUCTION FACILITY RATHER THAN LET IT DECAY.
SPEAKING OF PRODUCT--WHERE IS IT? THE RAW MATERIALS, YOU KNOW?
FORGIVE ME, BUT MR. OCASO AND I WILL BE INDISPOSED FOR A FEW MINUTES WHILE WE BEGIN THE PROCESS, PERHAPS MR. CAPRIO CAN EXPLAIN OUR PRODUCT TO YOU.
NO PROBLEM, DOC. SEE, GERRY, THERE IS NO RAW MATERIAL. THE WHOLE THING IS SYNTHETIC. THESE TWO GUYS, THEY'RE LIKE, CHEMICAL ENGINEERS OR SOMETHING.
INCREASE THE BOND ON MATRIX FORTY-FOUR, COULD YOU?
INCREASE?
ABOUT SIX PERCENT. FOR STABILITY. I THINK WE CAN GET A SHELF LIFE OF NINE DAYS PROVIDED IT STAYS LIGHT TIGHT.
THIS WHOLE DEAL IS ONE BIG FACTORY. THEY GET THEIR HEADS TOGETHER, TWEA THEIR LITTLE FORMULAS, ZAP THE SHIT WITH ELECTRICITY OR SOMETHING AND, JUST LIKE THAT...
...THE GREATEST GOD DAMN DRUG IN THE HISTORY OF NARCOTICS TRAFFICKING IS BORN.

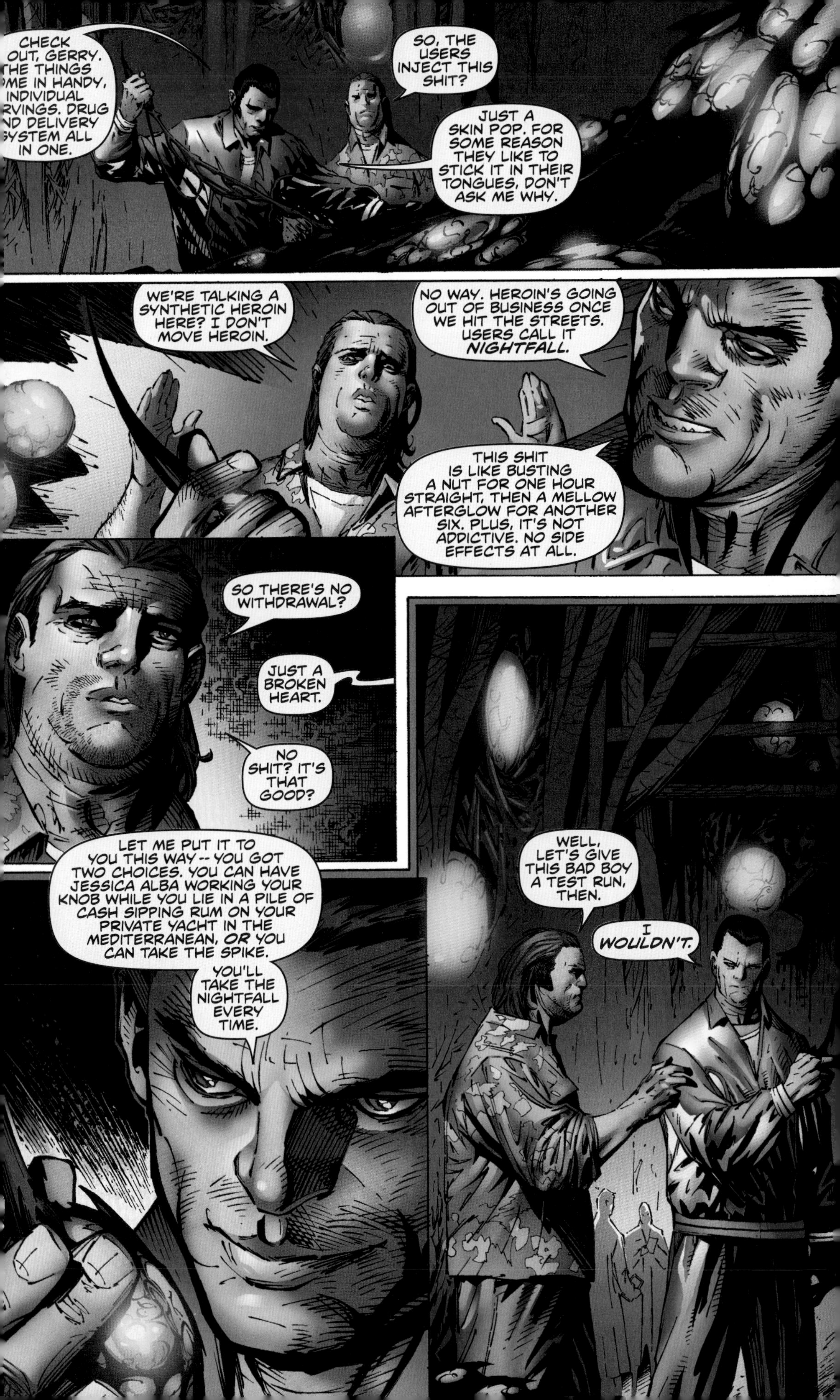
CHECK OUT, GERRY. THE THINGS OME IN HANDY, INDIVIDUAL RVINGS. DRUG ND DELIVERY SYSTEM ALL IN ONE.
SO, THE USERS INJECT THIS SHIT?
JUST A SKIN POP. FOR SOME REASON THEY LIKE TO STICK IT IN THEIR TONGUES, DON'T ASK ME WHY.
WE'RE TALKING A SYNTHETIC HEROIN HERE? I DON'T MOVE HEROIN.
NO WAY. HEROIN'S GOING OUT OF BUSINESS ONCE WE HIT THE STREETS. USERS CALL IT NIGHTFALL.
THIS SHIT IS LIKE BUSTING A NUT FOR ONE HOUR STRAIGHT, THEN A MELLOW AFTERGLOW FOR ANOTHER SIX. PLUS, IT'S NOT ADDICTIVE. NO SIDE EFFECTS AT ALL.
SO THERE'S NO WITHDRAWAL?
JUST A BROKEN HEART.
NO SHIT? IT'S THAT GOOD?
LET ME PUT IT TO YOU THIS WAY -- YOU GOT TWO CHOICES. YOU CAN HAVE JESSICA ALBA WORKING YOUR KNOB WHILE YOU LIE IN A PILE OF CASH SIPPING RUM ON YOUR PRIVATE YACHT IN THE MEDITERRANEAN, OR YOU CAN TAKE THE SPIKE.
YOU'LL TAKE THE NIGHTFALL EVERY TIME.
WELL, LET'S GIVE THIS BAD BOY A TEST RUN, THEN.
I WOULDN'T.

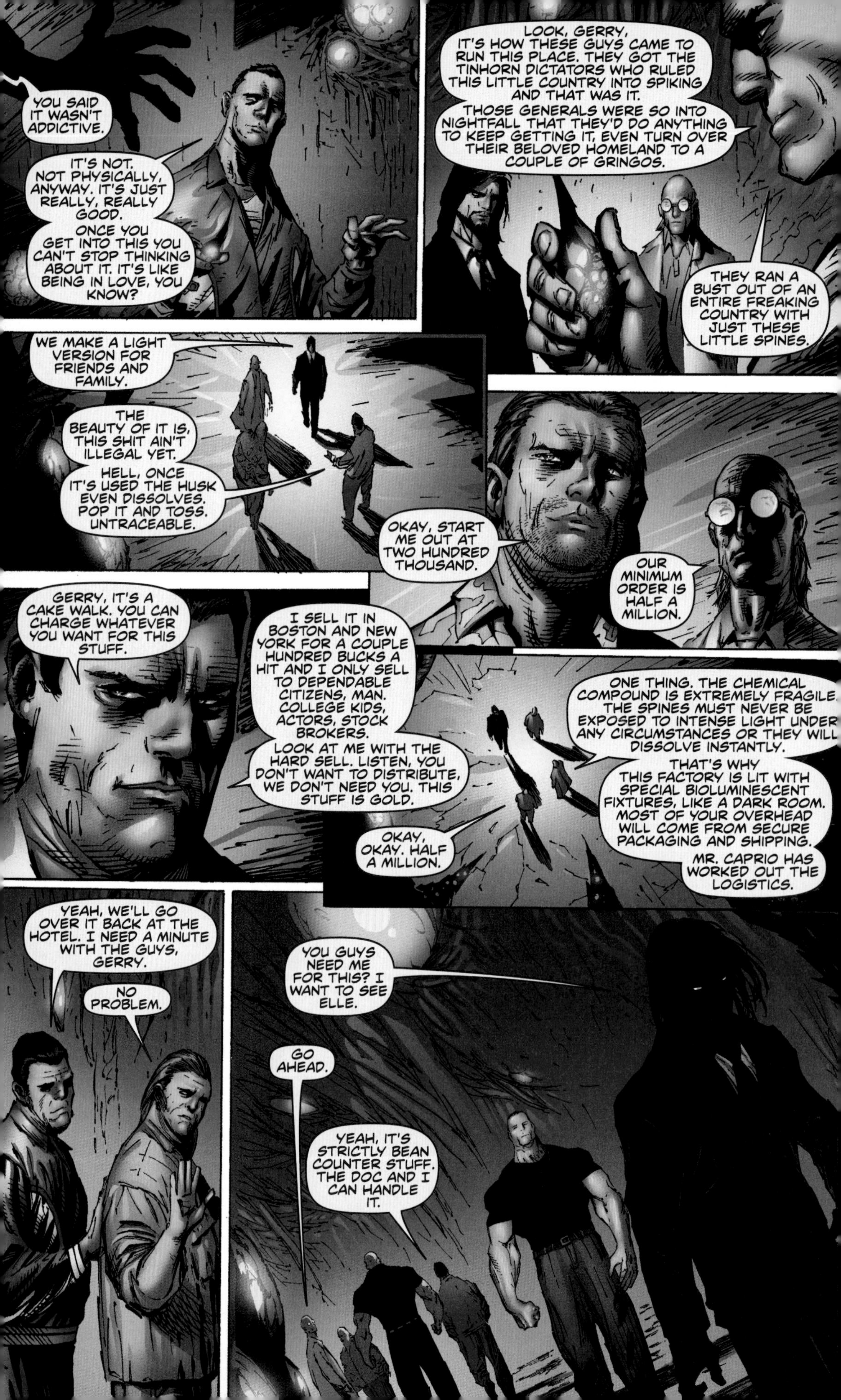
YOU SAID IT WASN'T ADDICTIVE.
IT'S NOT. NOT PHYSICALLY, ANYWAY. IT'S JUST REALLY, REALLY GOOD.
ONCE YOU GET INTO THIS YOU CAN'T STOP THINKING ABOUT IT. IT'S LIKE BEING IN LOVE, YOU KNOW?
LOOK, GERRY, IT'S HOW THESE GUYS CAME TO RUN THIS PLACE. THEY GOT THE TINHORN DICTATORS WHO RULED THIS LITTLE COUNTRY INTO SPIKING AND THAT WAS IT.
THOSE GENERALS WERE SO INTO NIGHTFALL THAT THEY'D DO ANYTHING TO KEEP GETTING IT, EVEN TURN OVER THEIR BELOVED HOMELAND TO A COUPLE OF GRINGOS.
THEY RAN A BUST OUT OF AN ENTIRE FREAKING COUNTRY WITH JUST THESE LITTLE SPINES.
WE MAKE A LIGHT VERSION FOR FRIENDS AND FAMILY.
THE BEAUTY OF IT IS, THIS SHIT AIN'T ILLEGAL YET.
HELL, ONCE IT'S USED THE HUSK EVEN DISSOLVES. POP IT AND TOSS. UNTRACEABLE.
OKAY, START ME OUT AT TWO HUNDRED THOUSAND.
OUR MINIMUM ORDER IS HALF A MILLION.
GERRY, IT'S A CAKE WALK. YOU CAN CHARGE WHATEVER YOU WANT FOR THIS STUFF.
I SELL IT IN BOSTON AND NEW YORK FOR A COUPLE HUNDRED BUCKS A HIT AND I ONLY SELL TO DEPENDABLE CITIZENS, MAN. COLLEGE KIDS, ACTORS, STOCK BROKERS.
LOOK AT ME WITH THE HARD SELL. LISTEN, YOU DON'T WANT TO DISTRIBUTE, WE DON'T NEED YOU. THIS STUFF IS GOLD.
OKAY, OKAY. HALF A MILLION.
ONE THING. THE CHEMICAL COMPOUND IS EXTREMELY FRAGILE. THE SPINES MUST NEVER BE EXPOSED TO INTENSE LIGHT UNDER ANY CIRCUMSTANCES OR THEY WILL DISSOLVE INSTANTLY.
THAT'S WHY THIS FACTORY IS LIT WITH SPECIAL BIOLUMINESCENT FIXTURES, LIKE A DARK ROOM. MOST OF YOUR OVERHEAD WILL COME FROM SECURE PACKAGING AND SHIPPING.
MR. CAPRIO HAS WORKED OUT THE LOGISTICS.
YEAH, WE'LL GO OVER IT BACK AT THE HOTEL. I NEED A MINUTE WITH THE GUYS, GERRY.
NO PROBLEM.
YOU GUYS NEED ME FOR THIS? I WANT TO SEE ELLE.
GO AHEAD.
YEAH, IT'S STRICTLY BEAN COUNTER STUFF. THE DOC AND I CAN HANDLE IT.

HANG ON A MIN--

HURRRKK!

AA-HAAUUUGH!

JESUS, YOU OKAY, MR. O?

YEAH. IT'S COOL, HECTOR. YOU CAN TAKE OFF. I'LL TAKE THE LABYRINTH HOME.

YOU SURE?

YEAH, IT'S JUST... SOMETHING I ATE.

More like everything I ate.

Ever since Professor Kirchner came along and helped me fine tune the Darkness, things have been upside down.

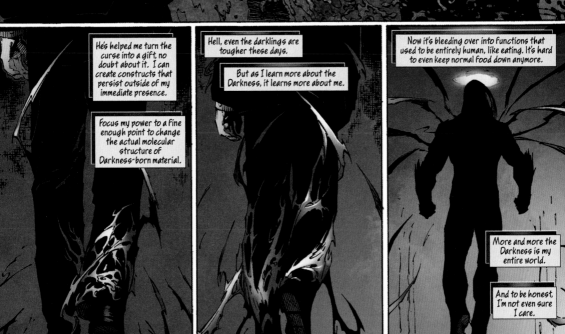

He's helped me turn the curse into a gift, no doubt about it. I can create constructs that persist outside of my immediate presence.

Focus my power to a fine enough point to change the actual molecular structure of Darkness-born material.

Hell, even the darklings are tougher these days.

But as I learn more about the Darkness, it learns more about me.

Now it's bleeding over into functions that used to be entirely human, like eating. It's hard to even keep normal food down anymore.

More and more the Darkness is my entire world.

And to be honest, I'm not even sure I care.

CAN I OFFER YOU SOMETHING TO DRINK?

NAH. LET'S GET RIGHT DOWN TO BUSINESS.

I SUPPOSE YOU WANT A DEEPER DISCOUNT FOR OPENING MIAMI UP TO US. IS THAT IT?

NOT ENTIRELY. I'M LOOKING FOR SOMETHING MORE LIKE A BONUS.

A BONUS?

YEAH. FOR STARTERS, I GET ALL THE PRODUCT I CAN MOVE FOR FREE, AND ON TOP OF THAT A ONE TIME FEE OF FIVE MILLION.

WHAT THE HELL ARE YOU TALKING ABOUT?

I'M TALKING ABOUT YOUR PARTNER.

MR. OCASO?

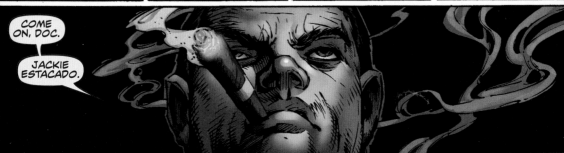

COME ON, DOC.

JACKIE ESTACADO.

IT TAKES MORE THAN GROWING A BEARD AND JUMPING A CONTINENT TO ESCAPE THE NOTICE OF OUR KIND. IT TOOK ME A WHILE TO PUT IT TOGETHER, BUT THE LOOKS, THE HAIR, THE NOCTURNAL HABITS.

GOD KNOWS, THE MOB ISN'T WHAT IT USED TO BE, BUT THE FRANCHETTI FAMILY STILL HAS FRIENDS THAT WOULD PAY DEARLY TO SEE THAT KID WITH A CHALK OUTLINE AROUND HIM.

NOT TO MENTION MY FRIENDS IN THE DEA. MY HELP COULD PUT A STOP TO A NEWBORN DRUG SCOURGE BEFORE IT SWEEPS THE STATES.

HELL, THIS IS THE KIND OF SHIT PRESIDENTS LOVE TO START WARS OVER, YOU KNOW?

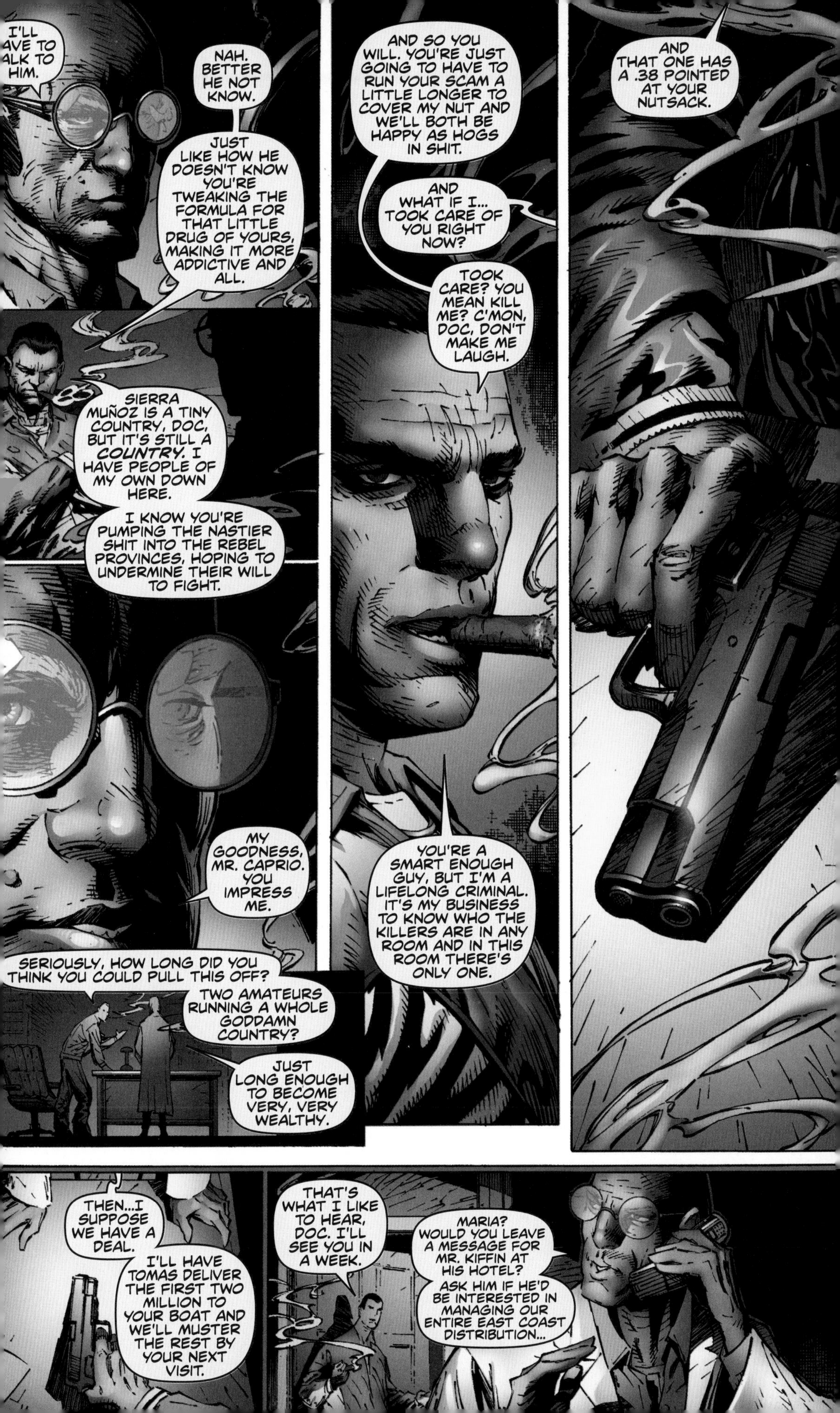
I'LL ...AVE TO ...ALK TO HIM.
NAH. BETTER HE NOT KNOW.
JUST LIKE HOW HE DOESN'T KNOW YOU'RE TWEAKING THE FORMULA FOR THAT LITTLE DRUG OF YOURS, MAKING IT MORE ADDICTIVE AND ALL.
SIERRA MUÑOZ IS A TINY COUNTRY, DOC, BUT IT'S STILL A COUNTRY. I HAVE PEOPLE OF MY OWN DOWN HERE.
I KNOW YOU'RE PUMPING THE NASTIER SHIT INTO THE REBEL PROVINCES, HOPING TO UNDERMINE THEIR WILL TO FIGHT.
MY GOODNESS, MR. CAPRIO. YOU IMPRESS ME.
SERIOUSLY, HOW LONG DID YOU THINK YOU COULD PULL THIS OFF?
TWO AMATEURS RUNNING A WHOLE GODDAMN COUNTRY?
JUST LONG ENOUGH TO BECOME VERY, VERY WEALTHY.
AND SO YOU WILL. YOU'RE JUST GOING TO HAVE TO RUN YOUR SCAM A LITTLE LONGER TO COVER MY NUT AND WE'LL BOTH BE HAPPY AS HOGS IN SHIT.
AND WHAT IF I... TOOK CARE OF YOU RIGHT NOW?
TOOK CARE? YOU MEAN KILL ME? C'MON, DOC, DON'T MAKE ME LAUGH.
YOU'RE A SMART ENOUGH GUY, BUT I'M A LIFELONG CRIMINAL. IT'S MY BUSINESS TO KNOW WHO THE KILLERS ARE IN ANY ROOM AND IN THIS ROOM THERE'S ONLY ONE.
AND THAT ONE HAS A .38 POINTED AT YOUR NUTSACK.
THEN...I SUPPOSE WE HAVE A DEAL.
I'LL HAVE TOMAS DELIVER THE FIRST TWO MILLION TO YOUR BOAT AND WE'LL MUSTER THE REST BY YOUR NEXT VISIT.
THAT'S WHAT I LIKE TO HEAR, DOC. I'LL SEE YOU IN A WEEK.
MARIA? WOULD YOU LEAVE A MESSAGE FOR MR. KIFFIN AT HIS HOTEL?
ASK HIM IF HE'D BE INTERESTED IN MANAGING OUR ENTIRE EAST COAST DISTRIBUTION...

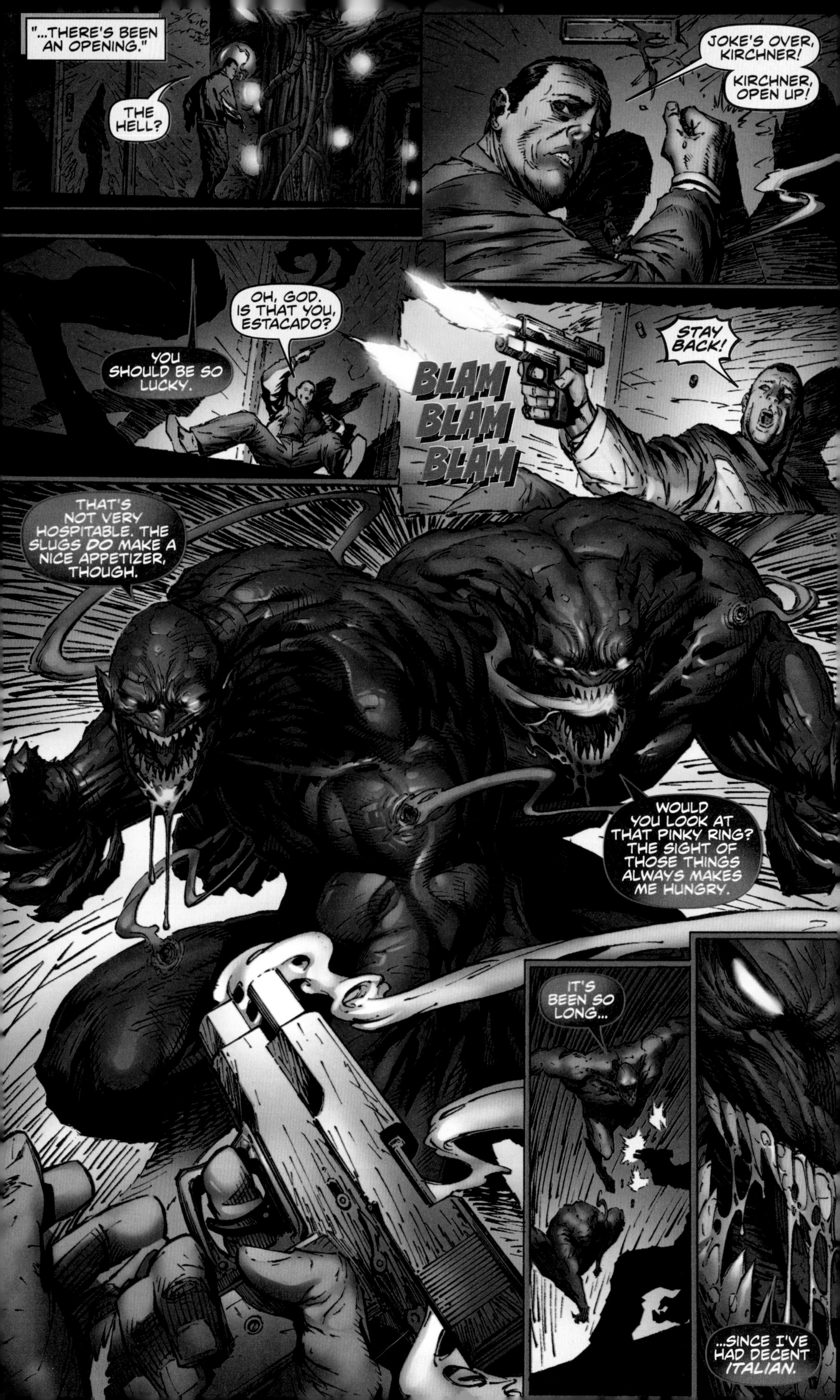
"...THERE'S BEEN AN OPENING."
THE HELL?
JOKE'S OVER, KIRCHNER!
KIRCHNER, OPEN UP!
OH, GOD. IS THAT YOU, ESTACADO?
YOU SHOULD BE SO LUCKY.
BLAM BLAM BLAM
STAY BACK!
THAT'S NOT VERY HOSPITABLE. THE SLUGS DO MAKE A NICE APPETIZER, THOUGH.
WOULD YOU LOOK AT THAT PINKY RING? THE SIGHT OF THOSE THINGS ALWAYS MAKES ME HUNGRY.
IT'S BEEN SO LONG...
...SINCE I'VE HAD DECENT ITALIAN.

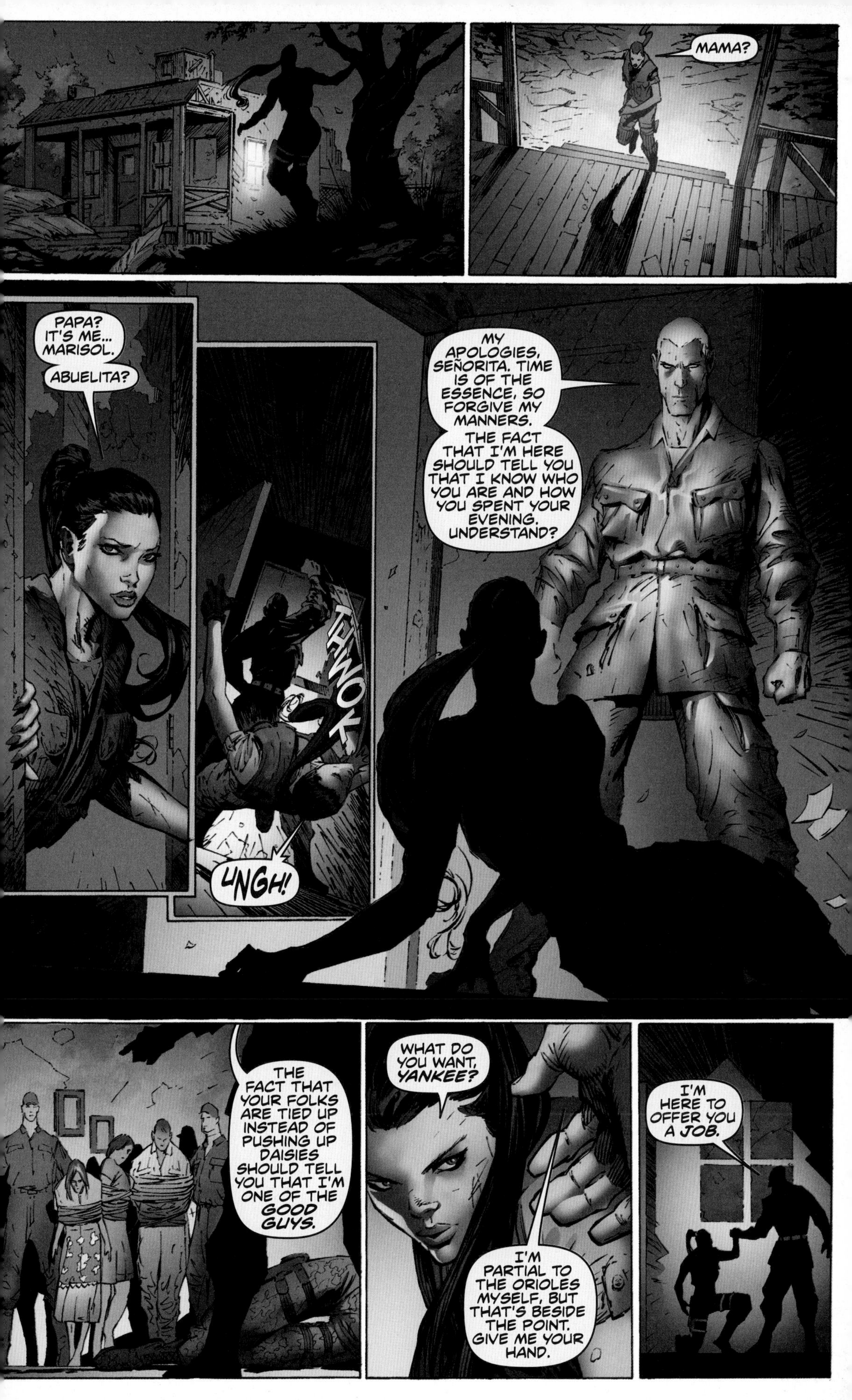
MAMA?
PAPA? IT'S ME... MARISOL.
ABUELITA?
THWOK
UNGH!
MY APOLOGIES, SEÑORITA. TIME IS OF THE ESSENCE, SO FORGIVE MY MANNERS.
THE FACT THAT I'M HERE SHOULD TELL YOU THAT I KNOW WHO YOU ARE AND HOW YOU SPENT YOUR EVENING. UNDERSTAND?
THE FACT THAT YOUR FOLKS ARE TIED UP INSTEAD OF PUSHING UP DAISIES SHOULD TELL YOU THAT I'M ONE OF THE GOOD GUYS.
WHAT DO YOU WANT, YANKEE?
I'M PARTIAL TO THE ORIOLES MYSELF, BUT THAT'S BESIDE THE POINT. GIVE ME YOUR HAND.
I'M HERE TO OFFER YOU A JOB.

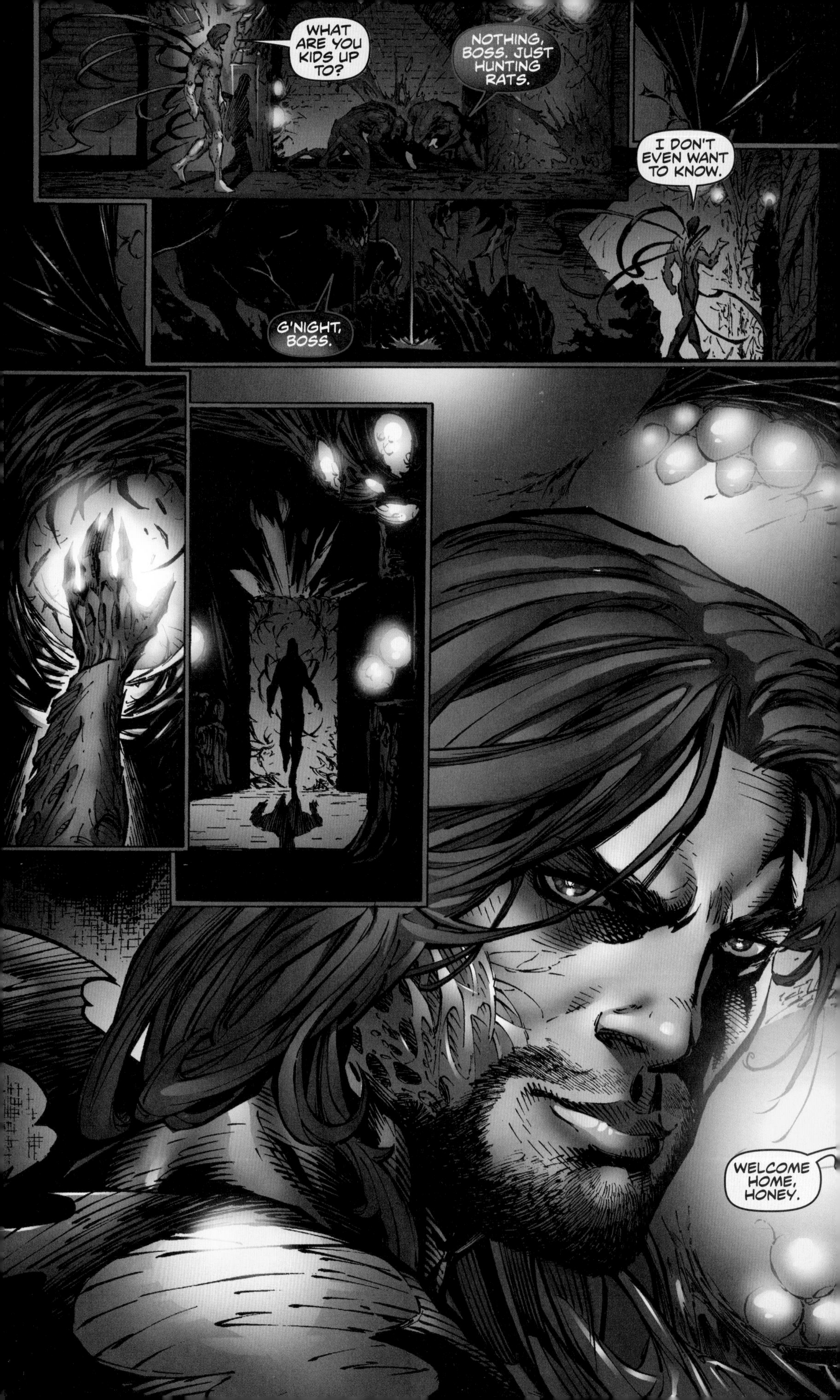
WHAT ARE YOU KIDS UP TO?
NOTHING, BOSS. JUST HUNTING RATS.
I DON'T EVEN WANT TO KNOW.
G'NIGHT, BOSS.
WELCOME HOME, HONEY.

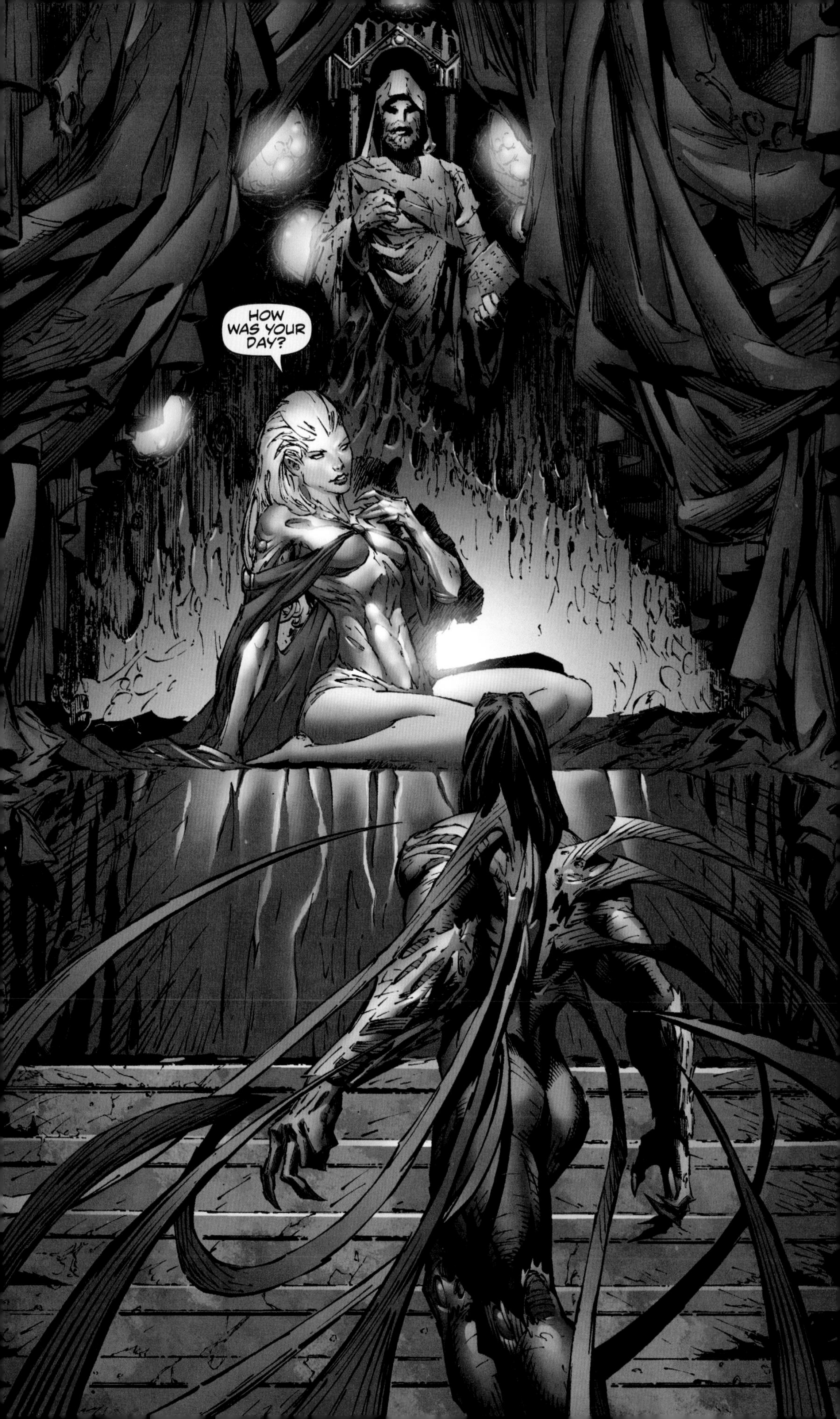
HOW WAS YOUR DAY?

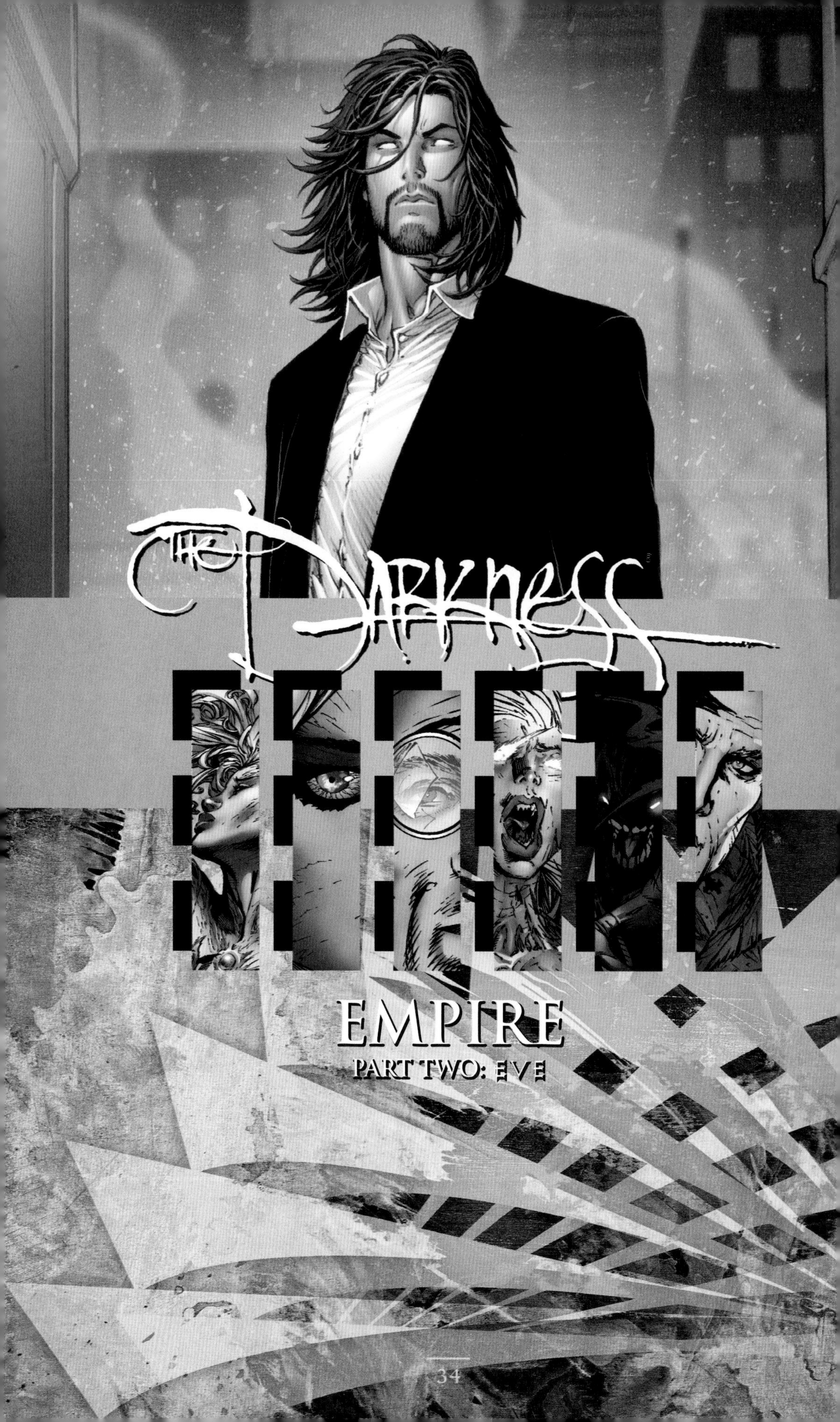
THE DARKNESS
EMPIRE
PART TWO: EVE

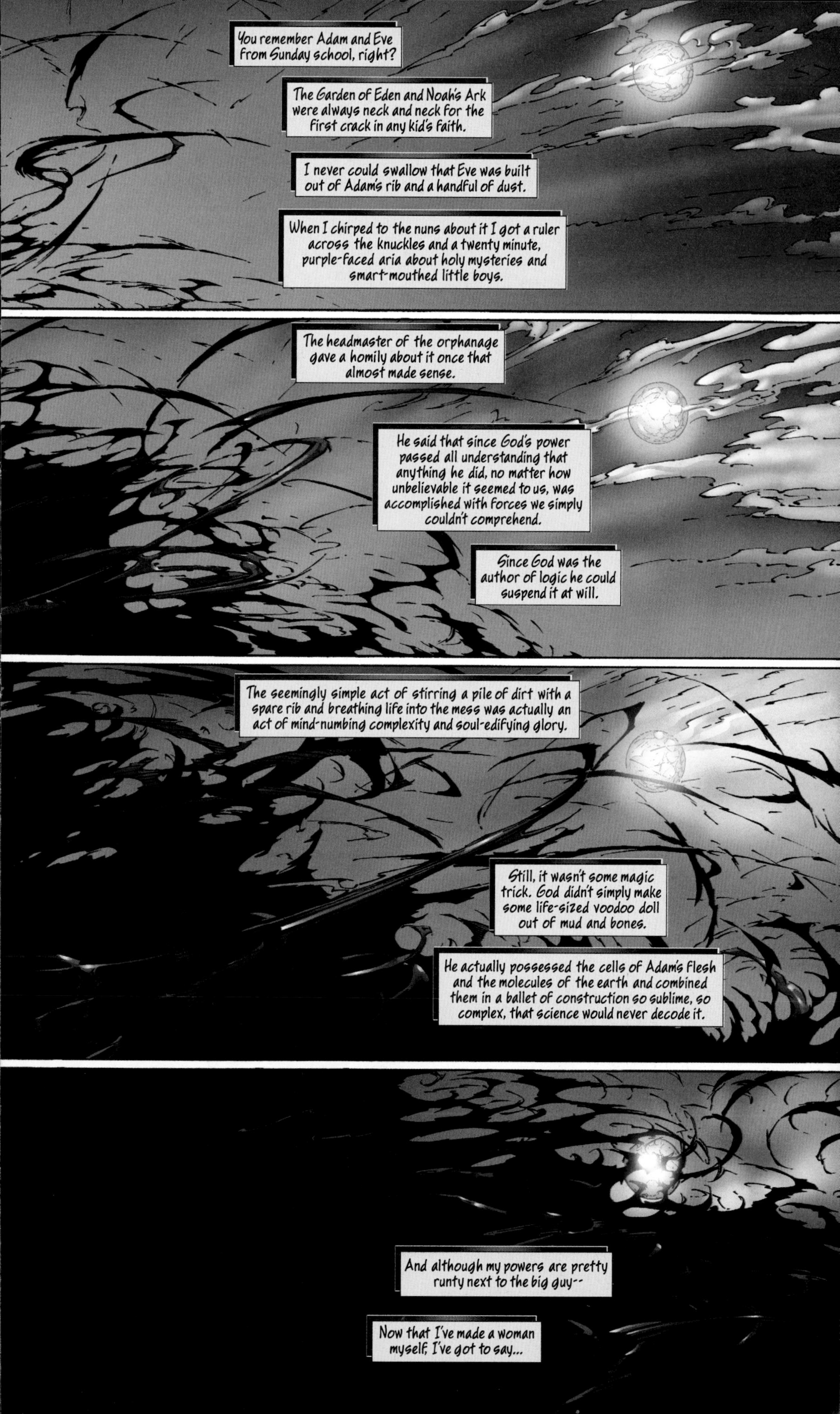
You remember Adam and Eve from Sunday school, right?
The Garden of Eden and Noah's Ark were always neck and neck for the first crack in any kid's faith.
I never could swallow that Eve was built out of Adam's rib and a handful of dust.
When I chirped to the nuns about it I got a ruler across the knuckles and a twenty minute, purple-faced aria about holy mysteries and smart-mouthed little boys.
The headmaster of the orphanage gave a homily about it once that almost made sense.
He said that since God's power passed all understanding that anything he did, no matter how unbelievable it seemed to us, was accomplished with forces we simply couldn't comprehend.
Since God was the author of logic he could suspend it at will.
The seemingly simple act of stirring a pile of dirt with a spare rib and breathing life into the mess was actually an act of mind-numbing complexity and soul-edifying glory.
Still, it wasn't some magic trick. God didn't simply make some life-sized voodoo doll out of mud and bones.
He actually possessed the cells of Adam's flesh and the molecules of the earth and combined them in a ballet of construction so sublime, so complex, that science would never decode it.
And although my powers are pretty runty next to the big guy--
Now that I've made a woman myself, I've got to say...

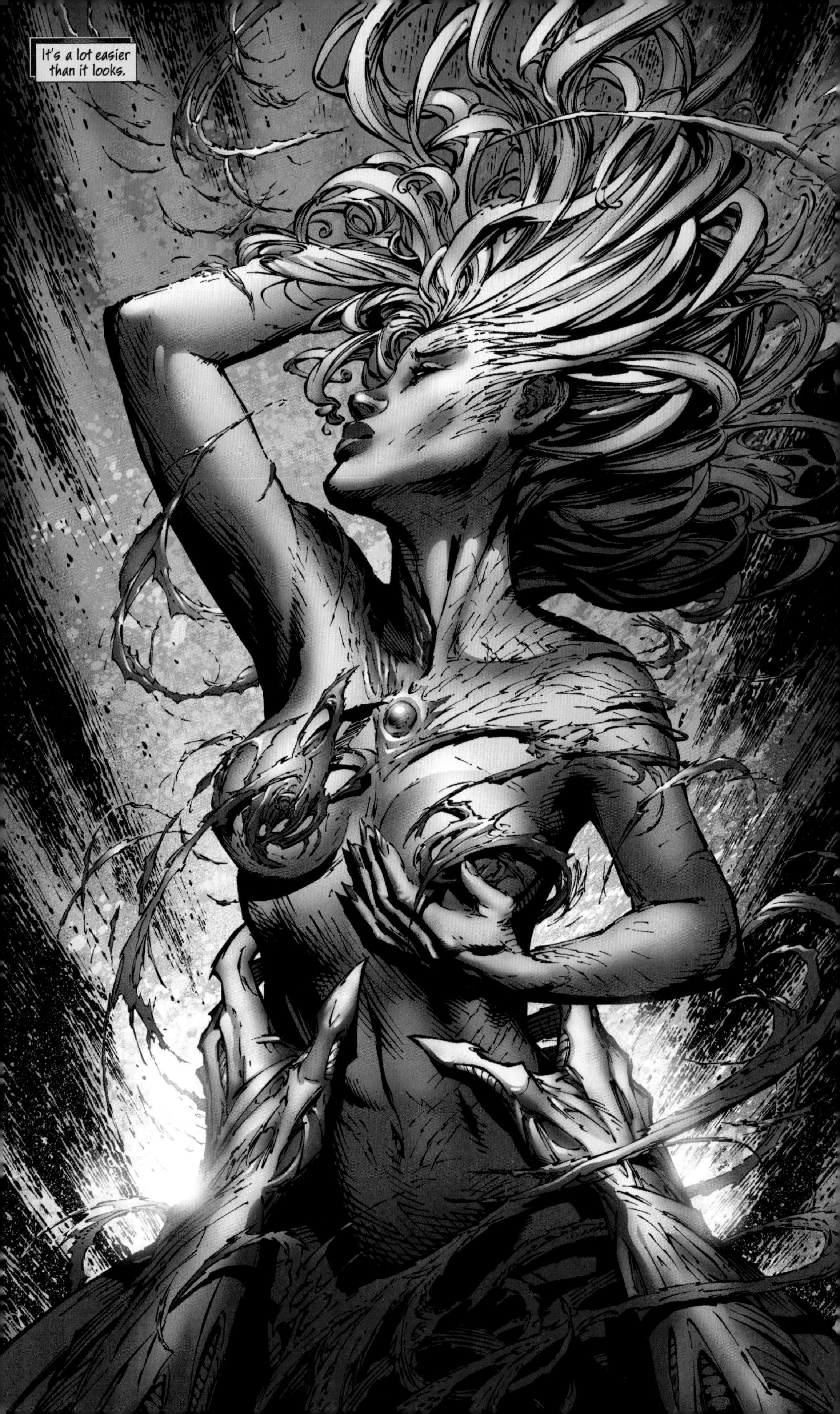
It's a lot easier than it looks.

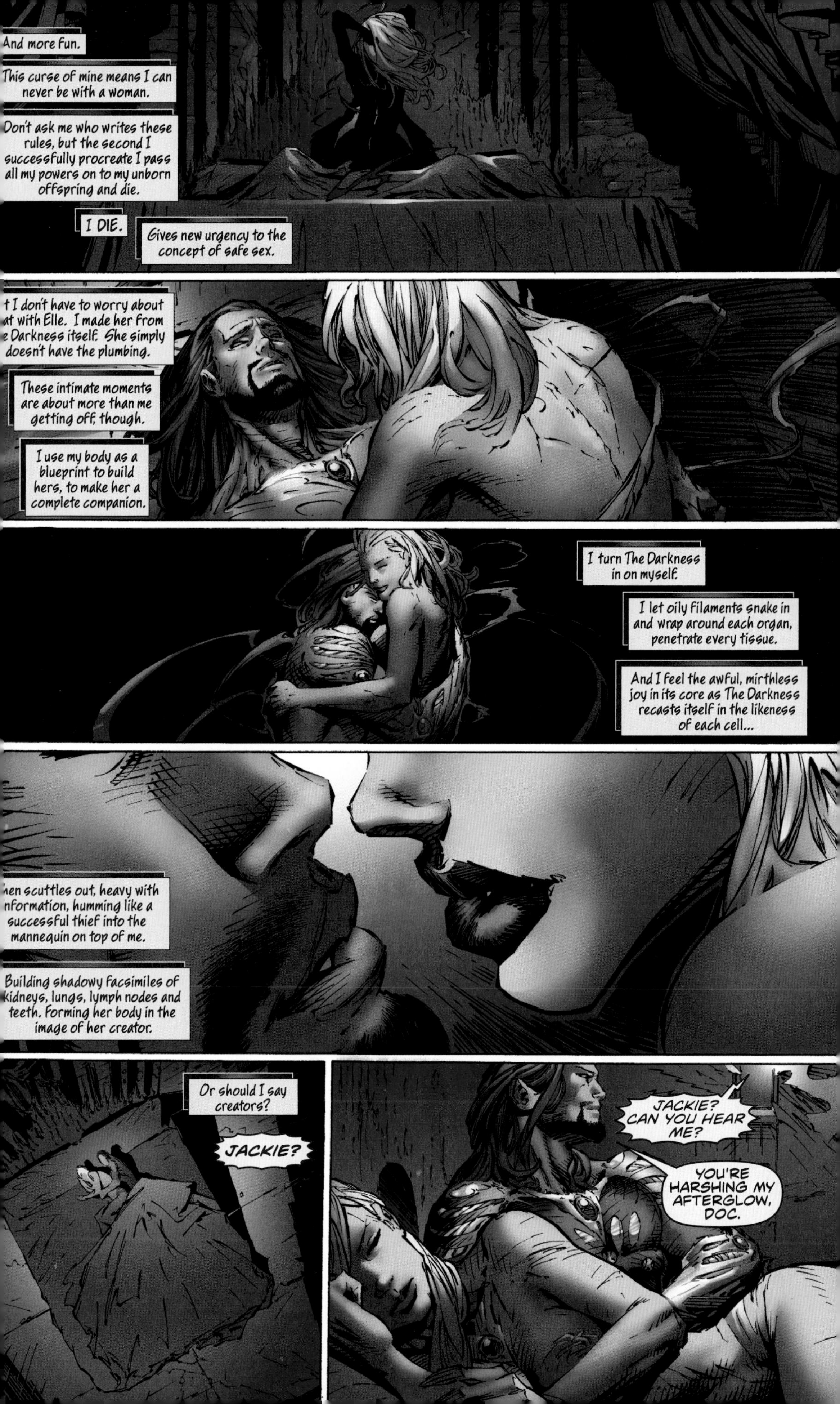

And more fun.
This curse of mine means I can never be with a woman.
Don't ask me who writes these rules, but the second I successfully procreate I pass all my powers on to my unborn offspring and die.
I DIE.
Gives new urgency to the concept of safe sex.
t I don't have to worry about at with Elle. I made her from e Darkness itself. She simply doesn't have the plumbing.
These intimate moments are about more than me getting off, though.
I use my body as a blueprint to build hers, to make her a complete companion.
I turn The Darkness in on myself.
I let oily filaments snake in and wrap around each organ, penetrate every tissue.
And I feel the awful, mirthless joy in its core as The Darkness recasts itself in the likeness of each cell...
hen scuttles out, heavy with nformation, humming like a successful thief into the mannequin on top of me.
Building shadowy facsimiles of kidneys, lungs, lymph nodes and teeth. Forming her body in the image of her creator.
Or should I say creators?
JACKIE?
JACKIE? CAN YOU HEAR ME?
YOU'RE HARSHING MY AFTERGLOW, DOC.

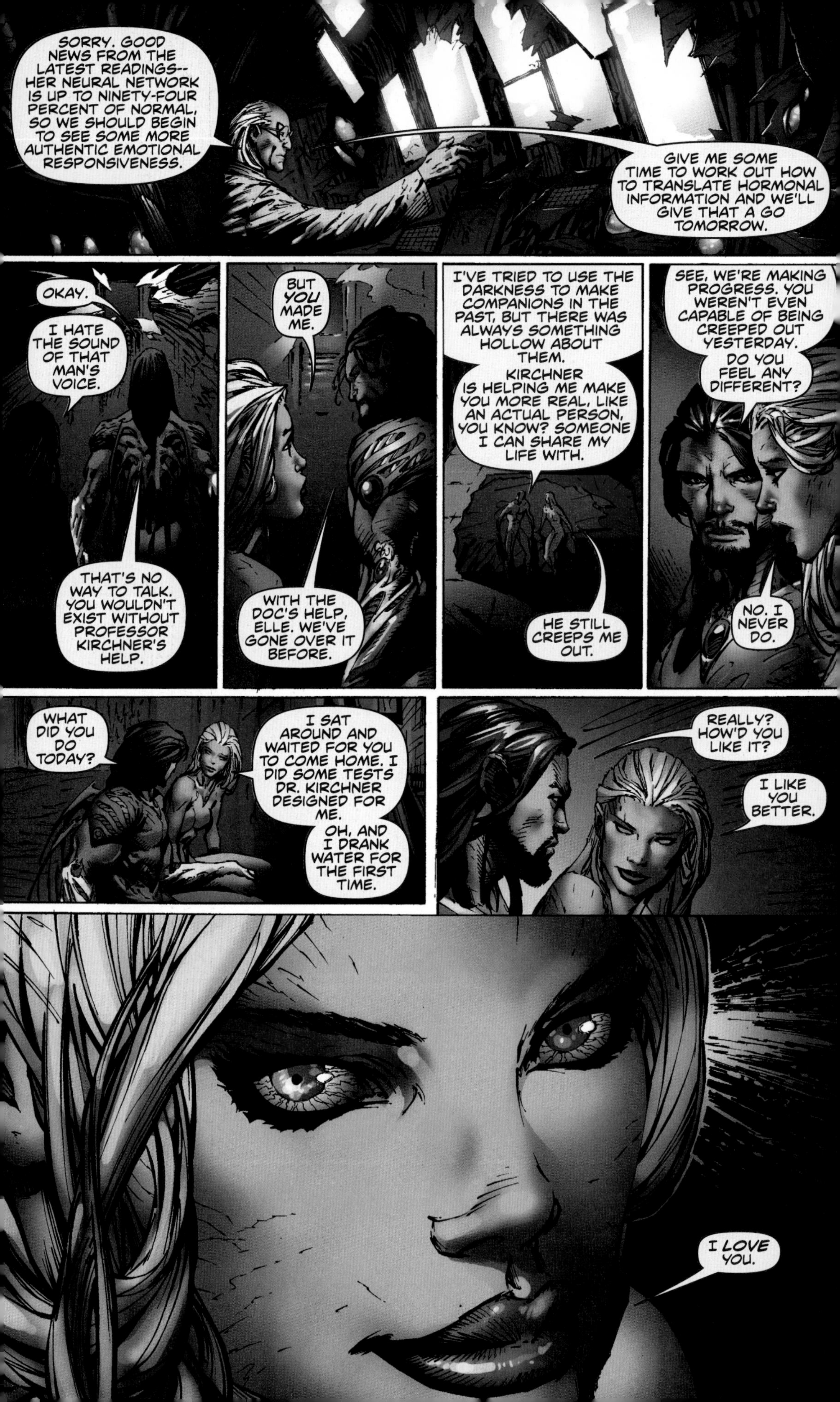
SORRY. GOOD NEWS FROM THE LATEST READINGS-- HER NEURAL NETWORK IS UP TO NINETY-FOUR PERCENT OF NORMAL, SO WE SHOULD BEGIN TO SEE SOME MORE AUTHENTIC EMOTIONAL RESPONSIVENESS.
GIVE ME SOME TIME TO WORK OUT HOW TO TRANSLATE HORMONAL INFORMATION AND WE'LL GIVE THAT A GO TOMORROW.
OKAY.
I HATE THE SOUND OF THAT MAN'S VOICE.
THAT'S NO WAY TO TALK. YOU WOULDN'T EXIST WITHOUT PROFESSOR KIRCHNER'S HELP.
BUT YOU MADE ME.
WITH THE DOC'S HELP, ELLE. WE'VE GONE OVER IT BEFORE.
I'VE TRIED TO USE THE DARKNESS TO MAKE COMPANIONS IN THE PAST, BUT THERE WAS ALWAYS SOMETHING HOLLOW ABOUT THEM.
KIRCHNER IS HELPING ME MAKE YOU MORE REAL, LIKE AN ACTUAL PERSON, YOU KNOW? SOMEONE I CAN SHARE MY LIFE WITH.
HE STILL CREEPS ME OUT.
SEE, WE'RE MAKING PROGRESS. YOU WEREN'T EVEN CAPABLE OF BEING CREEPED OUT YESTERDAY.
DO YOU FEEL ANY DIFFERENT?
NO. I NEVER DO.
WHAT DID YOU DO TODAY?
I SAT AROUND AND WAITED FOR YOU TO COME HOME. I DID SOME TESTS DR. KIRCHNER DESIGNED FOR ME.
OH, AND I DRANK WATER FOR THE FIRST TIME.
REALLY? HOW'D YOU LIKE IT?
I LIKE YOU BETTER.
I LOVE YOU.

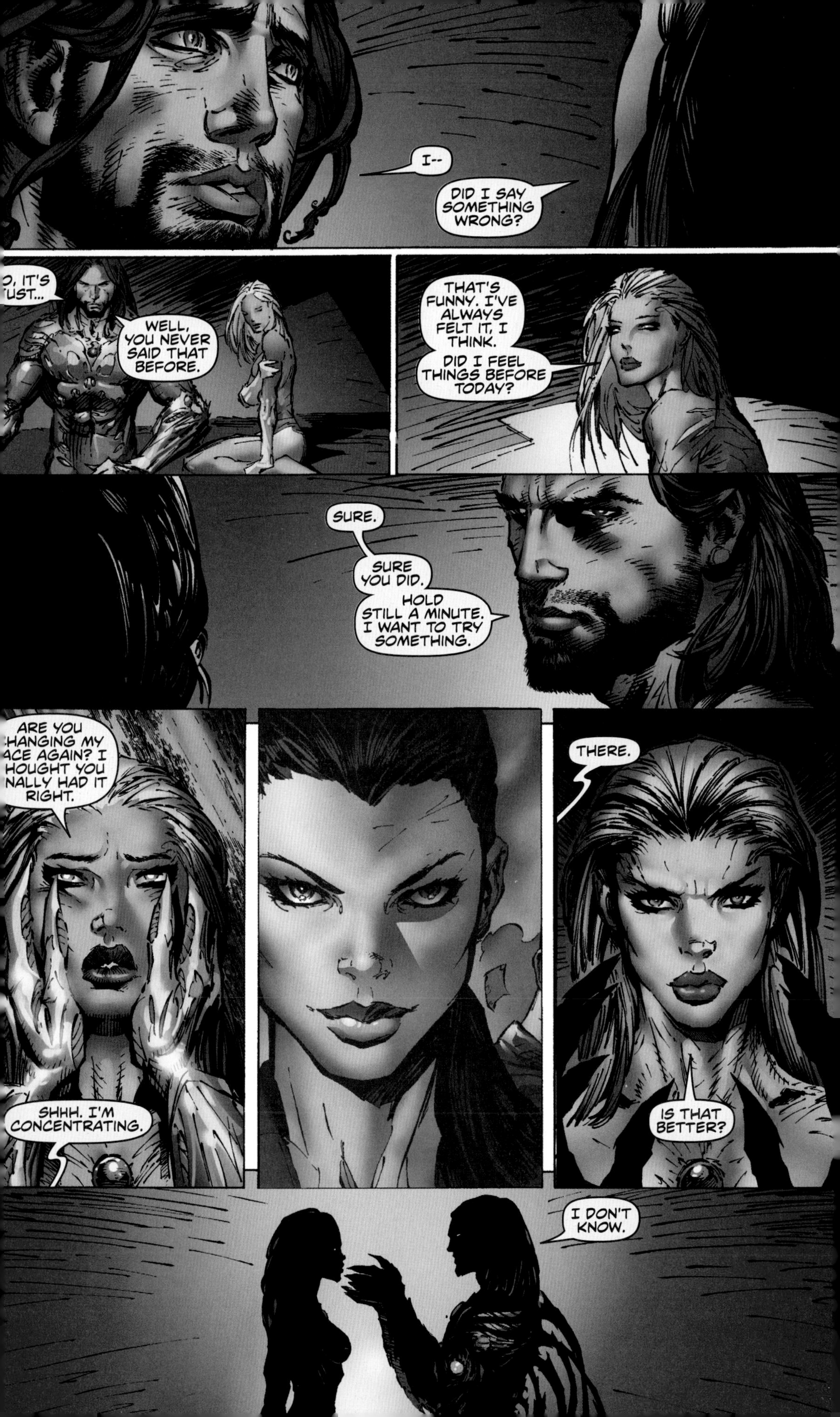
I--
DID I SAY SOMETHING WRONG?
O, IT'S JUST...
WELL, YOU NEVER SAID THAT BEFORE.
THAT'S FUNNY. I'VE ALWAYS FELT IT, I THINK.
DID I FEEL THINGS BEFORE TODAY?
SURE.
SURE YOU DID.
HOLD STILL A MINUTE. I WANT TO TRY SOMETHING.
ARE YOU CHANGING MY ACE AGAIN? I HOUGHT YOU NALLY HAD IT RIGHT.
SHHH. I'M CONCENTRATING.
THERE.
IS THAT BETTER?
I DON'T KNOW.

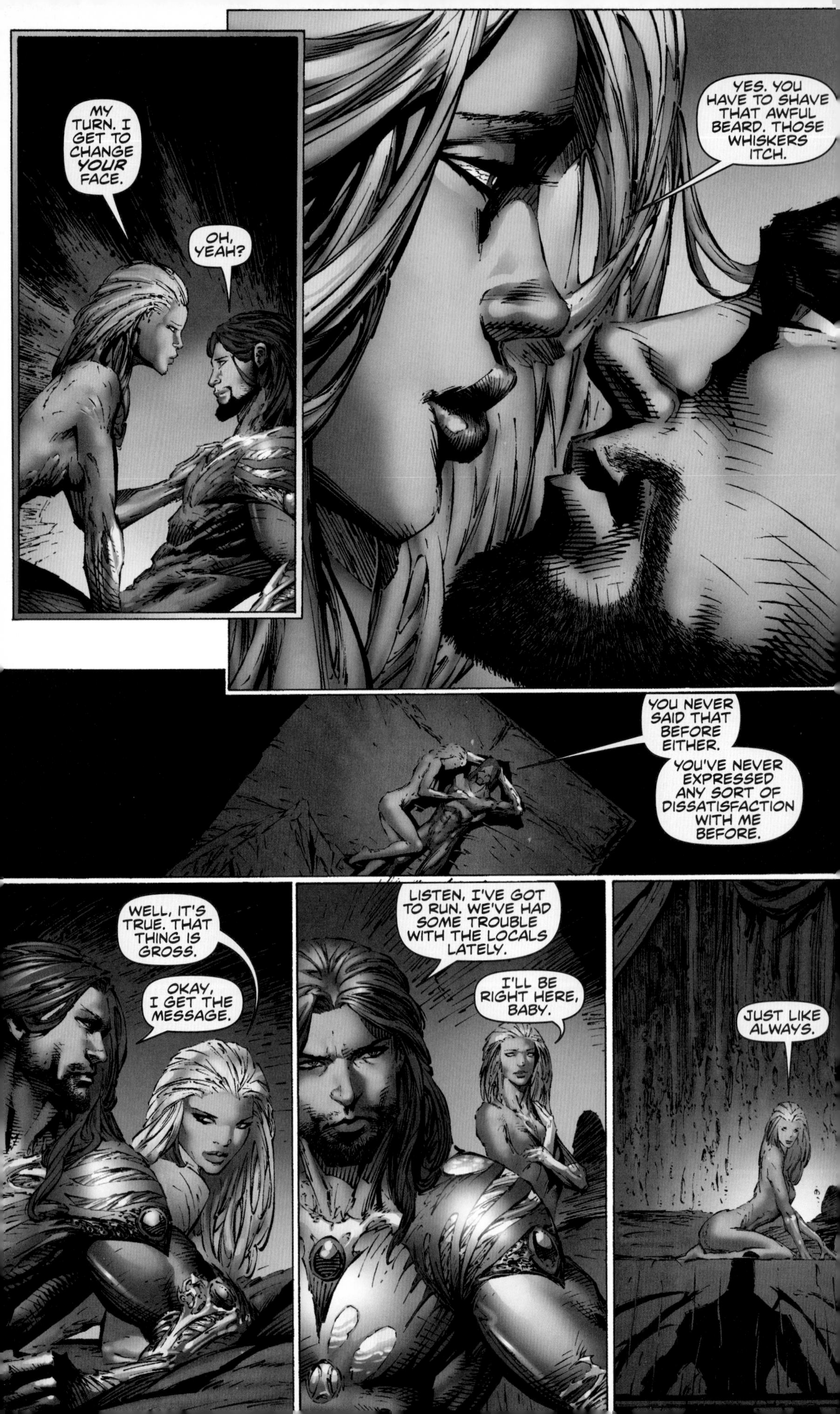
MY TURN. I GET TO CHANGE YOUR FACE.
OH, YEAH?
YES. YOU HAVE TO SHAVE THAT AWFUL BEARD. THOSE WHISKERS ITCH.
YOU NEVER SAID THAT BEFORE EITHER.
YOU'VE NEVER EXPRESSED ANY SORT OF DISSATISFACTION WITH ME BEFORE.
WELL, IT'S TRUE. THAT THING IS GROSS.
OKAY, I GET THE MESSAGE.
LISTEN, I'VE GOT TO RUN. WE'VE HAD SOME TROUBLE WITH THE LOCALS LATELY.
I'LL BE RIGHT HERE, BABY.
JUST LIKE ALWAYS.

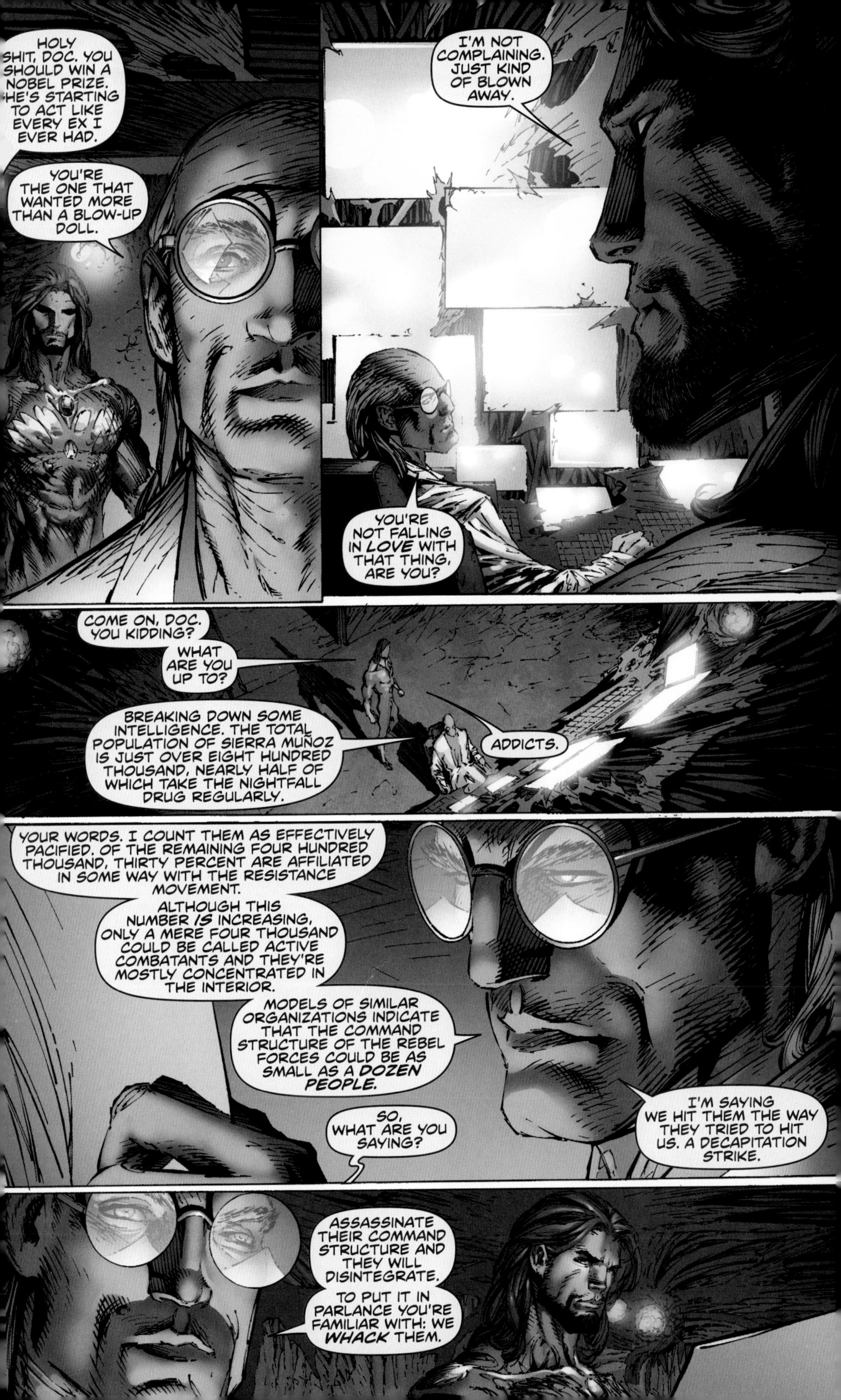

HOLY SHIT, DOC. YOU SHOULD WIN A NOBEL PRIZE. HE'S STARTING TO ACT LIKE EVERY EX I EVER HAD.
YOU'RE THE ONE THAT WANTED MORE THAN A BLOW-UP DOLL.
I'M NOT COMPLAINING. JUST KIND OF BLOWN AWAY.
YOU'RE NOT FALLING IN LOVE WITH THAT THING, ARE YOU?
COME ON, DOC. YOU KIDDING?
WHAT ARE YOU UP TO?
BREAKING DOWN SOME INTELLIGENCE. THE TOTAL POPULATION OF SIERRA MUÑOZ IS JUST OVER EIGHT HUNDRED THOUSAND, NEARLY HALF OF WHICH TAKE THE NIGHTFALL DRUG REGULARLY.
ADDICTS.
YOUR WORDS. I COUNT THEM AS EFFECTIVELY PACIFIED. OF THE REMAINING FOUR HUNDRED THOUSAND, THIRTY PERCENT ARE AFFILIATED IN SOME WAY WITH THE RESISTANCE MOVEMENT.
ALTHOUGH THIS NUMBER IS INCREASING, ONLY A MERE FOUR THOUSAND COULD BE CALLED ACTIVE COMBATANTS AND THEY'RE MOSTLY CONCENTRATED IN THE INTERIOR.
MODELS OF SIMILAR ORGANIZATIONS INDICATE THAT THE COMMAND STRUCTURE OF THE REBEL FORCES COULD BE AS SMALL AS A DOZEN PEOPLE.
SO, WHAT ARE YOU SAYING?
I'M SAYING WE HIT THEM THE WAY THEY TRIED TO HIT US. A DECAPITATION STRIKE.
ASSASSINATE THEIR COMMAND STRUCTURE AND THEY WILL DISINTEGRATE.
TO PUT IT IN PARLANCE YOU'RE FAMILIAR WITH: WE WHACK THEM.

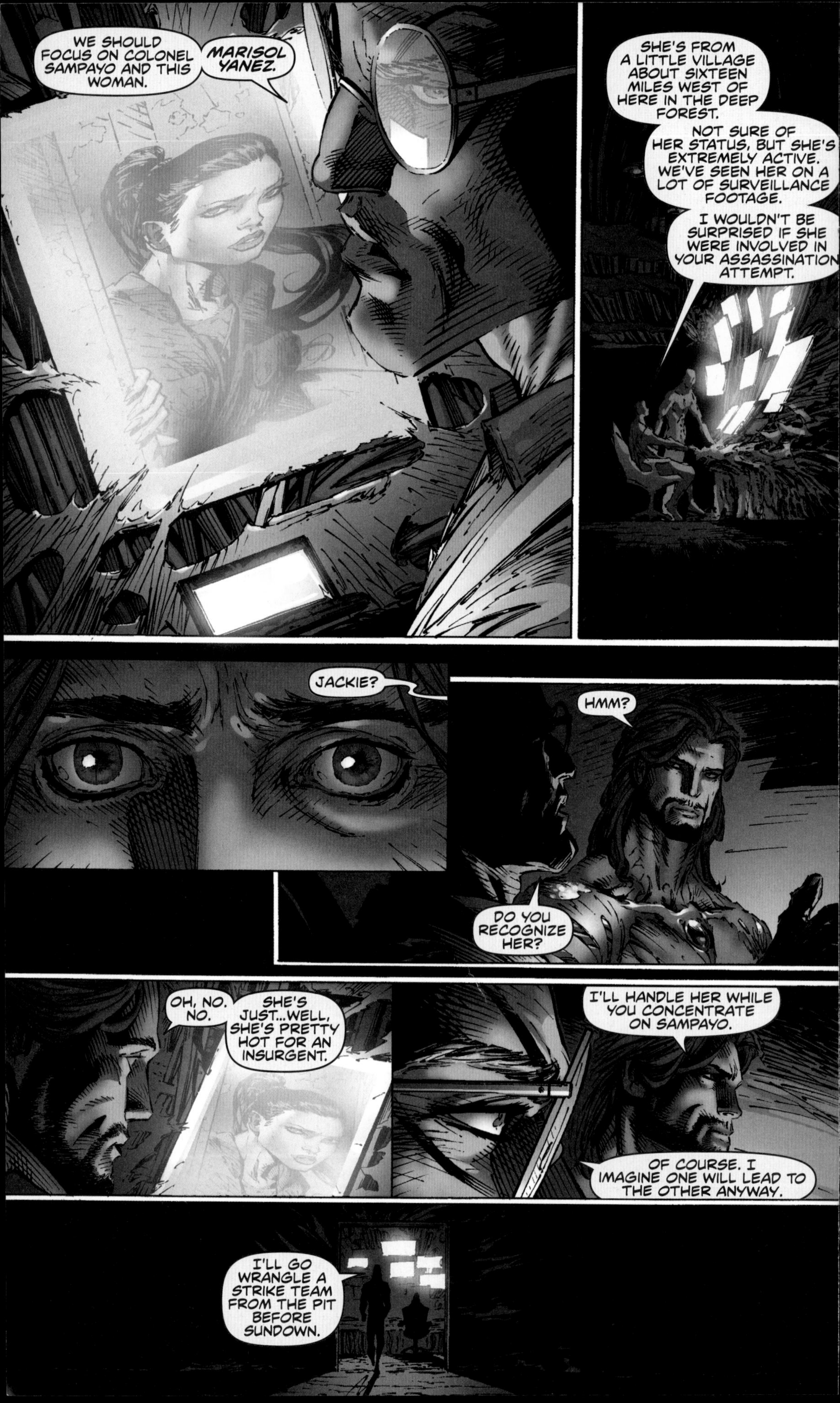
WE SHOULD FOCUS ON COLONEL SAMPAYO AND THIS WOMAN.
MARISOL YANEZ.
SHE'S FROM A LITTLE VILLAGE ABOUT SIXTEEN MILES WEST OF HERE IN THE DEEP FOREST.
NOT SURE OF HER STATUS, BUT SHE'S EXTREMELY ACTIVE. WE'VE SEEN HER ON A LOT OF SURVEILLANCE FOOTAGE.
I WOULDN'T BE SURPRISED IF SHE WERE INVOLVED IN YOUR ASSASSINATION ATTEMPT.
JACKIE?
HMM?
DO YOU RECOGNIZE HER?
OH, NO. NO.
SHE'S JUST...WELL, SHE'S PRETTY HOT FOR AN INSURGENT.
I'LL HANDLE HER WHILE YOU CONCENTRATE ON SAMPAYO.
OF COURSE. I IMAGINE ONE WILL LEAD TO THE OTHER ANYWAY.
I'LL GO WRANGLE A STRIKE TEAM FROM THE PIT BEFORE SUNDOWN.

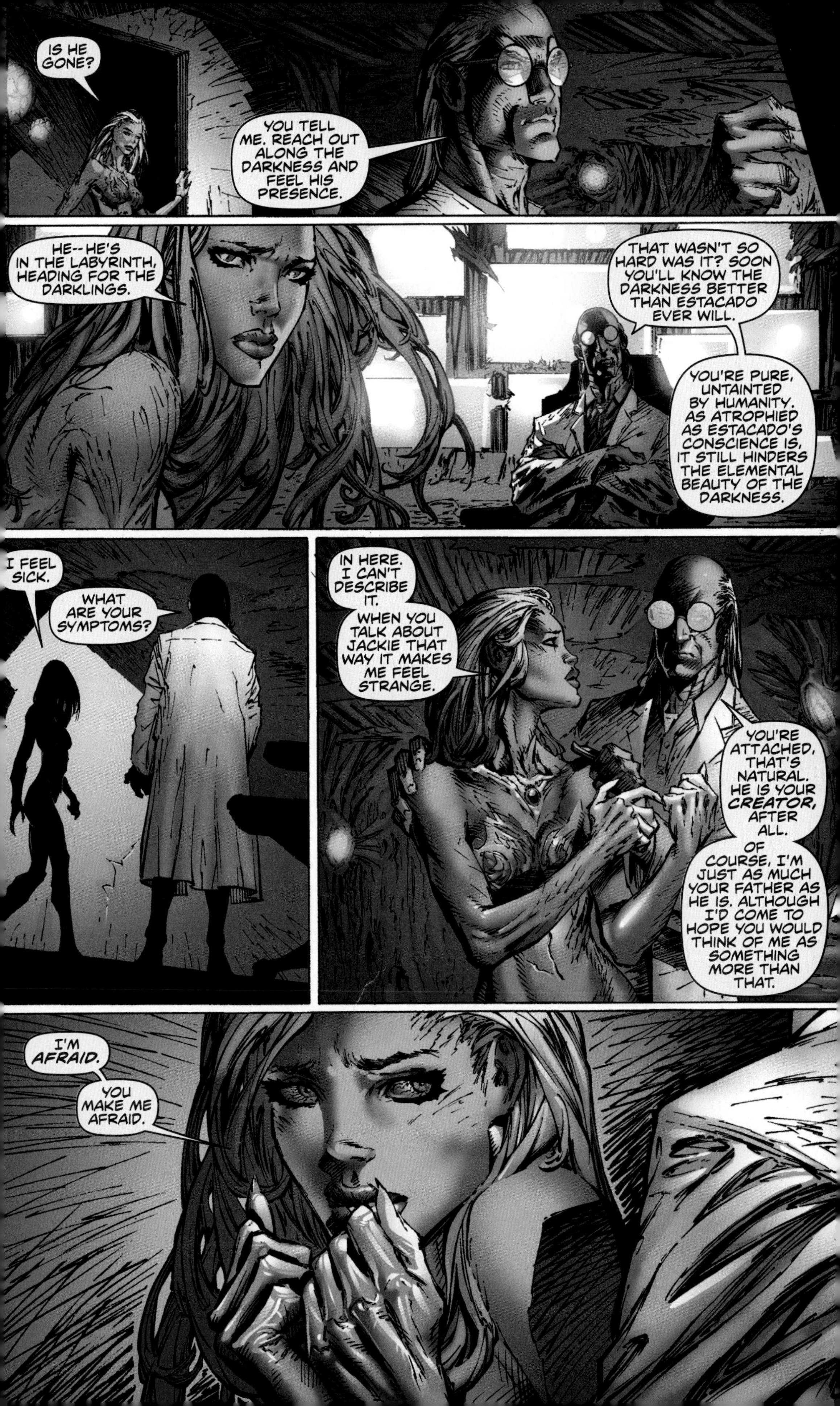
IS HE GONE?
YOU TELL ME. REACH OUT ALONG THE DARKNESS AND FEEL HIS PRESENCE.
HE--HE'S IN THE LABYRINTH, HEADING FOR THE DARKLINGS.
THAT WASN'T SO HARD WAS IT? SOON YOU'LL KNOW THE DARKNESS BETTER THAN ESTACADO EVER WILL.
YOU'RE PURE, UNTAINTED BY HUMANITY. AS ATROPHIED AS ESTACADO'S CONSCIENCE IS, IT STILL HINDERS THE ELEMENTAL BEAUTY OF THE DARKNESS.
I FEEL SICK.
WHAT ARE YOUR SYMPTOMS?
IN HERE. I CAN'T DESCRIBE IT.
WHEN YOU TALK ABOUT JACKIE THAT WAY IT MAKES ME FEEL STRANGE.
YOU'RE ATTACHED, THAT'S NATURAL. HE IS YOUR CREATOR, AFTER ALL.
OF COURSE, I'M JUST AS MUCH YOUR FATHER AS HE IS. ALTHOUGH I'D COME TO HOPE YOU WOULD THINK OF ME AS SOMETHING MORE THAN THAT.
I'M AFRAID.
YOU MAKE ME AFRAID.

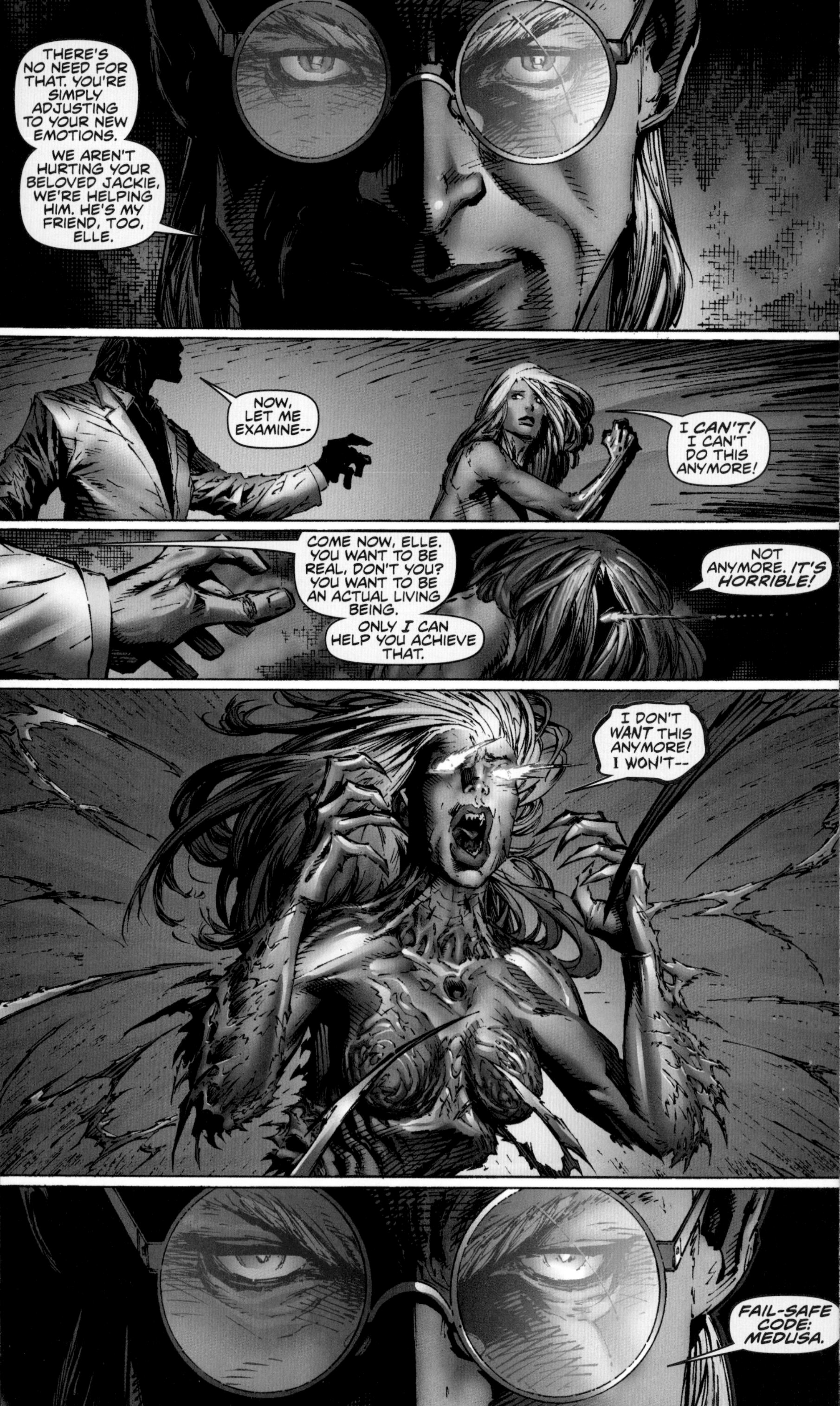
THERE'S NO NEED FOR THAT. YOU'RE SIMPLY ADJUSTING TO YOUR NEW EMOTIONS.
WE AREN'T HURTING YOUR BELOVED JACKIE, WE'RE HELPING HIM. HE'S MY FRIEND, TOO, ELLE.
NOW, LET ME EXAMINE--
I CAN'T! I CAN'T DO THIS ANYMORE!
COME NOW, ELLE. YOU WANT TO BE REAL, DON'T YOU? YOU WANT TO BE AN ACTUAL LIVING BEING.
ONLY I CAN HELP YOU ACHIEVE THAT.
NOT ANYMORE. IT'S HORRIBLE!
I DON'T WANT THIS ANYMORE! I WON'T--
FAIL-SAFE CODE: MEDUSA.

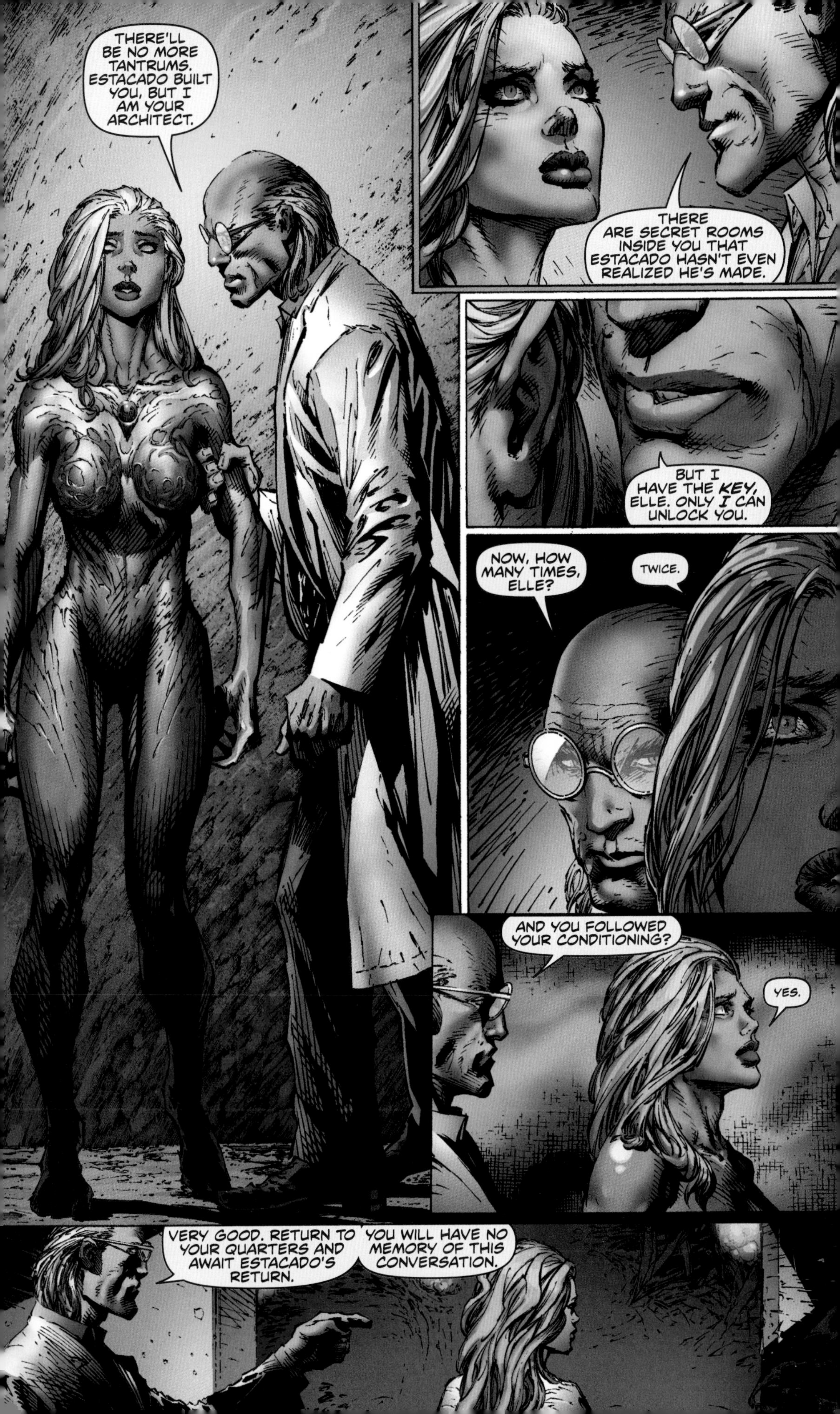
THERE'LL BE NO MORE TANTRUMS. ESTACADO BUILT YOU, BUT I AM YOUR ARCHITECT.
THERE ARE SECRET ROOMS INSIDE YOU THAT ESTACADO HASN'T EVEN REALIZED HE'S MADE.
BUT I HAVE THE **KEY**, ELLE. ONLY **I** CAN UNLOCK YOU.
NOW, HOW MANY TIMES, ELLE?
TWICE.
AND YOU FOLLOWED YOUR CONDITIONING?
YES.
VERY GOOD. RETURN TO YOUR QUARTERS AND AWAIT ESTACADO'S RETURN.
YOU WILL HAVE NO MEMORY OF THIS CONVERSATION.

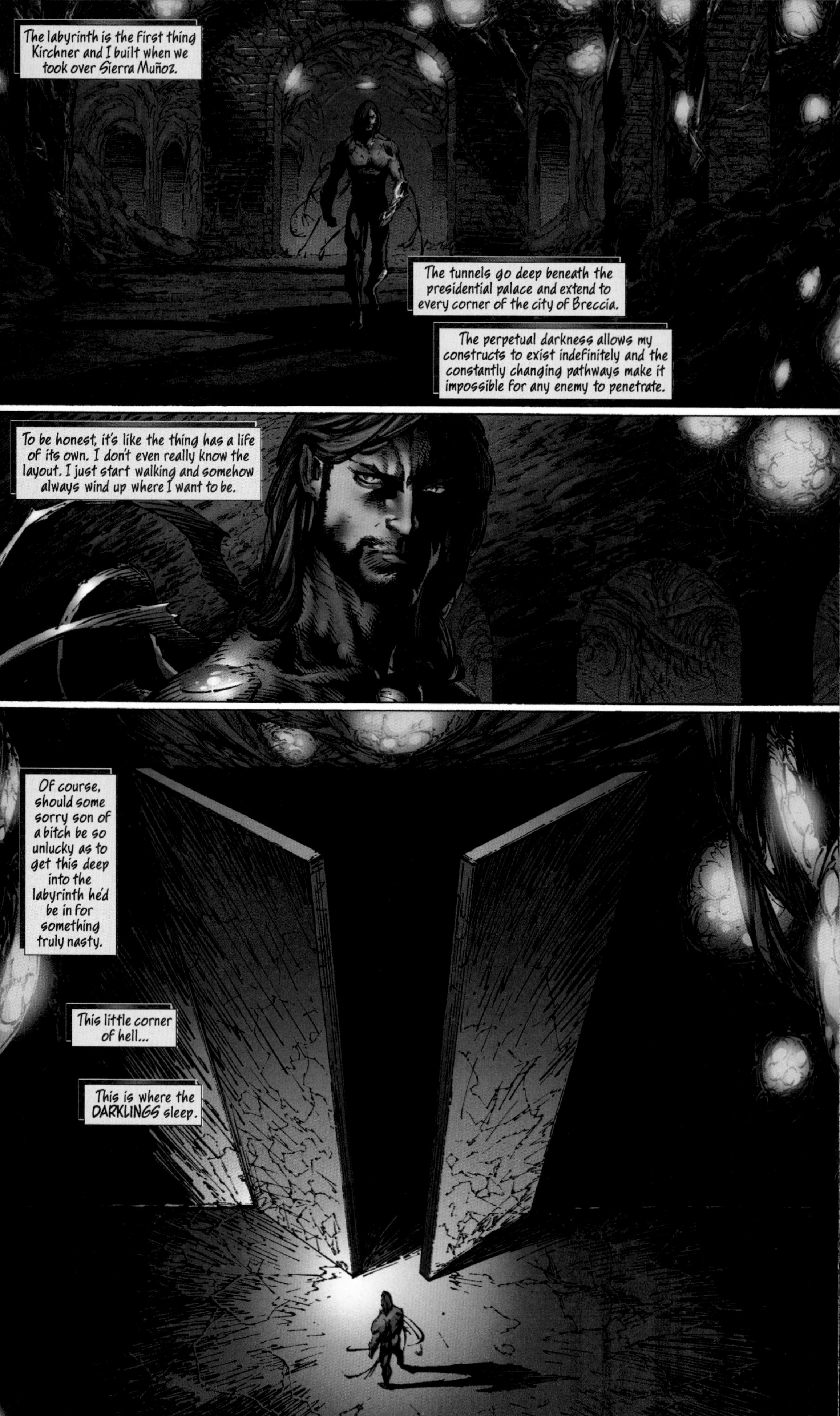
The labyrinth is the first thing Kirchner and I built when we took over Sierra Muñoz.
The tunnels go deep beneath the presidential palace and extend to every corner of the city of Breccia.
The perpetual darkness allows my constructs to exist indefinitely and the constantly changing pathways make it impossible for any enemy to penetrate.
To be honest, it's like the thing has a life of its own. I don't even really know the layout. I just start walking and somehow always wind up where I want to be.
Of course, should some sorry son of a bitch be so unlucky as to get this deep into the labyrinth he'd be in for something truly nasty.
This little corner of hell...
This is where the DARKLINGS sleep.

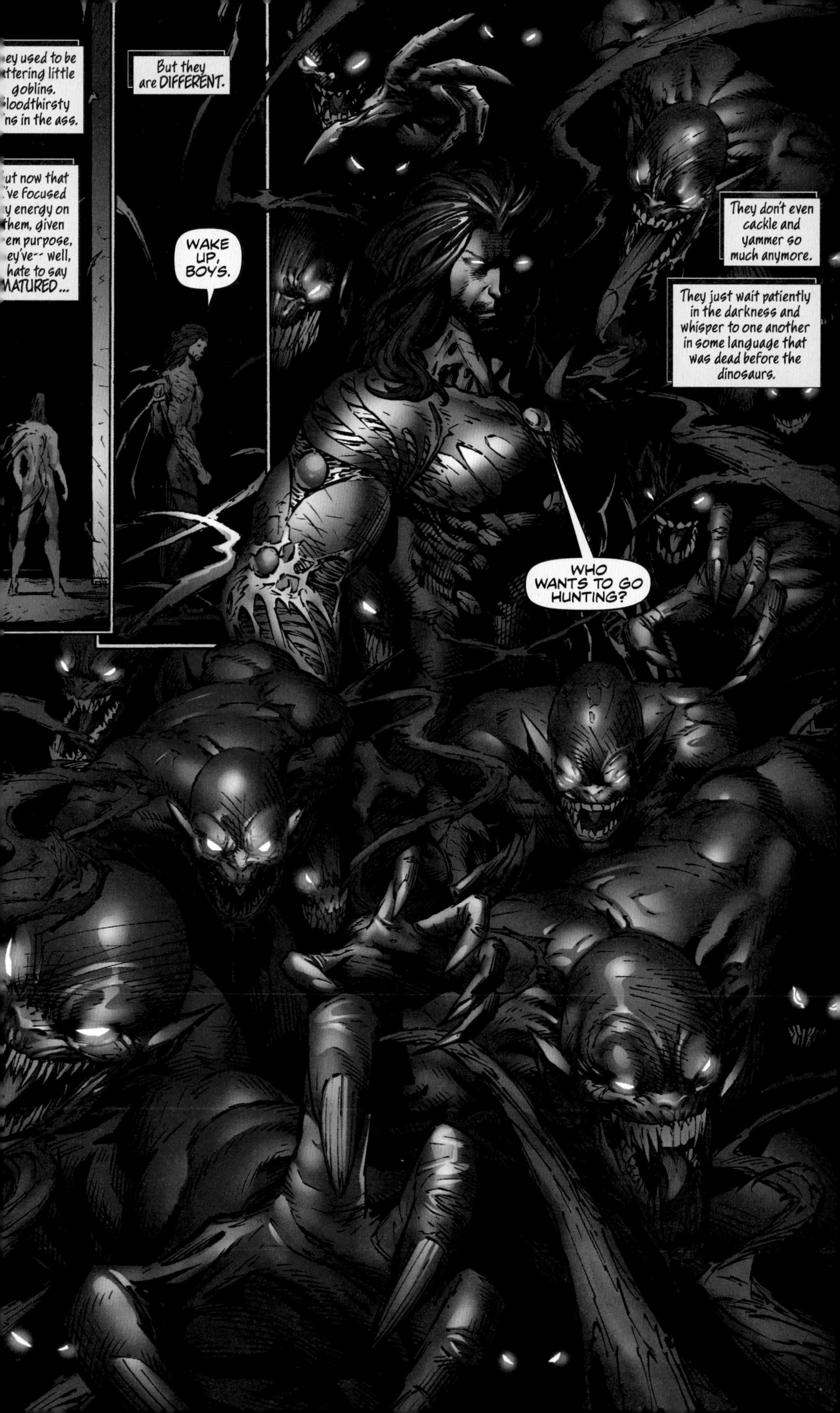

ey used to be
attering little
goblins.
loodthirsty
ns in the ass.
ut now that
've focused
y energy on
them, given
em purpose,
ey've-- well,
hate to say
MATURED...
But they
are DIFFERENT.
WAKE UP, BOYS.
They don't even cackle and yammer so much anymore.
They just wait patiently in the darkness and whisper to one another in some language that was dead before the dinosaurs.
WHO WANTS TO GO HUNTING?

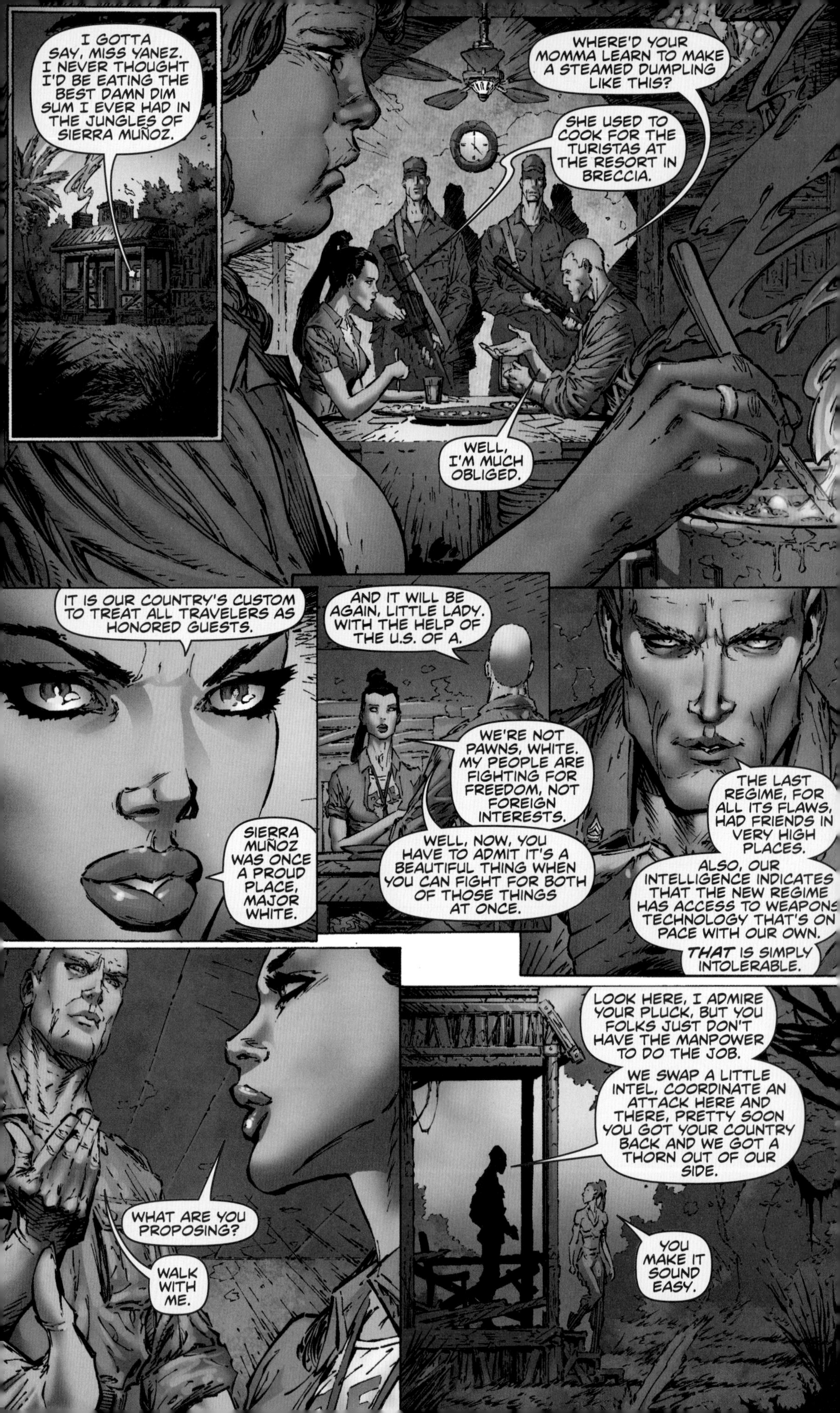
I GOTTA SAY, MISS YANEZ. I NEVER THOUGHT I'D BE EATING THE BEST DAMN DIM SUM I EVER HAD IN THE JUNGLES OF SIERRA MUÑOZ.
WHERE'D YOUR MOMMA LEARN TO MAKE A STEAMED DUMPLING LIKE THIS?
SHE USED TO COOK FOR THE TURISTAS AT THE RESORT IN BRECCIA.
WELL, I'M MUCH OBLIGED.
IT IS OUR COUNTRY'S CUSTOM TO TREAT ALL TRAVELERS AS HONORED GUESTS.
SIERRA MUÑOZ WAS ONCE A PROUD PLACE, MAJOR WHITE.
AND IT WILL BE AGAIN, LITTLE LADY. WITH THE HELP OF THE U.S. OF A.
WE'RE NOT PAWNS, WHITE. MY PEOPLE ARE FIGHTING FOR FREEDOM, NOT FOREIGN INTERESTS.
WELL, NOW, YOU HAVE TO ADMIT IT'S A BEAUTIFUL THING WHEN YOU CAN FIGHT FOR BOTH OF THOSE THINGS AT ONCE.
THE LAST REGIME, FOR ALL ITS FLAWS, HAD FRIENDS IN VERY HIGH PLACES.
ALSO, OUR INTELLIGENCE INDICATES THAT THE NEW REGIME HAS ACCESS TO WEAPONS TECHNOLOGY THAT'S ON PACE WITH OUR OWN.
THAT IS SIMPLY INTOLERABLE.
WHAT ARE YOU PROPOSING?
WALK WITH ME.
LOOK HERE, I ADMIRE YOUR PLUCK, BUT YOU FOLKS JUST DON'T HAVE THE MANPOWER TO DO THE JOB.
WE SWAP A LITTLE INTEL, COORDINATE AN ATTACK HERE AND THERE, PRETTY SOON YOU GOT YOUR COUNTRY BACK AND WE GOT A THORN OUT OF OUR SIDE.
YOU MAKE IT SOUND EASY.

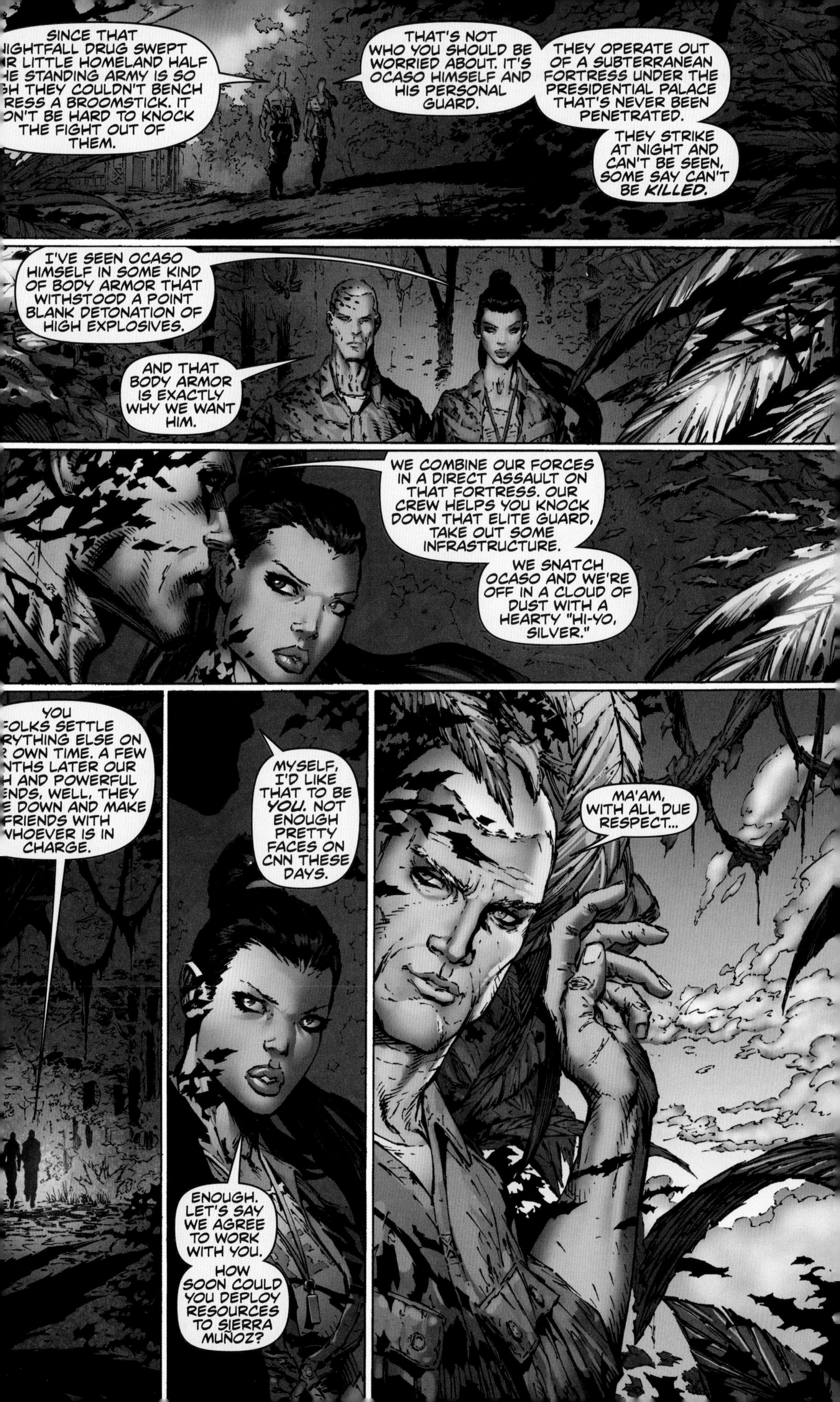

SINCE THAT NIGHTFALL DRUG SWEPT R LITTLE HOMELAND HALF HE STANDING ARMY IS SO GH THEY COULDN'T BENCH RESS A BROOMSTICK. IT ON'T BE HARD TO KNOCK THE FIGHT OUT OF THEM.
THAT'S NOT WHO YOU SHOULD BE WORRIED ABOUT. IT'S OCASO HIMSELF AND HIS PERSONAL GUARD.
THEY OPERATE OUT OF A SUBTERRANEAN FORTRESS UNDER THE PRESIDENTIAL PALACE THAT'S NEVER BEEN PENETRATED.
THEY STRIKE AT NIGHT AND CAN'T BE SEEN, SOME SAY CAN'T BE *KILLED.*
I'VE SEEN OCASO HIMSELF IN SOME KIND OF BODY ARMOR THAT WITHSTOOD A POINT BLANK DETONATION OF HIGH EXPLOSIVES.
AND THAT BODY ARMOR IS EXACTLY WHY WE WANT HIM.
WE COMBINE OUR FORCES IN A DIRECT ASSAULT ON THAT FORTRESS. OUR CREW HELPS YOU KNOCK DOWN THAT ELITE GUARD, TAKE OUT SOME INFRASTRUCTURE.
WE SNATCH OCASO AND WE'RE OFF IN A CLOUD OF DUST WITH A HEARTY "HI-YO, SILVER."
YOU FOLKS SETTLE RYTHING ELSE ON R OWN TIME. A FEW NTHS LATER OUR H AND POWERFUL ENDS, WELL, THEY E DOWN AND MAKE FRIENDS WITH WHOEVER IS IN CHARGE.
MYSELF, I'D LIKE THAT TO BE *YOU.* NOT ENOUGH PRETTY FACES ON CNN THESE DAYS.
MA'AM, WITH ALL DUE RESPECT...
ENOUGH. LET'S SAY WE AGREE TO WORK WITH YOU.
HOW SOON COULD YOU DEPLOY RESOURCES TO SIERRA MUÑOZ?

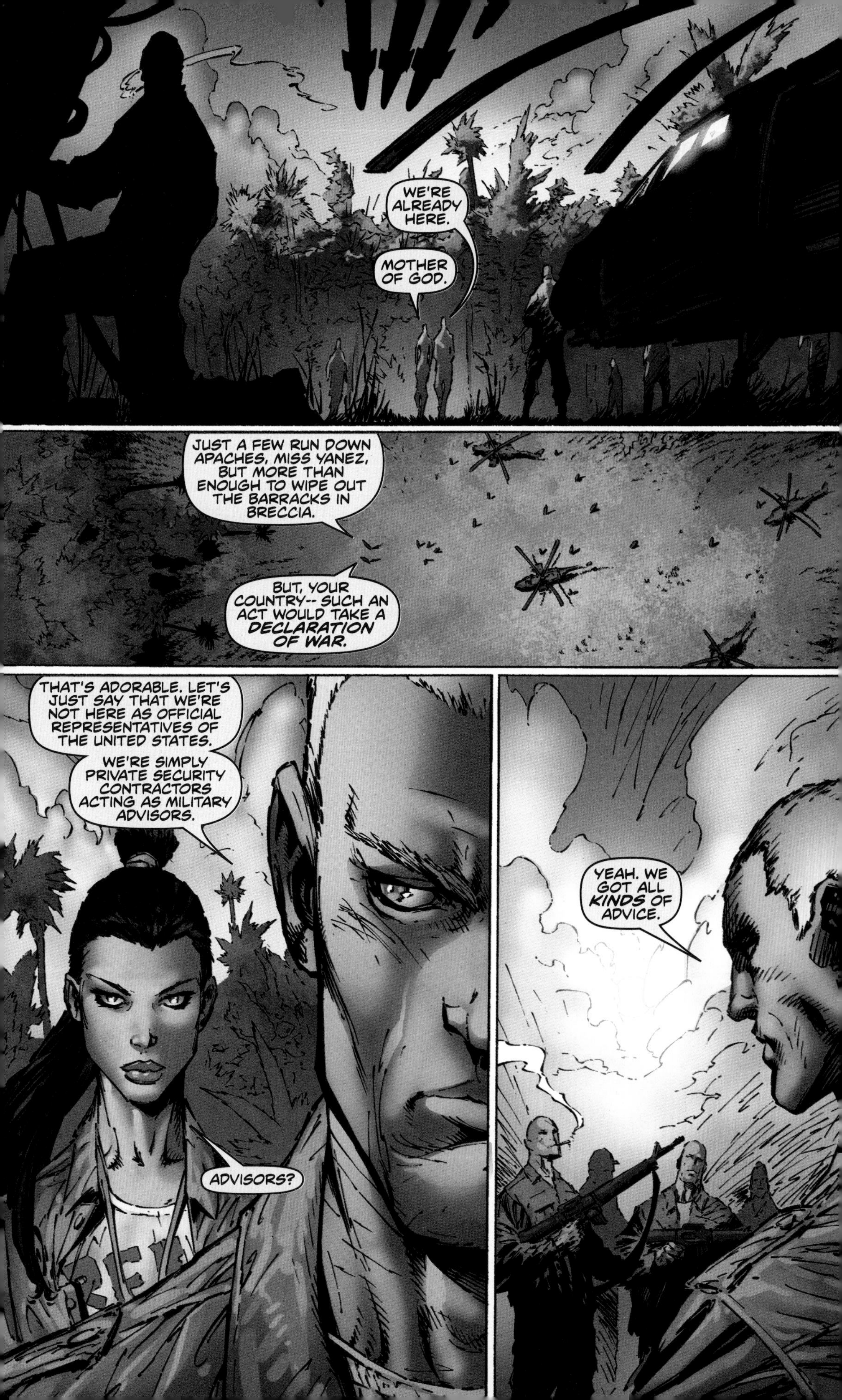
WE'RE ALREADY HERE.
MOTHER OF GOD.
JUST A FEW RUN DOWN APACHES, MISS YANEZ, BUT MORE THAN ENOUGH TO WIPE OUT THE BARRACKS IN BRECCIA.
BUT, YOUR COUNTRY-- SUCH AN ACT WOULD TAKE A DECLARATION OF WAR.
THAT'S ADORABLE. LET'S JUST SAY THAT WE'RE NOT HERE AS OFFICIAL REPRESENTATIVES OF THE UNITED STATES.
WE'RE SIMPLY PRIVATE SECURITY CONTRACTORS ACTING AS MILITARY ADVISORS.
ADVISORS?
YEAH. WE GOT ALL KINDS OF ADVICE.

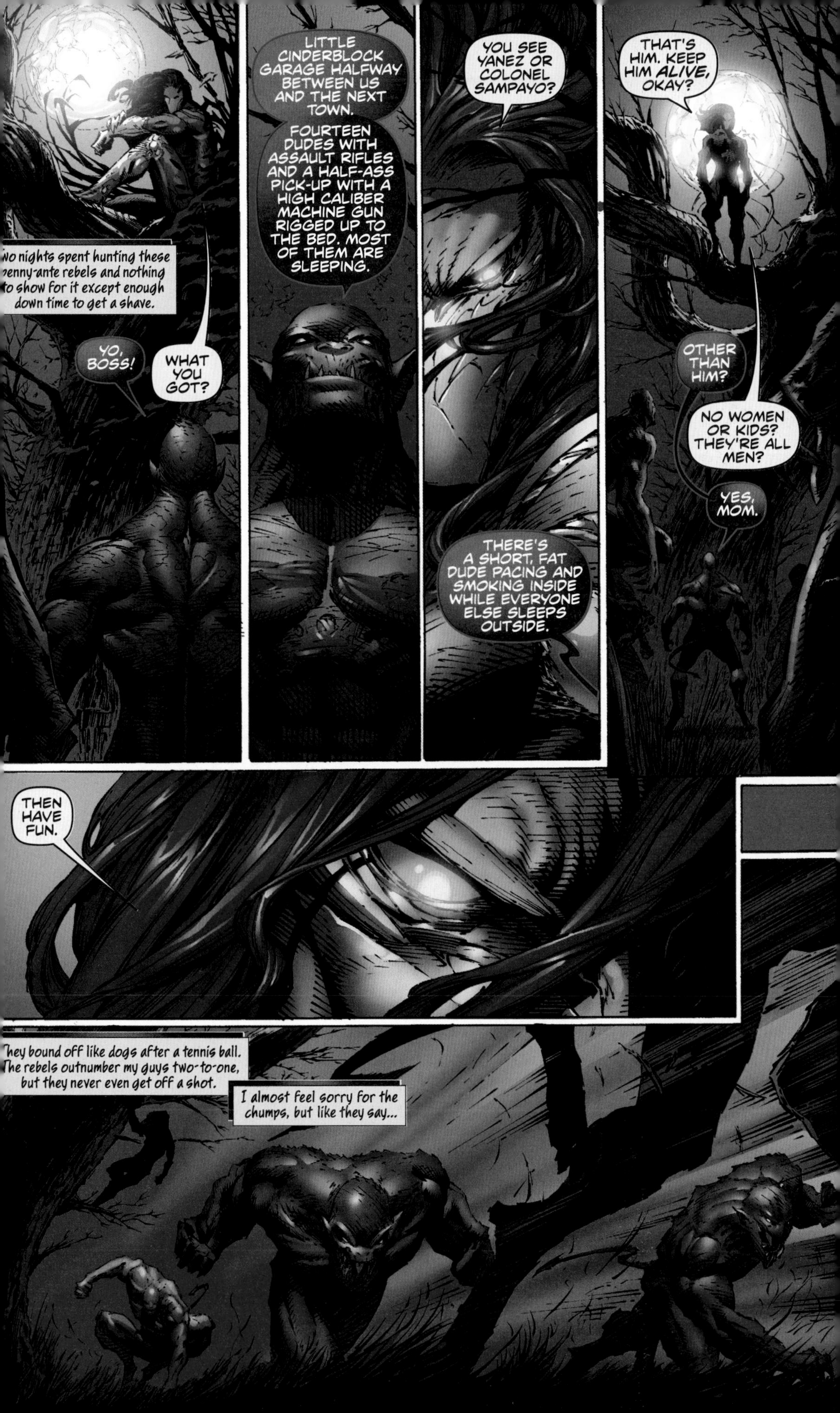

wo nights spent hunting these penny-ante rebels and nothing to show for it except enough down time to get a shave.
YO, BOSS!
WHAT YOU GOT?
LITTLE CINDERBLOCK GARAGE HALFWAY BETWEEN US AND THE NEXT TOWN.
FOURTEEN DUDES WITH ASSAULT RIFLES AND A HALF-ASS PICK-UP WITH A HIGH CALIBER MACHINE GUN RIGGED UP TO THE BED. MOST OF THEM ARE SLEEPING.
YOU SEE YANEZ OR COLONEL SAMPAYO?
THERE'S A SHORT, FAT DUDE PACING AND SMOKING INSIDE WHILE EVERYONE ELSE SLEEPS OUTSIDE.
THAT'S HIM. KEEP HIM ALIVE, OKAY?
OTHER THAN HIM?
NO WOMEN OR KIDS? THEY'RE ALL MEN?
YES, MOM.
THEN HAVE FUN.
hey bound off like dogs after a tennis ball. The rebels outnumber my guys two-to-one, but they never even get off a shot.
I almost feel sorry for the chumps, but like they say...

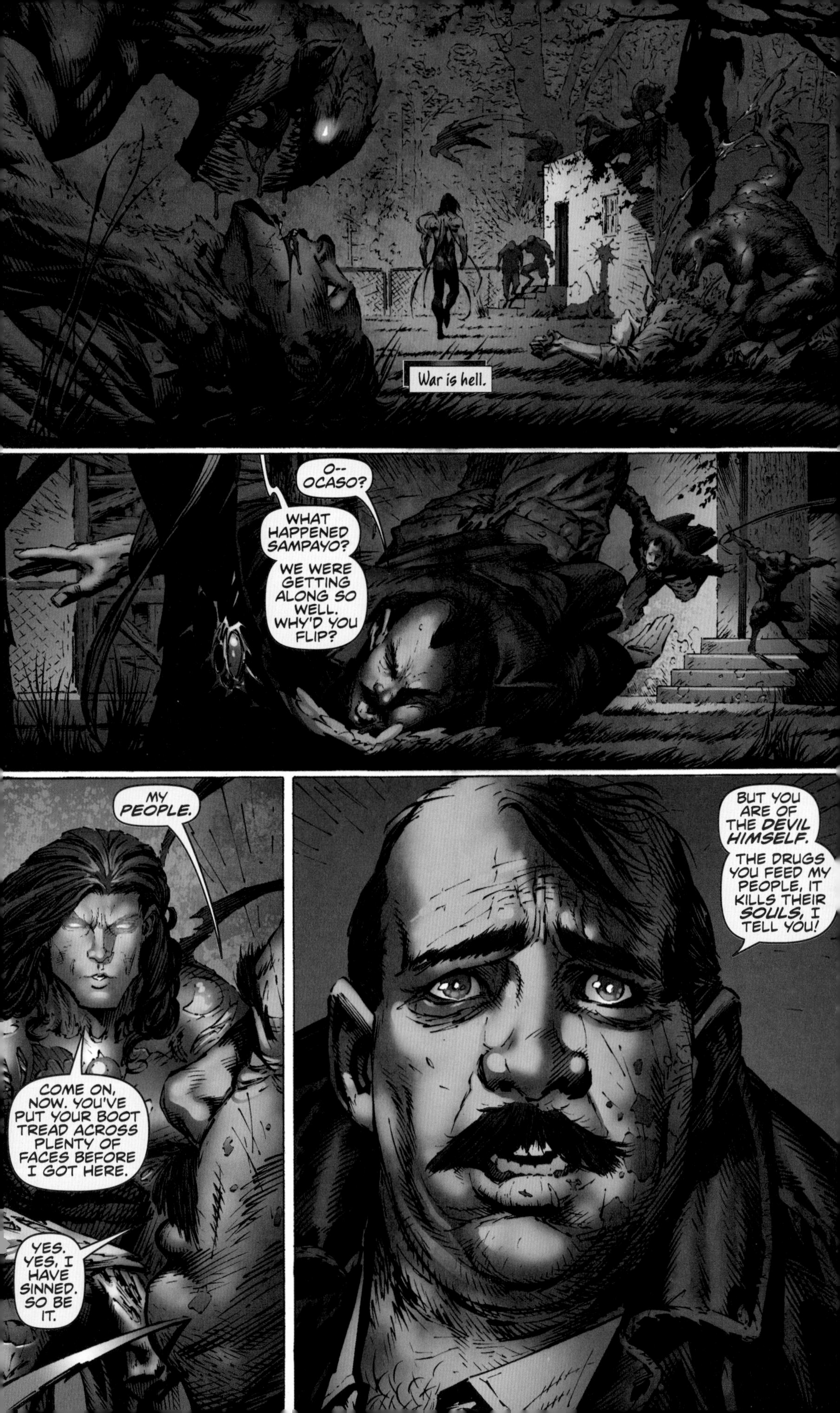
War is hell.
O-- OCASO?
WHAT HAPPENED SAMPAYO? WE WERE GETTING ALONG SO WELL. WHY'D YOU FLIP?
MY PEOPLE.
BUT YOU ARE OF THE DEVIL HIMSELF.
THE DRUGS YOU FEED MY PEOPLE, IT KILLS THEIR SOULS, I TELL YOU!
COME ON, NOW. YOU'VE PUT YOUR BOOT TREAD ACROSS PLENTY OF FACES BEFORE I GOT HERE.
YES. YES, I HAVE SINNED. SO BE IT.

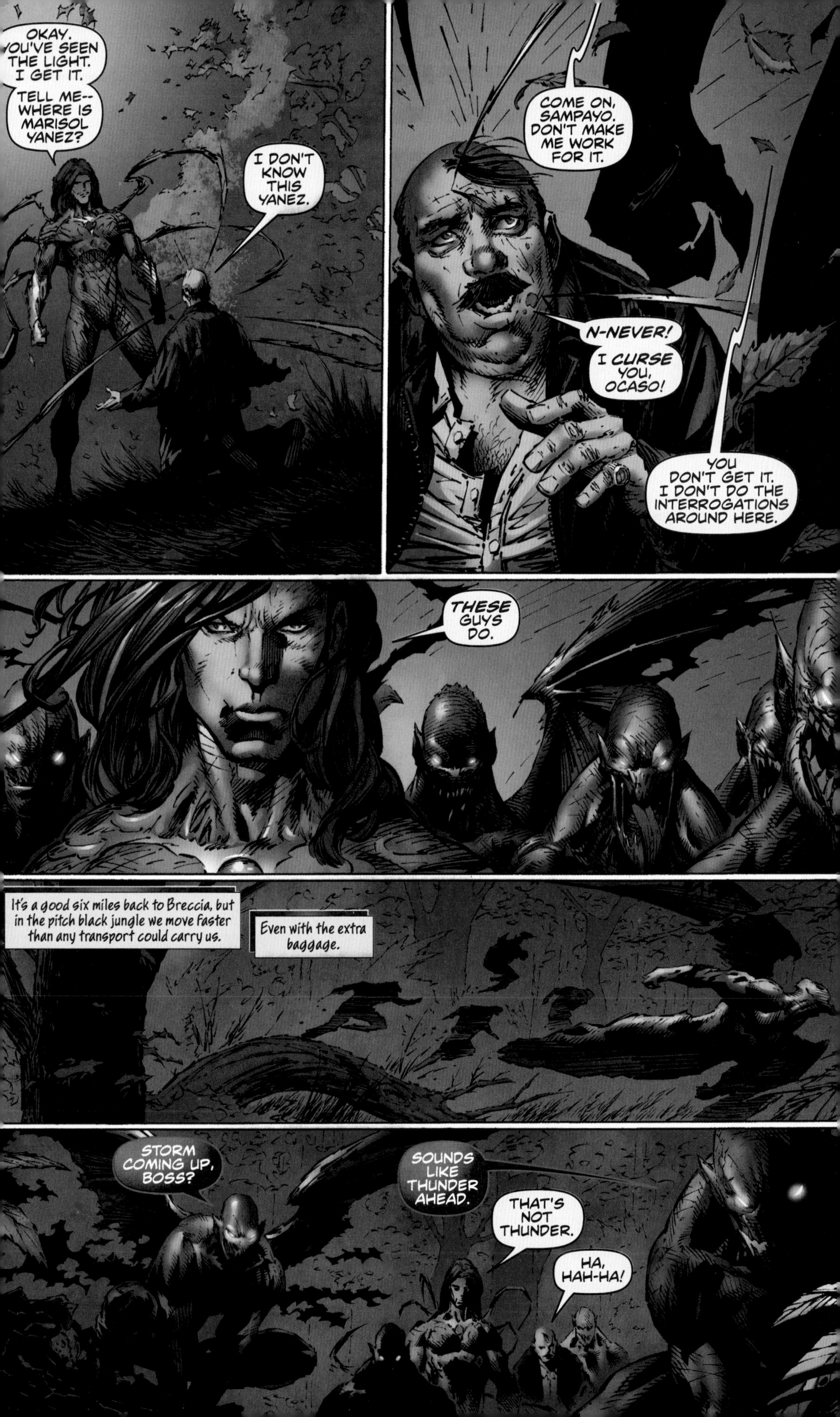

OKAY. YOU'VE SEEN THE LIGHT. I GET IT.
TELL ME-- WHERE IS MARISOL YANEZ?
I DON'T KNOW THIS YANEZ.
COME ON, SAMPAYO. DON'T MAKE ME WORK FOR IT.
N-NEVER!
I CURSE YOU, OCASO!
YOU DON'T GET IT. I DON'T DO THE INTERROGATIONS AROUND HERE.
THESE GUYS DO.
It's a good six miles back to Breccia, but in the pitch black jungle we move faster than any transport could carry us.
Even with the extra baggage.
STORM COMING UP, BOSS?
SOUNDS LIKE THUNDER AHEAD.
THAT'S NOT THUNDER.
HA, HAH-HA!

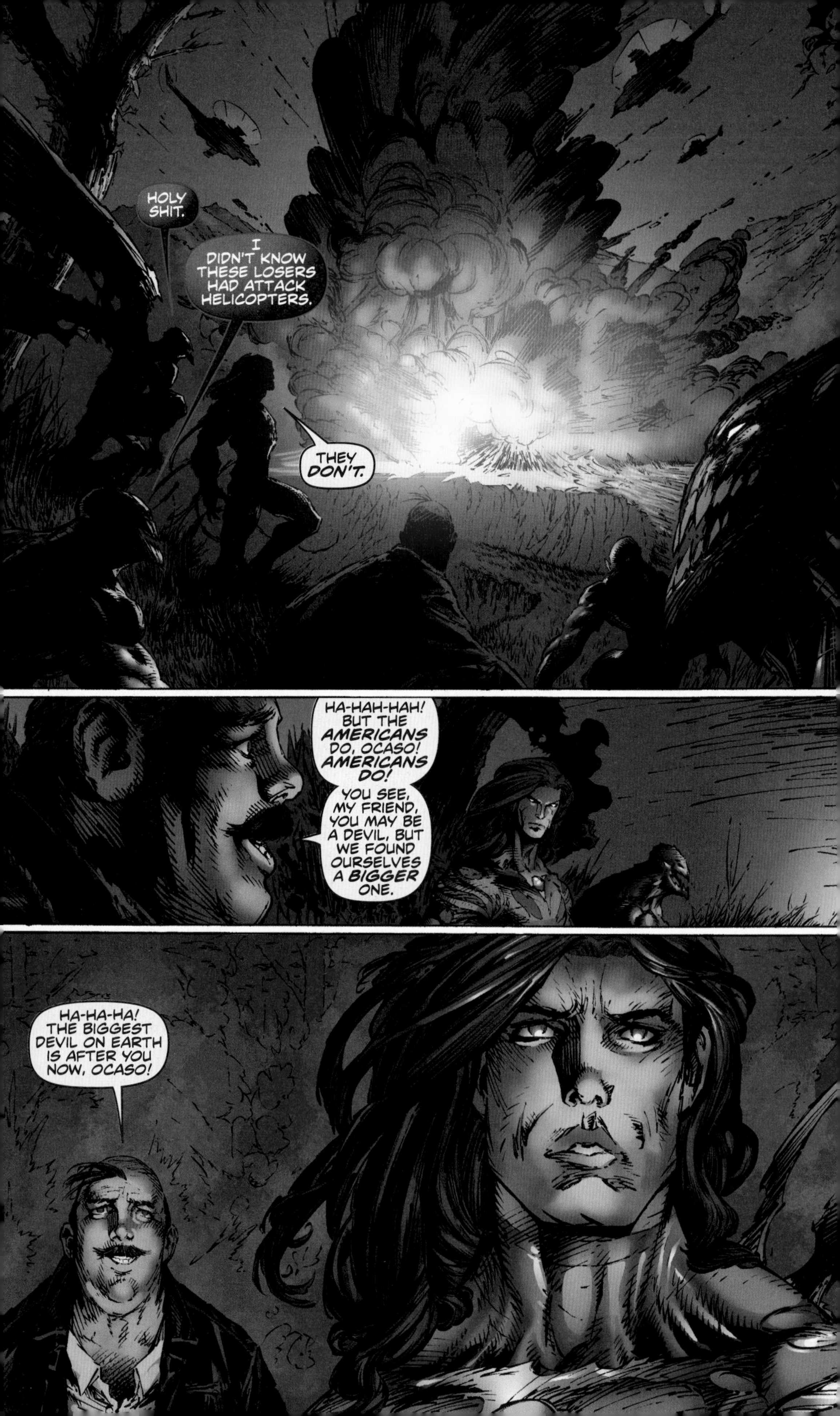
HOLY SHIT.
I DIDN'T KNOW THESE LOSERS HAD ATTACK HELICOPTERS.
THEY DON'T.
HA-HAH-HAH! BUT THE AMERICANS DO, OCASO! AMERICANS DO!
YOU SEE, MY FRIEND, YOU MAY BE A DEVIL, BUT WE FOUND OURSELVES A BIGGER ONE.
HA-HA-HA! THE BIGGEST DEVIL ON EARTH IS AFTER YOU NOW, OCASO!

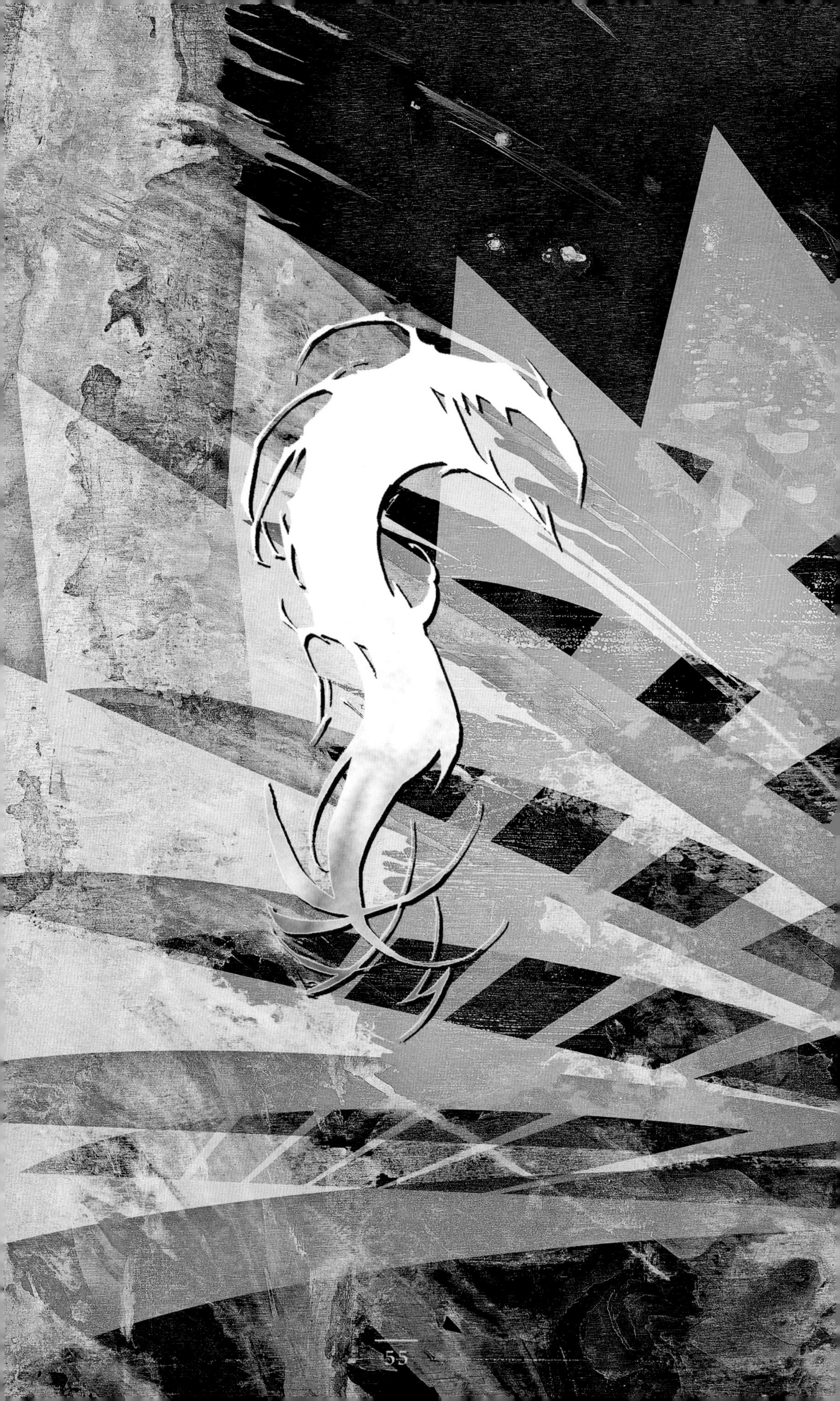

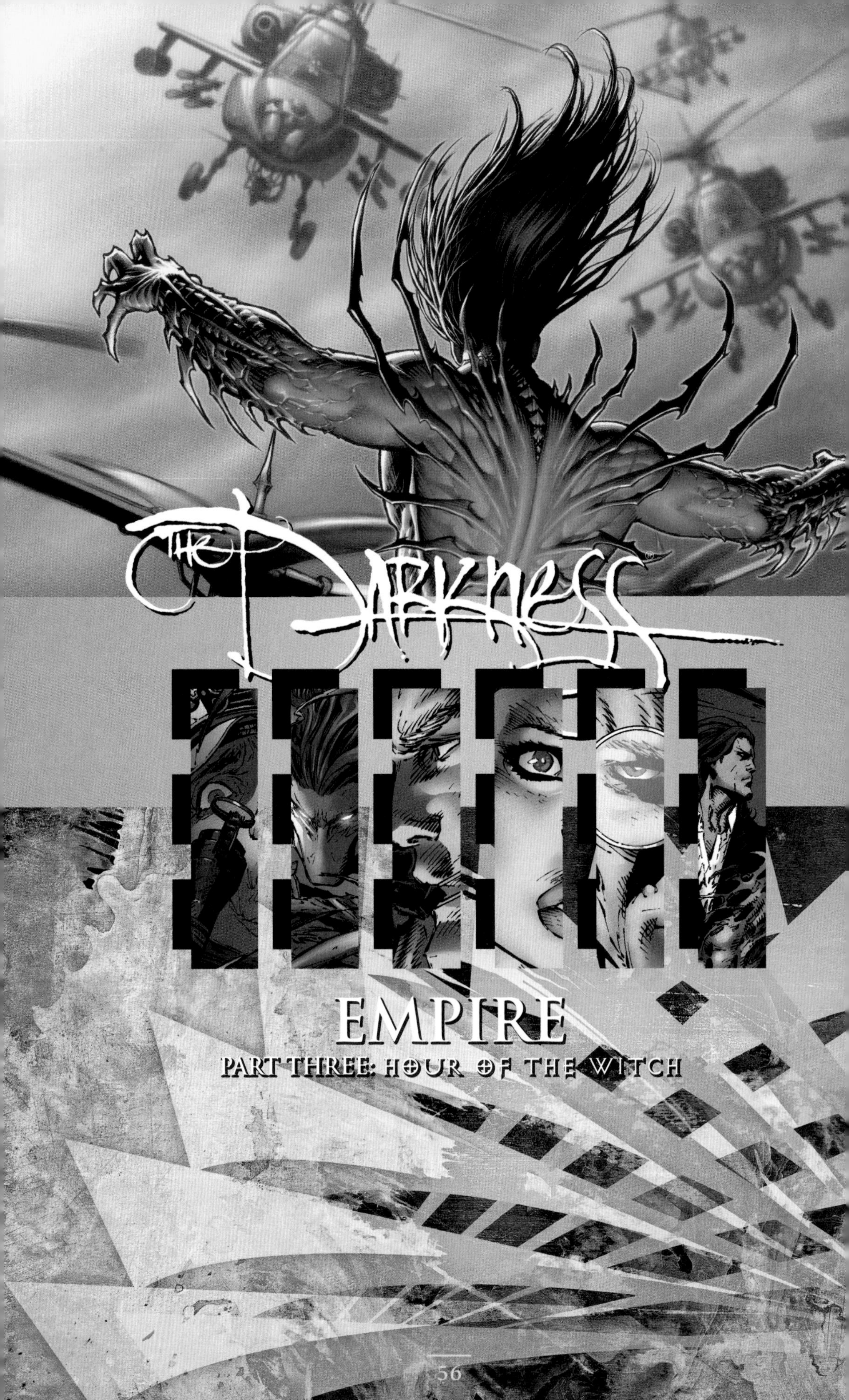
The Darkness®
EMPIRE
PART THREE: HOUR OF THE WITCH

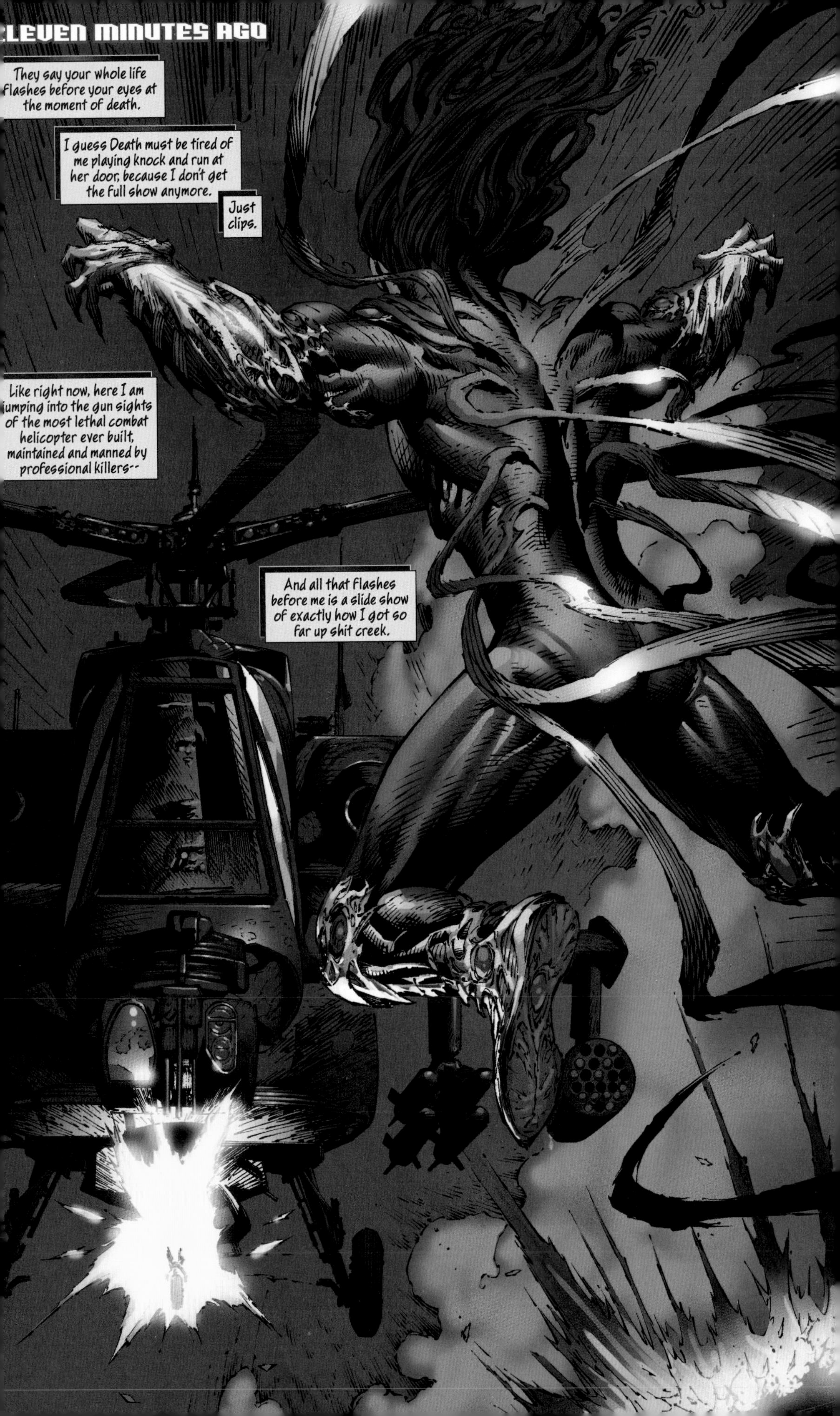

ELEVEN MINUTES AGO
They say your whole life flashes before your eyes at the moment of death.
I guess Death must be tired of me playing knock and run at her door, because I don't get the full show anymore.
Just clips.
Like right now, here I am jumping into the gun sights of the most lethal combat helicopter ever built, maintained and manned by professional killers--
And all that flashes before me is a slide show of exactly how I got so far up shit creek.

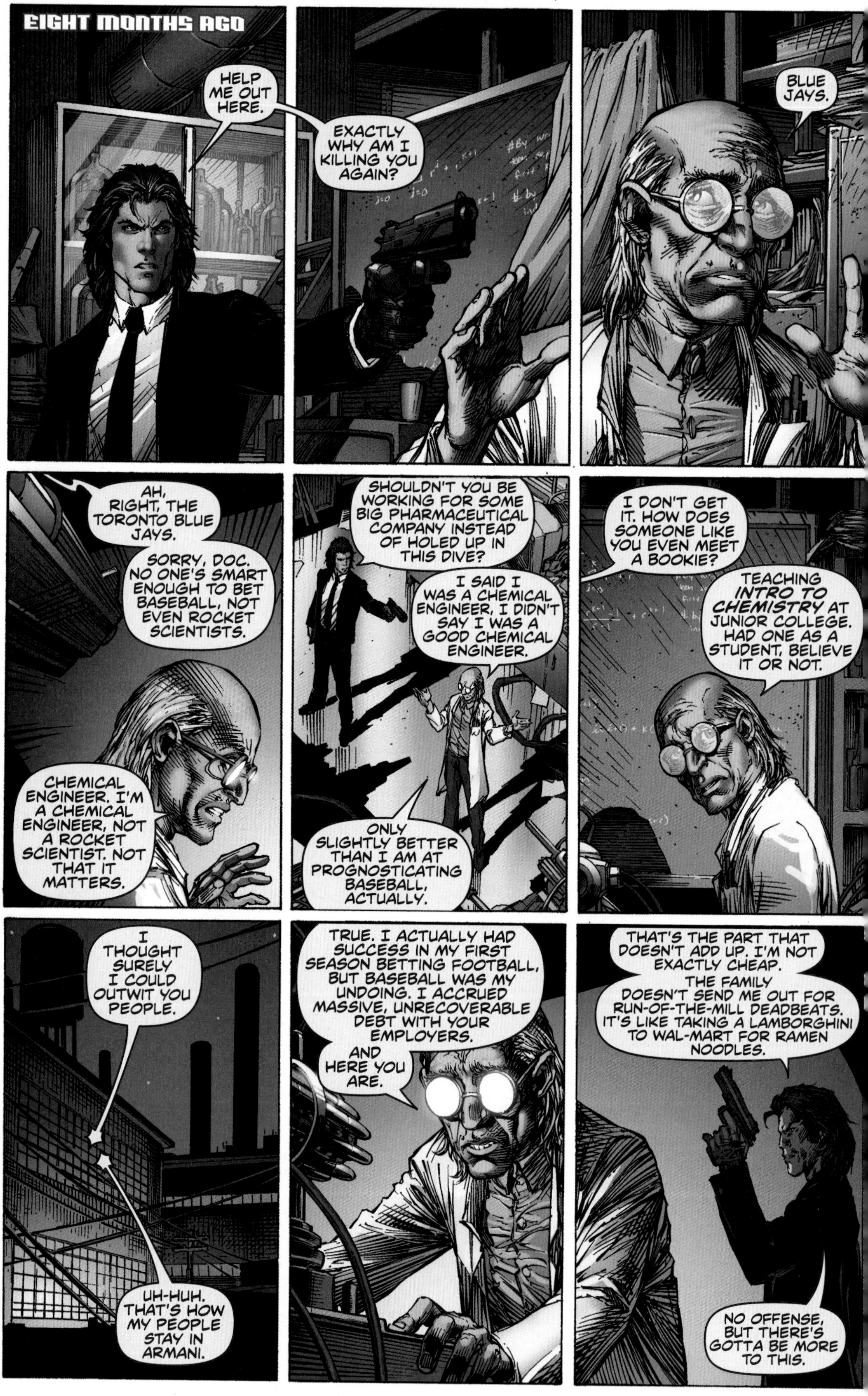
EIGHT MONTHS AGO
HELP ME OUT HERE.
EXACTLY WHY AM I KILLING YOU AGAIN?
BLUE JAYS.
AH, RIGHT, THE TORONTO BLUE JAYS.
SORRY, DOC. NO ONE'S SMART ENOUGH TO BET BASEBALL, NOT EVEN ROCKET SCIENTISTS.
CHEMICAL ENGINEER. I'M A CHEMICAL ENGINEER, NOT A ROCKET SCIENTIST. NOT THAT IT MATTERS.
SHOULDN'T YOU BE WORKING FOR SOME BIG PHARMACEUTICAL COMPANY INSTEAD OF HOLED UP IN THIS DIVE?
I SAID I WAS A CHEMICAL ENGINEER, I DIDN'T SAY I WAS A GOOD CHEMICAL ENGINEER.
ONLY SLIGHTLY BETTER THAN I AM AT PROGNOSTICATING BASEBALL, ACTUALLY.
I DON'T GET IT. HOW DOES SOMEONE LIKE YOU EVEN MEET A BOOKIE?
TEACHING INTRO TO CHEMISTRY AT JUNIOR COLLEGE. HAD ONE AS A STUDENT, BELIEVE IT OR NOT.
I THOUGHT SURELY I COULD OUTWIT YOU PEOPLE.
UH-HUH. THAT'S HOW MY PEOPLE STAY IN ARMANI.
TRUE. I ACTUALLY HAD SUCCESS IN MY FIRST SEASON BETTING FOOTBALL, BUT BASEBALL WAS MY UNDOING. I ACCRUED MASSIVE, UNRECOVERABLE DEBT WITH YOUR EMPLOYERS.
AND HERE YOU ARE.
THAT'S THE PART THAT DOESN'T ADD UP. I'M NOT EXACTLY CHEAP.
THE FAMILY DOESN'T SEND ME OUT FOR RUN-OF-THE-MILL DEADBEATS. IT'S LIKE TAKING A LAMBORGHINI TO WAL-MART FOR RAMEN NOODLES.
NO OFFENSE, BUT THERE'S GOTTA BE MORE TO THIS.

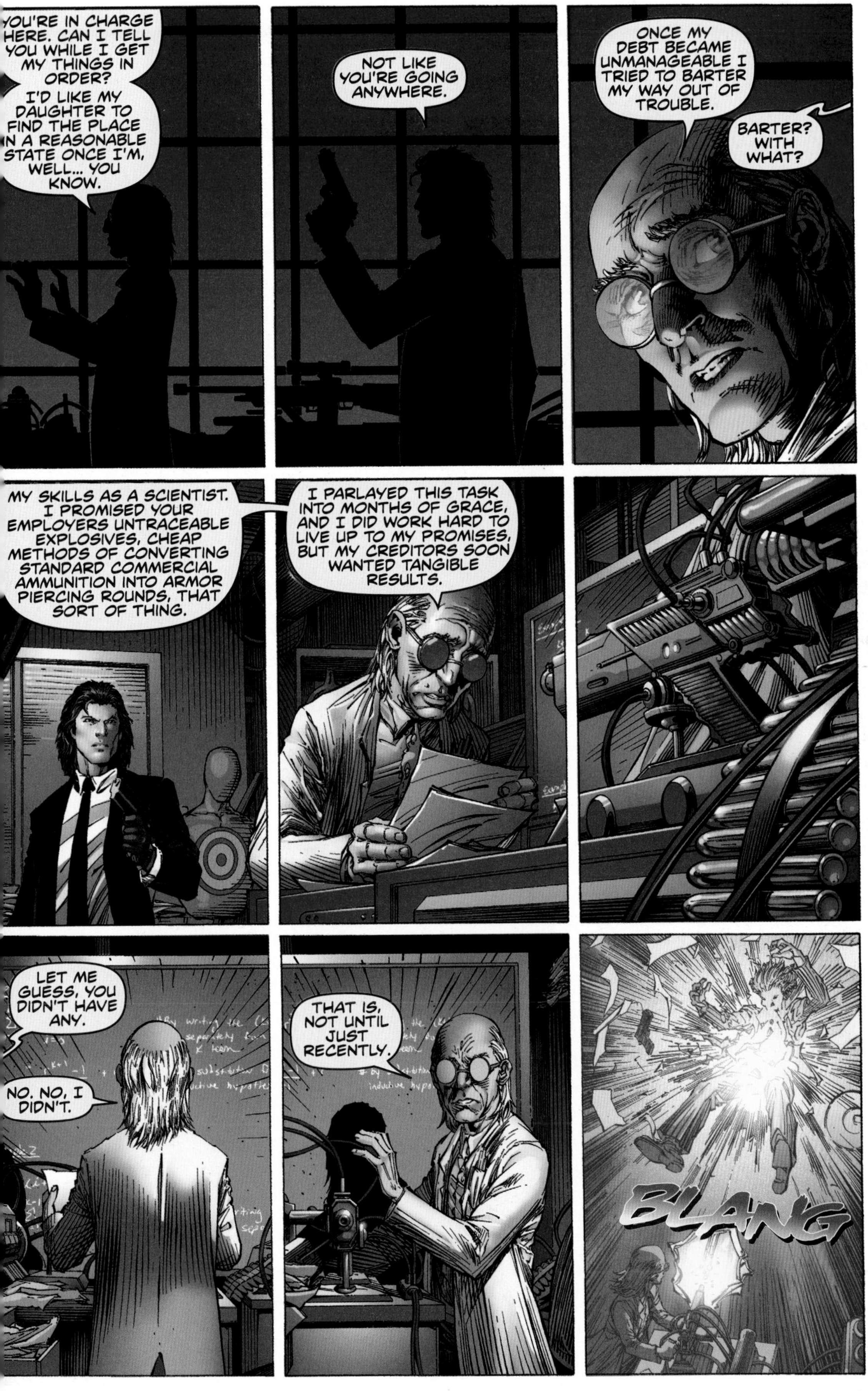
YOU'RE IN CHARGE HERE. CAN I TELL YOU WHILE I GET MY THINGS IN ORDER?
I'D LIKE MY DAUGHTER TO FIND THE PLACE IN A REASONABLE STATE ONCE I'M, WELL... YOU KNOW.
NOT LIKE YOU'RE GOING ANYWHERE.
ONCE MY DEBT BECAME UNMANAGEABLE I TRIED TO BARTER MY WAY OUT OF TROUBLE.
BARTER? WITH WHAT?
MY SKILLS AS A SCIENTIST. I PROMISED YOUR EMPLOYERS UNTRACEABLE EXPLOSIVES, CHEAP METHODS OF CONVERTING STANDARD COMMERCIAL AMMUNITION INTO ARMOR PIERCING ROUNDS, THAT SORT OF THING.
I PARLAYED THIS TASK INTO MONTHS OF GRACE, AND I DID WORK HARD TO LIVE UP TO MY PROMISES, BUT MY CREDITORS SOON WANTED TANGIBLE RESULTS.
LET ME GUESS, YOU DIDN'T HAVE ANY.
NO. NO, I DIDN'T.
THAT IS, NOT UNTIL JUST RECENTLY.
BLANG

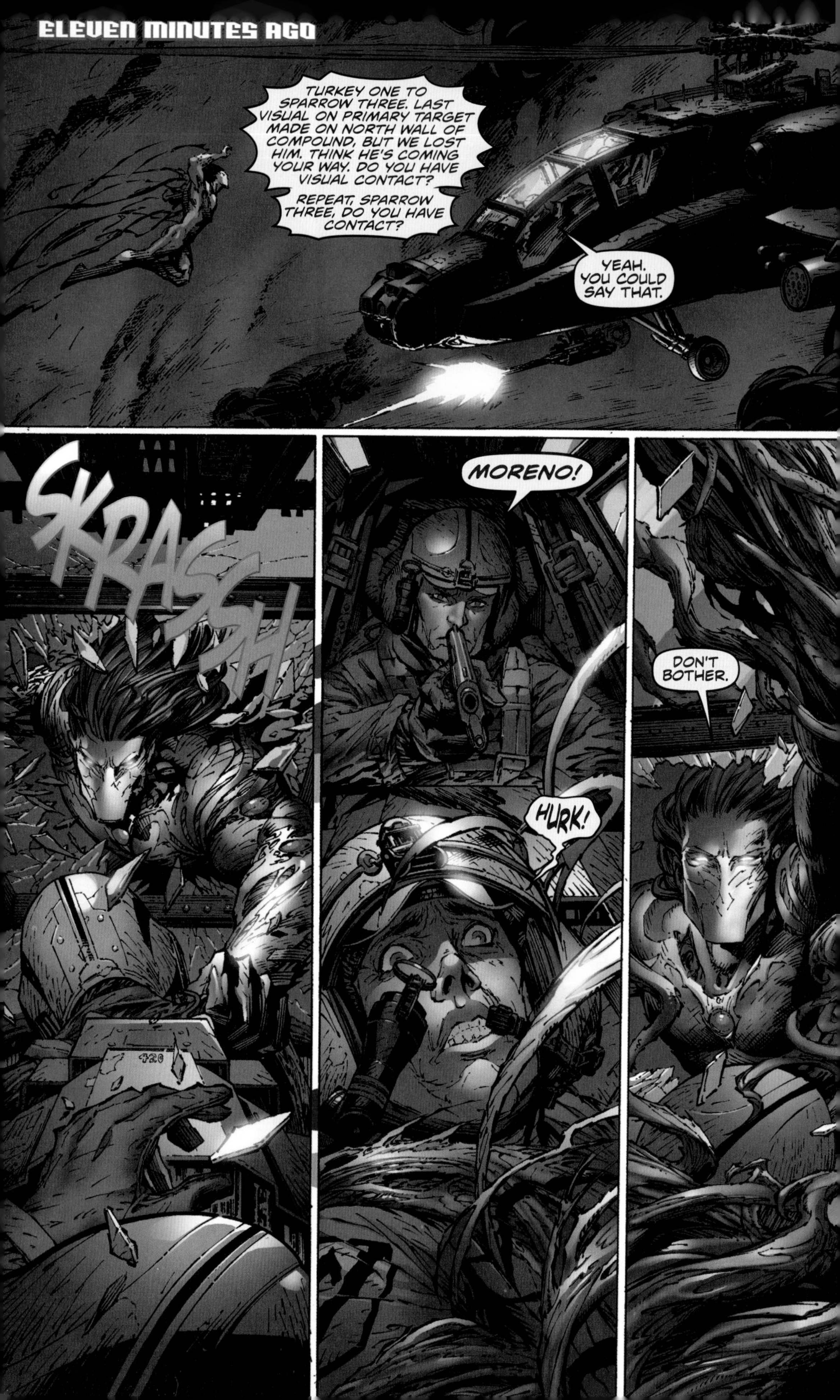
ELEVEN MINUTES AGO
TURKEY ONE TO SPARROW THREE. LAST VISUAL ON PRIMARY TARGET MADE ON NORTH WALL OF COMPOUND, BUT WE LOST HIM. THINK HE'S COMING YOUR WAY. DO YOU HAVE VISUAL CONTACT?
REPEAT, SPARROW THREE, DO YOU HAVE CONTACT?
YEAH. YOU COULD SAY THAT.
SKRASSH
MORENO!
HURK!
DON'T BOTHER.

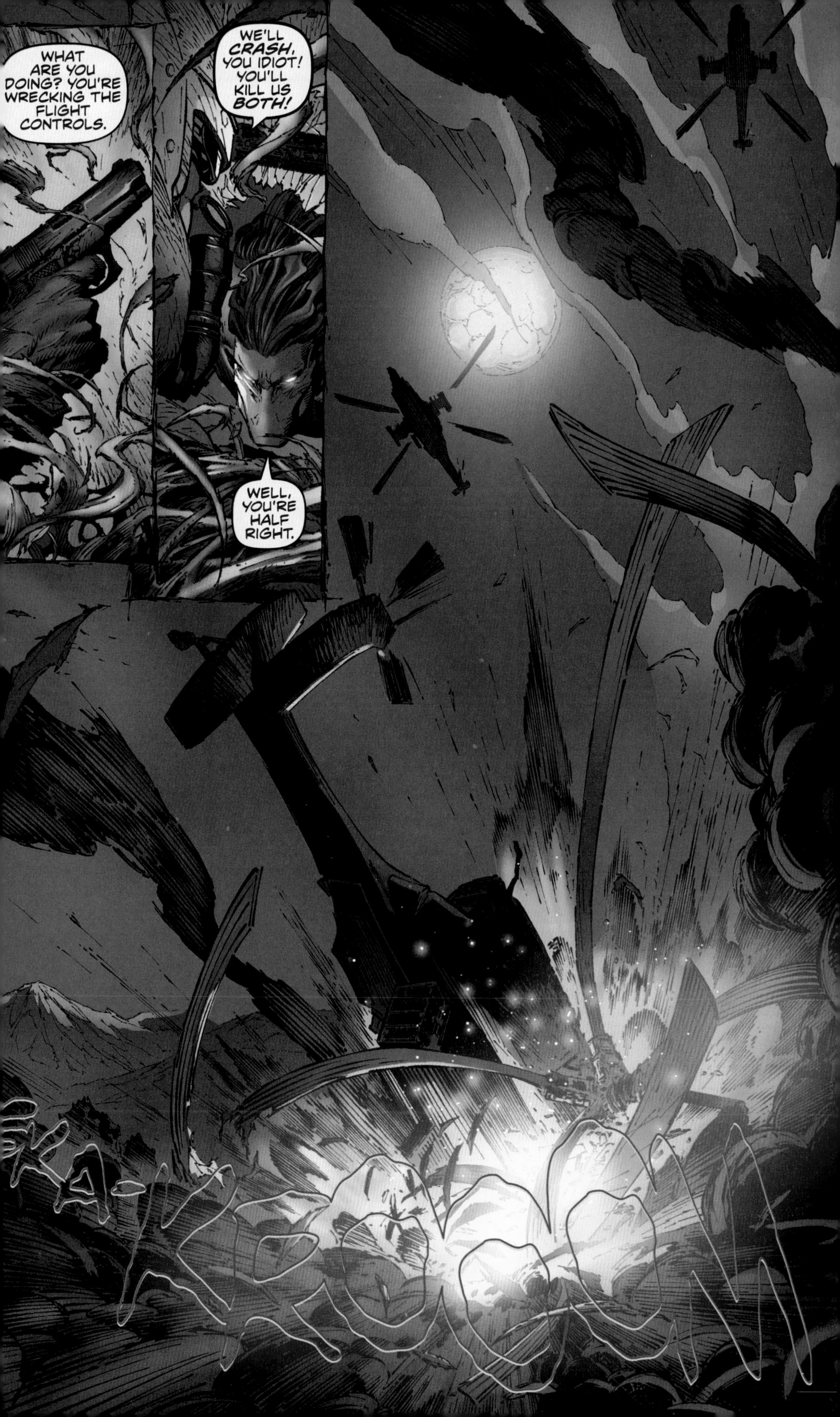
WHAT ARE YOU DOING? YOU'RE WRECKING THE FLIGHT CONTROLS.
WE'LL *CRASH*, YOU IDIOT! YOU'LL KILL US *BOTH*!
WELL, YOU'RE HALF RIGHT.
KA-KROOOOM

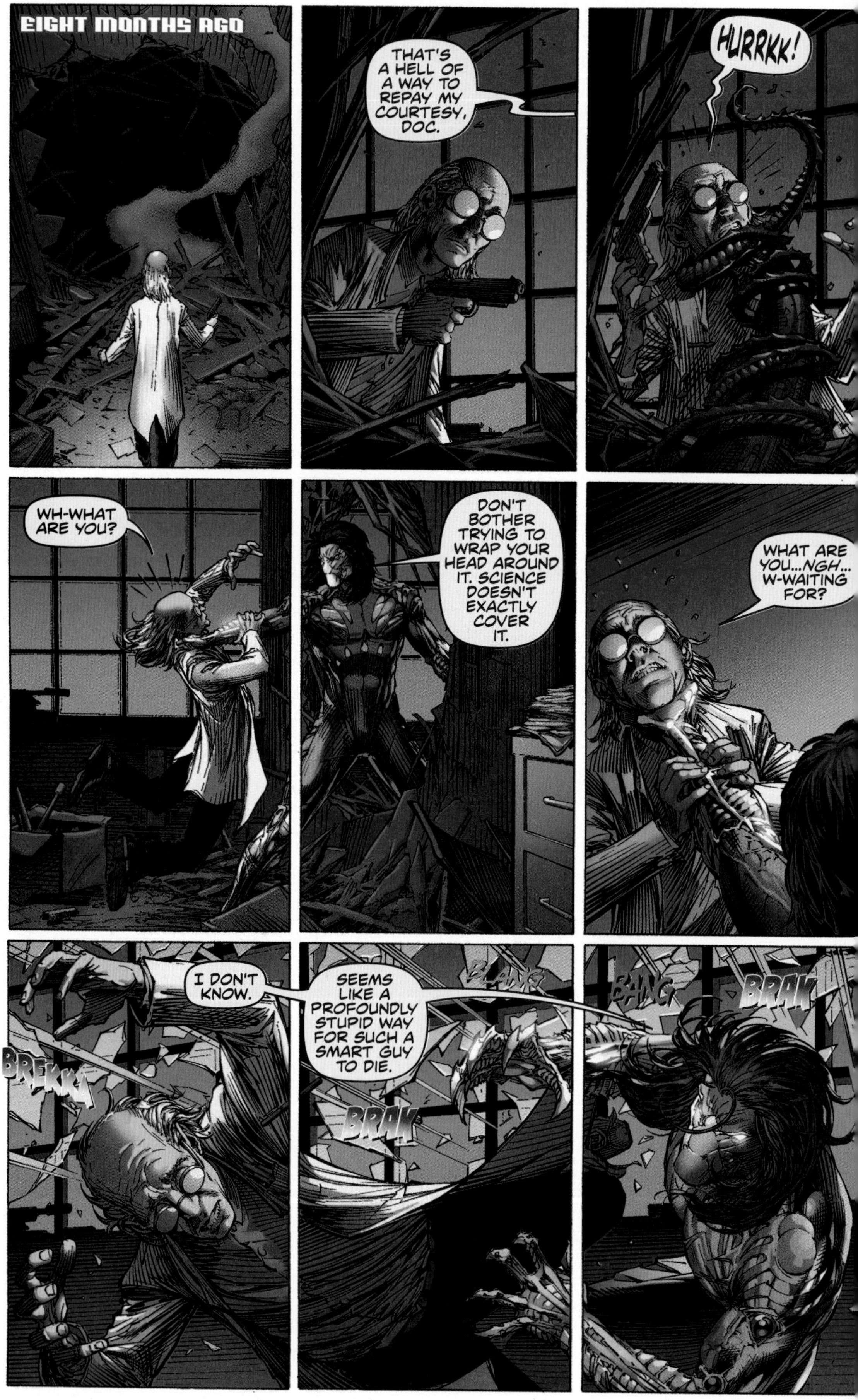
EIGHT MONTHS AGO
THAT'S A HELL OF A WAY TO REPAY MY COURTESY, DOC.
HURRKK!
WH-WHAT ARE YOU?
DON'T BOTHER TRYING TO WRAP YOUR HEAD AROUND IT. SCIENCE DOESN'T EXACTLY COVER IT.
WHAT ARE YOU...NGH... W-WAITING FOR?
I DON'T KNOW.
SEEMS LIKE A PROFOUNDLY STUPID WAY FOR SUCH A SMART GUY TO DIE.
BREKKA
BRAK
BLANG
BANG
BRAK

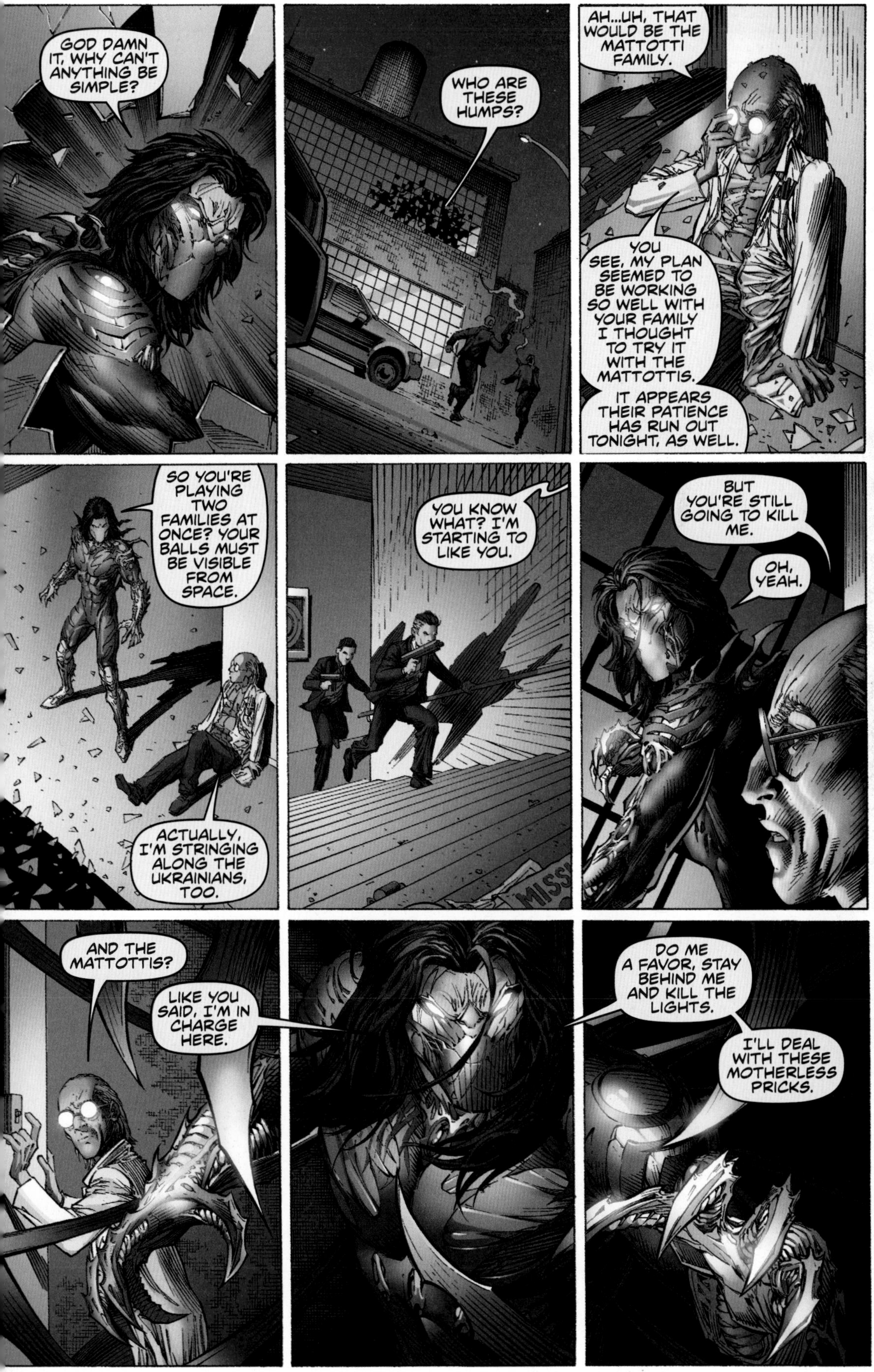
GOD DAMN IT, WHY CAN'T ANYTHING BE SIMPLE?
WHO ARE THESE HUMPS?
AH...UH, THAT WOULD BE THE MATTOTTI FAMILY.
YOU SEE, MY PLAN SEEMED TO BE WORKING SO WELL WITH YOUR FAMILY I THOUGHT TO TRY IT WITH THE MATTOTTIS.
IT APPEARS THEIR PATIENCE HAS RUN OUT TONIGHT, AS WELL.
SO YOU'RE PLAYING TWO FAMILIES AT ONCE? YOUR BALLS MUST BE VISIBLE FROM SPACE.
ACTUALLY, I'M STRINGING ALONG THE UKRAINIANS, TOO.
YOU KNOW WHAT? I'M STARTING TO LIKE YOU.
BUT YOU'RE STILL GOING TO KILL ME.
OH, YEAH.
AND THE MATTOTTIS?
LIKE YOU SAID, I'M IN CHARGE HERE.
DO ME A FAVOR, STAY BEHIND ME AND KILL THE LIGHTS.
I'LL DEAL WITH THESE MOTHERLESS PRICKS.

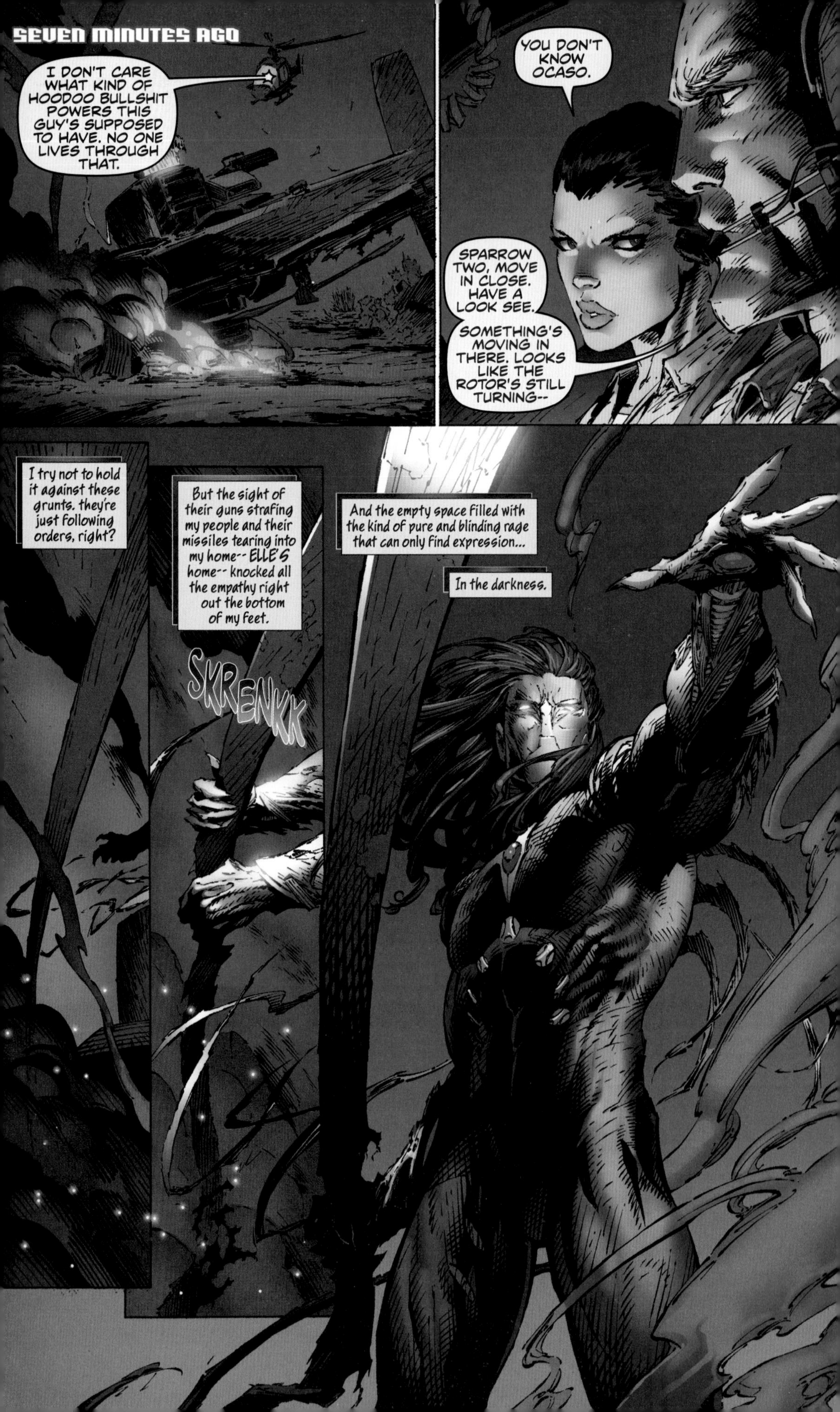
SEVEN MINUTES AGO
I DON'T CARE WHAT KIND OF HOODOO BULLSHIT POWERS THIS GUY'S SUPPOSED TO HAVE. NO ONE LIVES THROUGH THAT.
YOU DON'T KNOW OCASO.
SPARROW TWO, MOVE IN CLOSE. HAVE A LOOK SEE.
SOMETHING'S MOVING IN THERE. LOOKS LIKE THE ROTOR'S STILL TURNING--
I try not to hold it against these grunts. they're just following orders, right?
But the sight of their guns strafing my people and their missiles tearing into my home-- ELLE'S home-- knocked all the empathy right out the bottom of my feet.
SKRENKK
And the empty space filled with the kind of pure and blinding rage that can only find expression...
In the darkness.

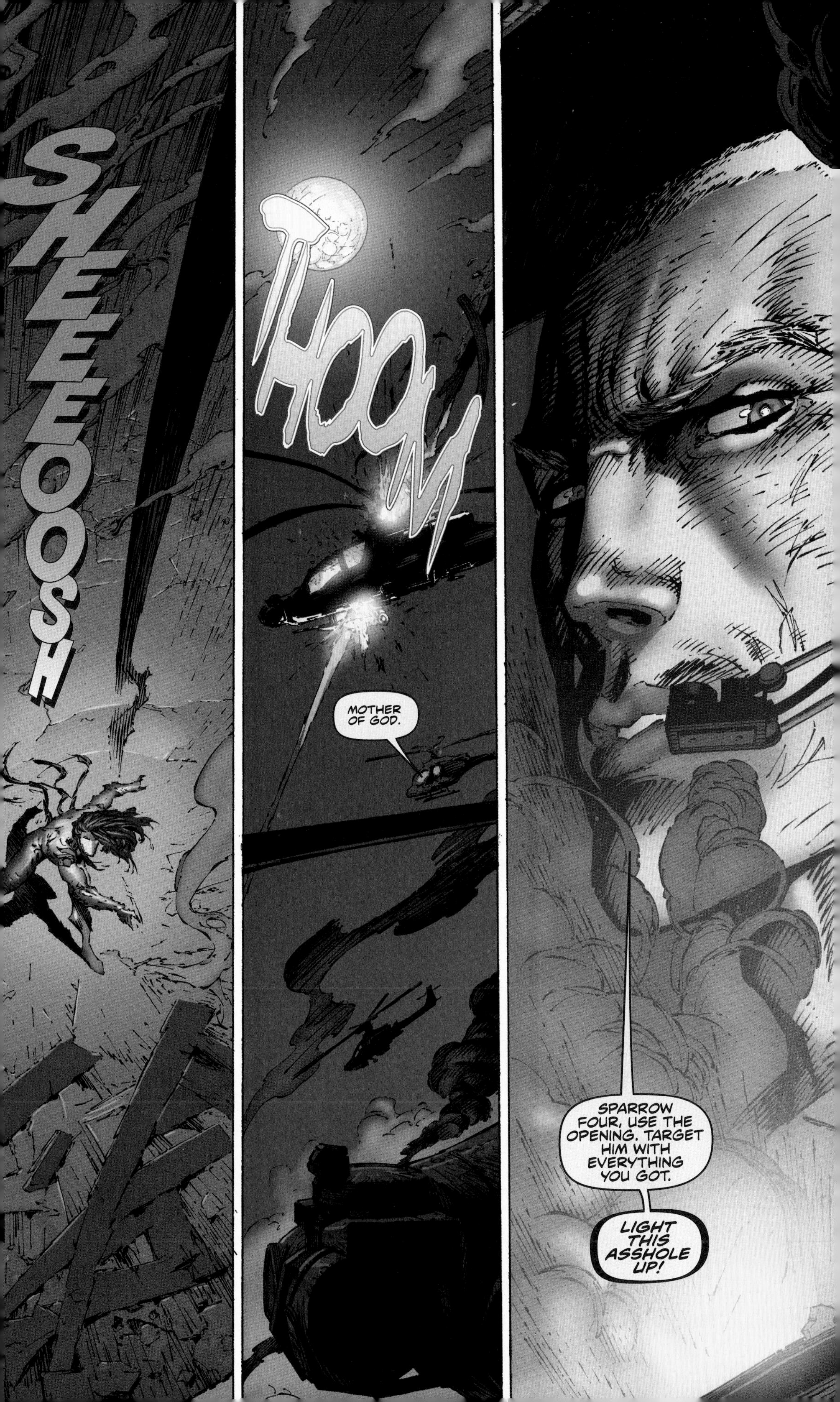
SHEEEOOOSH
THOOM
MOTHER OF GOD.
SPARROW FOUR, USE THE OPENING. TARGET HIM WITH EVERYTHING YOU GOT.
LIGHT THIS ASSHOLE UP!

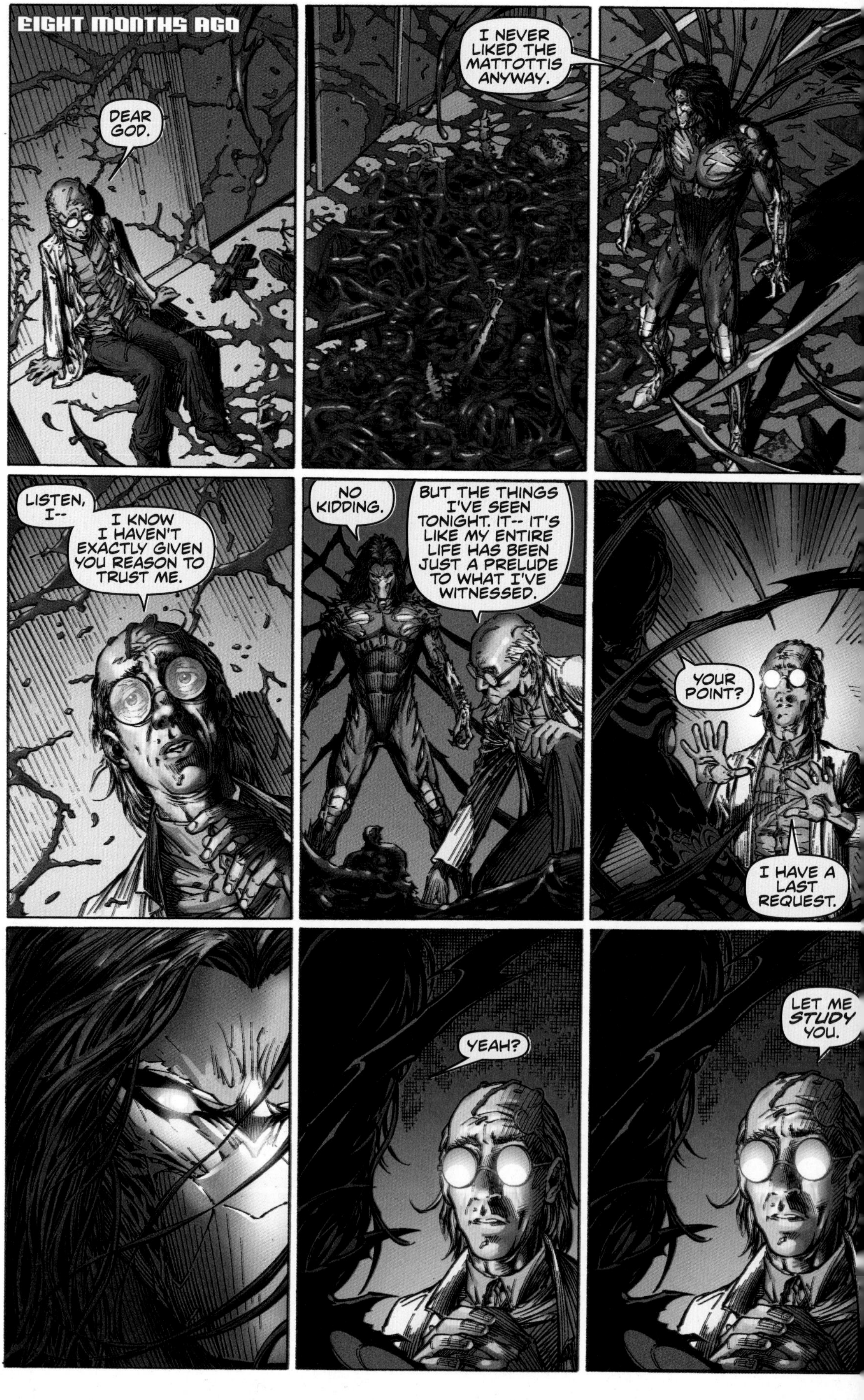
EIGHT MONTHS AGO
DEAR GOD.
I NEVER LIKED THE MATTOTTIS ANYWAY.
LISTEN, I--
I KNOW I HAVEN'T EXACTLY GIVEN YOU REASON TO TRUST ME.
NO KIDDING.
BUT THE THINGS I'VE SEEN TONIGHT. IT-- IT'S LIKE MY ENTIRE LIFE HAS BEEN JUST A PRELUDE TO WHAT I'VE WITNESSED.
YOUR POINT?
I HAVE A LAST REQUEST.
YEAH?
LET ME STUDY YOU.

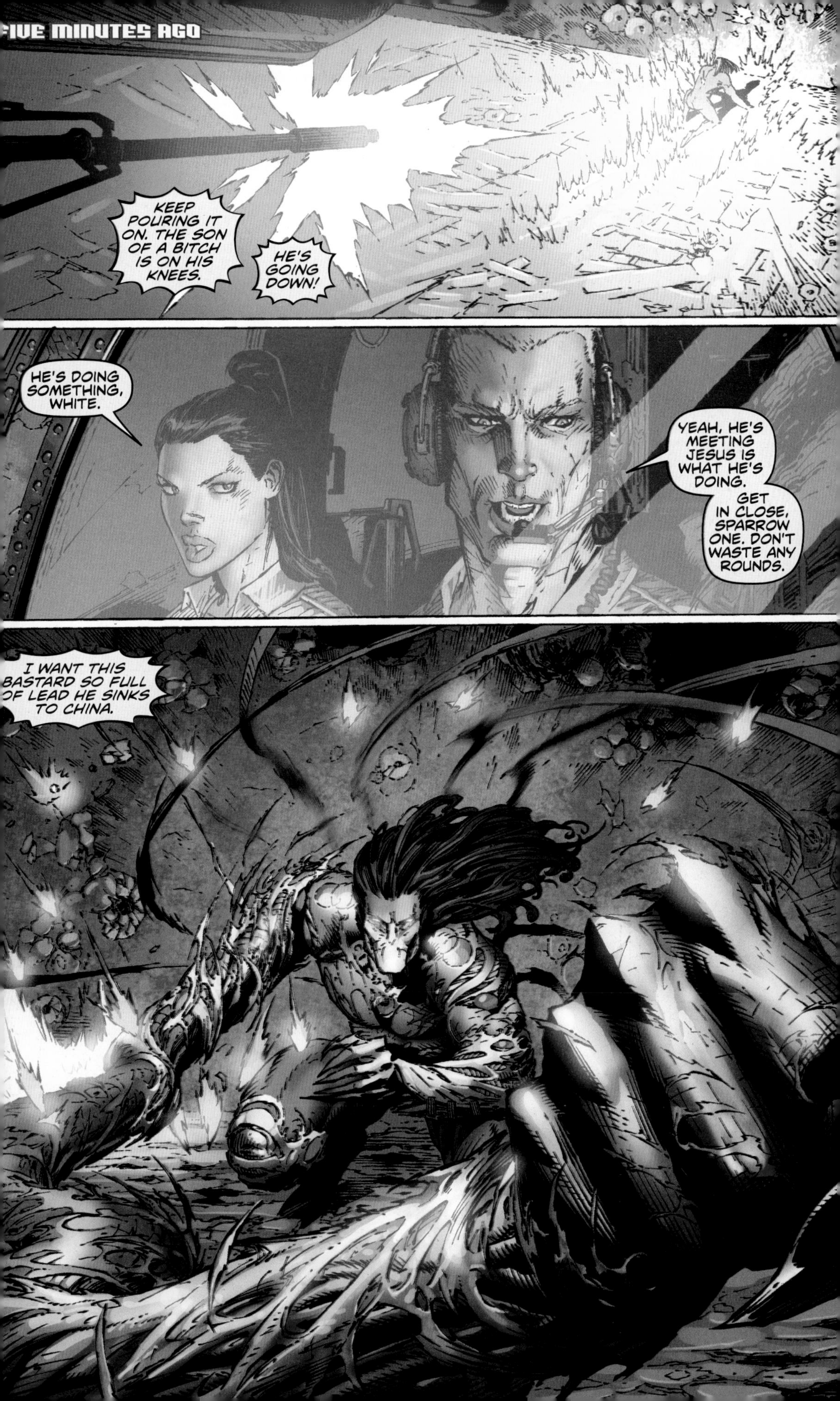
FIVE MINUTES AGO
KEEP POURING IT ON. THE SON OF A BITCH IS ON HIS KNEES.
HE'S GOING DOWN!
HE'S DOING SOMETHING, WHITE.
YEAH, HE'S MEETING JESUS IS WHAT HE'S DOING.
GET IN CLOSE, SPARROW ONE. DON'T WASTE ANY ROUNDS.
I WANT THIS BASTARD SO FULL OF LEAD HE SINKS TO CHINA.

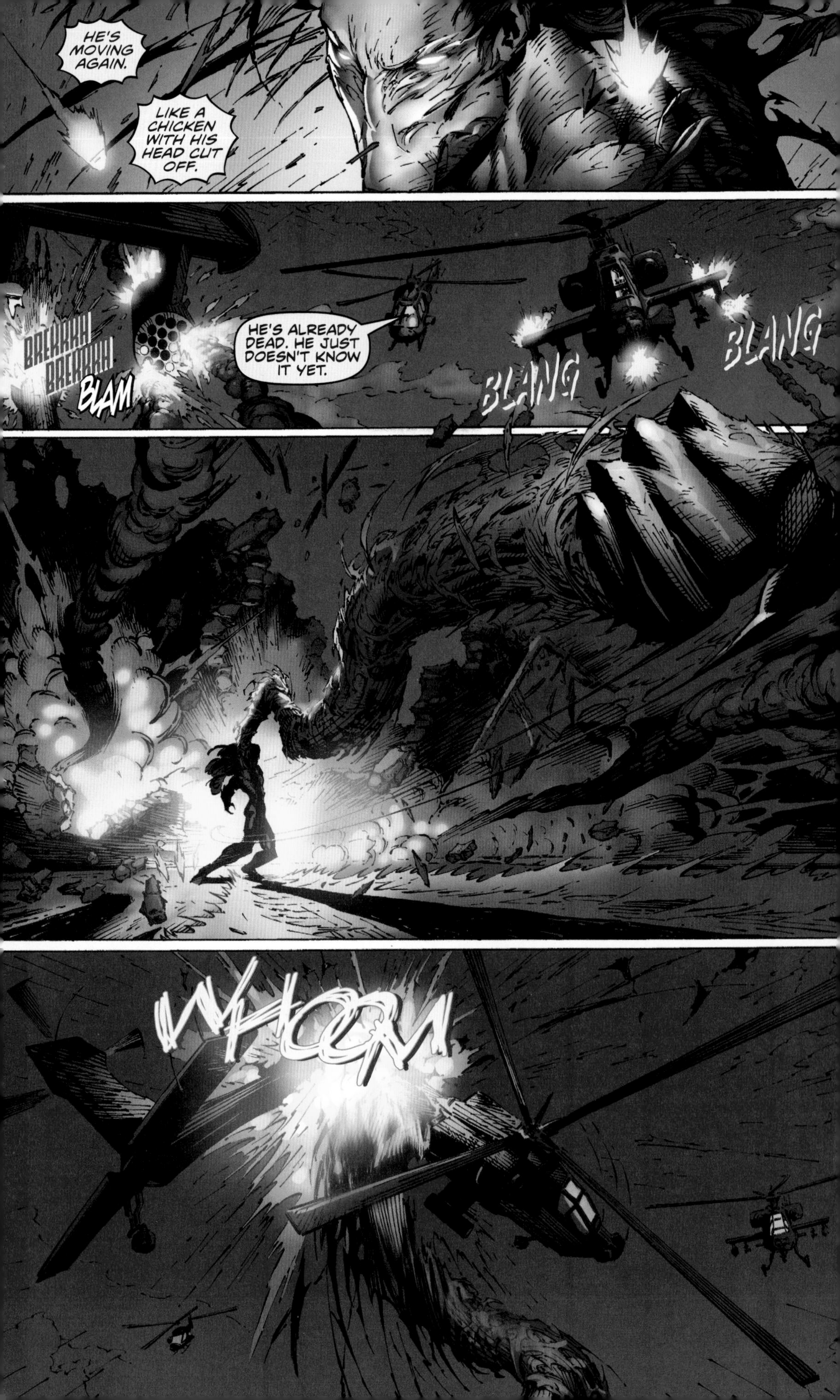

HE'S MOVING AGAIN.
LIKE A CHICKEN WITH HIS HEAD CUT OFF.
BREKKKH BREKKKH
BLAM
HE'S ALREADY DEAD. HE JUST DOESN'T KNOW IT YET.
BLANG
BLANG
WHOOM

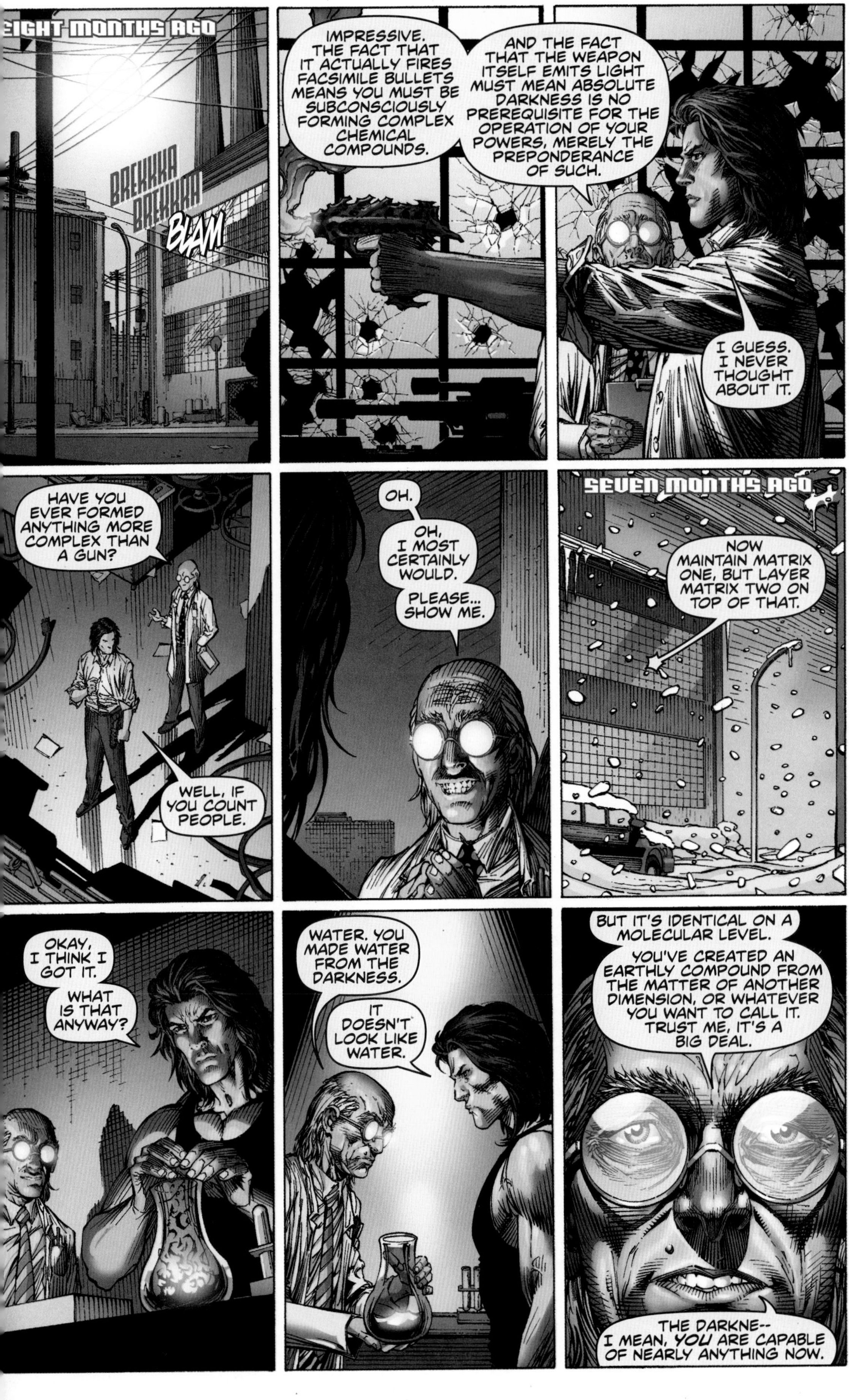
EIGHT MONTHS AGO
BREKKKA BREKKKA
BLAM
IMPRESSIVE. THE FACT THAT IT ACTUALLY FIRES FACSIMILE BULLETS MEANS YOU MUST BE SUBCONSCIOUSLY FORMING COMPLEX CHEMICAL COMPOUNDS.
AND THE FACT THAT THE WEAPON ITSELF EMITS LIGHT MUST MEAN ABSOLUTE DARKNESS IS NO PREREQUISITE FOR THE OPERATION OF YOUR POWERS, MERELY THE PREPONDERANCE OF SUCH.
I GUESS. I NEVER THOUGHT ABOUT IT.
HAVE YOU EVER FORMED ANYTHING MORE COMPLEX THAN A GUN?
WELL, IF YOU COUNT PEOPLE.
OH.
OH, I MOST CERTAINLY WOULD.
PLEASE... SHOW ME.
SEVEN MONTHS AGO
NOW MAINTAIN MATRIX ONE, BUT LAYER MATRIX TWO ON TOP OF THAT.
OKAY, I THINK I GOT IT.
WHAT IS THAT ANYWAY?
WATER. YOU MADE WATER FROM THE DARKNESS.
IT DOESN'T LOOK LIKE WATER.
BUT IT'S IDENTICAL ON A MOLECULAR LEVEL.
YOU'VE CREATED AN EARTHLY COMPOUND FROM THE MATTER OF ANOTHER DIMENSION, OR WHATEVER YOU WANT TO CALL IT. TRUST ME, IT'S A BIG DEAL.
THE DARKNE-- I MEAN, *YOU* ARE CAPABLE OF NEARLY ANYTHING NOW.

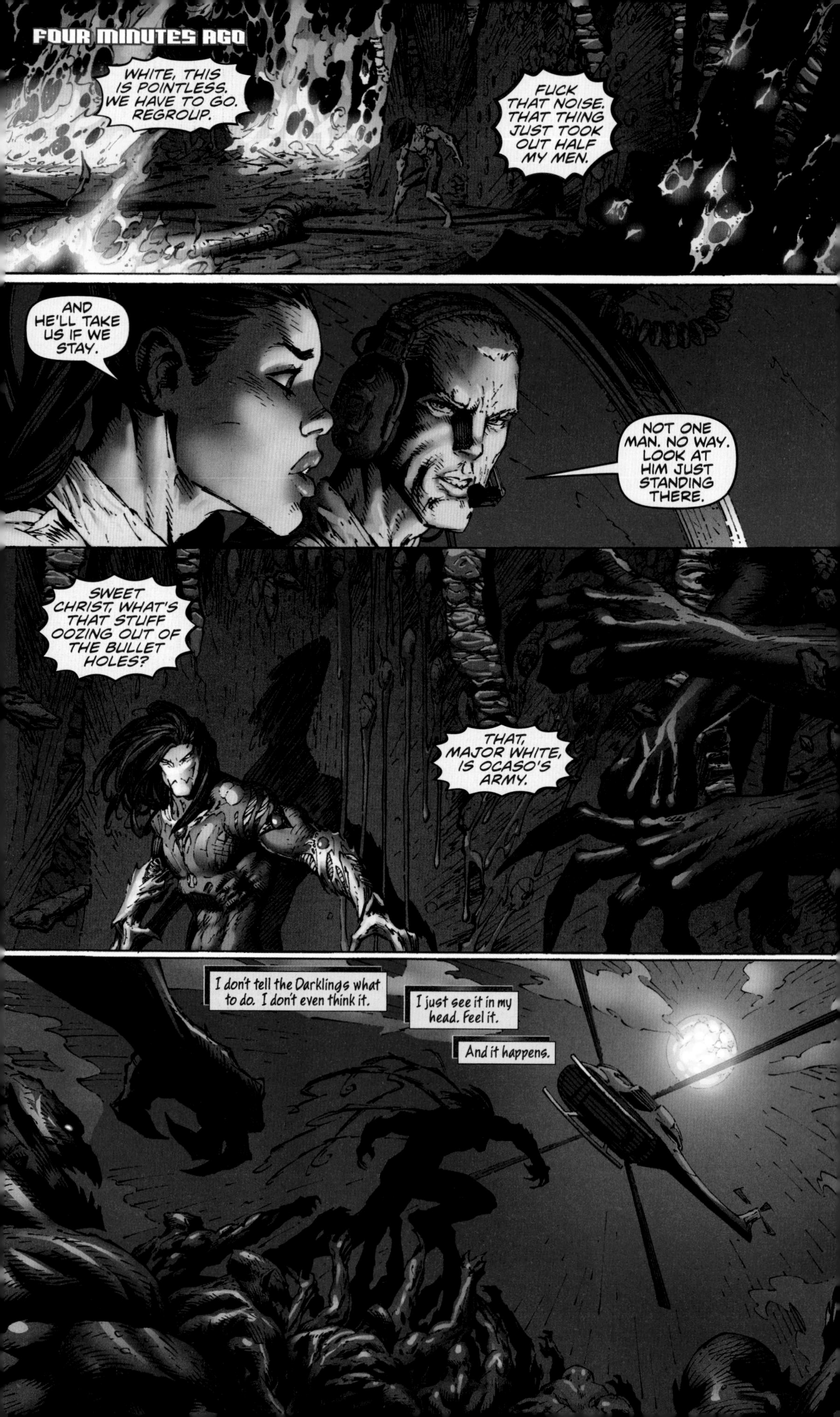
FOUR MINUTES AGO
WHITE, THIS IS POINTLESS. WE HAVE TO GO. REGROUP.
FUCK THAT NOISE. THAT THING JUST TOOK OUT HALF MY MEN.
AND HE'LL TAKE US IF WE STAY.
NOT ONE MAN. NO WAY. LOOK AT HIM JUST STANDING THERE.
SWEET CHRIST, WHAT'S THAT STUFF OOZING OUT OF THE BULLET HOLES?
THAT, MAJOR WHITE, IS OCASO'S ARMY.
I don't tell the Darklings what to do. I don't even think it.
I just see it in my head. Feel it.
And it happens.

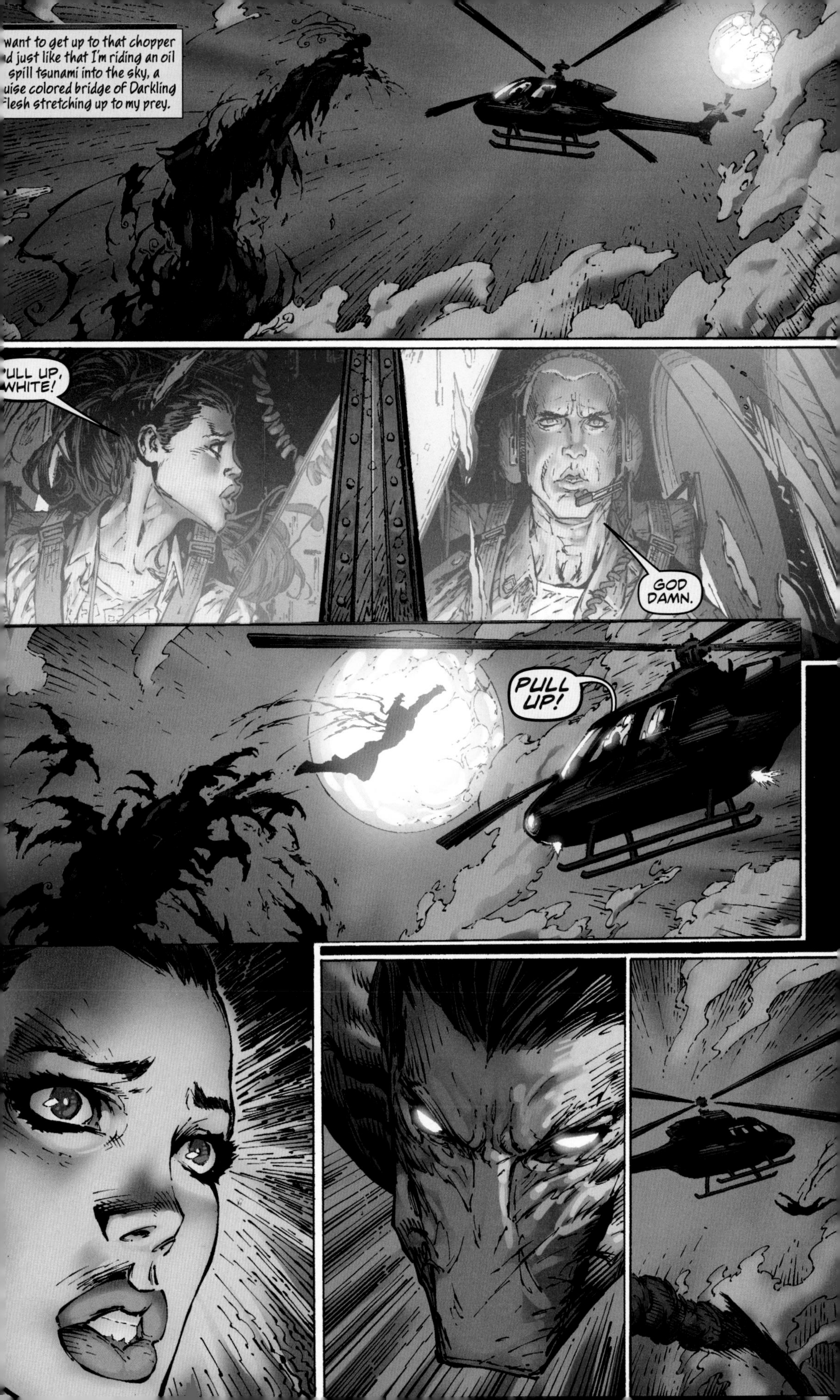
want to get up to that chopper
d just like that I'm riding an oil
spill tsunami into the sky, a
uise colored bridge of Darkling
Flesh stretching up to my prey.
ULL UP,
WHITE!
GOD
DAMN.
PULL
UP!

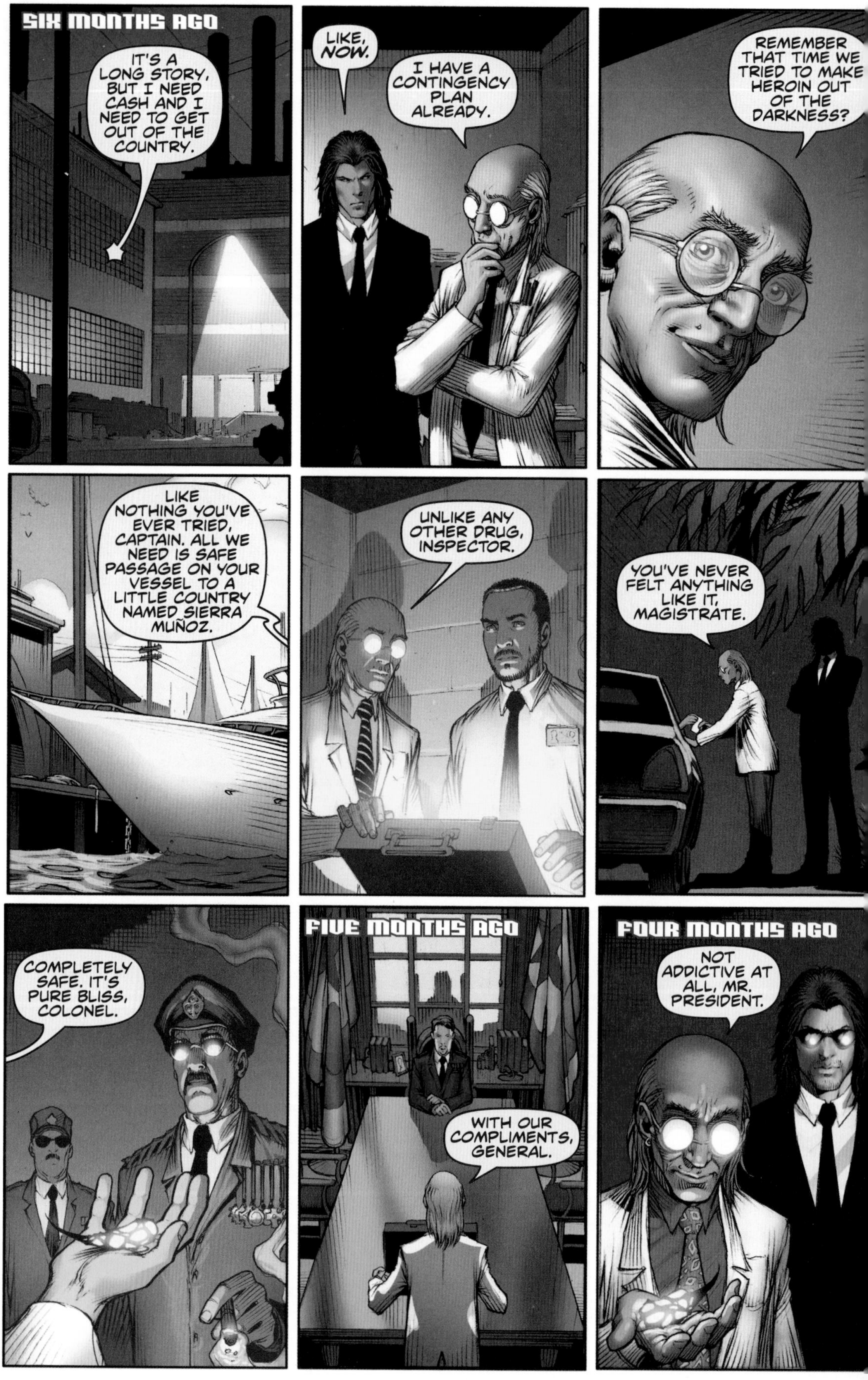
SIX MONTHS AGO
IT'S A LONG STORY, BUT I NEED CASH AND I NEED TO GET OUT OF THE COUNTRY.
LIKE, NOW.
I HAVE A CONTINGENCY PLAN ALREADY.
REMEMBER THAT TIME WE TRIED TO MAKE HEROIN OUT OF THE DARKNESS?
LIKE NOTHING YOU'VE EVER TRIED, CAPTAIN. ALL WE NEED IS SAFE PASSAGE ON YOUR VESSEL TO A LITTLE COUNTRY NAMED SIERRA MUÑOZ.
UNLIKE ANY OTHER DRUG, INSPECTOR.
YOU'VE NEVER FELT ANYTHING LIKE IT, MAGISTRATE.
COMPLETELY SAFE. IT'S PURE BLISS, COLONEL.
FIVE MONTHS AGO
WITH OUR COMPLIMENTS, GENERAL.
FOUR MONTHS AGO
NOT ADDICTIVE AT ALL, MR. PRESIDENT.

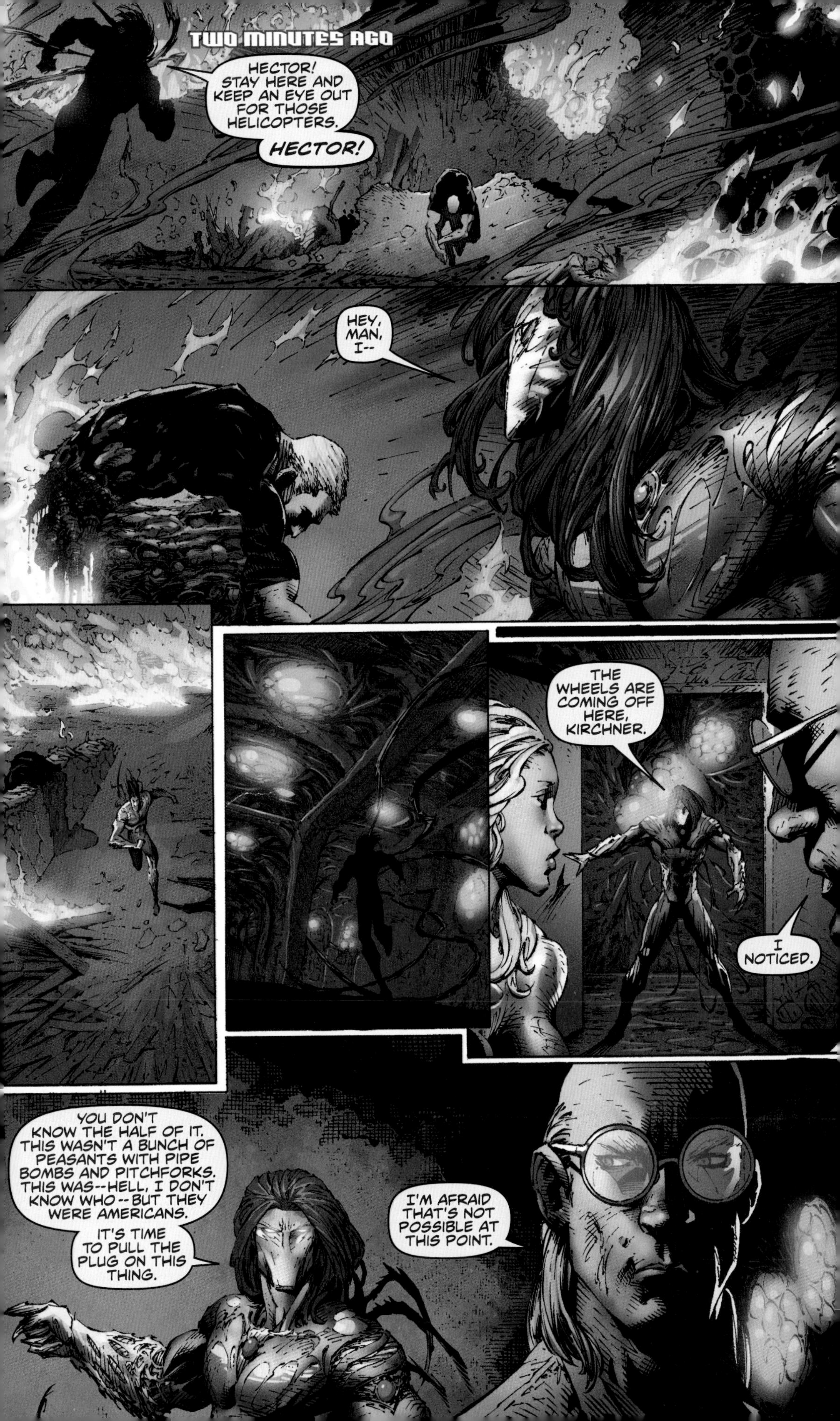
TWO MINUTES AGO
HECTOR! STAY HERE AND KEEP AN EYE OUT FOR THOSE HELICOPTERS.
HECTOR!
HEY, MAN, I--
THE WHEELS ARE COMING OFF HERE, KIRCHNER.
I NOTICED.
YOU DON'T KNOW THE HALF OF IT. THIS WASN'T A BUNCH OF PEASANTS WITH PIPE BOMBS AND PITCHFORKS. THIS WAS--HELL, I DON'T KNOW WHO--BUT THEY WERE AMERICANS.
IT'S TIME TO PULL THE PLUG ON THIS THING.
I'M AFRAID THAT'S NOT POSSIBLE AT THIS POINT.

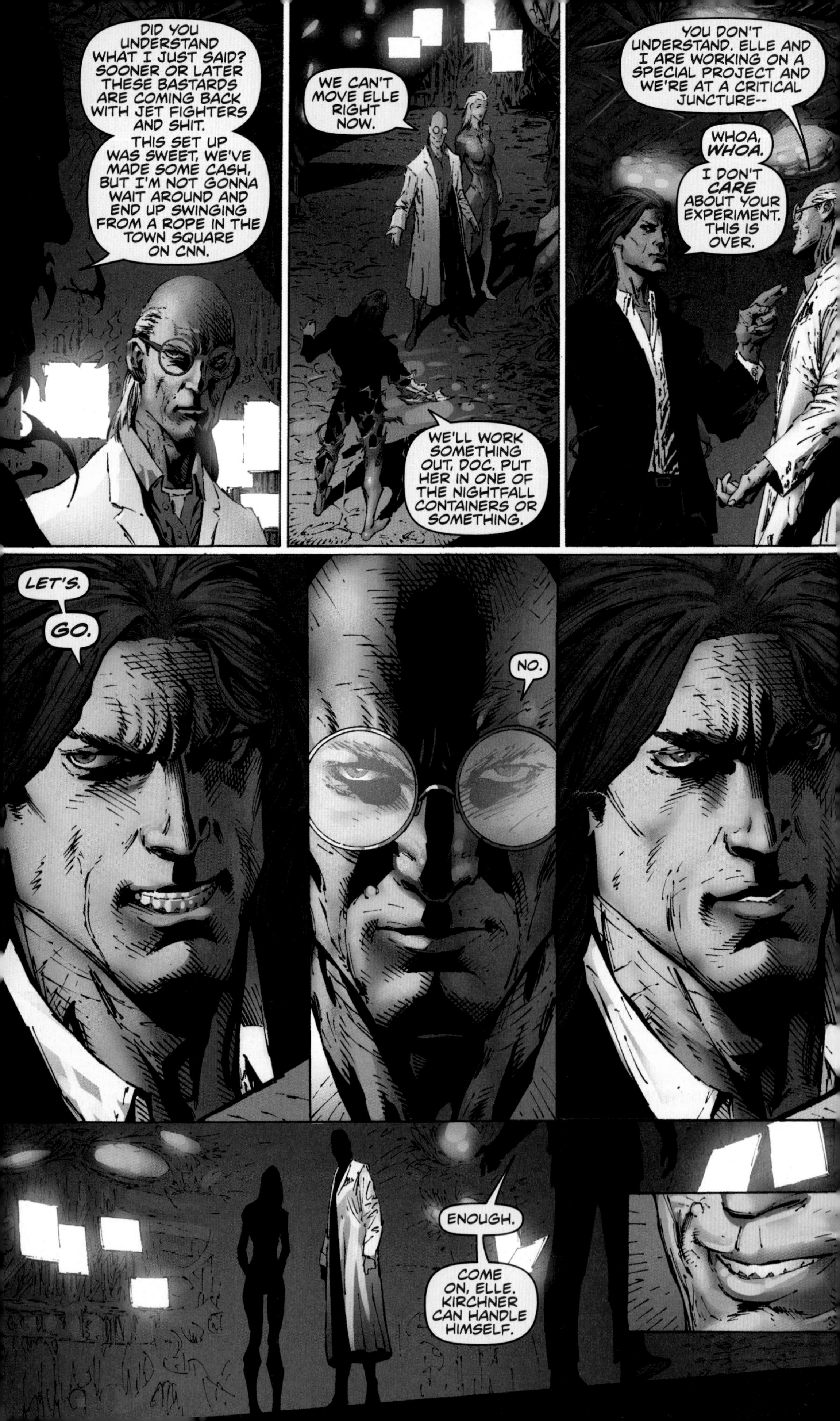
DID YOU UNDERSTAND WHAT I JUST SAID? SOONER OR LATER THESE BASTARDS ARE COMING BACK WITH JET FIGHTERS AND SHIT.
THIS SET UP WAS SWEET, WE'VE MADE SOME CASH, BUT I'M NOT GONNA WAIT AROUND AND END UP SWINGING FROM A ROPE IN THE TOWN SQUARE ON CNN.
WE CAN'T MOVE ELLE RIGHT NOW.
WE'LL WORK SOMETHING OUT, DOC. PUT HER IN ONE OF THE NIGHTFALL CONTAINERS OR SOMETHING.
YOU DON'T UNDERSTAND. ELLE AND I ARE WORKING ON A SPECIAL PROJECT AND WE'RE AT A CRITICAL JUNCTURE--
WHOA, *WHOA.*
I DON'T *CARE* ABOUT YOUR EXPERIMENT. THIS IS OVER.
LET'S.
GO.
NO.
ENOUGH.
COME ON, ELLE. KIRCHNER CAN HANDLE HIMSELF.

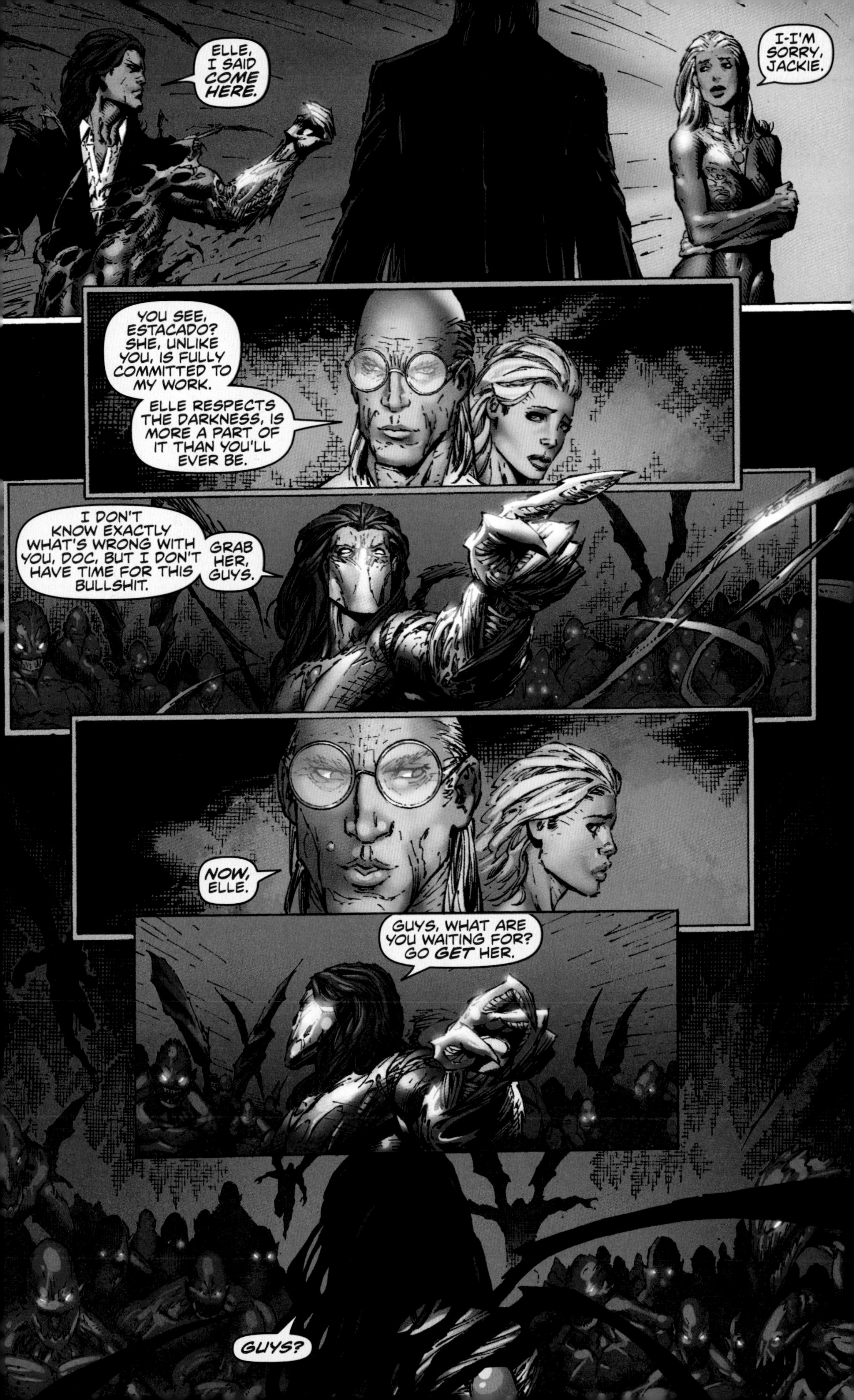

ELLE, I SAID COME HERE.
I-I'M SORRY, JACKIE.
YOU SEE, ESTACADO? SHE, UNLIKE YOU, IS FULLY COMMITTED TO MY WORK.
ELLE RESPECTS THE DARKNESS, IS MORE A PART OF IT THAN YOU'LL EVER BE.
I DON'T KNOW EXACTLY WHAT'S WRONG WITH YOU, DOC, BUT I DON'T HAVE TIME FOR THIS BULLSHIT.
GRAB HER, GUYS.
NOW, ELLE.
GUYS, WHAT ARE YOU WAITING FOR? GO GET HER.
GUYS?

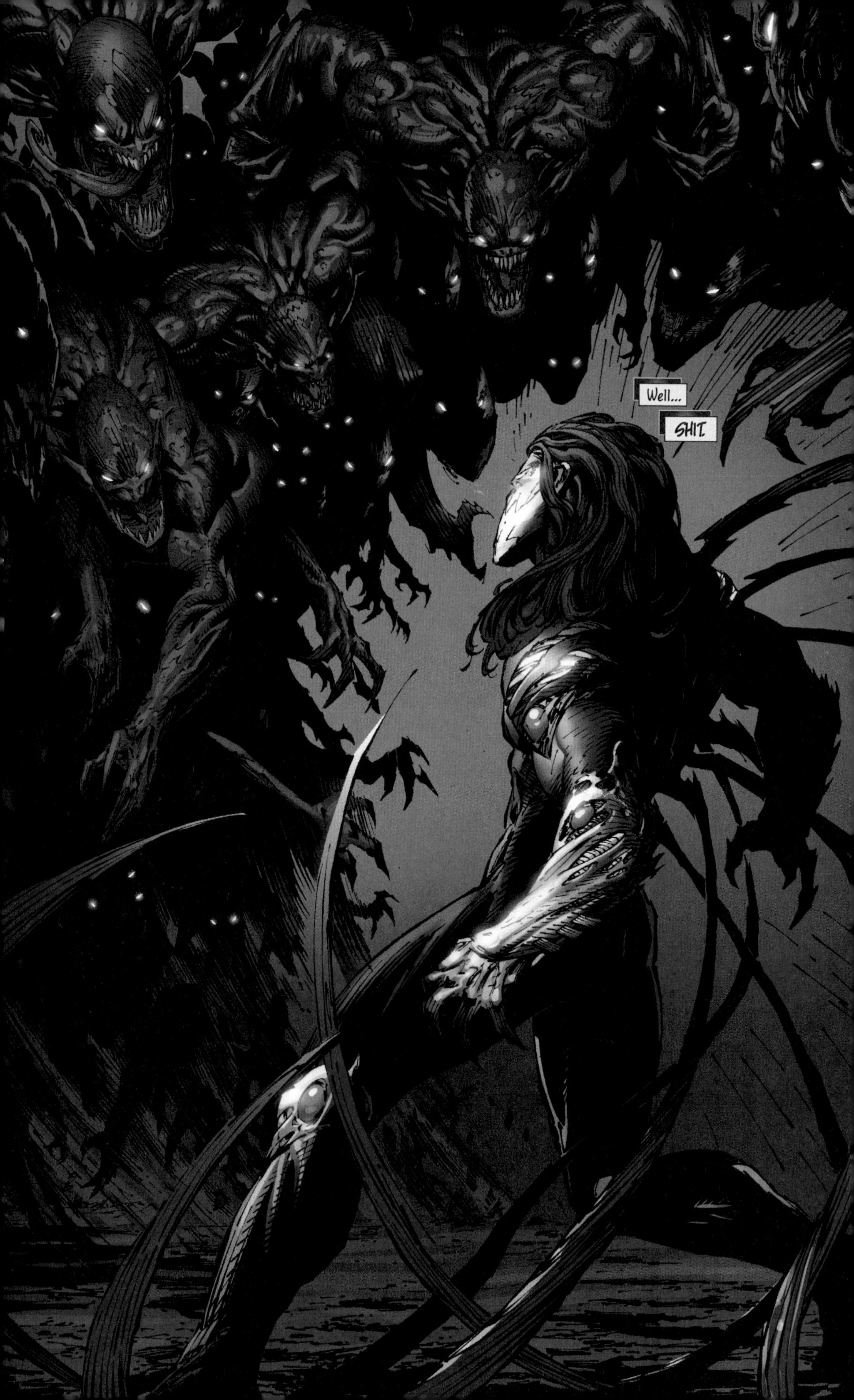
Well...
SHIT.

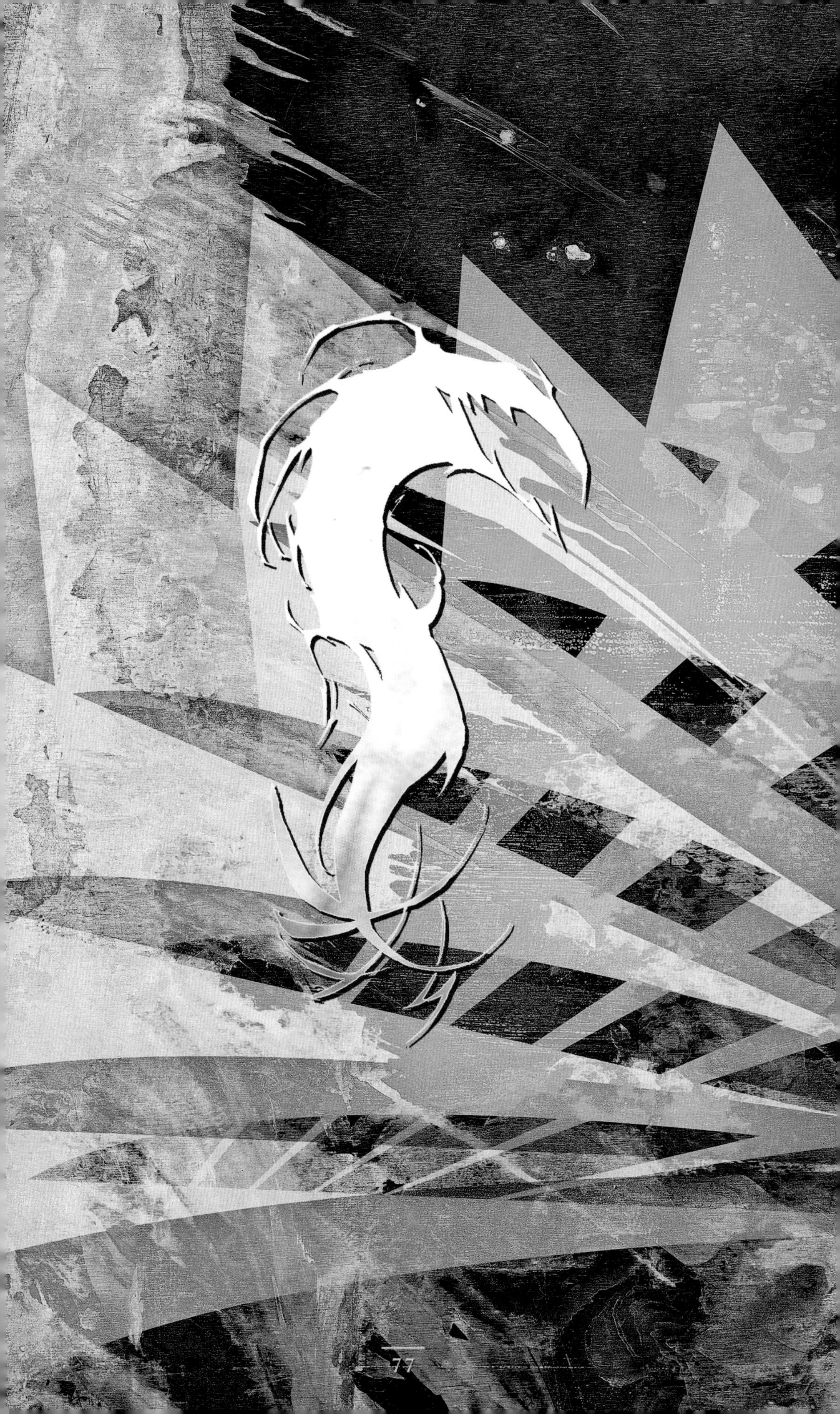

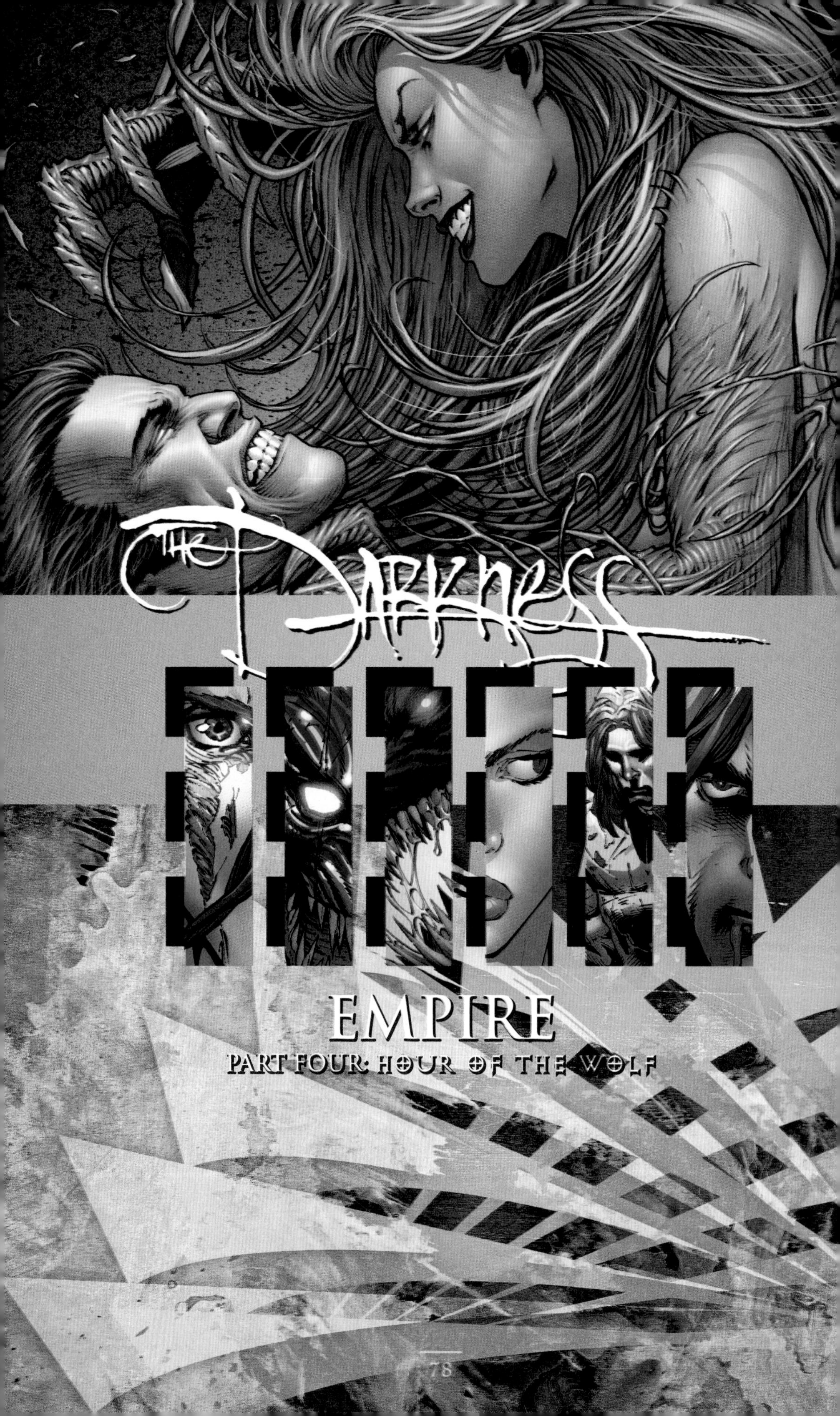
THE DARKNESS
EMPIRE
PART FOUR: HOUR OF THE WOLF

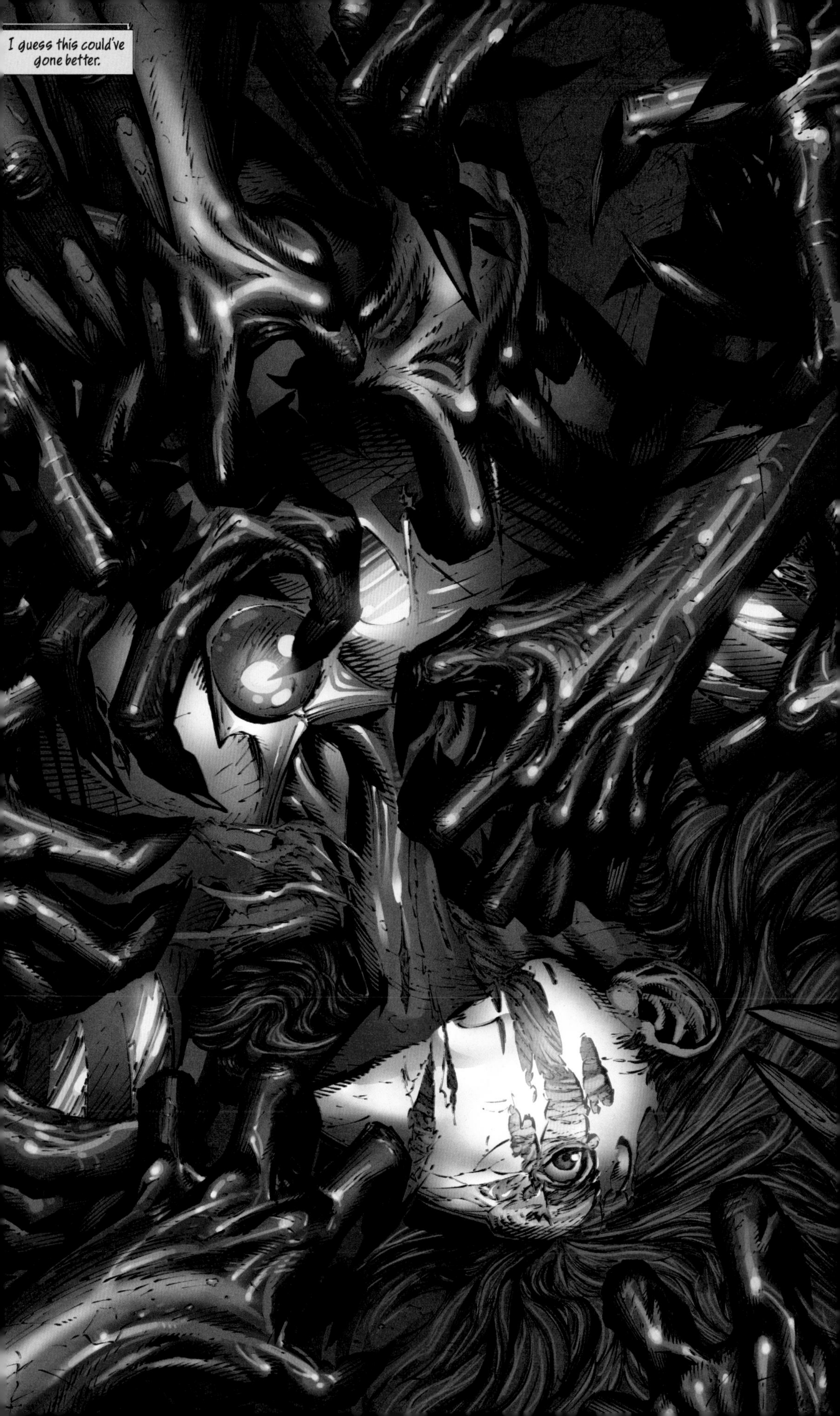
I guess this could've gone better.

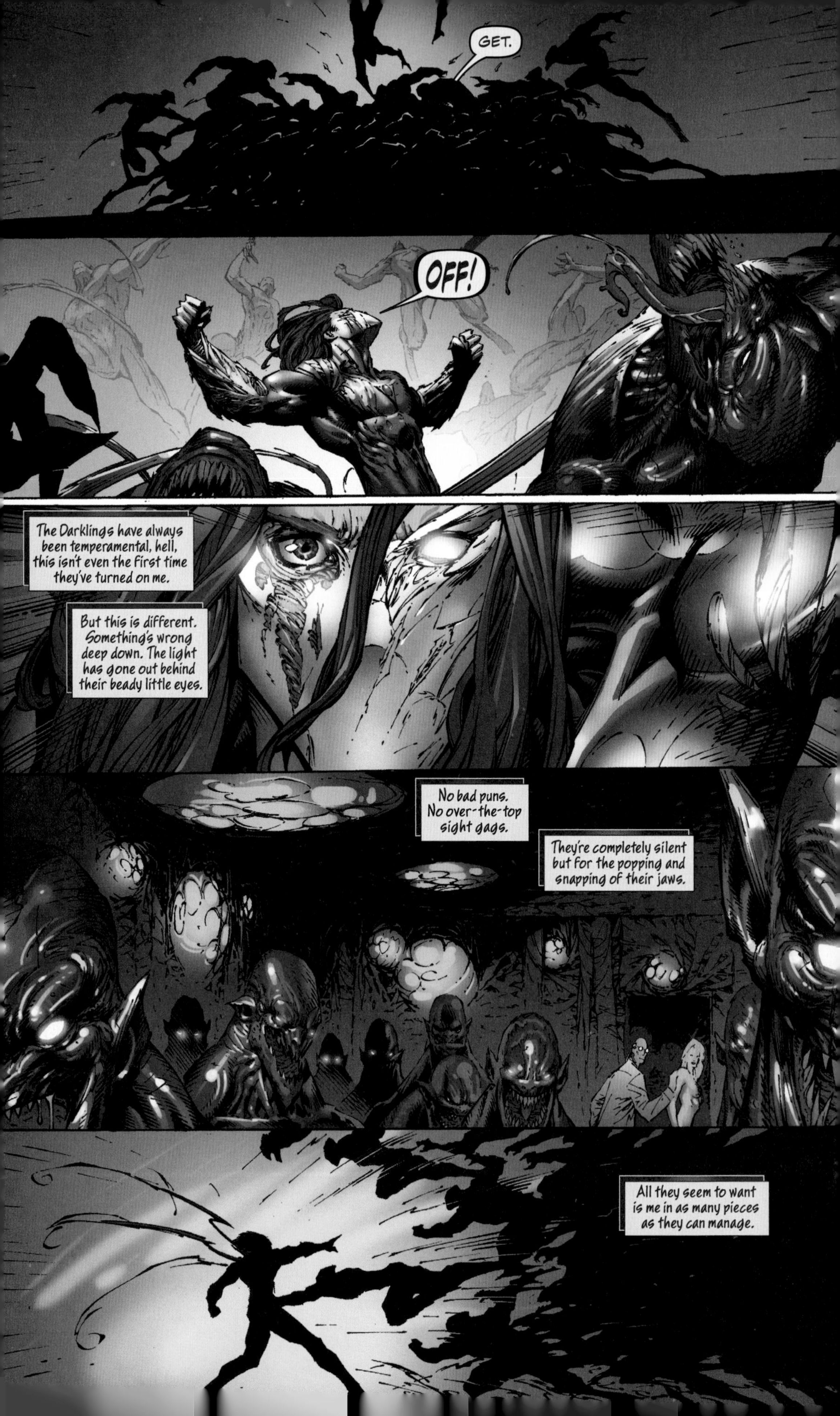
GET.
OFF!
The Darklings have always been temperamental, hell, this isn't even the first time they've turned on me.
But this is different. Something's wrong deep down. The light has gone out behind their beady little eyes.
No bad puns. No over-the-top sight gags.
They're completely silent but for the popping and snapping of their jaws.
All they seem to want is me in as many pieces as they can manage.

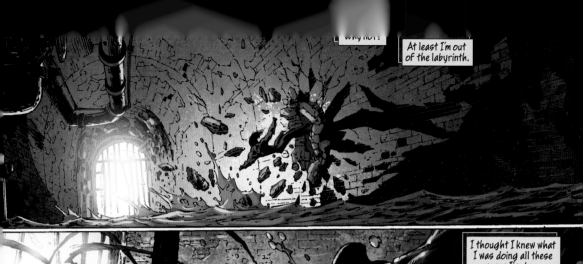

At least I'm out of the labyrinth.

I thought I knew what I was doing all these years I've been siccing these rabid little pricks on people.

But now that I'm on the receiving end, I've got to say...

It's pretty God damned horrible.

Never been so happy...

To see the dawn.

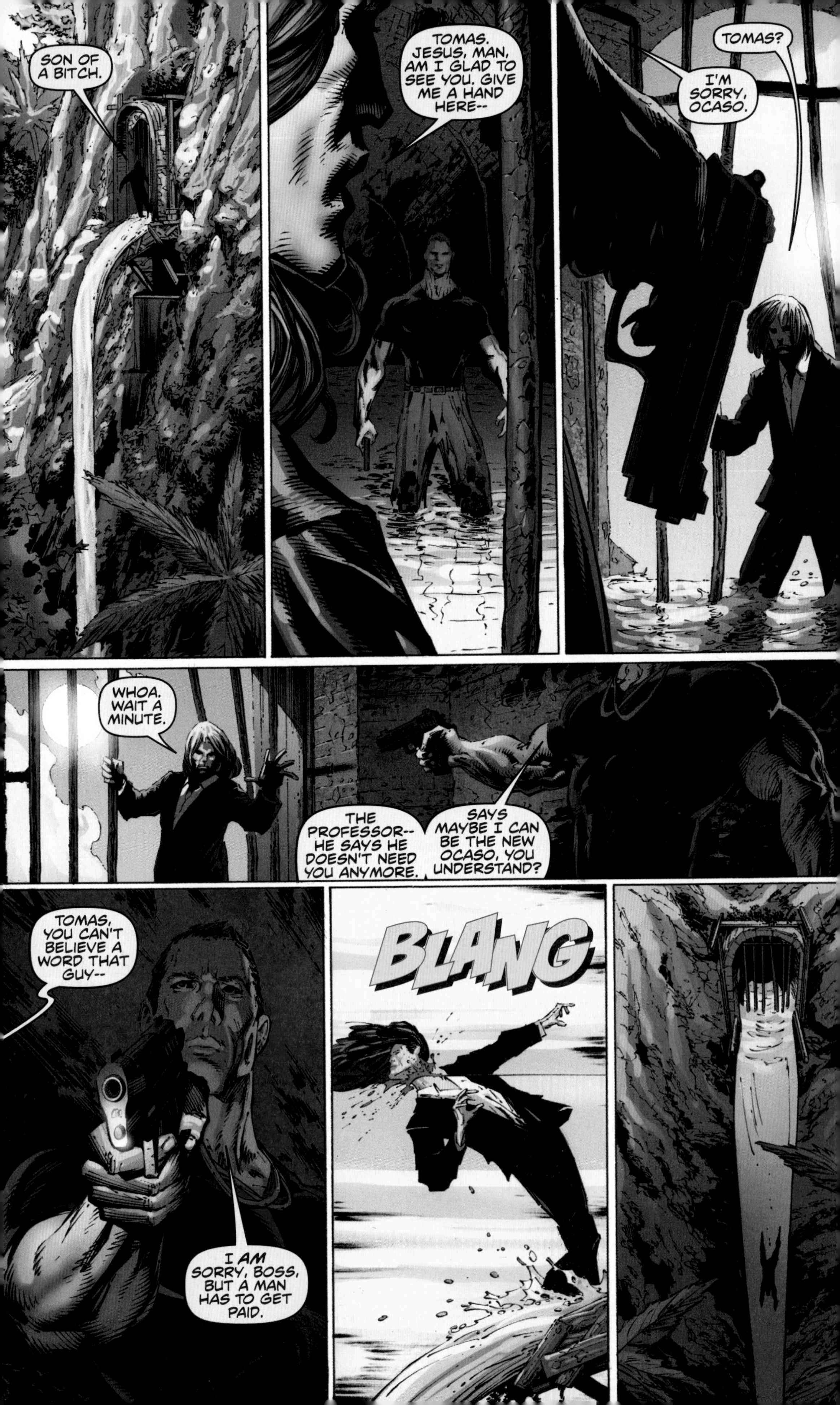
SON OF A BITCH.
TOMAS. JESUS, MAN, AM I GLAD TO SEE YOU. GIVE ME A HAND HERE--
TOMAS?
I'M SORRY, OCASO.
WHOA. WAIT A MINUTE.
THE PROFESSOR-- HE SAYS HE DOESN'T NEED YOU ANYMORE.
SAYS MAYBE I CAN BE THE NEW OCASO, YOU UNDERSTAND?
TOMAS, YOU CAN'T BELIEVE A WORD THAT GUY--
I AM SORRY, BOSS, BUT A MAN HAS TO GET PAID.
BLANG

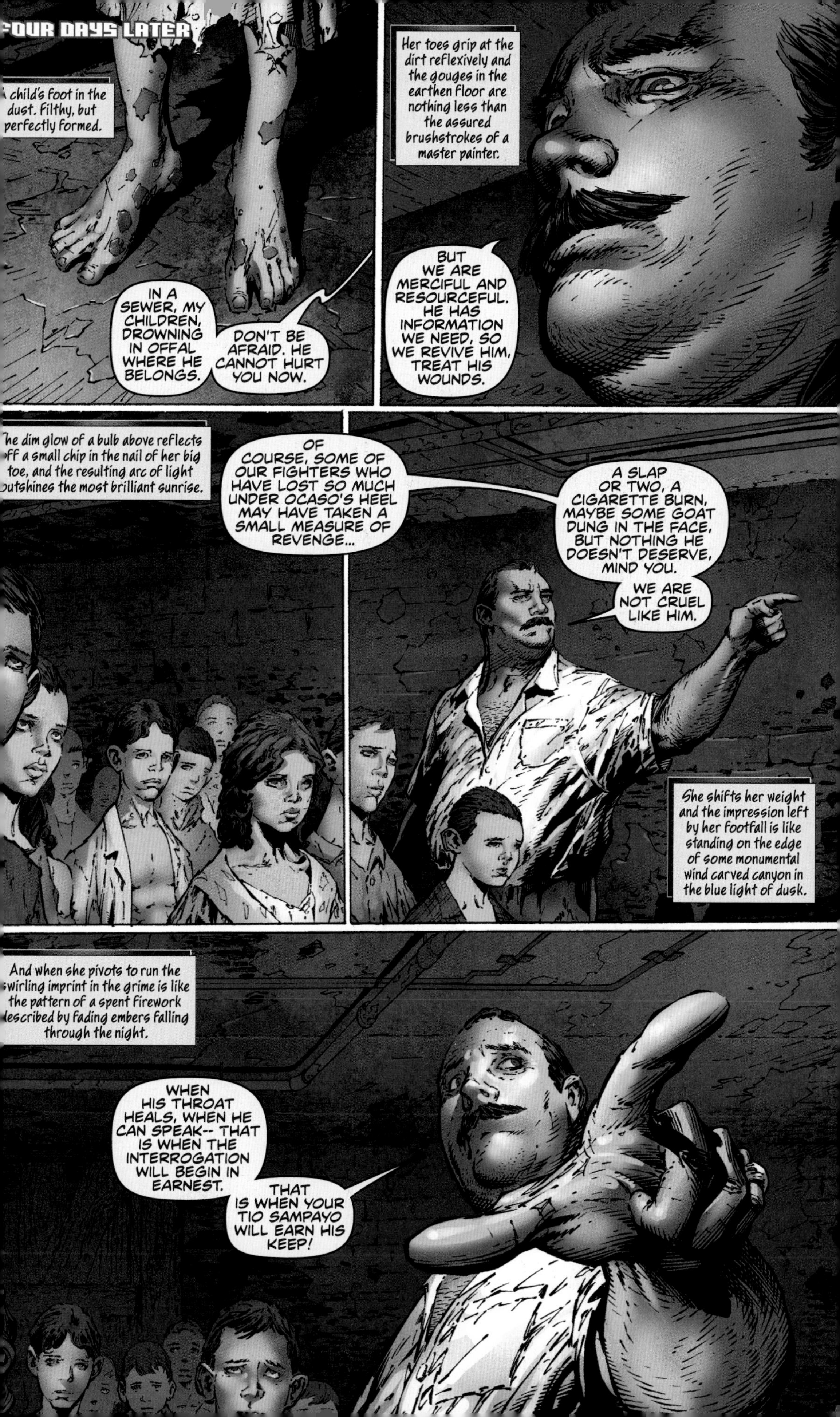
FOUR DAYS LATER
A child's foot in the dust. Filthy, but perfectly formed.
IN A SEWER, MY CHILDREN, DROWNING IN OFFAL WHERE HE BELONGS.
DON'T BE AFRAID. HE CANNOT HURT YOU NOW.
Her toes grip at the dirt reflexively and the gouges in the earthen floor are nothing less than the assured brushstrokes of a master painter.
BUT WE ARE MERCIFUL AND RESOURCEFUL. HE HAS INFORMATION WE NEED, SO WE REVIVE HIM, TREAT HIS WOUNDS.
The dim glow of a bulb above reflects off a small chip in the nail of her big toe, and the resulting arc of light outshines the most brilliant sunrise.
OF COURSE, SOME OF OUR FIGHTERS WHO HAVE LOST SO MUCH UNDER OCASO'S HEEL MAY HAVE TAKEN A SMALL MEASURE OF REVENGE...
A SLAP OR TWO, A CIGARETTE BURN, MAYBE SOME GOAT DUNG IN THE FACE, BUT NOTHING HE DOESN'T DESERVE, MIND YOU.
WE ARE NOT CRUEL LIKE HIM.
She shifts her weight and the impression left by her footfall is like standing on the edge of some monumental wind carved canyon in the blue light of dusk.
And when she pivots to run the swirling imprint in the grime is like the pattern of a spent firework described by fading embers falling through the night.
WHEN HIS THROAT HEALS, WHEN HE CAN SPEAK-- THAT IS WHEN THE INTERROGATION WILL BEGIN IN EARNEST.
THAT IS WHEN YOUR TIO SAMPAYO WILL EARN HIS KEEP!

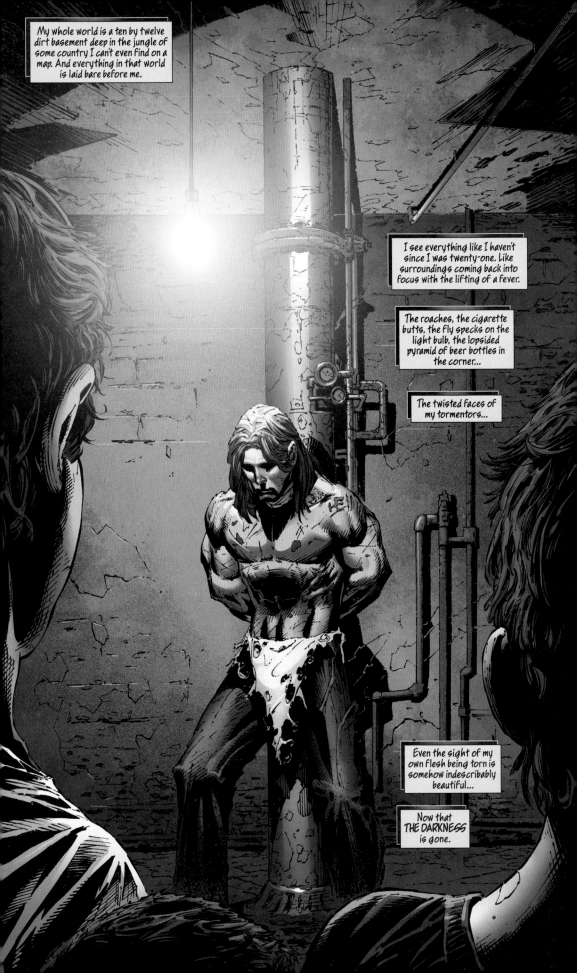

My whole world is a ten by twelve dirt basement deep in the jungle of some country I can't even find on a map. And everything in that world is laid bare before me.

I see everything like I haven't since I was twenty-one. Like surroundings coming back into focus with the lifting of a fever.

The roaches, the cigarette butts, the fly specks on the light bulb, the lopsided pyramid of beer bottles in the corner...

The twisted faces of my tormentors...

Even the sight of my own flesh being torn is somehow indescribably beautiful...

Now that THE DARKNESS is gone.

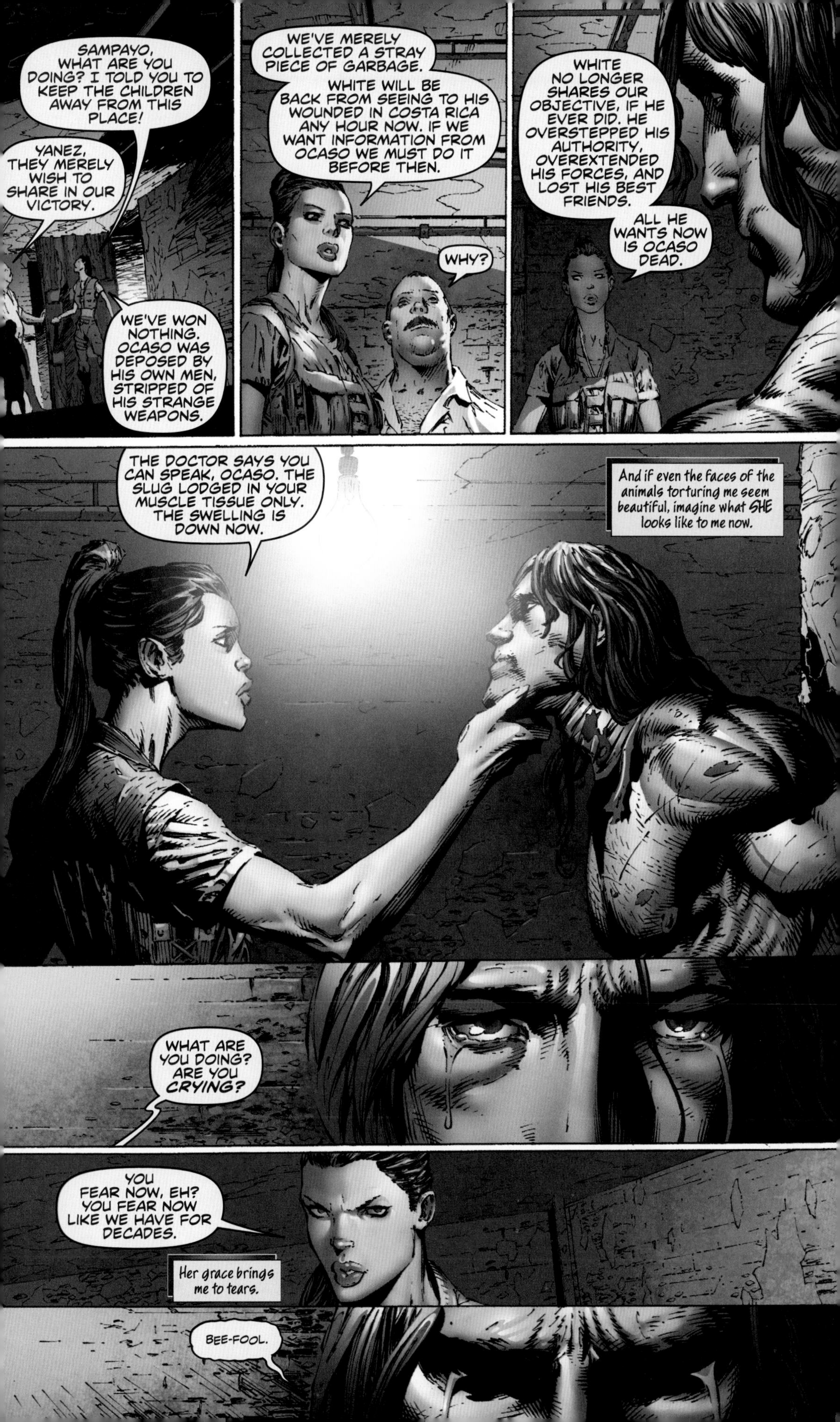
SAMPAYO, WHAT ARE YOU DOING? I TOLD YOU TO KEEP THE CHILDREN AWAY FROM THIS PLACE!
YANEZ, THEY MERELY WISH TO SHARE IN OUR VICTORY.
WE'VE WON NOTHING. OCASO WAS DEPOSED BY HIS OWN MEN, STRIPPED OF HIS STRANGE WEAPONS.
WE'VE MERELY COLLECTED A STRAY PIECE OF GARBAGE.
WHITE WILL BE BACK FROM SEEING TO HIS WOUNDED IN COSTA RICA ANY HOUR NOW. IF WE WANT INFORMATION FROM OCASO WE MUST DO IT BEFORE THEN.
WHY?
WHITE NO LONGER SHARES OUR OBJECTIVE, IF HE EVER DID. HE OVERSTEPPED HIS AUTHORITY, OVEREXTENDED HIS FORCES, AND LOST HIS BEST FRIENDS.
ALL HE WANTS NOW IS OCASO DEAD.
THE DOCTOR SAYS YOU CAN SPEAK, OCASO. THE SLUG LODGED IN YOUR MUSCLE TISSUE ONLY. THE SWELLING IS DOWN NOW.
And if even the faces of the animals torturing me seem beautiful, imagine what SHE looks like to me now.
WHAT ARE YOU DOING? ARE YOU CRYING?
YOU FEAR NOW, EH? YOU FEAR NOW LIKE WE HAVE FOR DECADES.
Her grace brings me to tears.
BEE-FOOL.

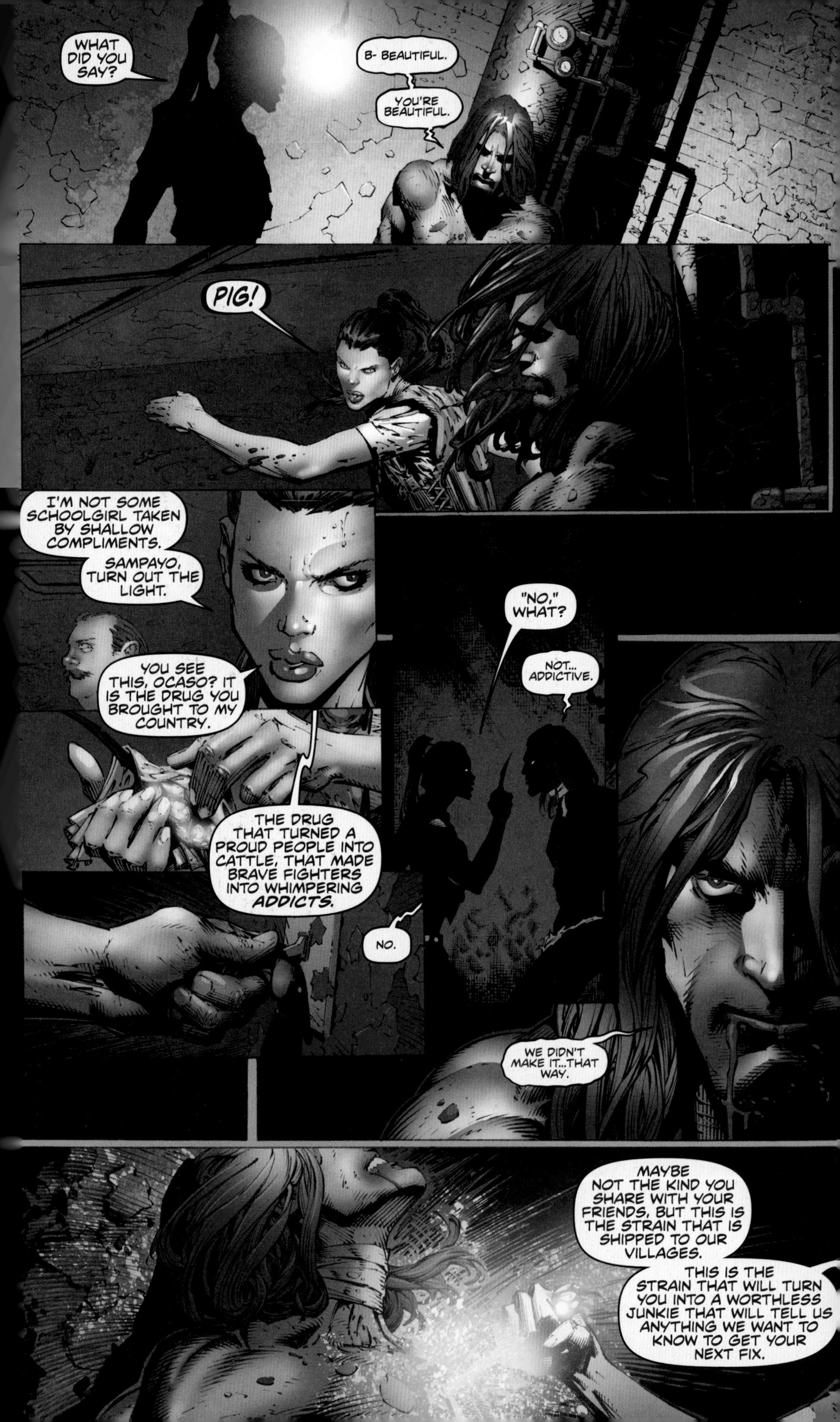
WHAT DID YOU SAY?
B- BEAUTIFUL.
YOU'RE BEAUTIFUL.
PIG!
I'M NOT SOME SCHOOLGIRL TAKEN BY SHALLOW COMPLIMENTS.
SAMPAYO, TURN OUT THE LIGHT.
YOU SEE THIS, OCASO? IT IS THE DRUG YOU BROUGHT TO MY COUNTRY.
THE DRUG THAT TURNED A PROUD PEOPLE INTO CATTLE, THAT MADE BRAVE FIGHTERS INTO WHIMPERING *ADDICTS*.
NO.
"NO," WHAT?
NOT... ADDICTIVE.
WE DIDN'T MAKE IT...THAT WAY.
MAYBE NOT THE KIND YOU SHARE WITH YOUR FRIENDS, BUT THIS IS THE STRAIN THAT IS SHIPPED TO OUR VILLAGES.
THIS IS THE STRAIN THAT WILL TURN YOU INTO A WORTHLESS JUNKIE THAT WILL TELL US ANYTHING WE WANT TO KNOW TO GET YOUR NEXT FIX.

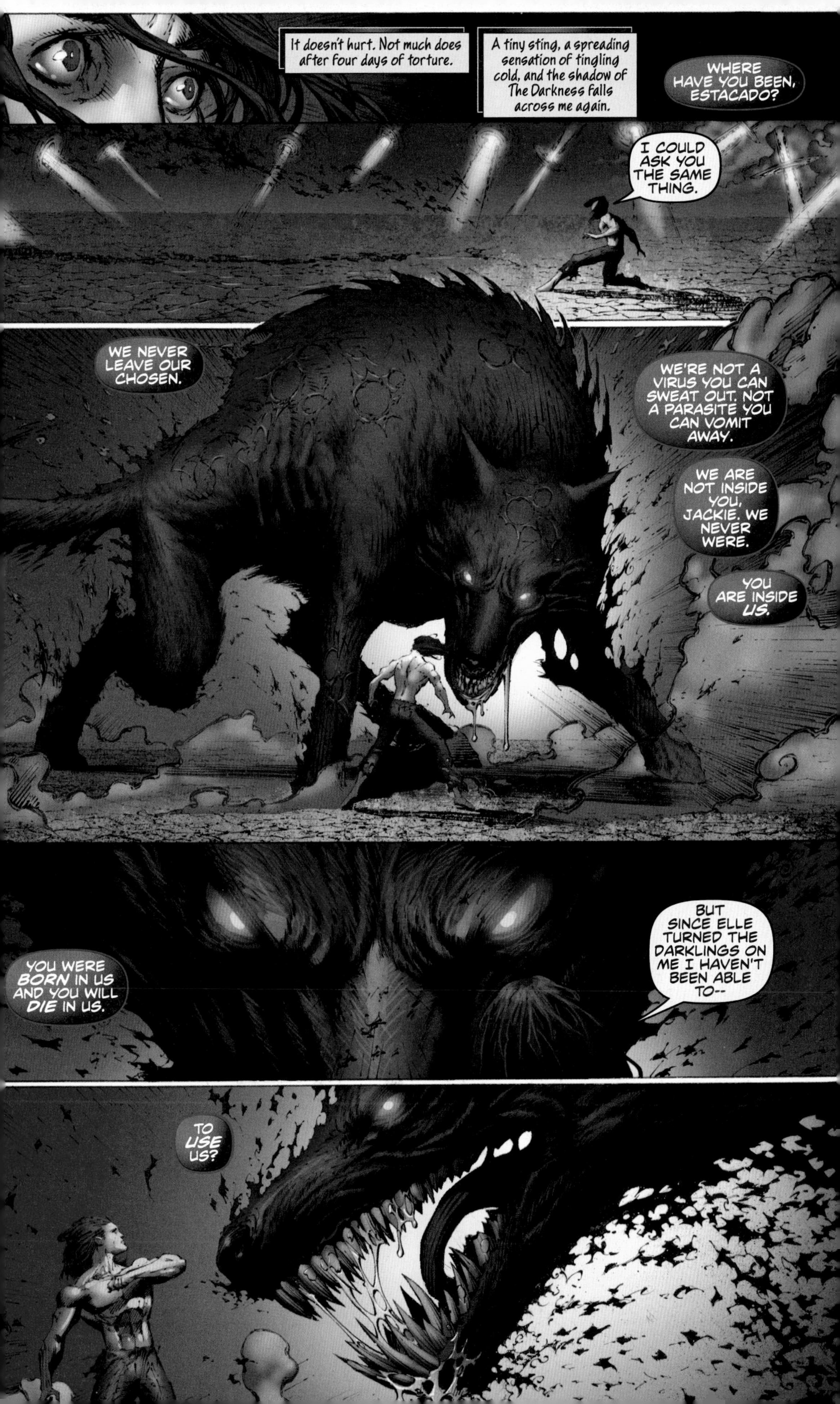
It doesn't hurt. Not much does after four days of torture.
A tiny sting, a spreading sensation of tingling cold, and the shadow of The Darkness falls across me again.
WHERE HAVE YOU BEEN, ESTACADO?
I COULD ASK YOU THE SAME THING.
WE NEVER LEAVE OUR CHOSEN.
WE'RE NOT A VIRUS YOU CAN SWEAT OUT. NOT A PARASITE YOU CAN VOMIT AWAY.
WE ARE NOT INSIDE YOU, JACKIE. WE NEVER WERE.
YOU ARE INSIDE US.
YOU WERE BORN IN US AND YOU WILL DIE IN US.
BUT SINCE ELLE TURNED THE DARKLINGS ON ME I HAVEN'T BEEN ABLE TO--
TO USE US?

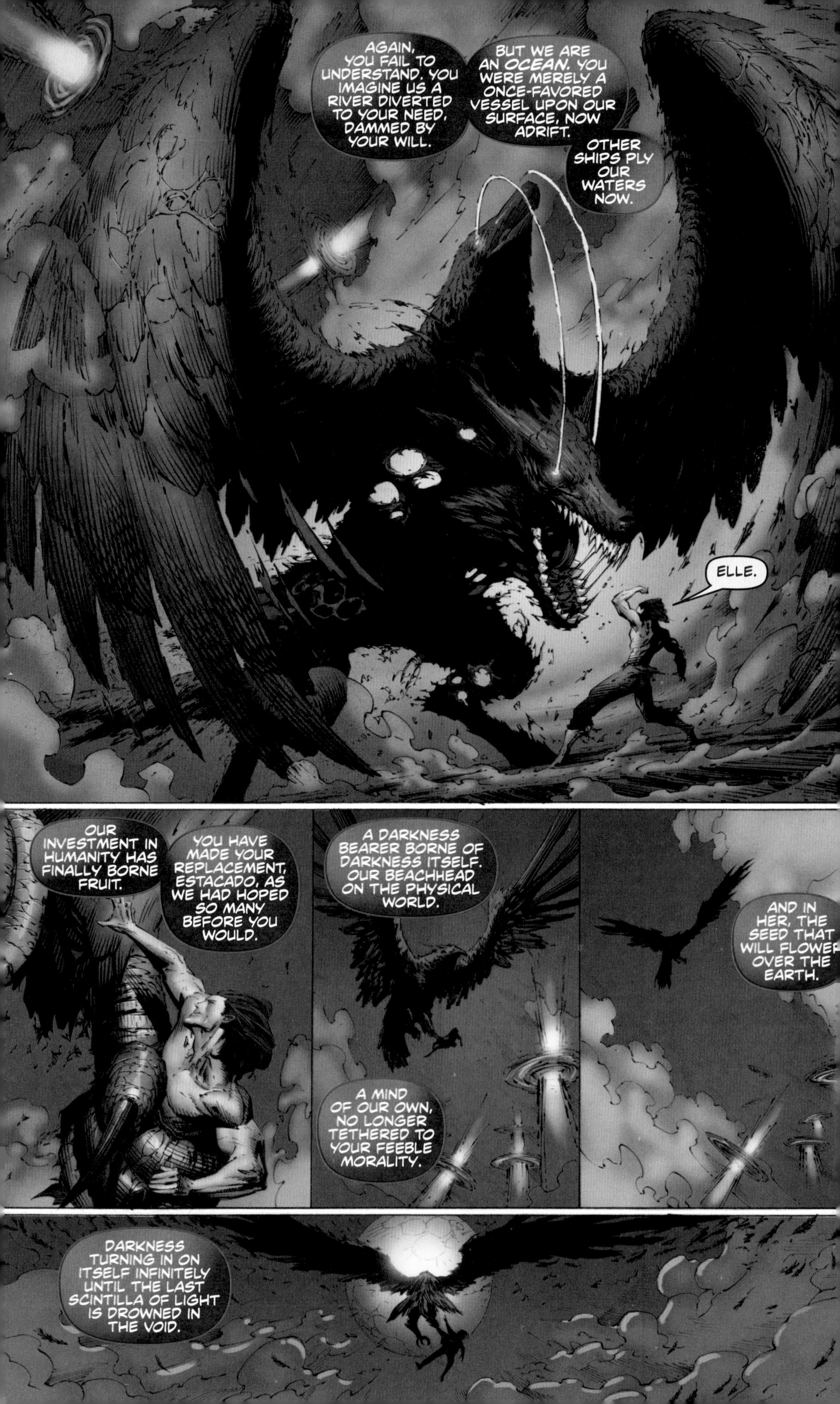

AGAIN, YOU FAIL TO UNDERSTAND. YOU IMAGINE US A RIVER DIVERTED TO YOUR NEED, DAMMED BY YOUR WILL.
BUT WE ARE AN *OCEAN.* YOU WERE MERELY A ONCE-FAVORED VESSEL UPON OUR SURFACE, NOW ADRIFT.
OTHER SHIPS PLY OUR WATERS NOW.
ELLE.
OUR INVESTMENT IN HUMANITY HAS FINALLY BORNE FRUIT.
YOU HAVE MADE YOUR REPLACEMENT, ESTACADO, AS WE HAD HOPED SO MANY BEFORE YOU WOULD.
A DARKNESS BEARER BORNE OF DARKNESS ITSELF. OUR BEACHHEAD ON THE PHYSICAL WORLD.
A MIND OF OUR OWN, NO LONGER TETHERED TO YOUR FEEBLE MORALITY.
AND IN HER, THE SEED THAT WILL FLOWER OVER THE EARTH.
DARKNESS TURNING IN ON ITSELF INFINITELY UNTIL THE LAST SCINTILLA OF LIGHT IS DROWNED IN THE VOID.

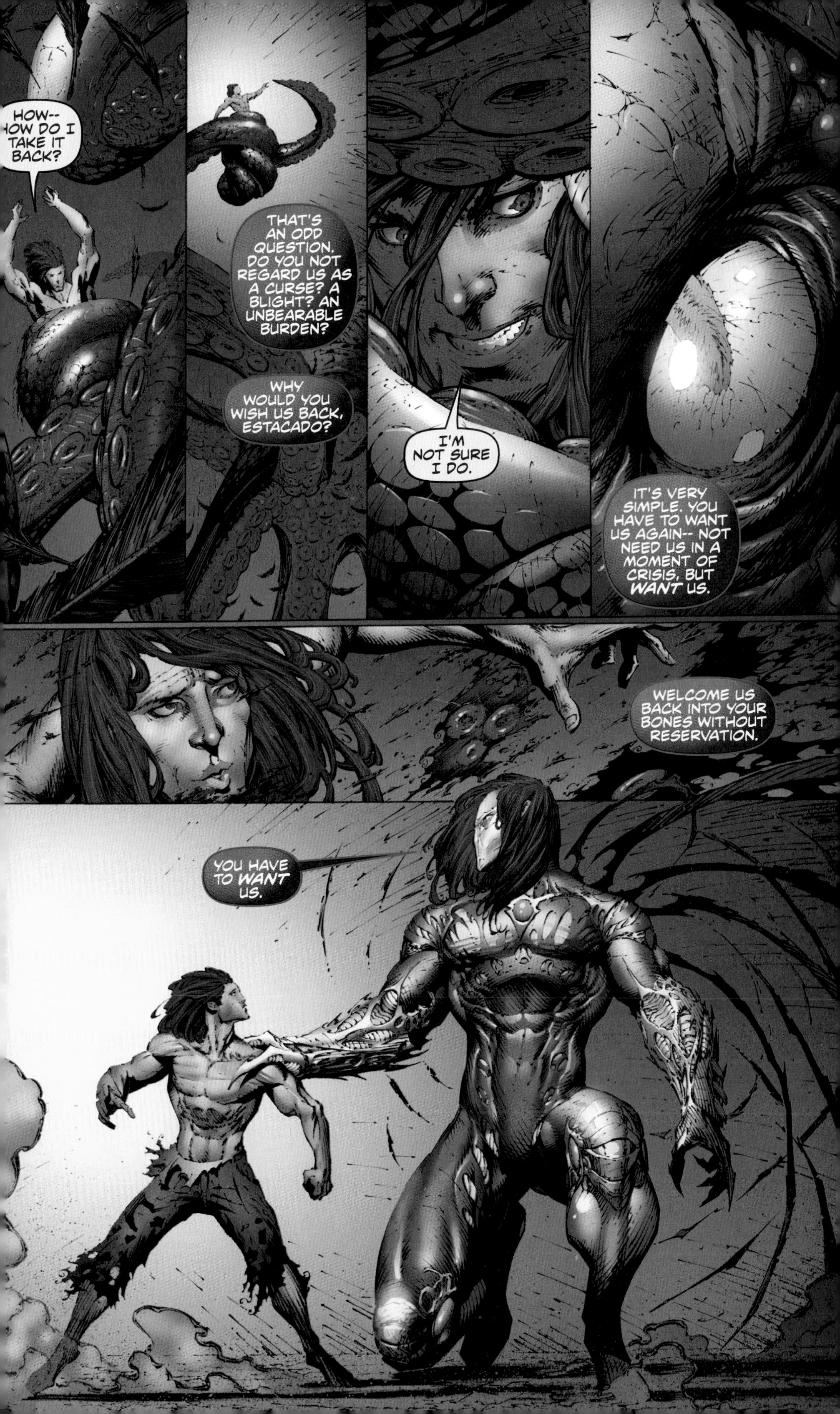
HOW--
HOW DO I TAKE IT BACK?
THAT'S AN ODD QUESTION. DO YOU NOT REGARD US AS A CURSE? A BLIGHT? AN UNBEARABLE BURDEN?
WHY WOULD YOU WISH US BACK, ESTACADO?
I'M NOT SURE I DO.
IT'S VERY SIMPLE. YOU HAVE TO WANT US AGAIN-- NOT NEED US IN A MOMENT OF CRISIS, BUT *WANT* US.
WELCOME US BACK INTO YOUR BONES WITHOUT RESERVATION.
YOU HAVE TO *WANT* US.

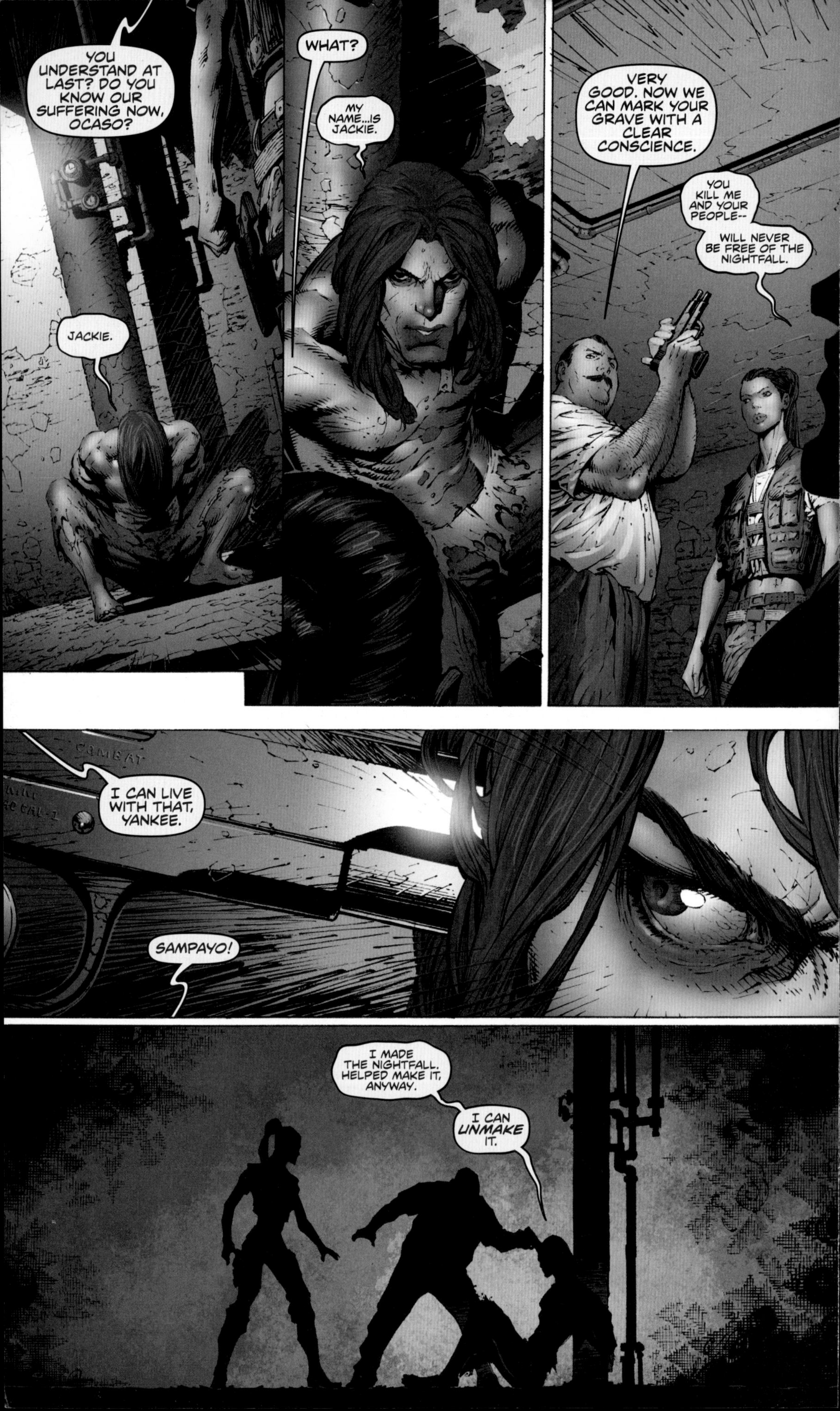
YOU UNDERSTAND AT LAST? DO YOU KNOW OUR SUFFERING NOW, OCASO?
JACKIE.
WHAT?
MY NAME...IS JACKIE.
VERY GOOD. NOW WE CAN MARK YOUR GRAVE WITH A CLEAR CONSCIENCE.
YOU KILL ME AND YOUR PEOPLE--
WILL NEVER BE FREE OF THE NIGHTFALL.
I CAN LIVE WITH THAT, YANKEE.
SAMPAYO!
I MADE THE NIGHTFALL. HELPED MAKE IT, ANYWAY.
I CAN *UNMAKE* IT.

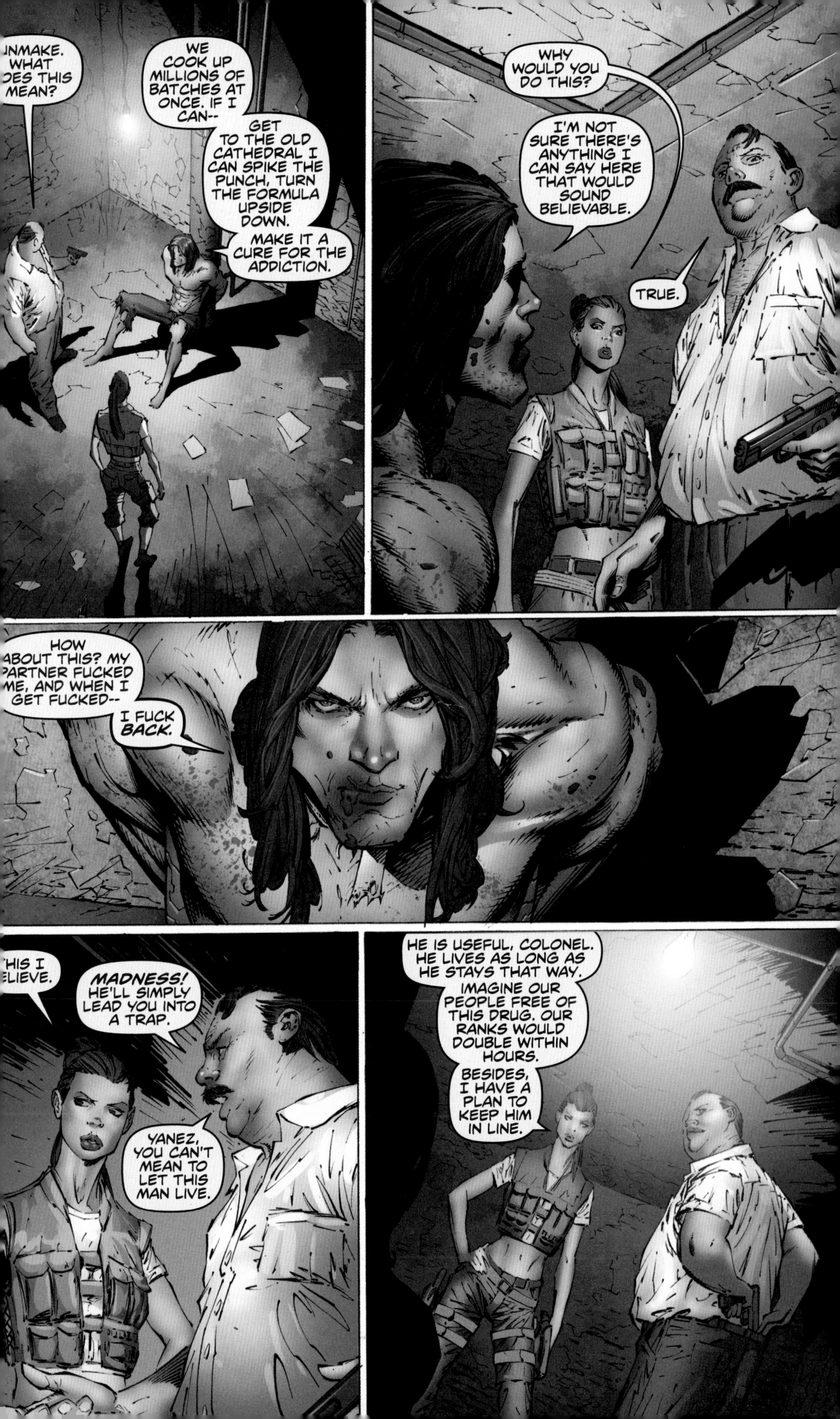

UNMAKE. WHAT DOES THIS MEAN?
WE COOK UP MILLIONS OF BATCHES AT ONCE. IF I CAN--
GET TO THE OLD CATHEDRAL I CAN SPIKE THE PUNCH, TURN THE FORMULA UPSIDE DOWN.
MAKE IT A CURE FOR THE ADDICTION.
WHY WOULD YOU DO THIS?
I'M NOT SURE THERE'S ANYTHING I CAN SAY HERE THAT WOULD SOUND BELIEVABLE.
TRUE.
HOW ABOUT THIS? MY PARTNER FUCKED ME, AND WHEN I GET FUCKED--
I FUCK *BACK.*
THIS I BELIEVE.
MADNESS! HE'LL SIMPLY LEAD YOU INTO A TRAP.
YANEZ, YOU CAN'T MEAN TO LET THIS MAN LIVE.
HE IS USEFUL, COLONEL. HE LIVES AS LONG AS HE STAYS THAT WAY.
IMAGINE OUR PEOPLE FREE OF THIS DRUG. OUR RANKS WOULD DOUBLE WITHIN HOURS.
BESIDES, I HAVE A PLAN TO KEEP HIM IN LINE.

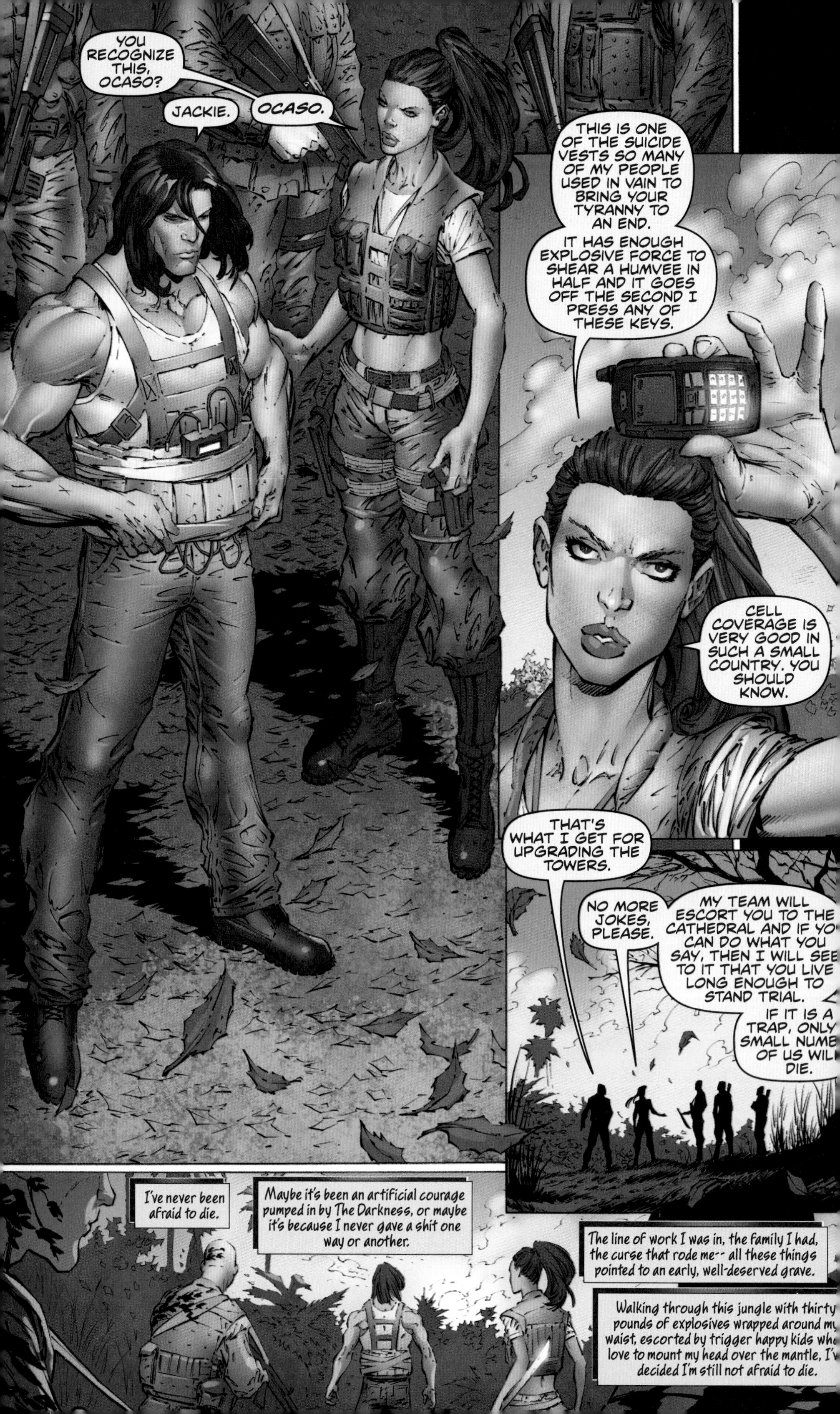
YOU RECOGNIZE THIS, OCASO?
JACKIE.
OCASO.
THIS IS ONE OF THE SUICIDE VESTS SO MANY OF MY PEOPLE USED IN VAIN TO BRING YOUR TYRANNY TO AN END.
IT HAS ENOUGH EXPLOSIVE FORCE TO SHEAR A HUMVEE IN HALF AND IT GOES OFF THE SECOND I PRESS ANY OF THESE KEYS.
CELL COVERAGE IS VERY GOOD IN SUCH A SMALL COUNTRY. YOU SHOULD KNOW.
THAT'S WHAT I GET FOR UPGRADING THE TOWERS.
NO MORE JOKES, PLEASE.
MY TEAM WILL ESCORT YOU TO THE CATHEDRAL AND IF YO CAN DO WHAT YOU SAY, THEN I WILL SEE TO IT THAT YOU LIVE LONG ENOUGH TO STAND TRIAL.
IF IT IS A TRAP, ONLY SMALL NUMB OF US WIL DIE.
I've never been afraid to die.
Maybe it's been an artificial courage pumped in by The Darkness, or maybe it's because I never gave a shit one way or another.
The line of work I was in, the family I had, the curse that rode me-- all these things pointed to an early, well-deserved grave.
Walking through this jungle with thirty pounds of explosives wrapped around m waist, escorted by trigger happy kids wh love to mount my head over the mantle, I' decided I'm still not afraid to die.

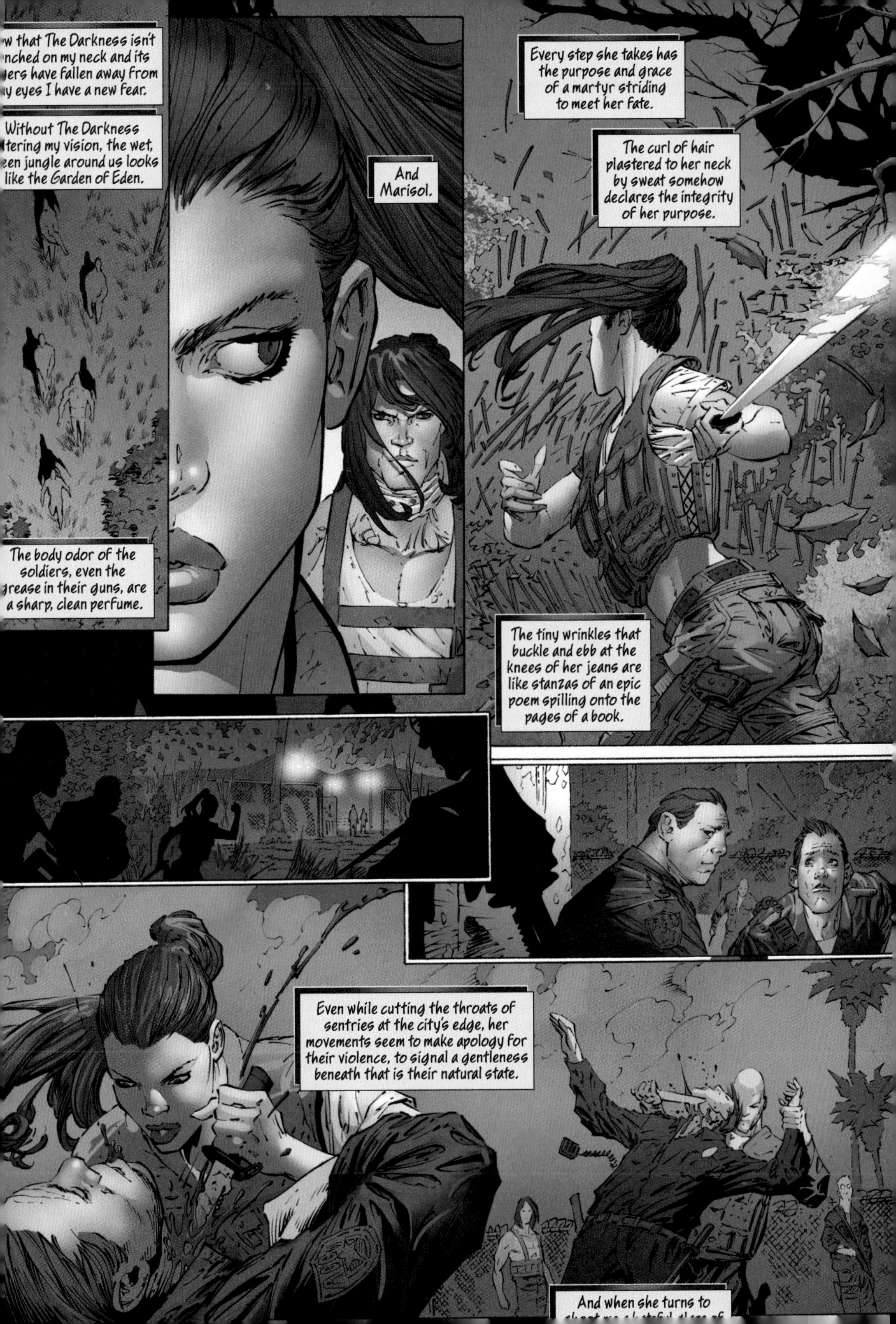

w that The Darkness isn't nched on my neck and its ers have fallen away from y eyes I have a new fear.
Without The Darkness tering my vision, the wet, een jungle around us looks like the Garden of Eden.
The body odor of the soldiers, even the grease in their guns, are a sharp, clean perfume.
And Marisol.
Every step she takes has the purpose and grace of a martyr striding to meet her fate.
The curl of hair plastered to her neck by sweat somehow declares the integrity of her purpose.
The tiny wrinkles that buckle and ebb at the knees of her jeans are like stanzas of an epic poem spilling onto the pages of a book.
Even while cutting the throats of sentries at the city's edge, her movements seem to make apology for their violence, to signal a gentleness beneath that is their natural state.
And when she turns to

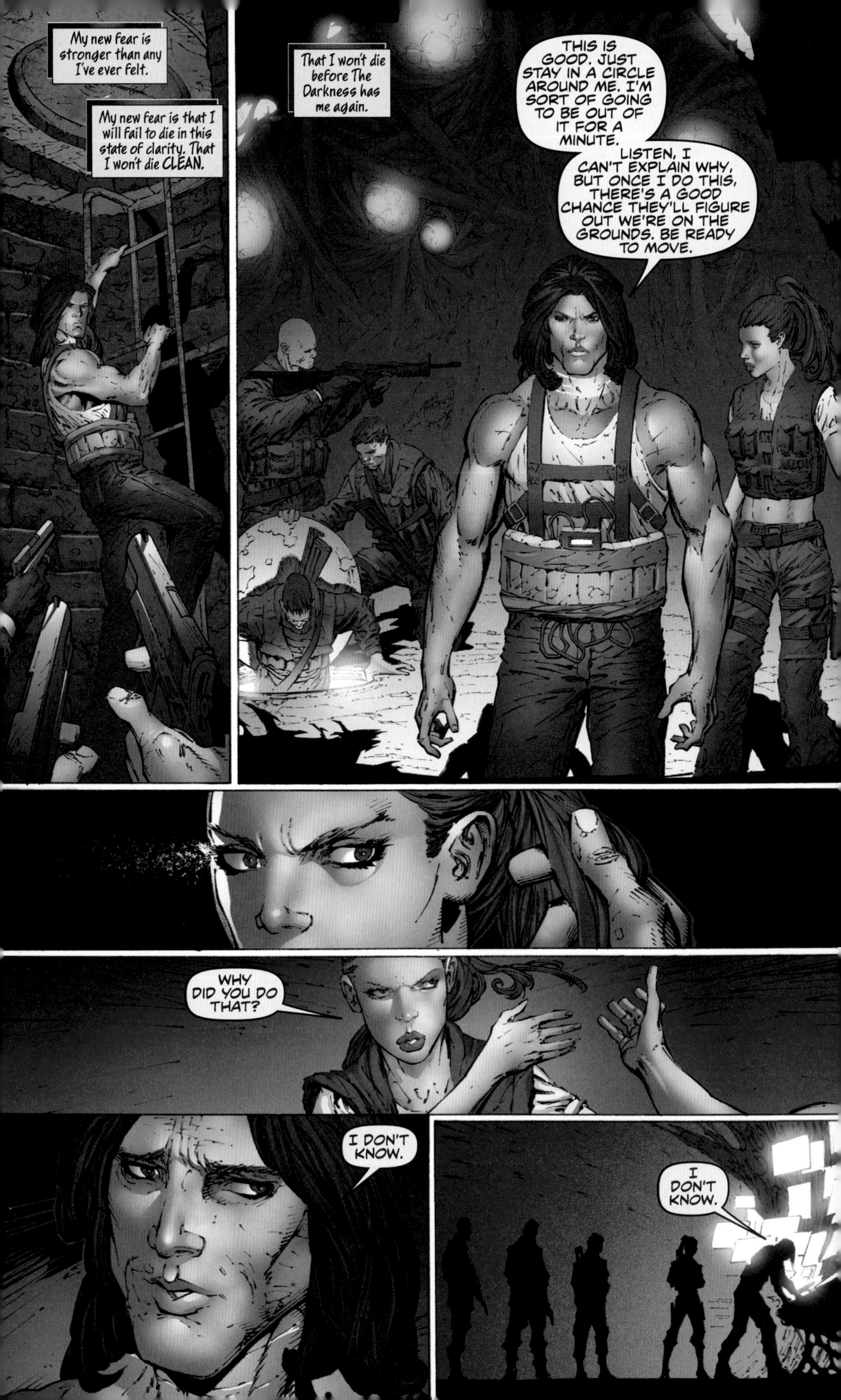

My new fear is stronger than any I've ever felt.
My new fear is that I will fail to die in this state of clarity. That I won't die CLEAN.
That I won't die before The Darkness has me again.
THIS IS GOOD. JUST STAY IN A CIRCLE AROUND ME. I'M SORT OF GOING TO BE OUT OF IT FOR A MINUTE.
LISTEN, I CAN'T EXPLAIN WHY, BUT ONCE I DO THIS, THERE'S A GOOD CHANCE THEY'LL FIGURE OUT WE'RE ON THE GROUNDS. BE READY TO MOVE.
WHY DID YOU DO THAT?
I DON'T KNOW.
I DON'T KNOW.

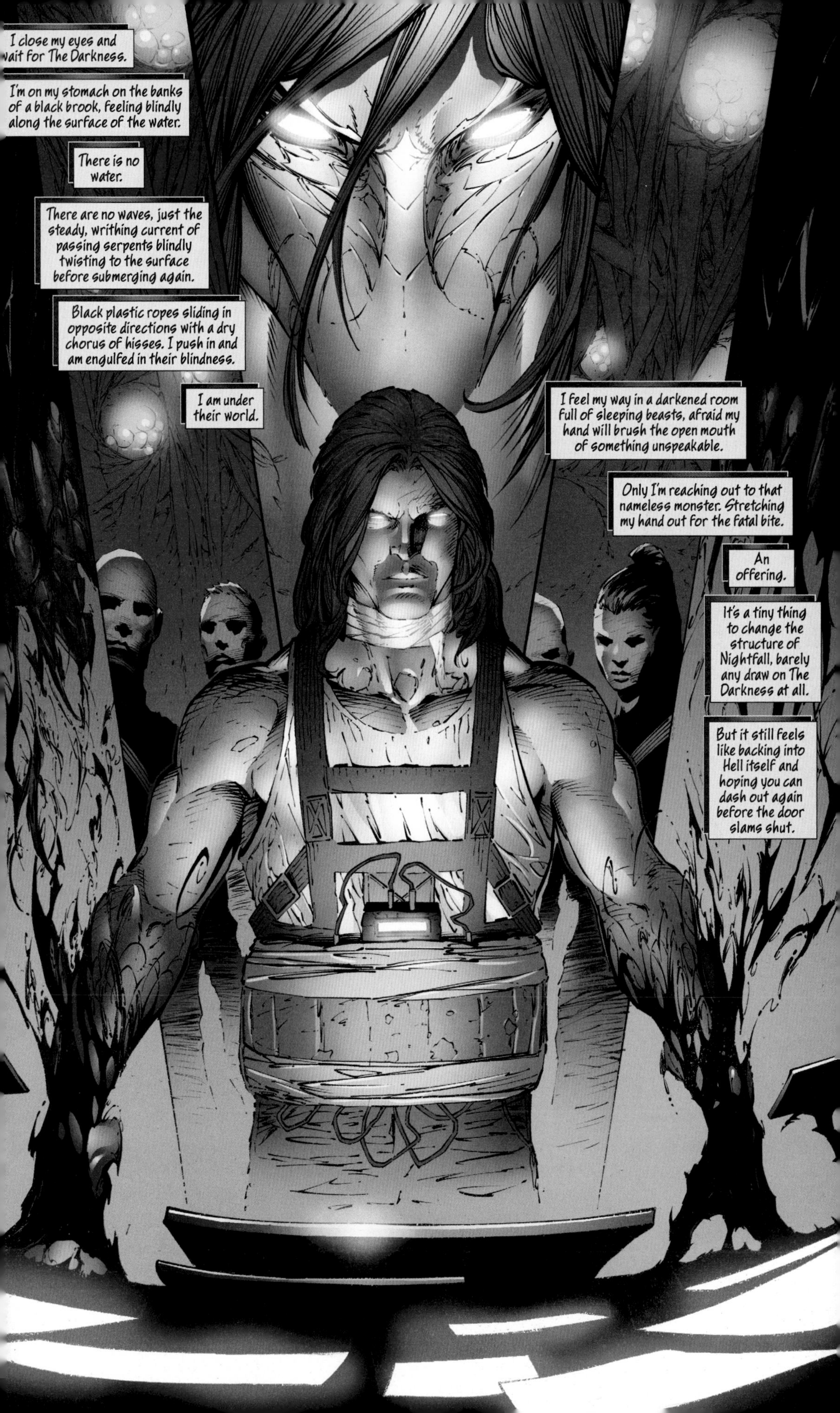
I close my eyes and wait for The Darkness.
I'm on my stomach on the banks of a black brook, feeling blindly along the surface of the water.
There is no water.
There are no waves, just the steady, writhing current of passing serpents blindly twisting to the surface before submerging again.
Black plastic ropes sliding in opposite directions with a dry chorus of hisses. I push in and am engulfed in their blindness.
I am under their world.
I feel my way in a darkened room full of sleeping beasts, afraid my hand will brush the open mouth of something unspeakable.
Only I'm reaching out to that nameless monster. Stretching my hand out for the fatal bite.
An offering.
It's a tiny thing to change the structure of Nightfall, barely any draw on The Darkness at all.
But it still feels like backing into Hell itself and hoping you can dash out again before the door slams shut.

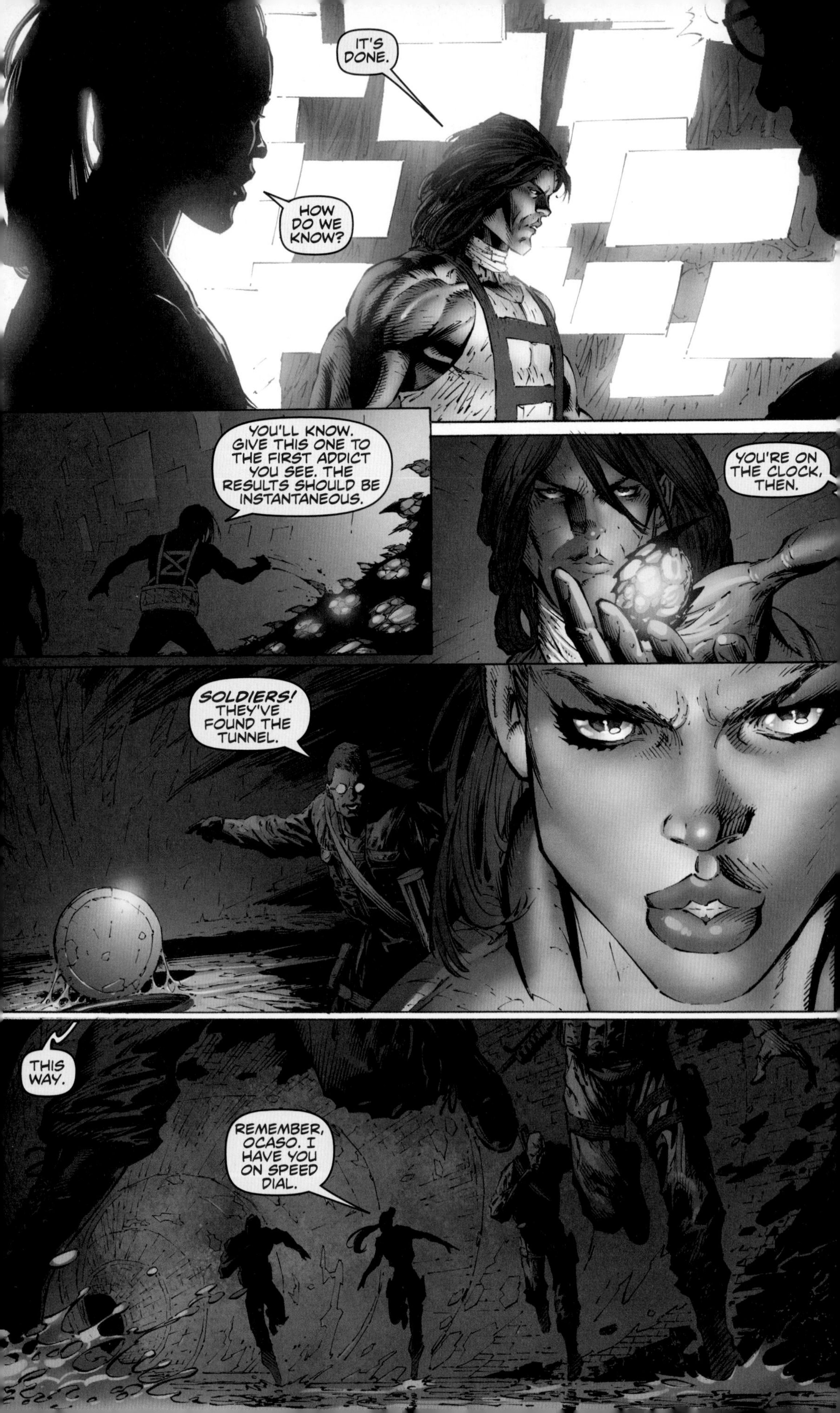
IT'S DONE.
HOW DO WE KNOW?
YOU'LL KNOW. GIVE THIS ONE TO THE FIRST ADDICT YOU SEE. THE RESULTS SHOULD BE INSTANTANEOUS.
YOU'RE ON THE CLOCK, THEN.
SOLDIERS! THEY'VE FOUND THE TUNNEL.
THIS WAY.
REMEMBER, OCASO. I HAVE YOU ON SPEED DIAL.

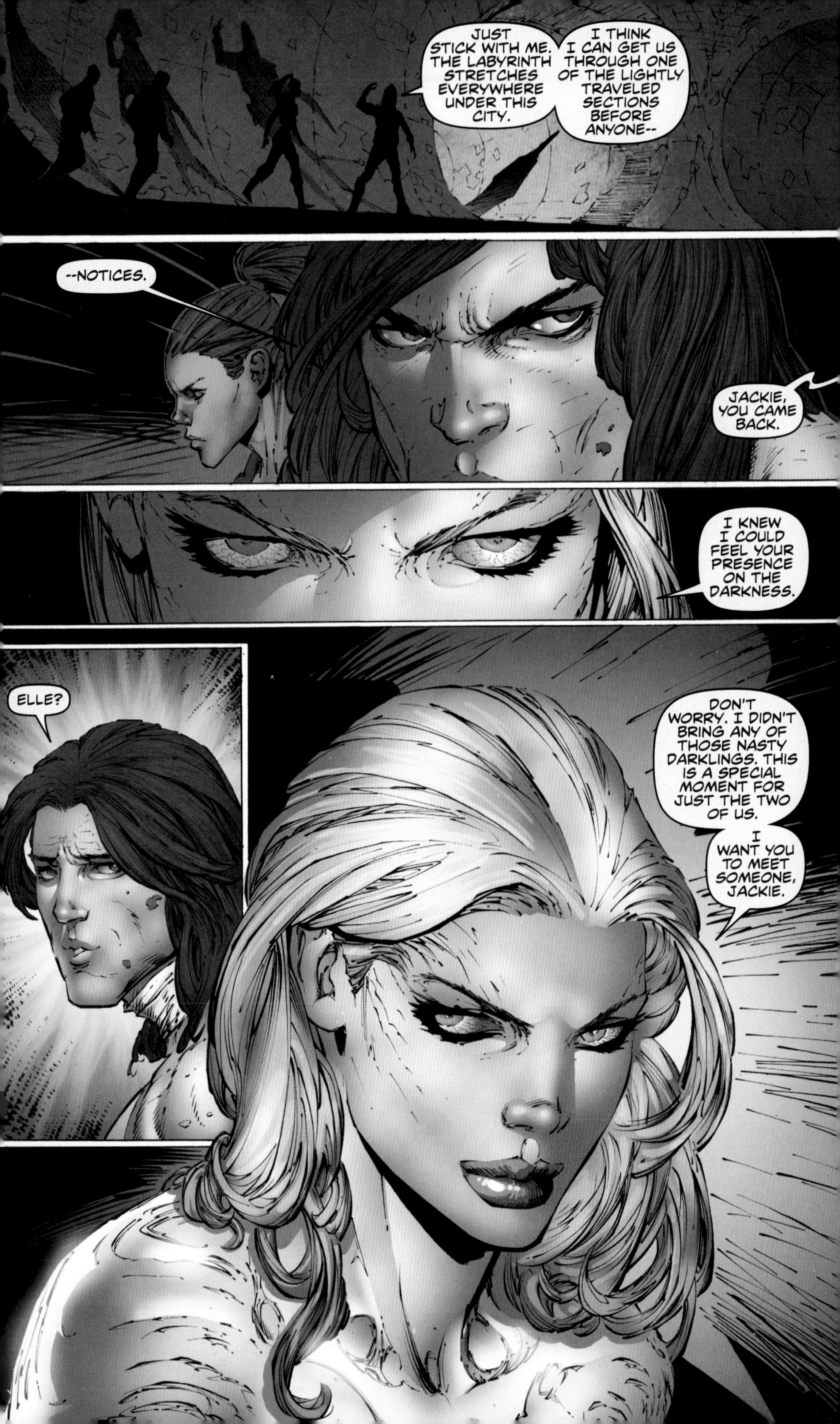
JUST STICK WITH ME. THE LABYRINTH STRETCHES EVERYWHERE UNDER THIS CITY.
I THINK I CAN GET US THROUGH ONE OF THE LIGHTLY TRAVELED SECTIONS BEFORE ANYONE--
--NOTICES.
JACKIE, YOU CAME BACK.
I KNEW I COULD FEEL YOUR PRESENCE ON THE DARKNESS.
ELLE?
DON'T WORRY. I DIDN'T BRING ANY OF THOSE NASTY DARKLINGS. THIS IS A SPECIAL MOMENT FOR JUST THE TWO OF US.
I WANT YOU TO MEET SOMEONE, JACKIE.

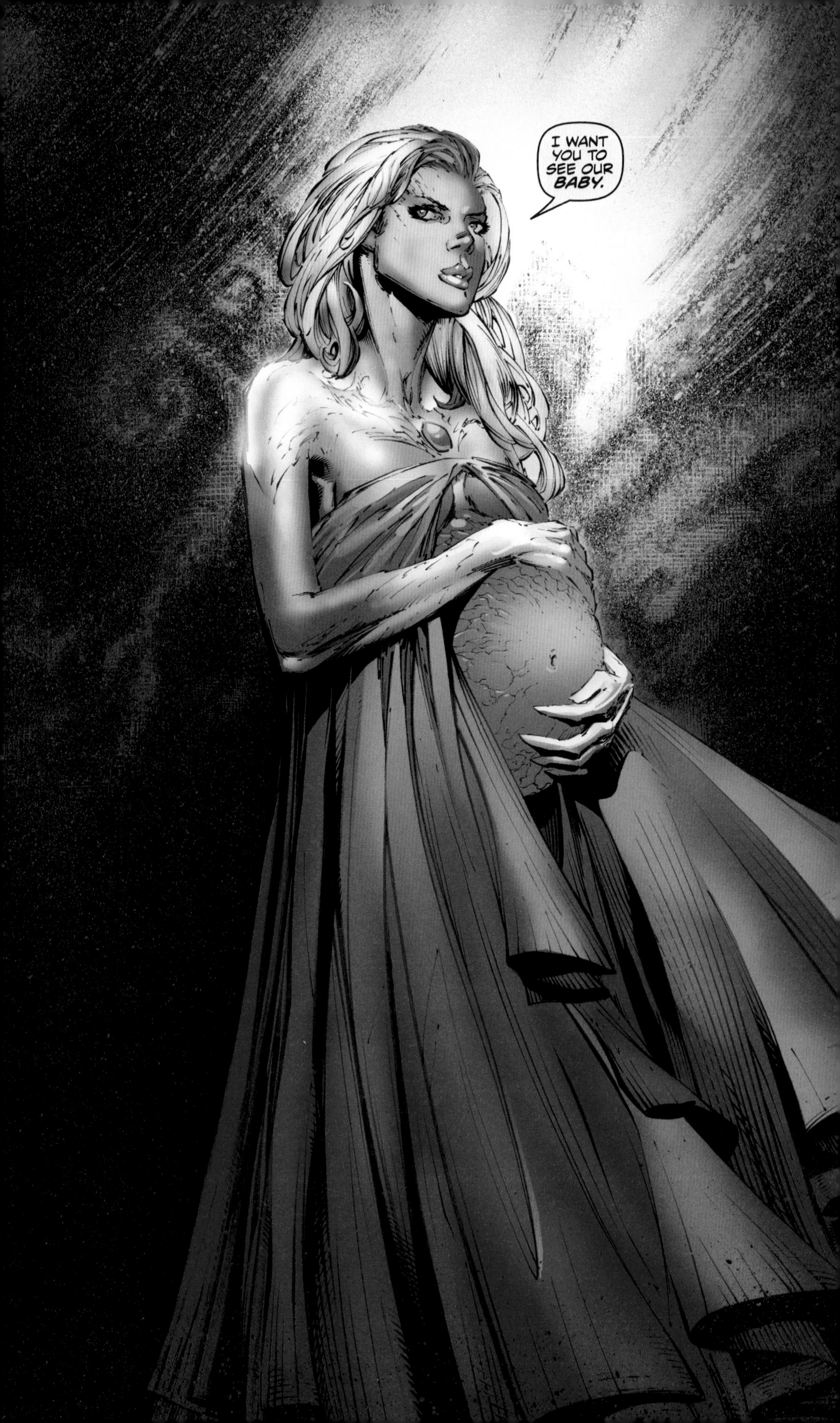
I WANT YOU TO SEE OUR BABY.

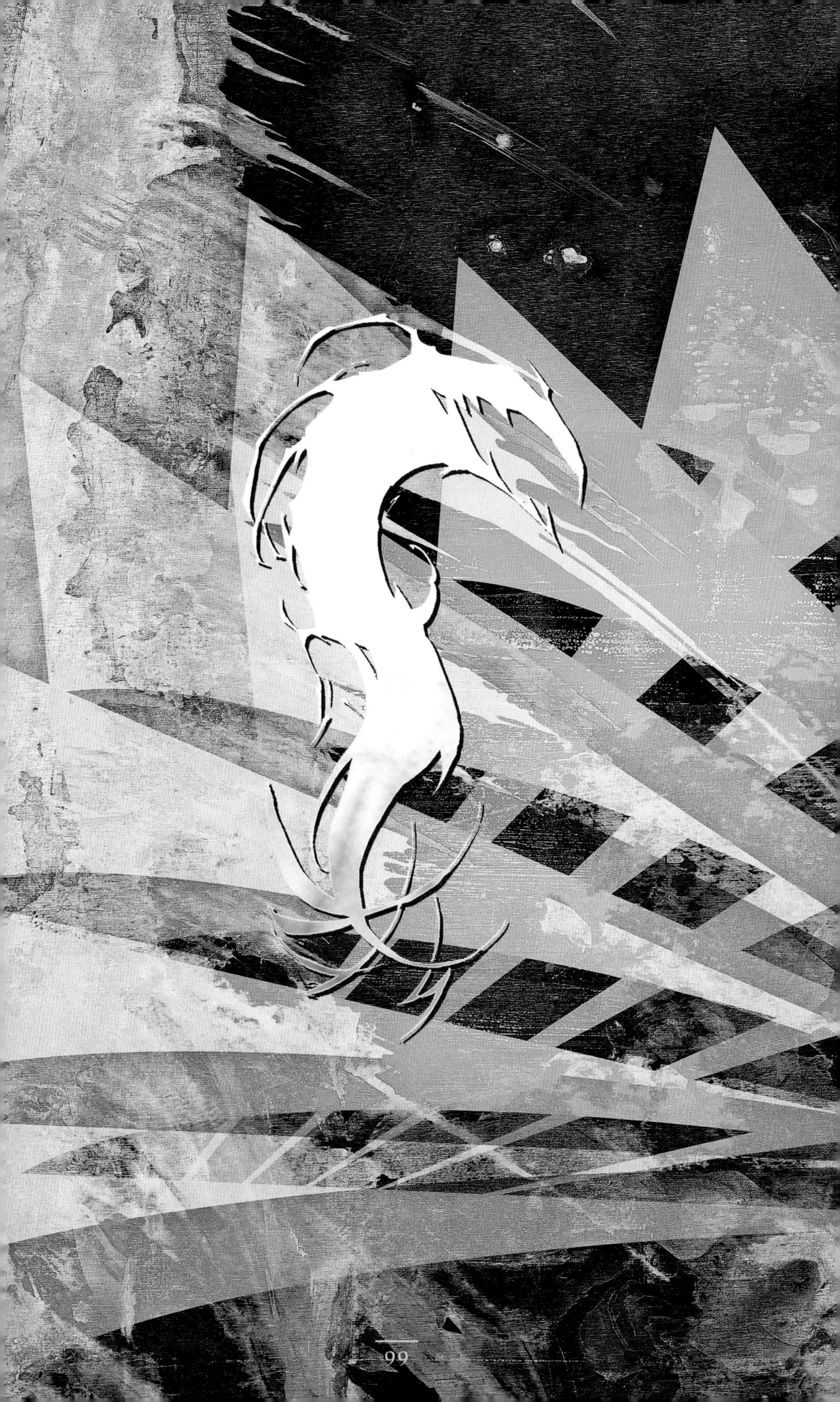

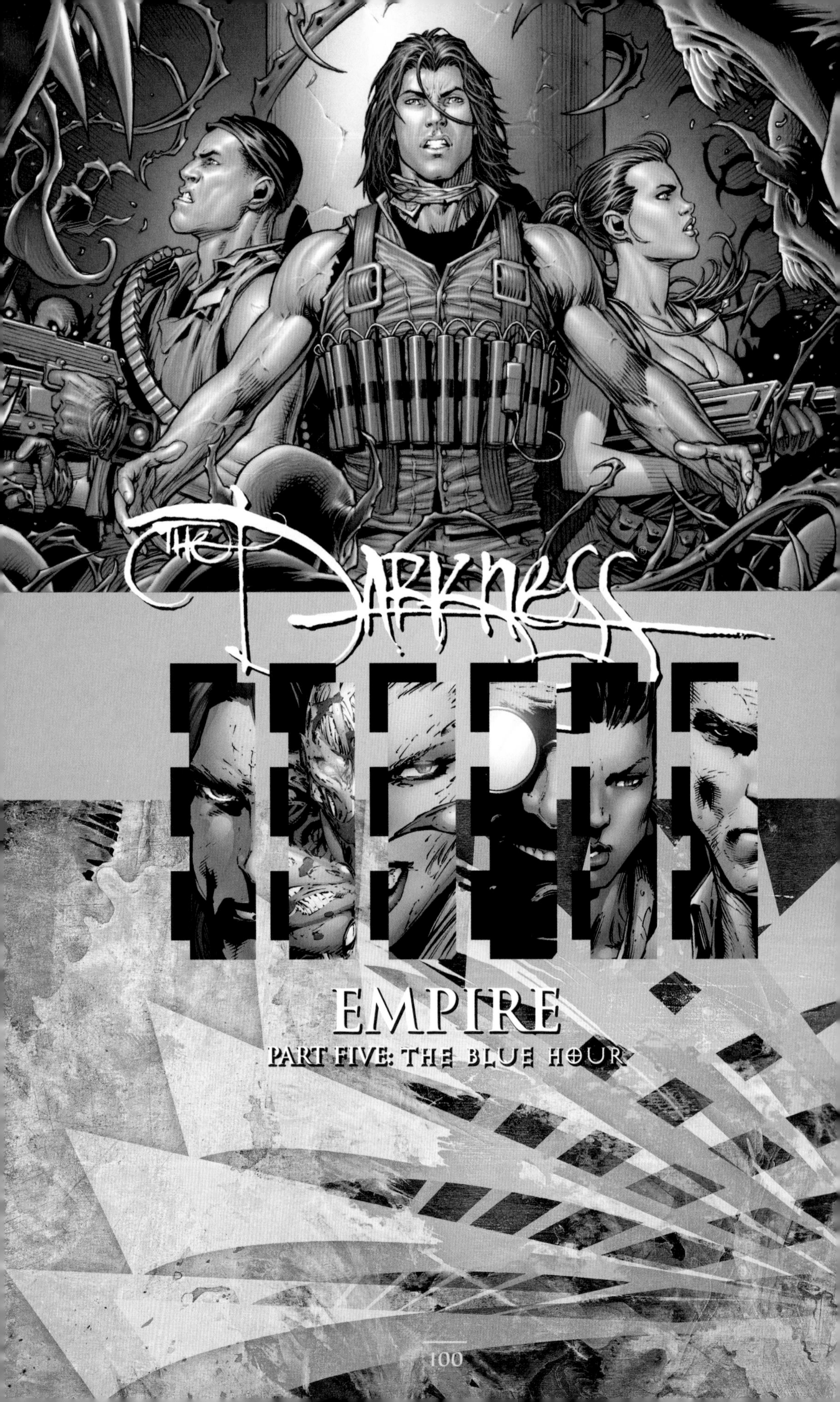

The Darkness
EMPIRE
PART FIVE: THE BLUE HOUR

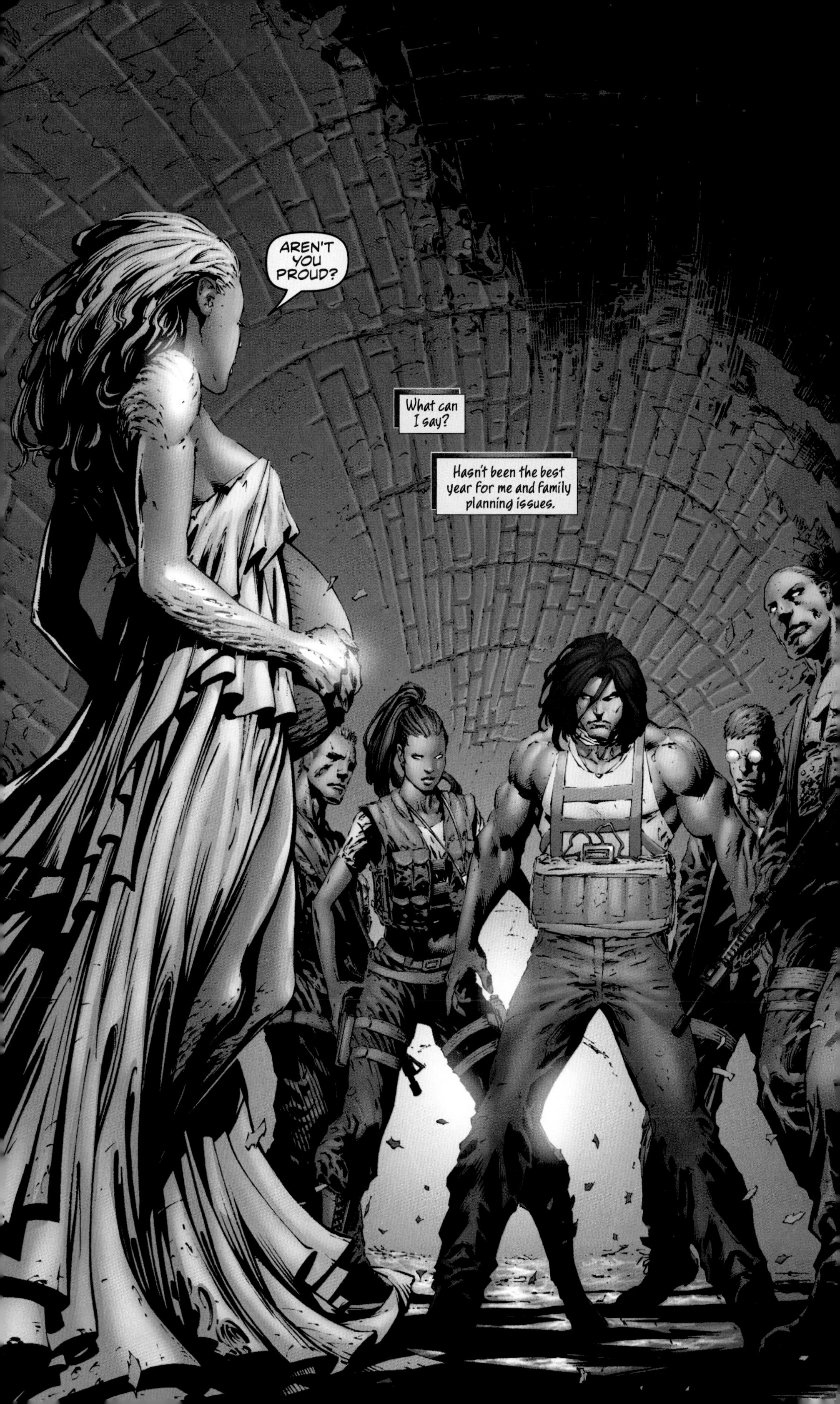
ARE'NT YOU PROUD?
What can I say?
Hasn't been the best year for me and family planning issues.

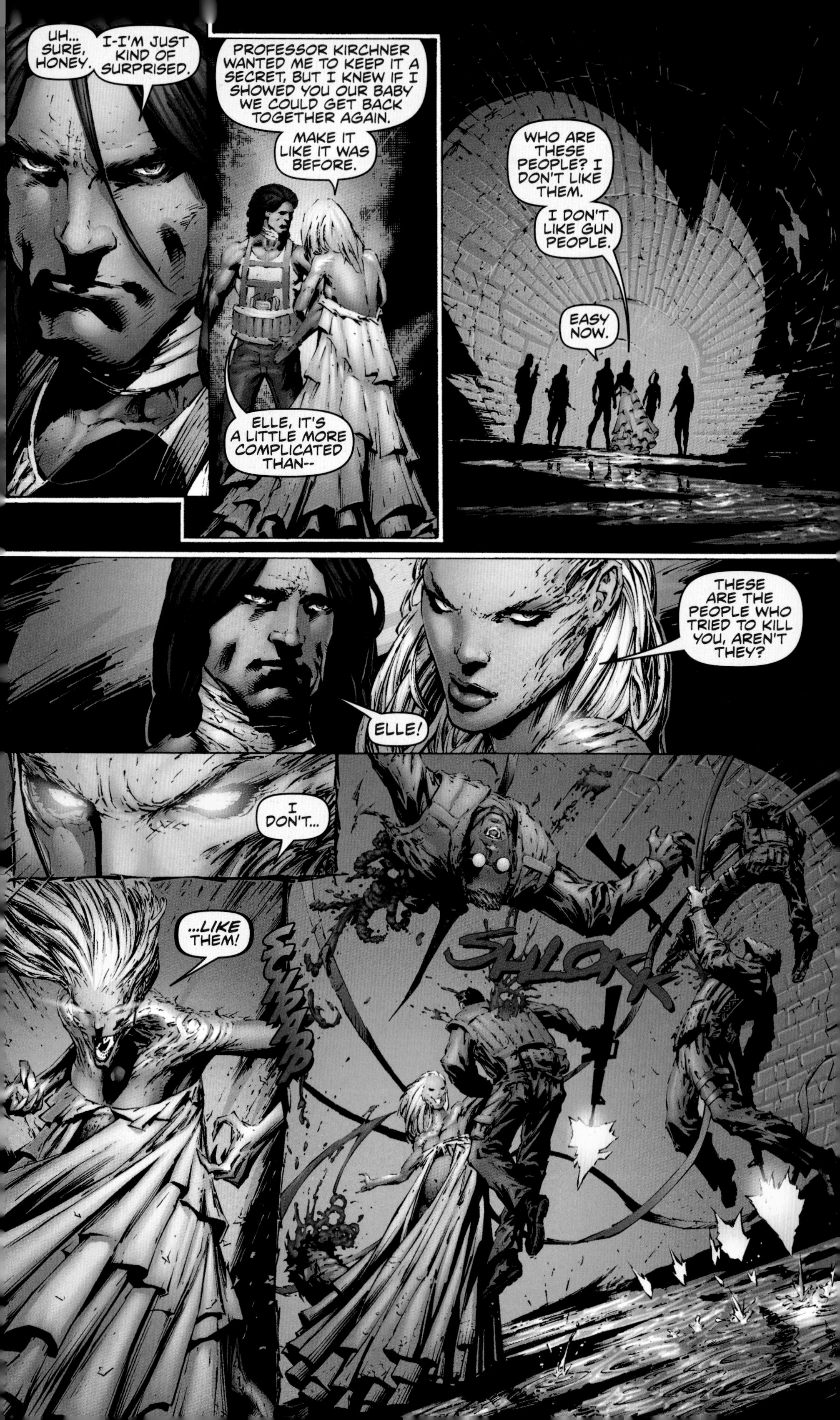
UH... SURE, HONEY.
I-I'M JUST KIND OF SURPRISED.
PROFESSOR KIRCHNER WANTED ME TO KEEP IT A SECRET, BUT I KNEW IF I SHOWED YOU OUR BABY WE COULD GET BACK TOGETHER AGAIN.
MAKE IT LIKE IT WAS BEFORE.
ELLE, IT'S A LITTLE MORE COMPLICATED THAN--
WHO ARE THESE PEOPLE? I DON'T LIKE THEM.
I DON'T LIKE GUN PEOPLE.
EASY NOW.
THESE ARE THE PEOPLE WHO TRIED TO KILL YOU, AREN'T THEY?
ELLE!
I DON'T...
...LIKE THEM!
SHLOKK

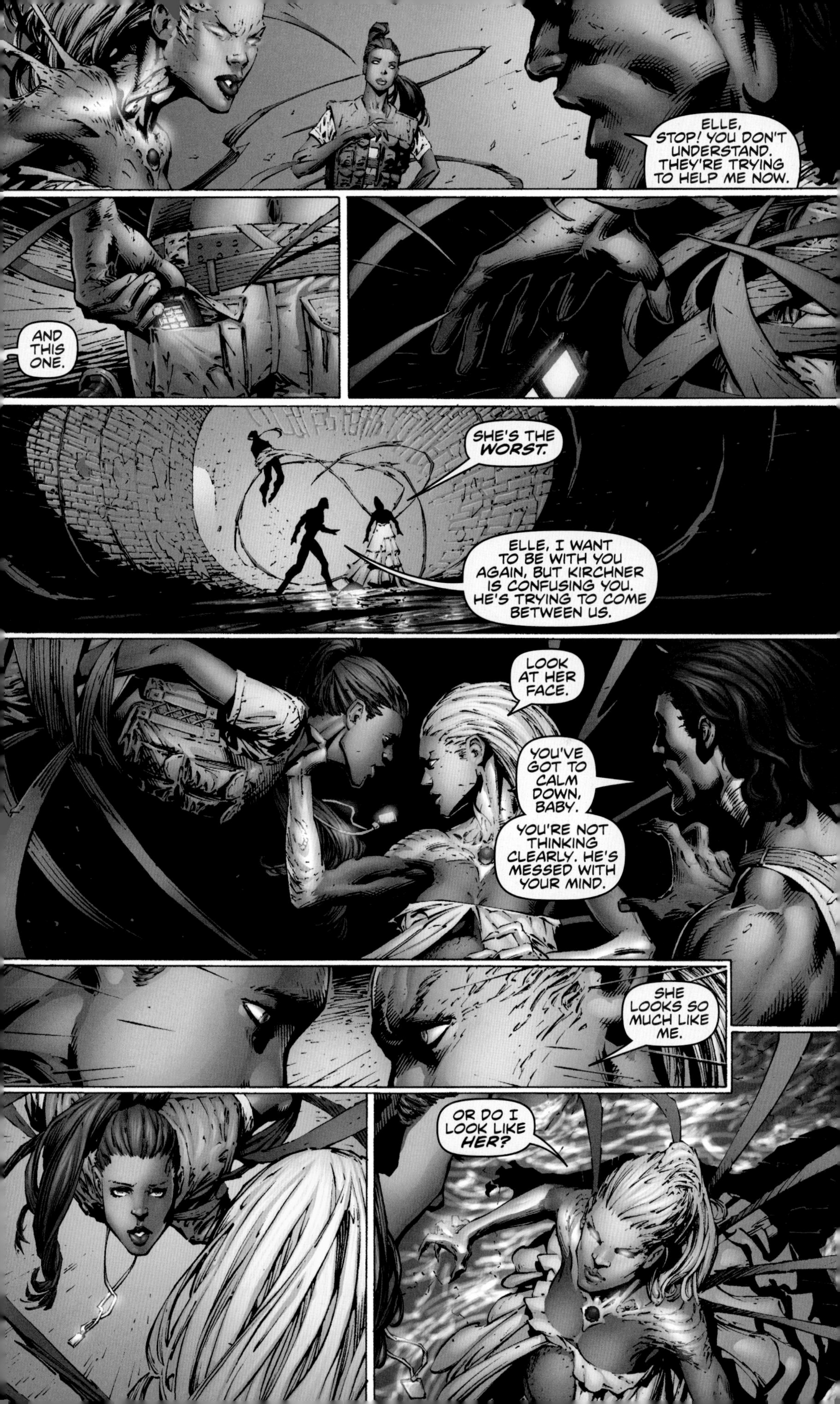
ELLE, STOP! YOU DON'T UNDERSTAND. THEY'RE TRYING TO HELP ME NOW.
AND THIS ONE.
SHE'S THE *WORST.*
ELLE, I WANT TO BE WITH YOU AGAIN, BUT KIRCHNER IS CONFUSING YOU. HE'S TRYING TO COME BETWEEN US.
LOOK AT HER FACE.
YOU'VE GOT TO CALM DOWN, BABY.
YOU'RE NOT THINKING CLEARLY. HE'S MESSED WITH YOUR MIND.
SHE LOOKS SO MUCH LIKE ME.
OR DO I LOOK LIKE *HER?*

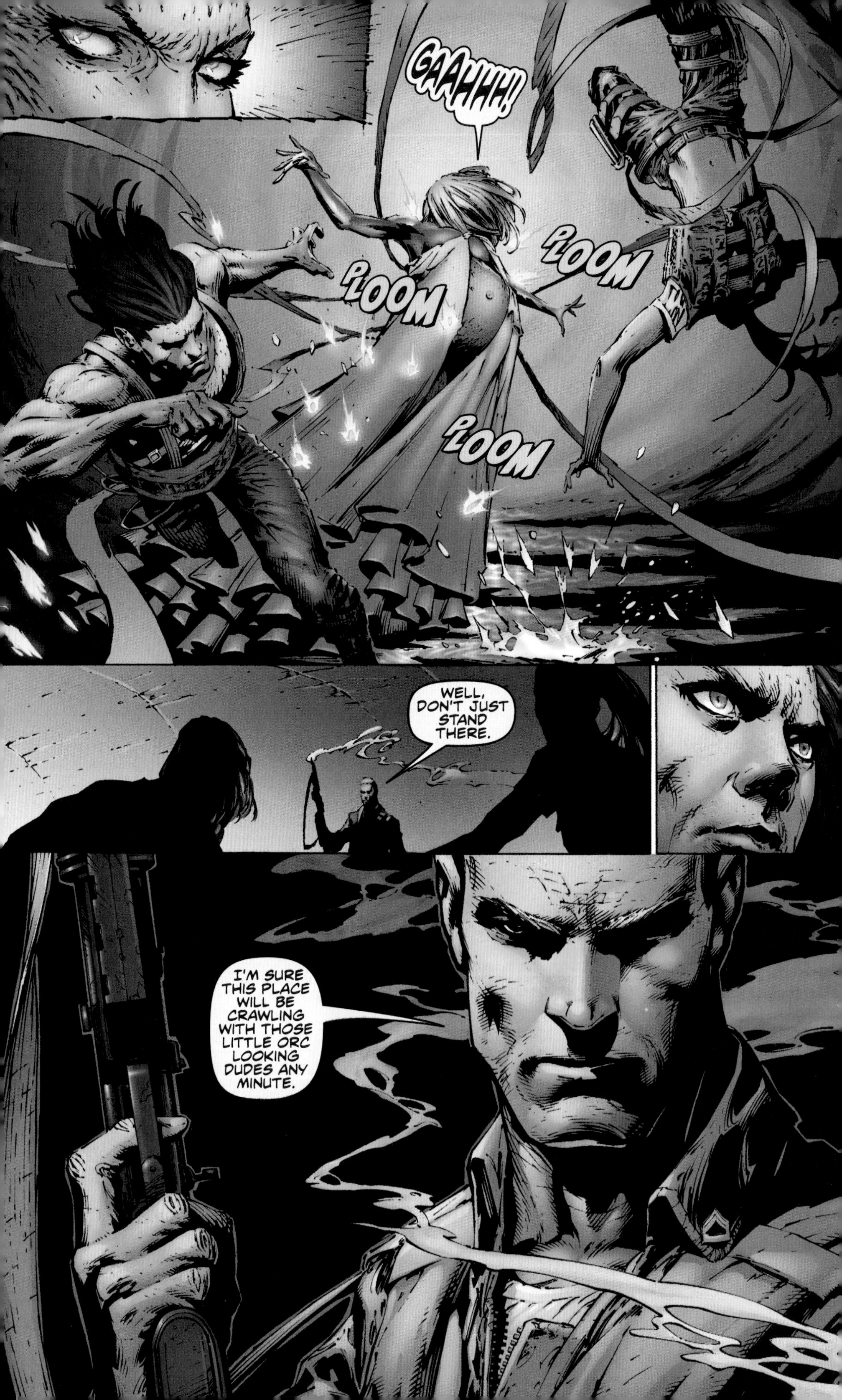
GAAHHH!
PLOOM
PLOOM
PLOOM
WELL, DON'T JUST STAND THERE.
I'M SURE THIS PLACE WILL BE CRAWLING WITH THOSE LITTLE ORC LOOKING DUDES ANY MINUTE.

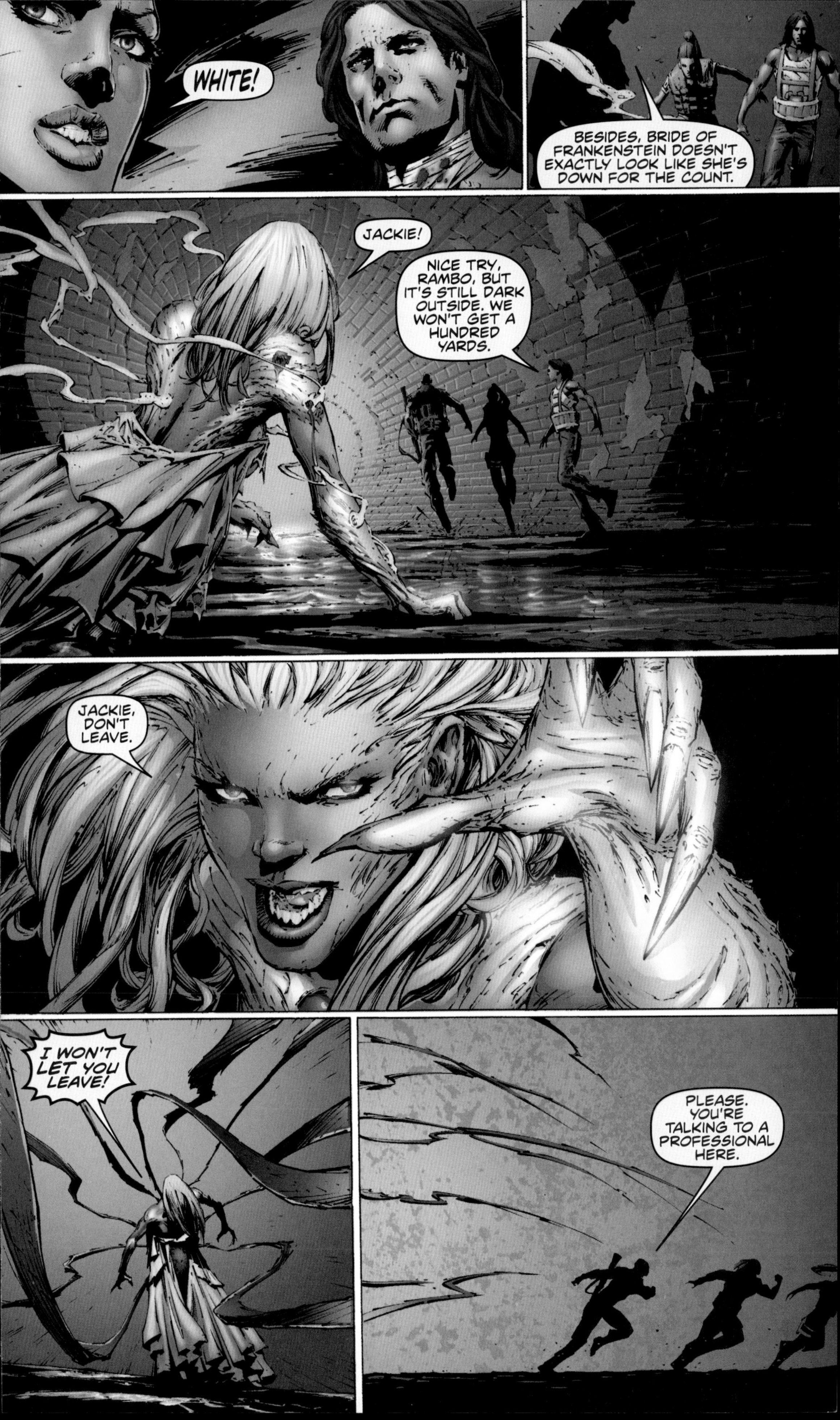
WHITE!
BESIDES, BRIDE OF FRANKENSTEIN DOESN'T EXACTLY LOOK LIKE SHE'S DOWN FOR THE COUNT.
JACKIE!
NICE TRY, RAMBO, BUT IT'S STILL DARK OUTSIDE. WE WON'T GET A HUNDRED YARDS.
JACKIE, DON'T LEAVE.
I WON'T LET YOU LEAVE!
PLEASE. YOU'RE TALKING TO A PROFESSIONAL HERE.

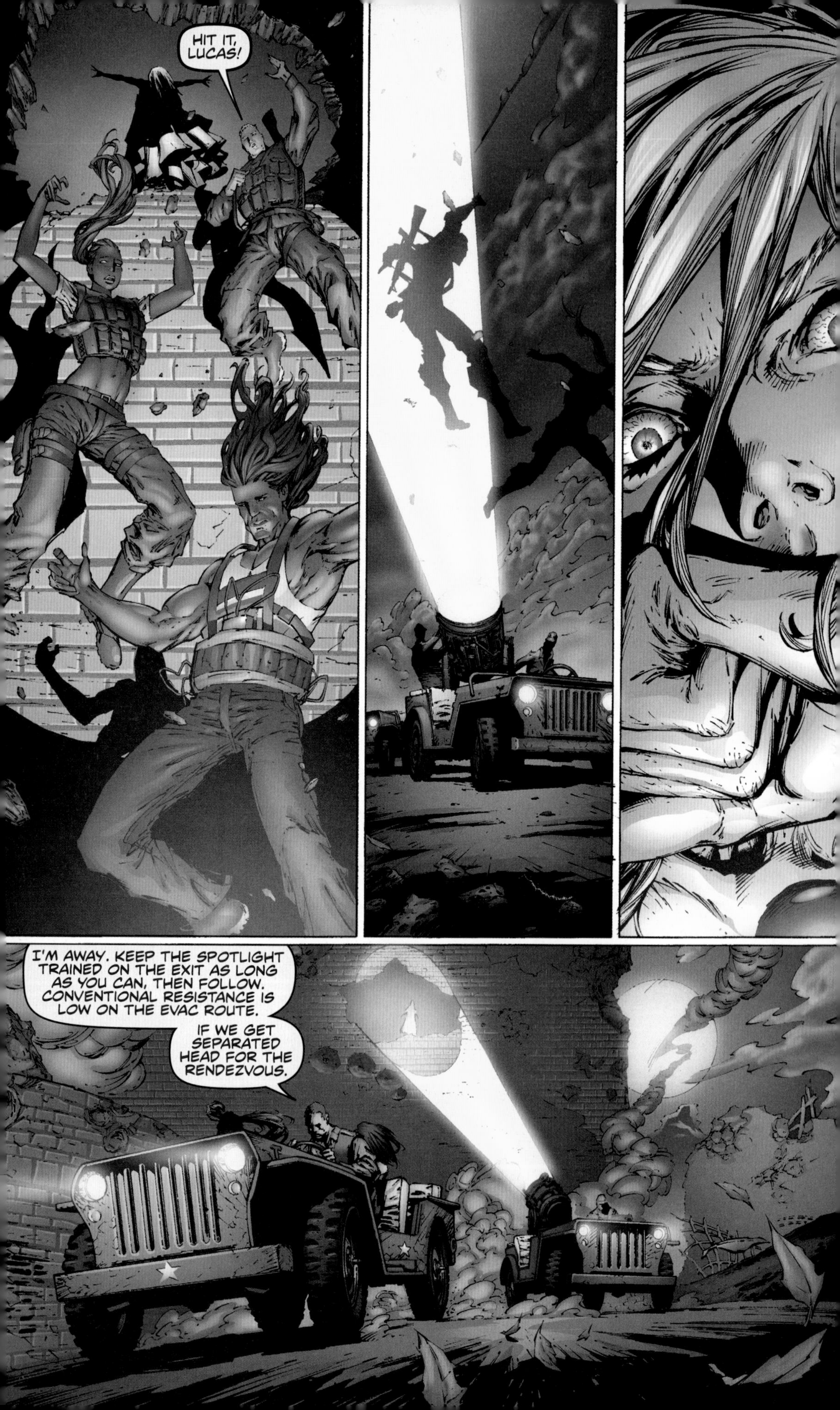
HIT IT, LUCAS!
I'M AWAY. KEEP THE SPOTLIGHT TRAINED ON THE EXIT AS LONG AS YOU CAN, THEN FOLLOW. CONVENTIONAL RESISTANCE IS LOW ON THE EVAC ROUTE.
IF WE GET SEPARATED HEAD FOR THE RENDEZVOUS.

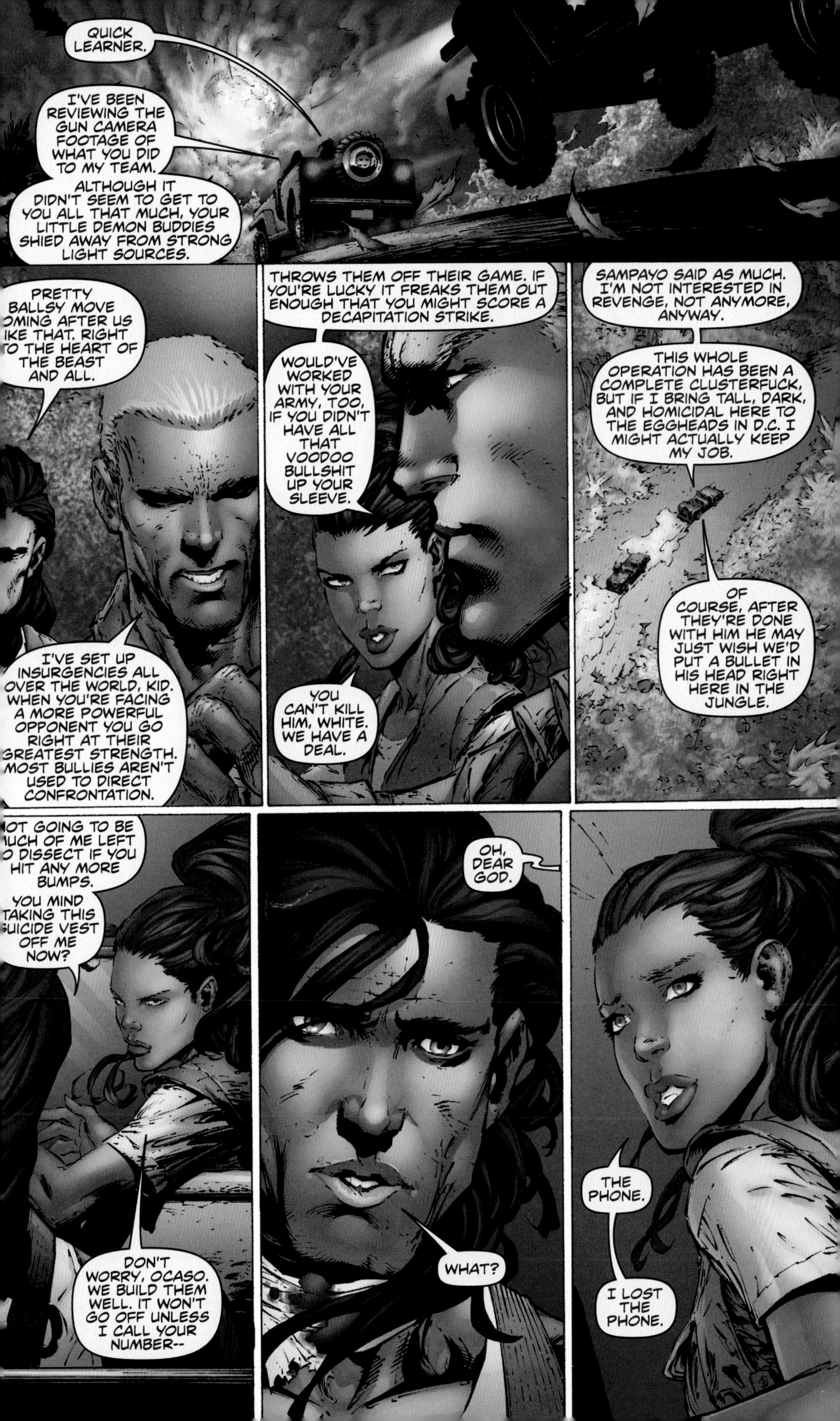
QUICK LEARNER.
I'VE BEEN REVIEWING THE GUN CAMERA FOOTAGE OF WHAT YOU DID TO MY TEAM.
ALTHOUGH IT DIDN'T SEEM TO GET TO YOU ALL THAT MUCH, YOUR LITTLE DEMON BUDDIES SHIED AWAY FROM STRONG LIGHT SOURCES.
PRETTY BALLSY MOVE OMING AFTER US IKE THAT. RIGHT O THE HEART OF THE BEAST AND ALL.
I'VE SET UP INSURGENCIES ALL OVER THE WORLD, KID. WHEN YOU'RE FACING A MORE POWERFUL OPPONENT YOU GO RIGHT AT THEIR GREATEST STRENGTH. MOST BULLIES AREN'T USED TO DIRECT CONFRONTATION.
THROWS THEM OFF THEIR GAME. IF YOU'RE LUCKY IT FREAKS THEM OUT ENOUGH THAT YOU MIGHT SCORE A DECAPITATION STRIKE.
WOULD'VE WORKED WITH YOUR ARMY, TOO, IF YOU DIDN'T HAVE ALL THAT VOODOO BULLSHIT UP YOUR SLEEVE.
YOU CAN'T KILL HIM, WHITE. WE HAVE A DEAL.
SAMPAYO SAID AS MUCH. I'M NOT INTERESTED IN REVENGE, NOT ANYMORE, ANYWAY.
THIS WHOLE OPERATION HAS BEEN A COMPLETE CLUSTERFUCK, BUT IF I BRING TALL, DARK, AND HOMICIDAL HERE TO THE EGGHEADS IN D.C. I MIGHT ACTUALLY KEEP MY JOB.
OF COURSE, AFTER THEY'RE DONE WITH HIM HE MAY JUST WISH WE'D PUT A BULLET IN HIS HEAD RIGHT HERE IN THE JUNGLE.
OT GOING TO BE UCH OF ME LEFT O DISSECT IF YOU HIT ANY MORE BUMPS.
YOU MIND TAKING THIS UICIDE VEST OFF ME NOW?
DON'T WORRY, OCASO. WE BUILD THEM WELL. IT WON'T GO OFF UNLESS I CALL YOUR NUMBER--
OH, DEAR GOD.
WHAT?
THE PHONE.
I LOST THE PHONE.

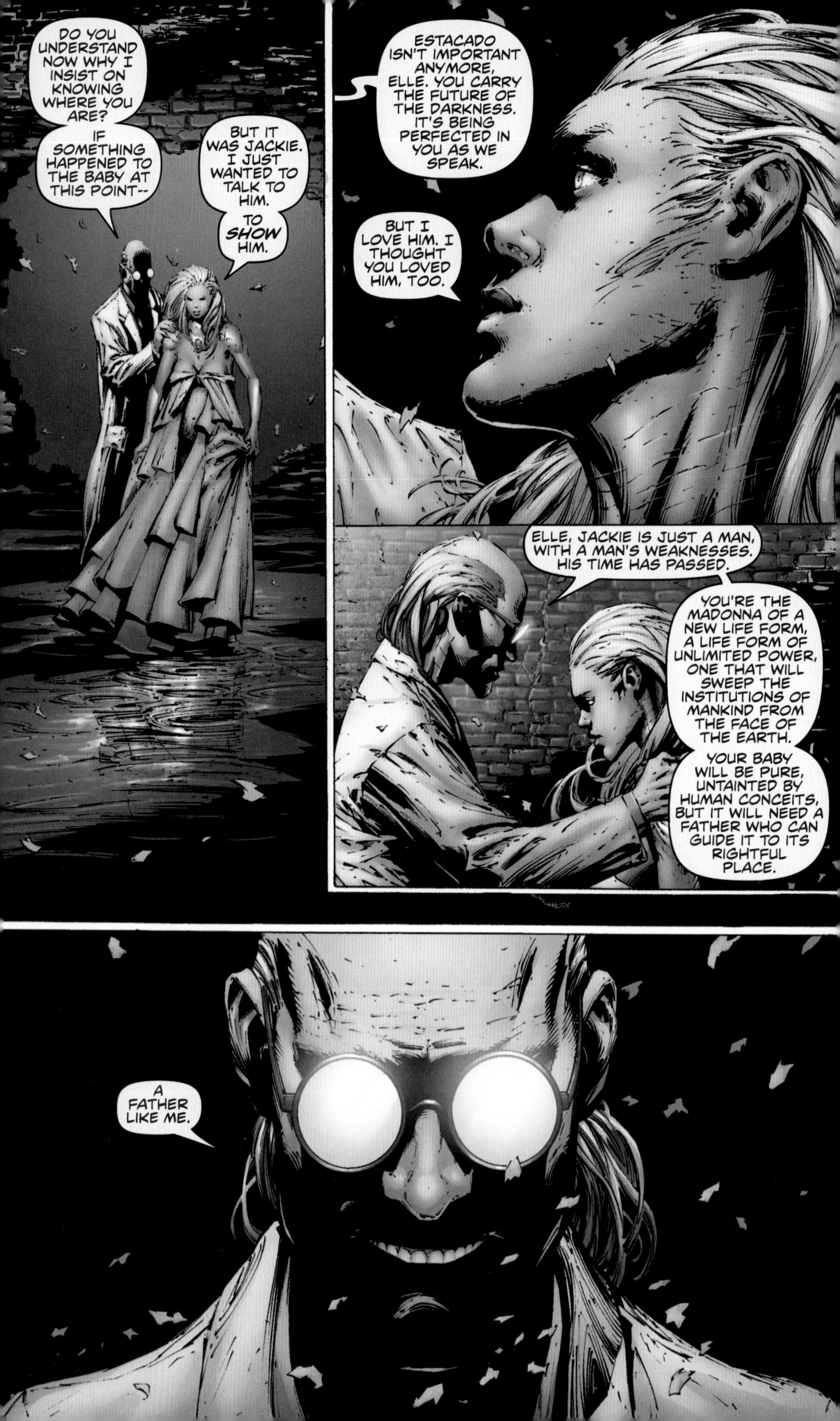
DO YOU UNDERSTAND NOW WHY I INSIST ON KNOWING WHERE YOU ARE?
IF SOMETHING HAPPENED TO THE BABY AT THIS POINT--
BUT IT WAS JACKIE. I JUST WANTED TO TALK TO HIM.
TO SHOW HIM.
ESTACADO ISN'T IMPORTANT ANYMORE, ELLE. YOU CARRY THE FUTURE OF THE DARKNESS. IT'S BEING PERFECTED IN YOU AS WE SPEAK.
BUT I LOVE HIM. I THOUGHT YOU LOVED HIM, TOO.
ELLE, JACKIE IS JUST A MAN, WITH A MAN'S WEAKNESSES. HIS TIME HAS PASSED.
YOU'RE THE MADONNA OF A NEW LIFE FORM, A LIFE FORM OF UNLIMITED POWER, ONE THAT WILL SWEEP THE INSTITUTIONS OF MANKIND FROM THE FACE OF THE EARTH.
YOUR BABY WILL BE PURE, UNTAINTED BY HUMAN CONCEITS, BUT IT WILL NEED A FATHER WHO CAN GUIDE IT TO ITS RIGHTFUL PLACE.
A FATHER LIKE ME.

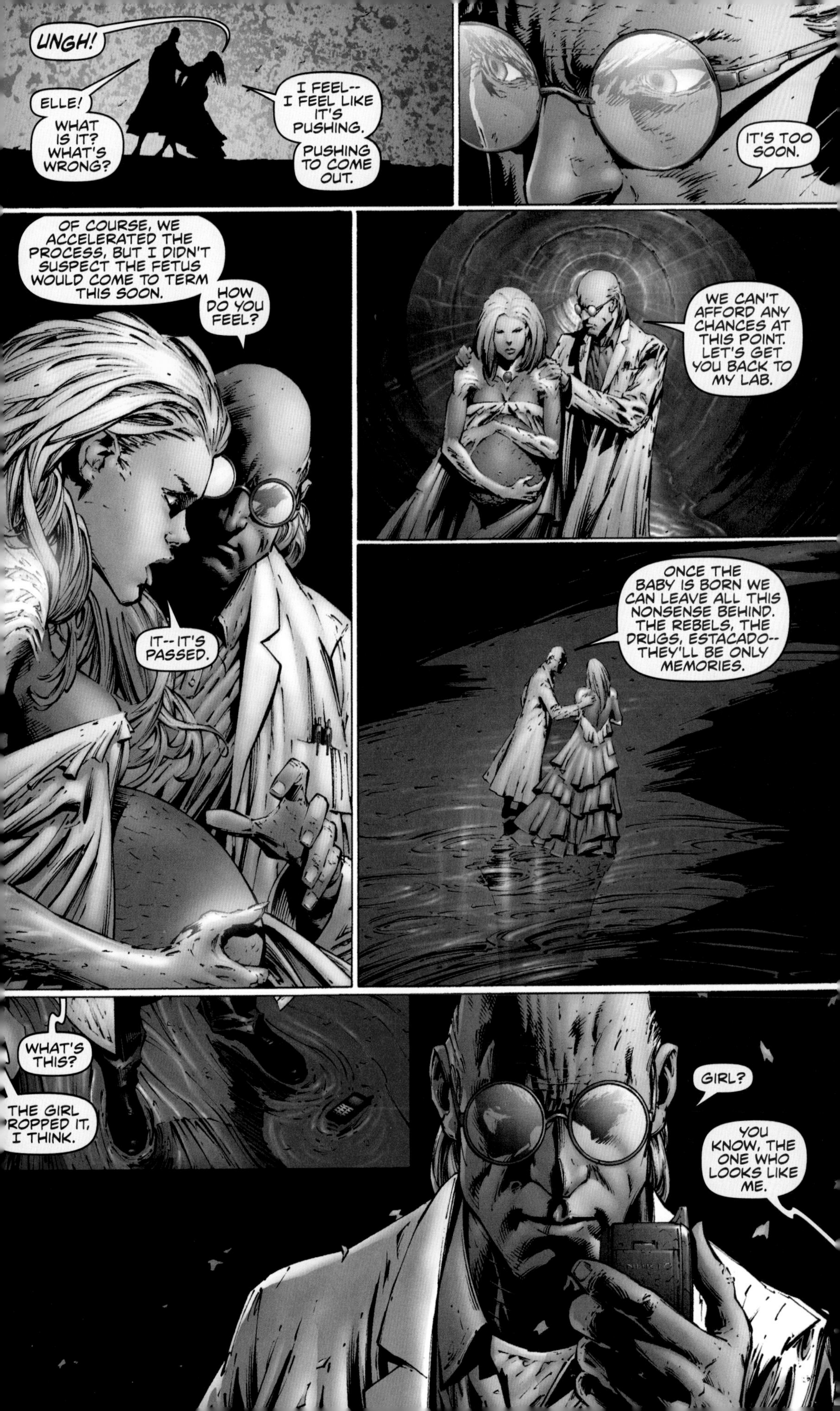
UNGH!
ELLE!
WHAT IS IT? WHAT'S WRONG?
I FEEL-- I FEEL LIKE IT'S PUSHING.
PUSHING TO COME OUT.
IT'S TOO SOON.
OF COURSE, WE ACCELERATED THE PROCESS, BUT I DIDN'T SUSPECT THE FETUS WOULD COME TO TERM THIS SOON.
HOW DO YOU FEEL?
IT--IT'S PASSED.
WE CAN'T AFFORD ANY CHANCES AT THIS POINT. LET'S GET YOU BACK TO MY LAB.
ONCE THE BABY IS BORN WE CAN LEAVE ALL THIS NONSENSE BEHIND. THE REBELS, THE DRUGS, ESTACADO-- THEY'LL BE ONLY MEMORIES.
WHAT'S THIS?
THE GIRL ROPPED IT, I THINK.
GIRL?
YOU KNOW, THE ONE WHO LOOKS LIKE ME.

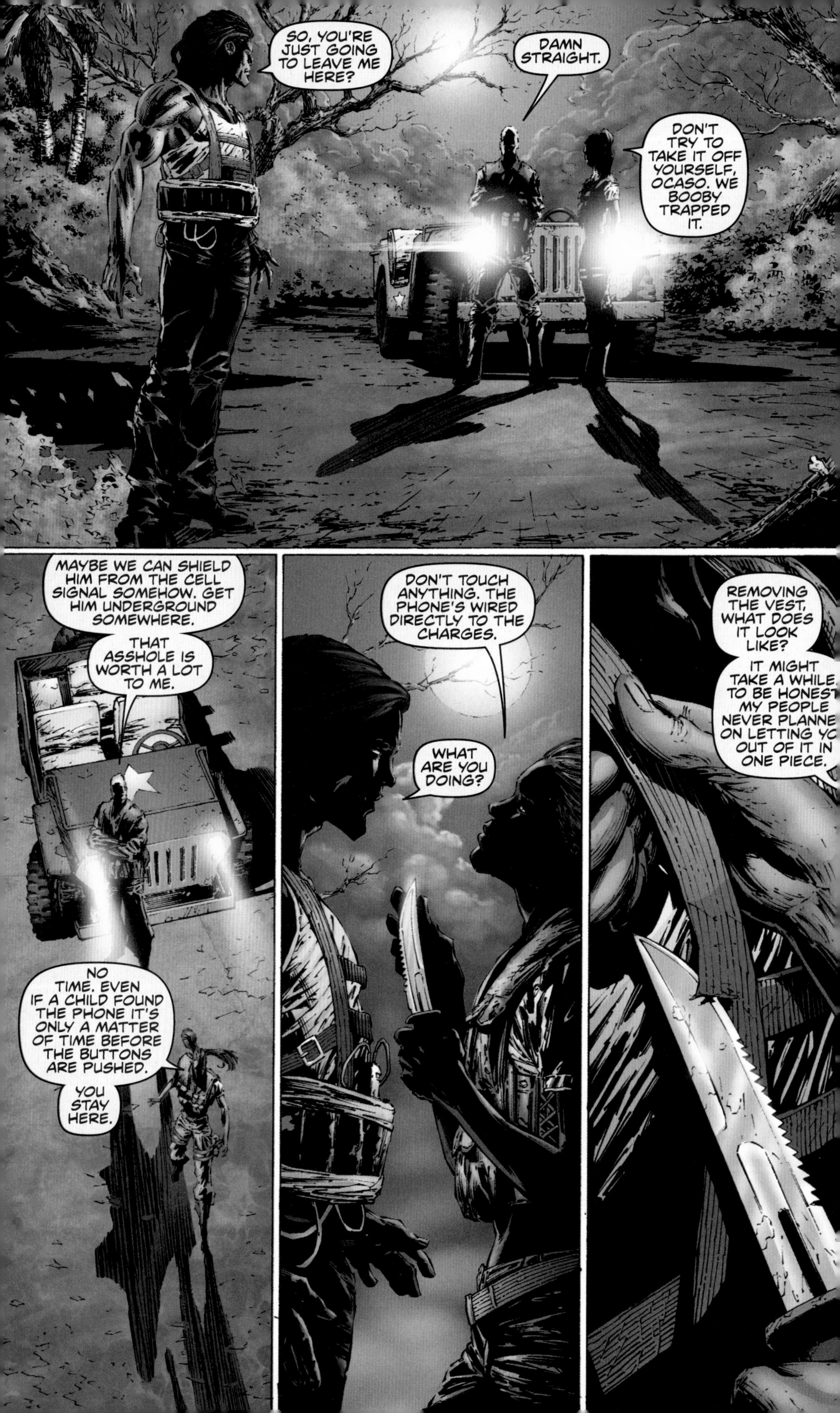
SO, YOU'RE JUST GOING TO LEAVE ME HERE?
DAMN STRAIGHT.
DON'T TRY TO TAKE IT OFF YOURSELF, OCASO. WE BOOBY TRAPPED IT.
MAYBE WE CAN SHIELD HIM FROM THE CELL SIGNAL SOMEHOW. GET HIM UNDERGROUND SOMEWHERE.
THAT ASSHOLE IS WORTH A LOT TO ME.
NO TIME. EVEN IF A CHILD FOUND THE PHONE IT'S ONLY A MATTER OF TIME BEFORE THE BUTTONS ARE PUSHED.
YOU STAY HERE.
DON'T TOUCH ANYTHING. THE PHONE'S WIRED DIRECTLY TO THE CHARGES.
WHAT ARE YOU DOING?
REMOVING THE VEST, WHAT DOES IT LOOK LIKE?
IT MIGHT TAKE A WHILE. TO BE HONEST MY PEOPLE NEVER PLANNE ON LETTING YO OUT OF IT IN ONE PIECE.

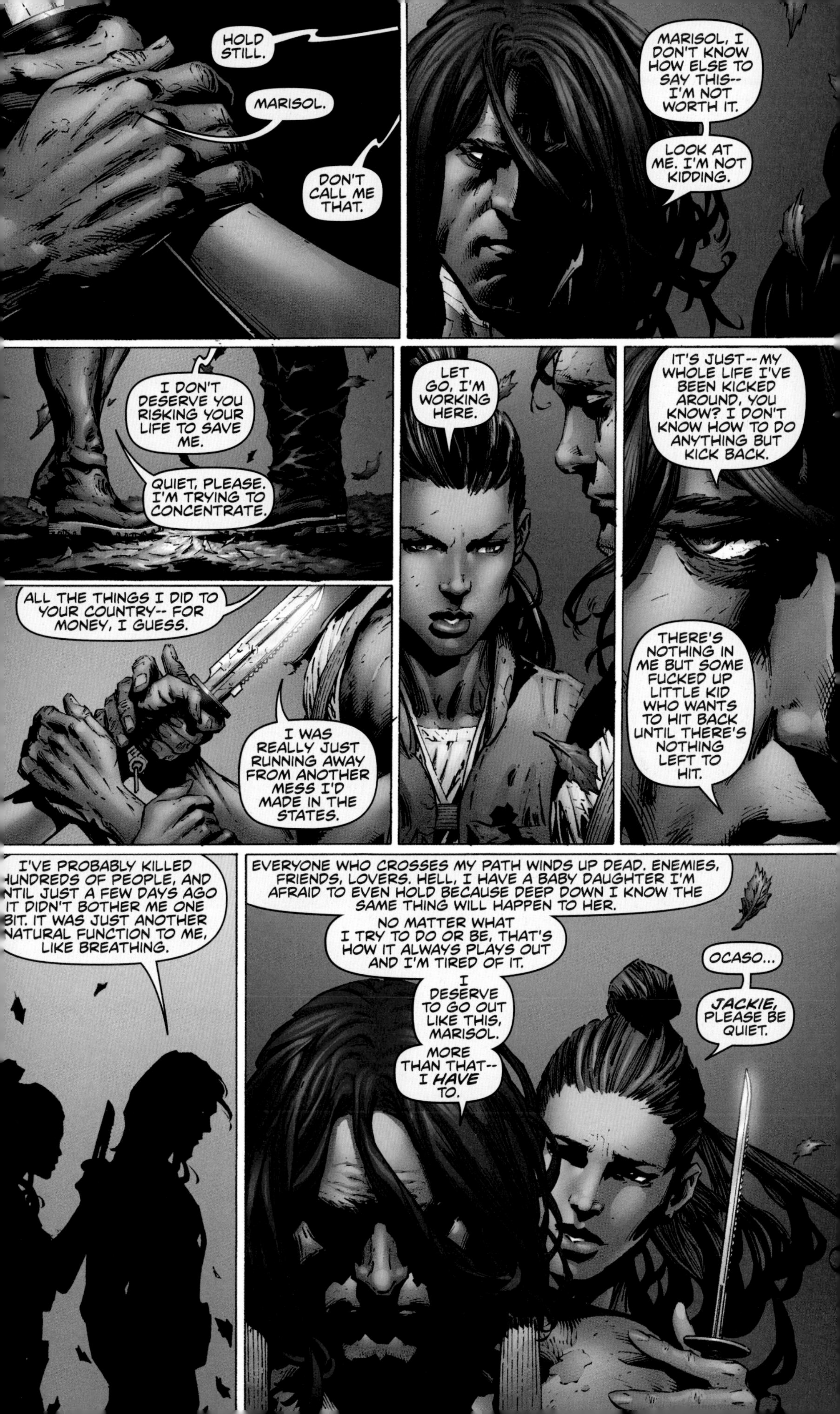
HOLD STILL.
MARISOL.
DON'T CALL ME THAT.
MARISOL, I DON'T KNOW HOW ELSE TO SAY THIS-- I'M NOT WORTH IT.
LOOK AT ME. I'M NOT KIDDING.
I DON'T DESERVE YOU RISKING YOUR LIFE TO SAVE ME.
QUIET, PLEASE. I'M TRYING TO CONCENTRATE.
LET GO, I'M WORKING HERE.
IT'S JUST--MY WHOLE LIFE I'VE BEEN KICKED AROUND, YOU KNOW? I DON'T KNOW HOW TO DO ANYTHING BUT KICK BACK.
ALL THE THINGS I DID TO YOUR COUNTRY-- FOR MONEY, I GUESS.
I WAS REALLY JUST RUNNING AWAY FROM ANOTHER MESS I'D MADE IN THE STATES.
THERE'S NOTHING IN ME BUT SOME FUCKED UP LITTLE KID WHO WANTS TO HIT BACK UNTIL THERE'S NOTHING LEFT TO HIT.
I'VE PROBABLY KILLED HUNDREDS OF PEOPLE, AND UNTIL JUST A FEW DAYS AGO IT DIDN'T BOTHER ME ONE BIT. IT WAS JUST ANOTHER NATURAL FUNCTION TO ME, LIKE BREATHING.
EVERYONE WHO CROSSES MY PATH WINDS UP DEAD. ENEMIES, FRIENDS, LOVERS. HELL, I HAVE A BABY DAUGHTER I'M AFRAID TO EVEN HOLD BECAUSE DEEP DOWN I KNOW THE SAME THING WILL HAPPEN TO HER.
NO MATTER WHAT I TRY TO DO OR BE, THAT'S HOW IT ALWAYS PLAYS OUT AND I'M TIRED OF IT.
I DESERVE TO GO OUT LIKE THIS, MARISOL.
MORE THAN THAT-- I *HAVE* TO.
OCASO...
JACKIE, PLEASE BE QUIET.

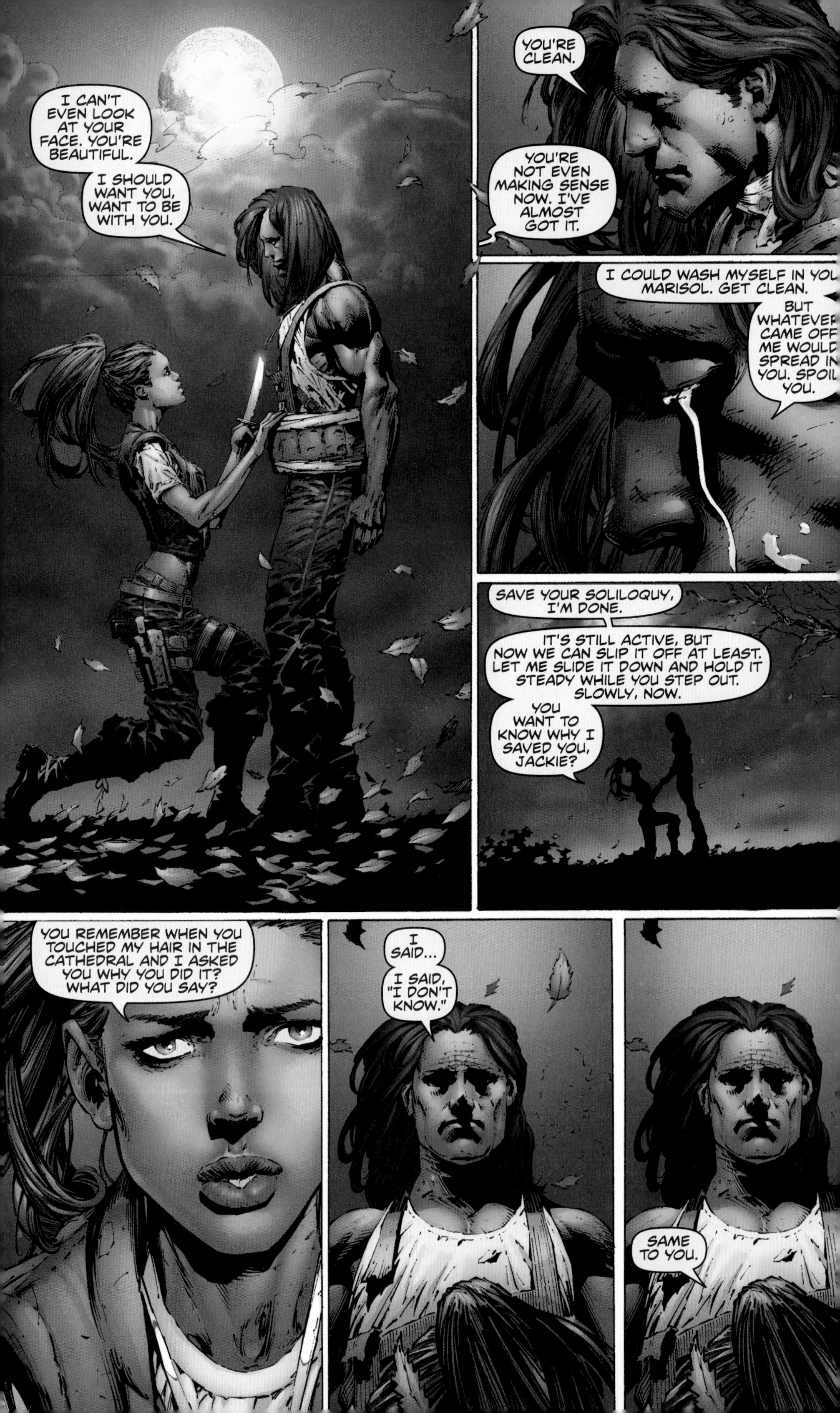

I CAN'T EVEN LOOK AT YOUR FACE. YOU'RE BEAUTIFUL.
I SHOULD WANT YOU, WANT TO BE WITH YOU.
YOU'RE CLEAN.
YOU'RE NOT EVEN MAKING SENSE NOW. I'VE ALMOST GOT IT.
I COULD WASH MYSELF IN YOU MARISOL. GET CLEAN.
BUT WHATEVER CAME OFF ME WOULD SPREAD IN YOU. SPOIL YOU.
SAVE YOUR SOLILOQUY, I'M DONE.
IT'S STILL ACTIVE, BUT NOW WE CAN SLIP IT OFF AT LEAST. LET ME SLIDE IT DOWN AND HOLD IT STEADY WHILE YOU STEP OUT. SLOWLY, NOW.
YOU WANT TO KNOW WHY I SAVED YOU, JACKIE?
YOU REMEMBER WHEN YOU TOUCHED MY HAIR IN THE CATHEDRAL AND I ASKED YOU WHY YOU DID IT? WHAT DID YOU SAY?
I SAID...
I SAID, "I DON'T KNOW."
SAME TO YOU.

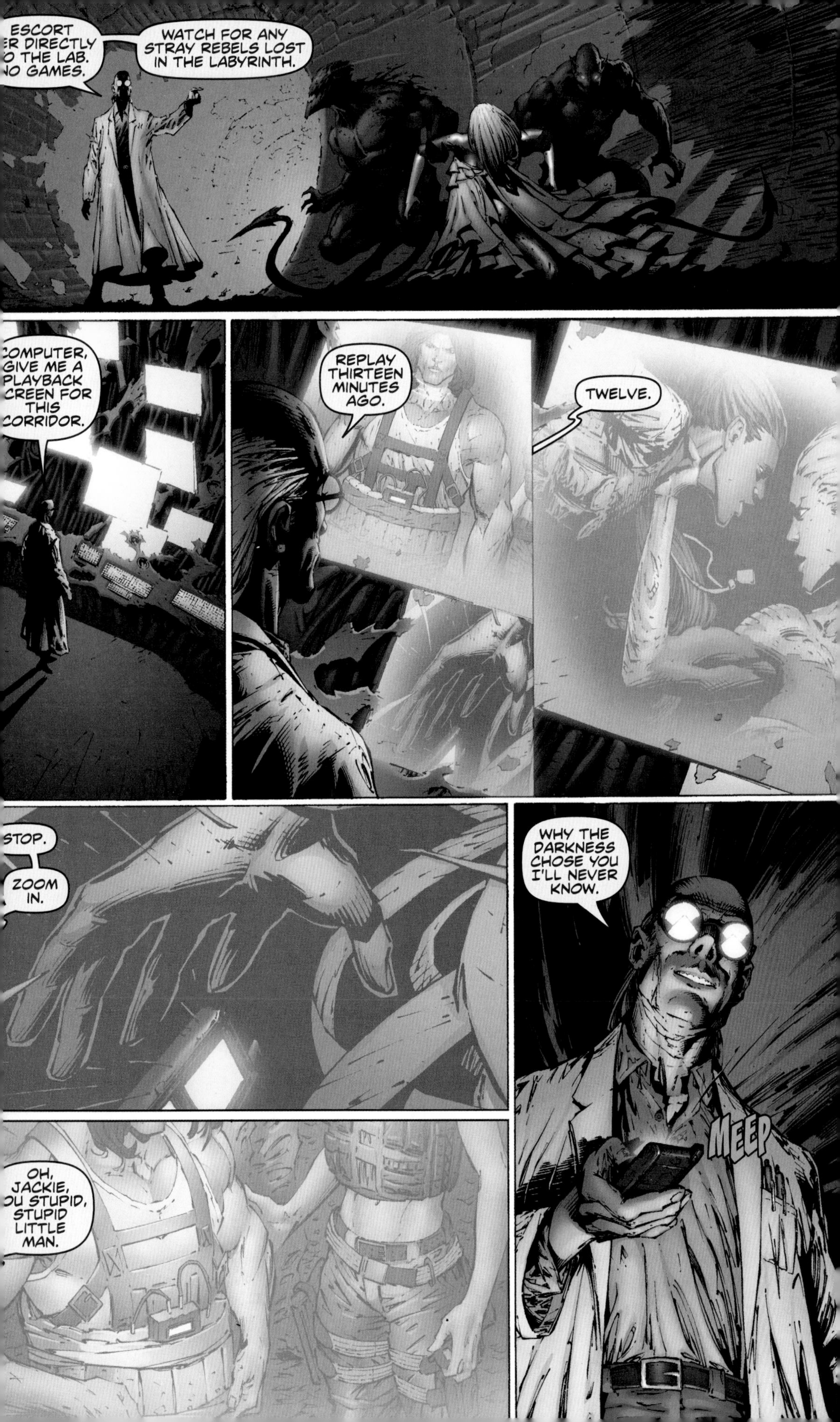
ESCORT ER DIRECTLY O THE LAB. NO GAMES.
WATCH FOR ANY STRAY REBELS LOST IN THE LABYRINTH.
COMPUTER, GIVE ME A PLAYBACK CREEN FOR THIS CORRIDOR.
REPLAY THIRTEEN MINUTES AGO.
TWELVE.
STOP.
ZOOM IN.
OH, JACKIE, OU STUPID, STUPID LITTLE MAN.
WHY THE DARKNESS CHOSE YOU I'LL NEVER KNOW.
MEEP

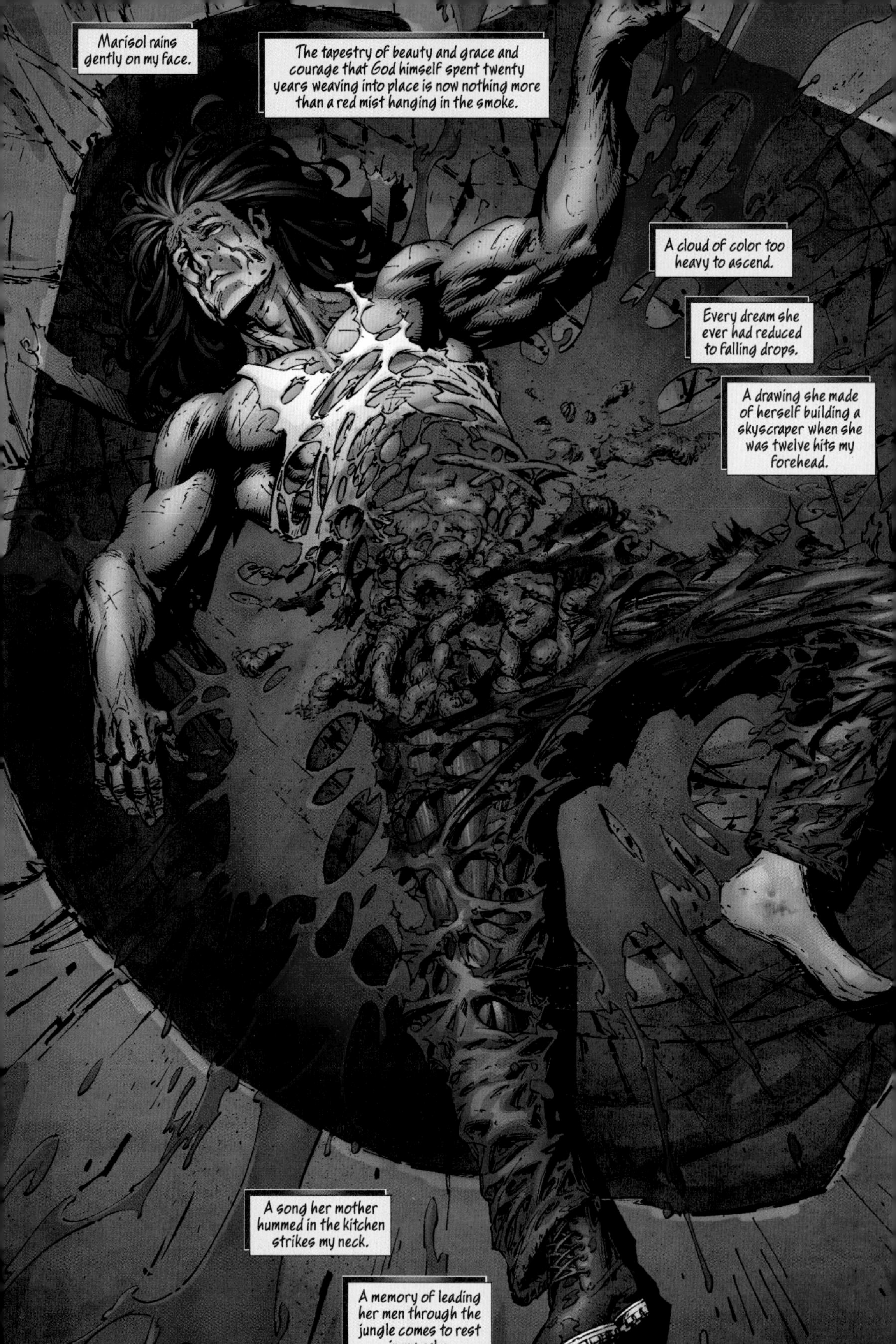
Marisol rains gently on my face.
The tapestry of beauty and grace and courage that God himself spent twenty years weaving into place is now nothing more than a red mist hanging in the smoke.
A cloud of color too heavy to ascend.
Every dream she ever had reduced to falling drops.
A drawing she made of herself building a skyscraper when she was twelve hits my forehead.
A song her mother hummed in the kitchen strikes my neck.
A memory of leading her men through the jungle comes to rest in my palm.

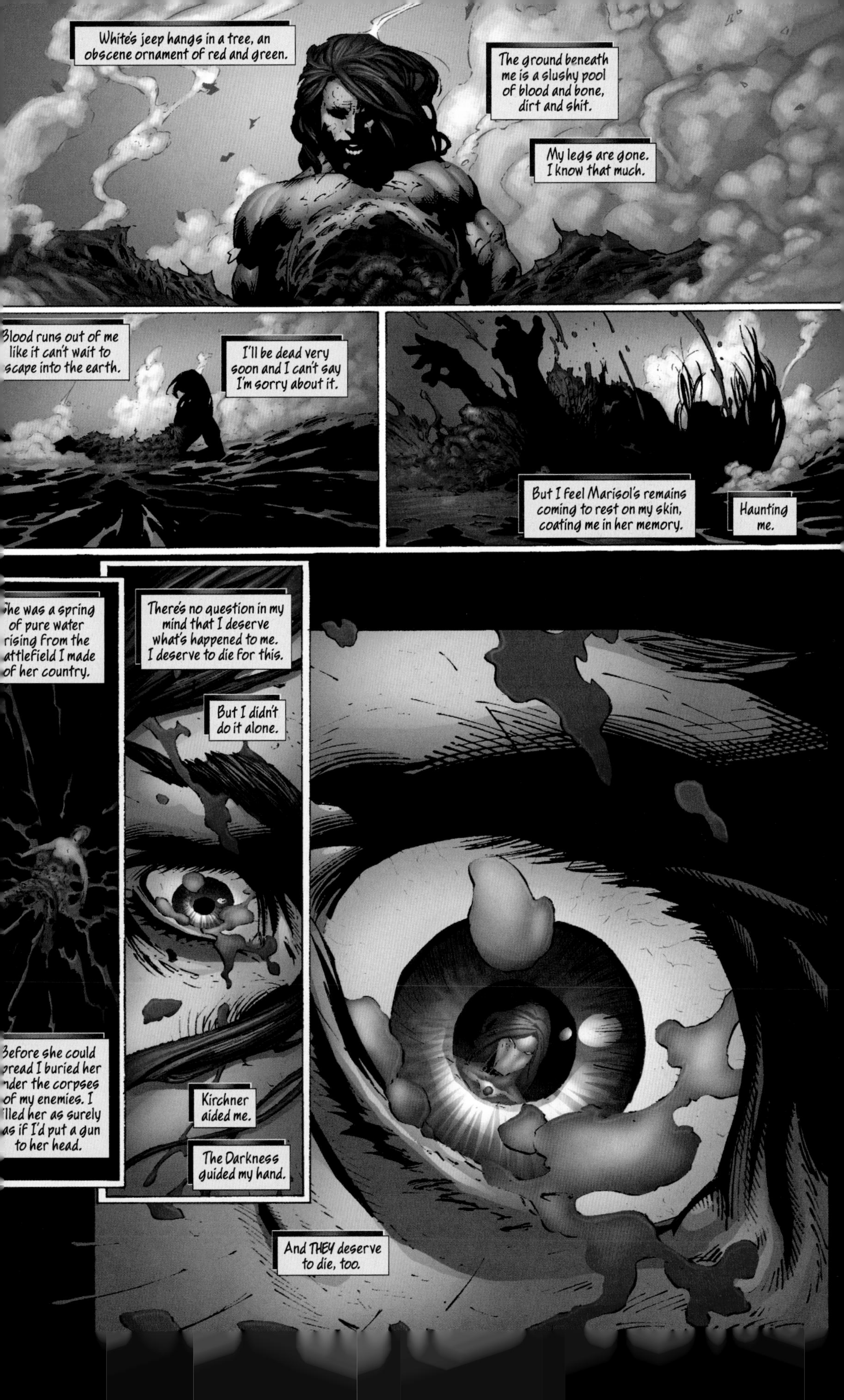

White's jeep hangs in a tree, an obscene ornament of red and green.
The ground beneath me is a slushy pool of blood and bone, dirt and shit.
My legs are gone. I know that much.
Blood runs out of me like it can't wait to scape into the earth.
I'll be dead very soon and I can't say I'm sorry about it.
But I feel Marisol's remains coming to rest on my skin, coating me in her memory.
Haunting me.
he was a spring of pure water rising from the attlefield I made of her country.
There's no question in my mind that I deserve what's happened to me. I deserve to die for this.
But I didn't do it alone.
Before she could pread I buried her nder the corpses of my enemies. I illed her as surely as if I'd put a gun to her head.
Kirchner aided me.
The Darkness guided my hand.
And THEY deserve to die, too.

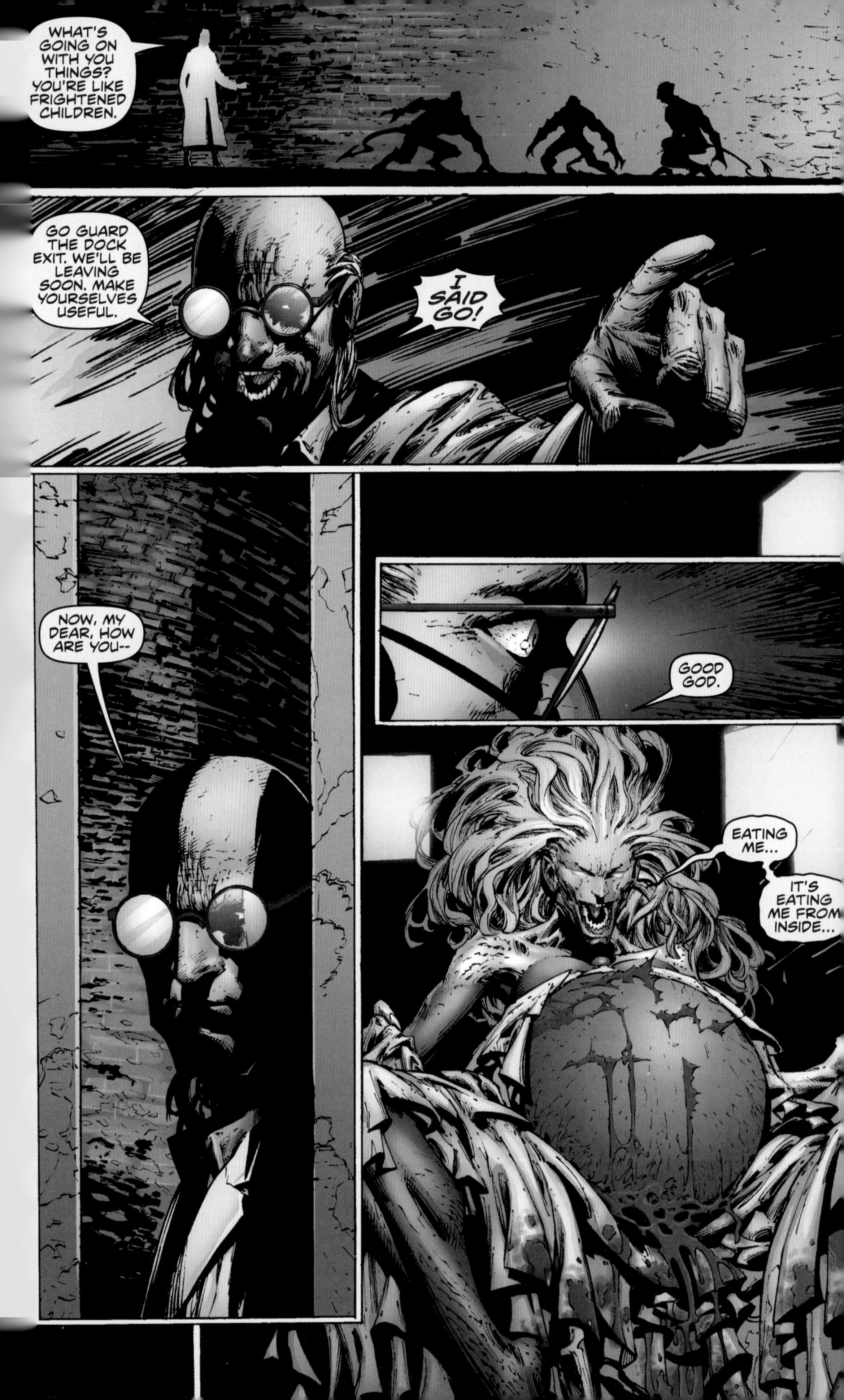
WHAT'S GOING ON WITH YOU THINGS? YOU'RE LIKE FRIGHTENED CHILDREN.
GO GUARD THE DOCK EXIT. WE'LL BE LEAVING SOON. MAKE YOURSELVES USEFUL.
I SAID GO!
NOW, MY DEAR, HOW ARE YOU--
GOOD GOD.
EATING ME...
IT'S EATING ME FROM INSIDE...

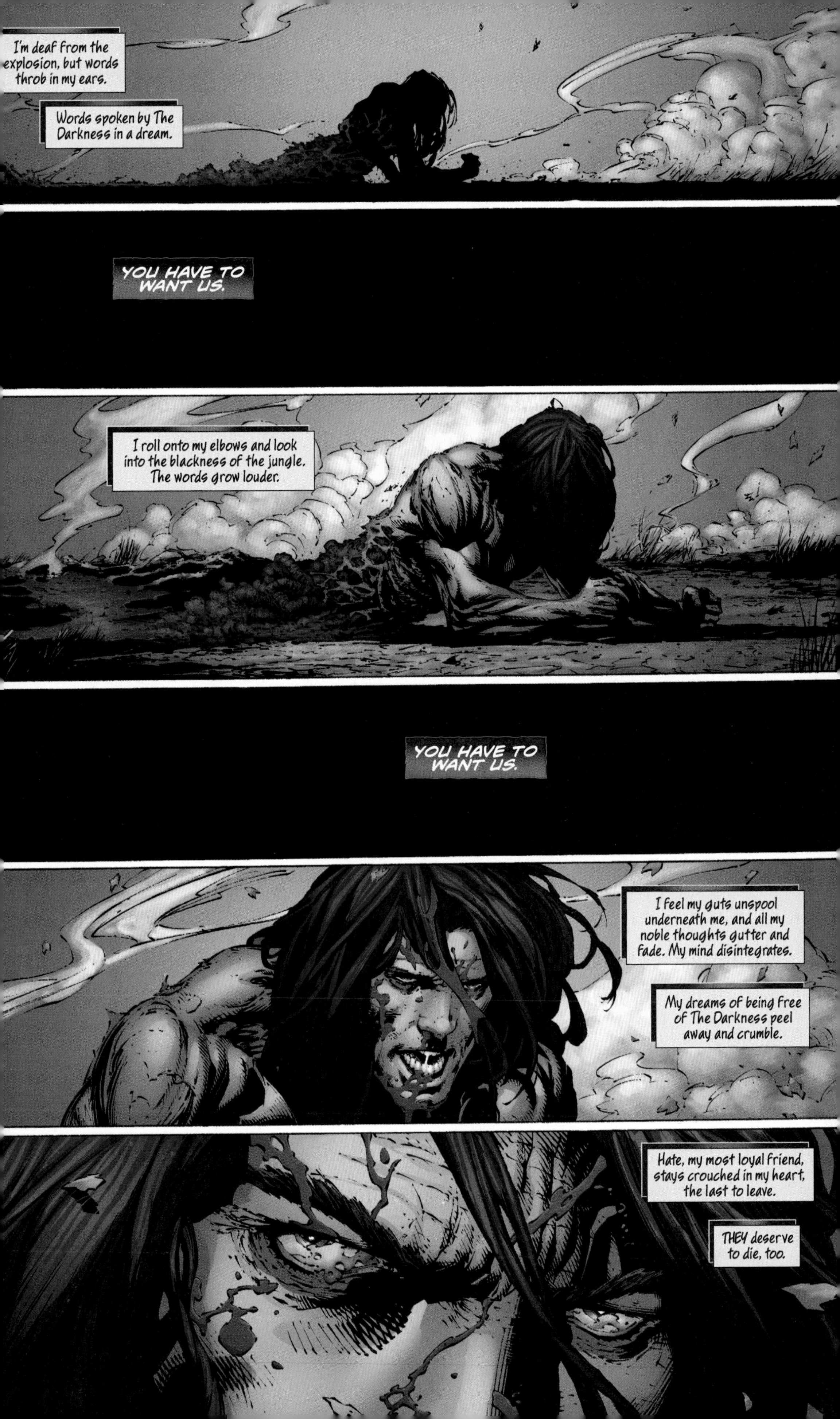

I'm deaf from the explosion, but words throb in my ears.
Words spoken by The Darkness in a dream.
YOU HAVE TO WANT US.
I roll onto my elbows and look into the blackness of the jungle. The words grow louder.
YOU HAVE TO WANT US.
I feel my guts unspool underneath me, and all my noble thoughts gutter and fade. My mind disintegrates.
My dreams of being free of The Darkness peel away and crumble.
Hate, my most loyal friend, stays crouched in my heart, the last to leave.
THEY deserve to die, too.

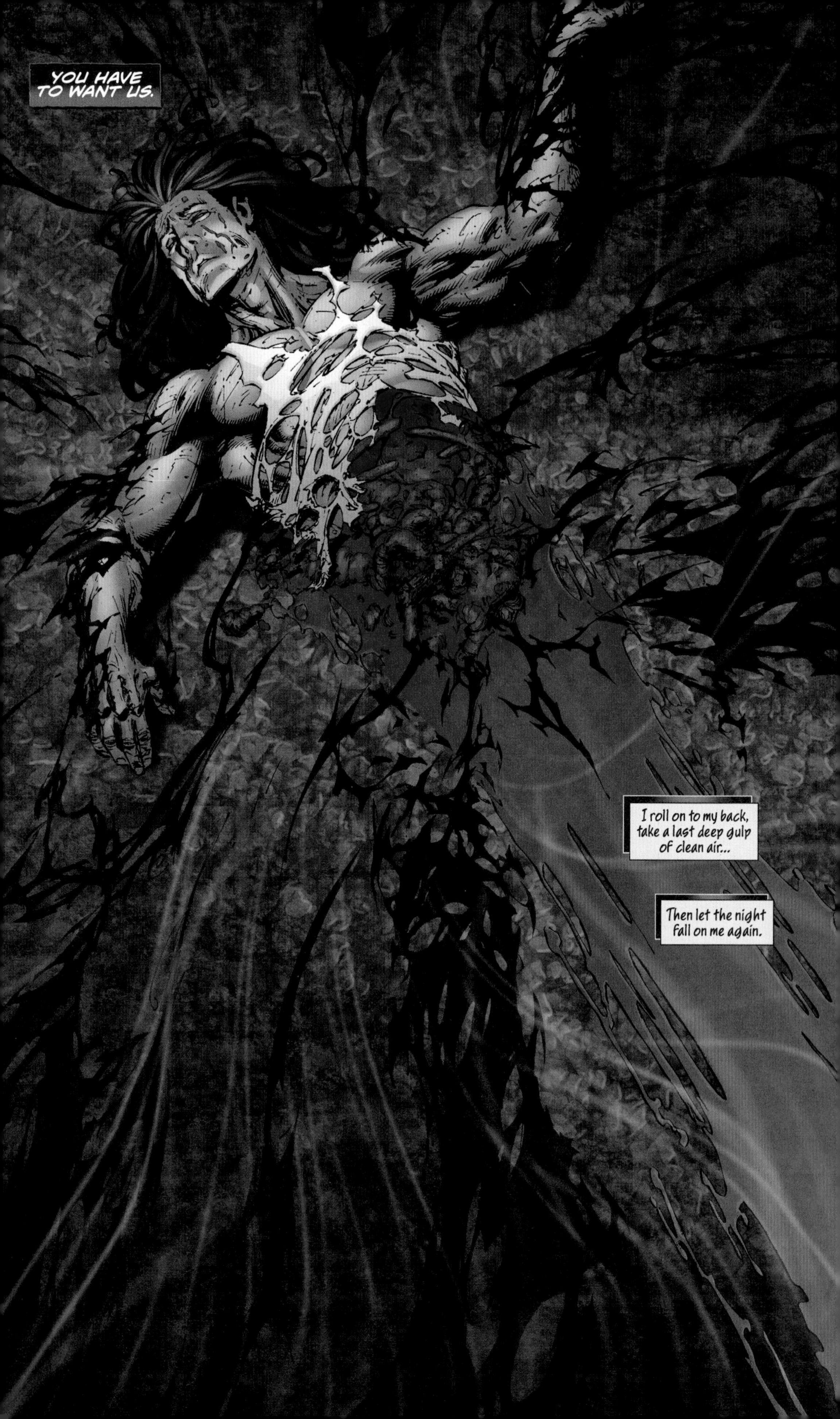
YOU HAVE TO WANT US.
I roll on to my back, take a last deep gulp of clean air...
Then let the night fall on me again.

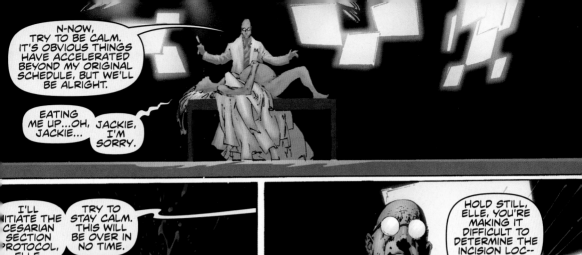

N-NOW, TRY TO BE CALM. IT'S OBVIOUS THINGS HAVE ACCELERATED BEYOND MY ORIGINAL SCHEDULE, BUT WE'LL BE ALRIGHT.

EATING ME UP...OH, JACKIE... JACKIE, I'M SORRY.

I'LL INITIATE THE CESARIAN SECTION PROTOCOL, ELLE.

TRY TO STAY CALM. THIS WILL BE OVER IN NO TIME.

THERE'S NOTHING LEFT... NOTHING LEFT IN ME... I'M HOLLOW.

HOLD STILL, ELLE, YOU'RE MAKING IT DIFFICULT TO DETERMINE THE INCISION LOC-- AAAHH!

FORGET THE INCISION.

I'M SORRY, JACKIE.

SCHRIPP

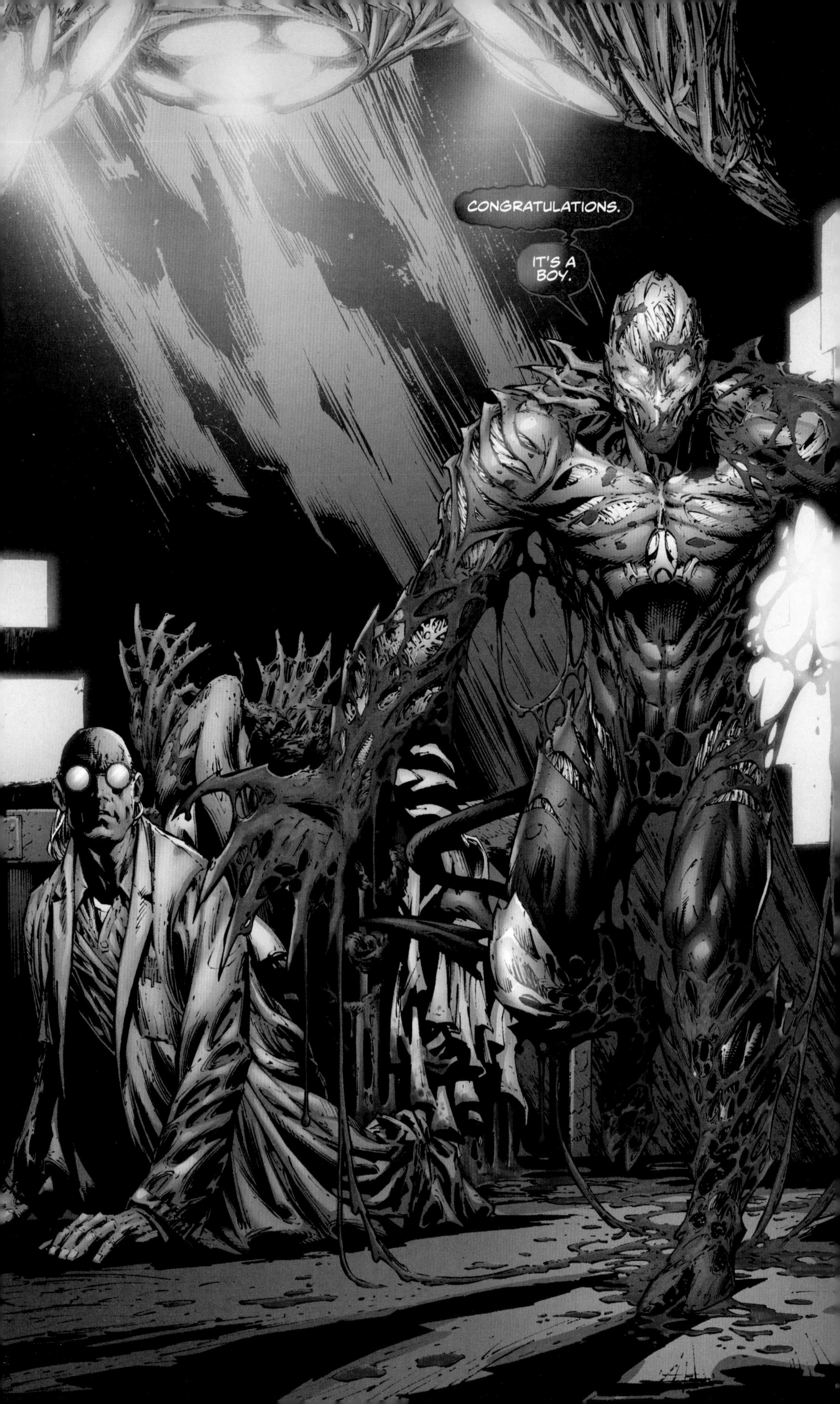
CONGRATULATIONS.
IT'S A BOY.

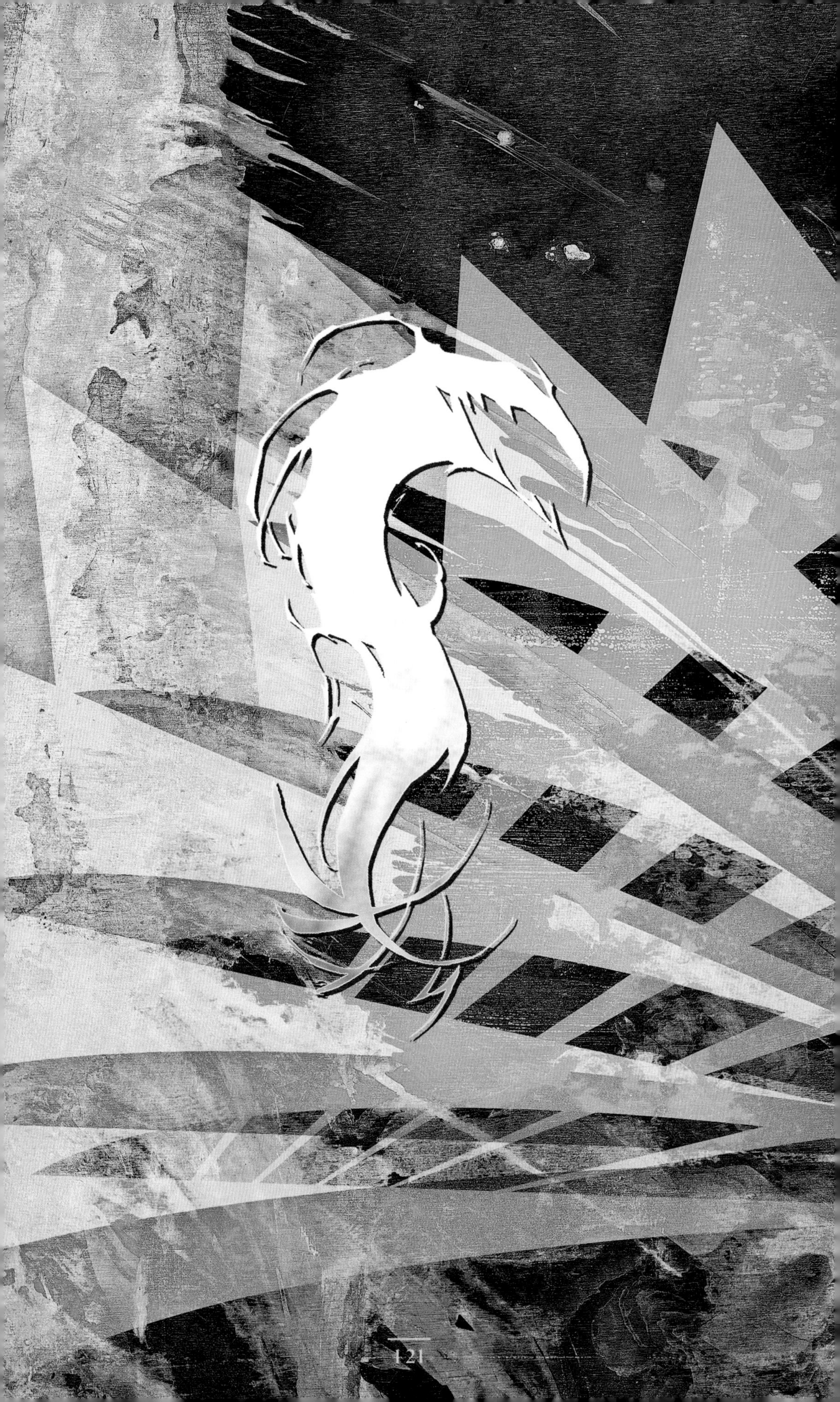

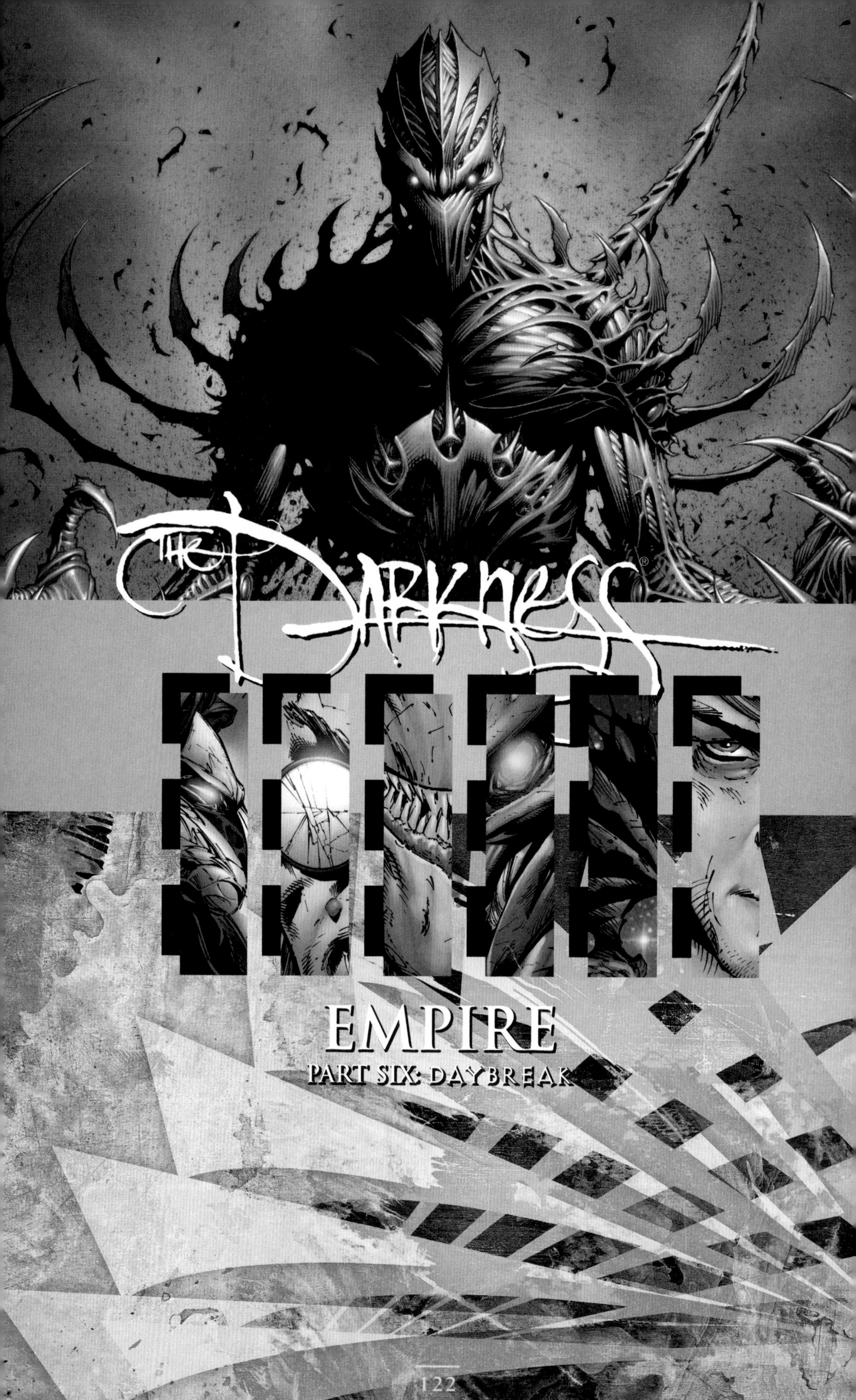
The Darkness®
EMPIRE
PART SIX: DAYBREAK

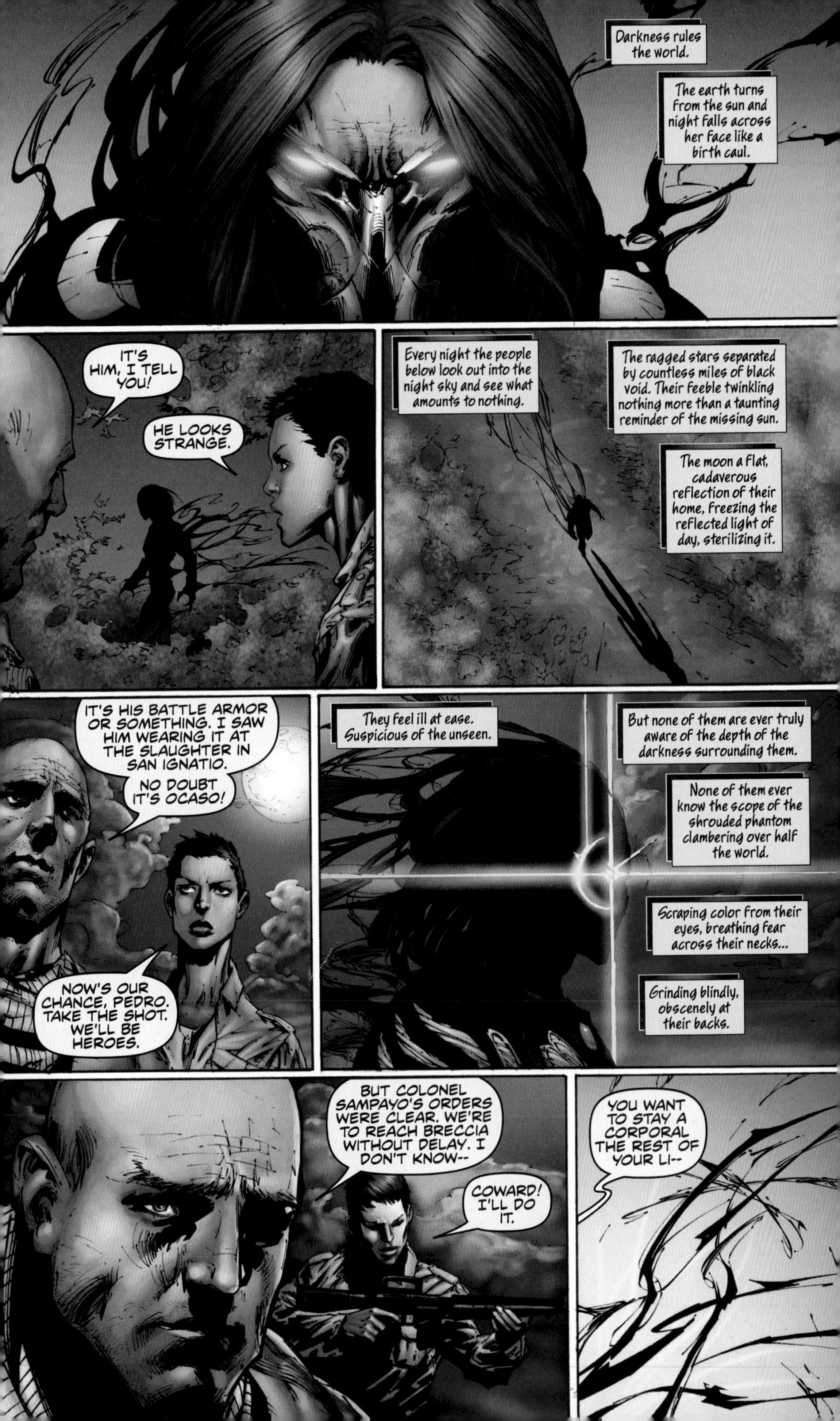
Darkness rules the world.
The earth turns from the sun and night falls across her face like a birth caul.
IT'S HIM, I TELL YOU!
HE LOOKS STRANGE.
Every night the people below look out into the night sky and see what amounts to nothing.
The ragged stars separated by countless miles of black void. Their feeble twinkling nothing more than a taunting reminder of the missing sun.
The moon a flat, cadaverous reflection of their home, freezing the reflected light of day, sterilizing it.
IT'S HIS BATTLE ARMOR OR SOMETHING. I SAW HIM WEARING IT AT THE SLAUGHTER IN SAN IGNATIO.
NO DOUBT IT'S OCASO!
NOW'S OUR CHANCE, PEDRO. TAKE THE SHOT. WE'LL BE HEROES.
They feel ill at ease. Suspicious of the unseen.
But none of them are ever truly aware of the depth of the darkness surrounding them.
None of them ever know the scope of the shrouded phantom clambering over half the world.
Scraping color from their eyes, breathing fear across their necks...
Grinding blindly, obscenely at their backs.
BUT COLONEL SAMPAYO'S ORDERS WERE CLEAR. WE'RE TO REACH BRECCIA WITHOUT DELAY. I DON'T KNOW--
COWARD! I'LL DO IT.
YOU WANT TO STAY A CORPORAL THE REST OF YOUR LI--

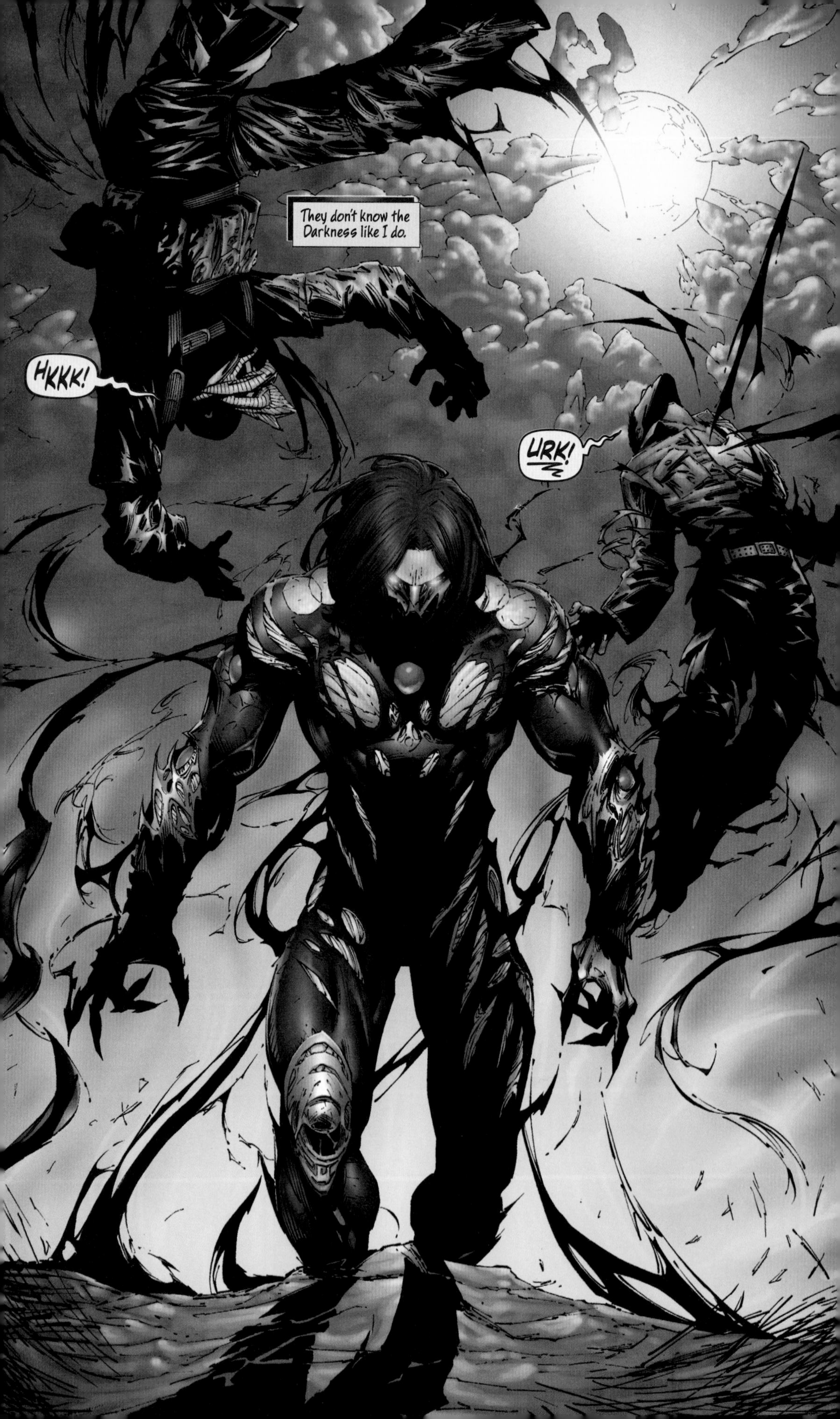
They don't know the Darkness like I do.
HKKK!
URK!

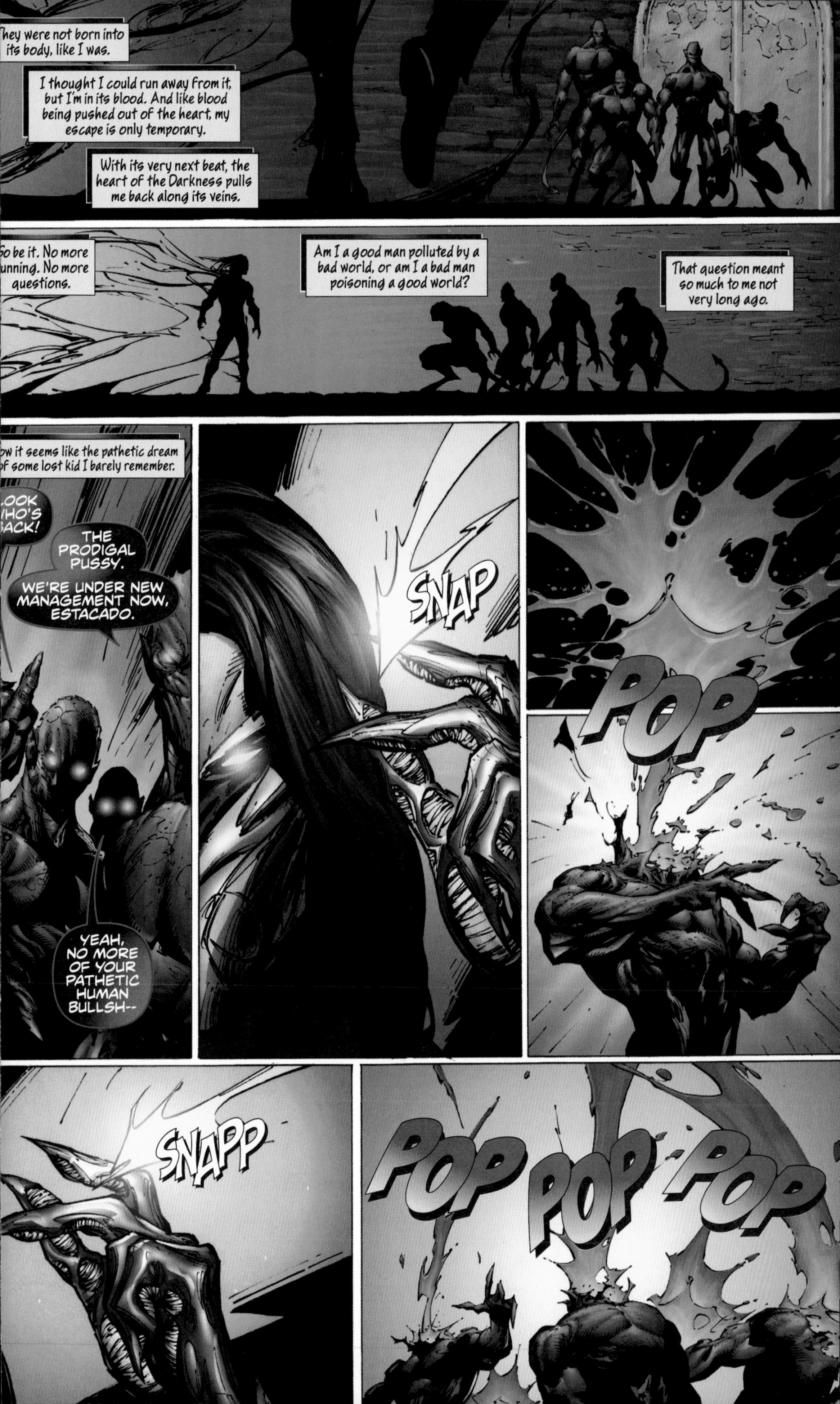

hey were not born into its body, like I was.
I thought I could run away from it, but I'm in its blood. And like blood being pushed out of the heart, my escape is only temporary.
With its very next beat, the heart of the Darkness pulls me back along its veins.
So be it. No more running. No more questions.
Am I a good man polluted by a bad world, or am I a bad man poisoning a good world?
That question meant so much to me not very long ago.
ow it seems like the pathetic dream of some lost kid I barely remember.
LOOK WHO'S BACK!
THE PRODIGAL PUSSY.
WE'RE UNDER NEW MANAGEMENT NOW, ESTACADO.
YEAH, NO MORE OF YOUR PATHETIC HUMAN BULLSH--
SNAP
POP
SNAPP
POP POP POP

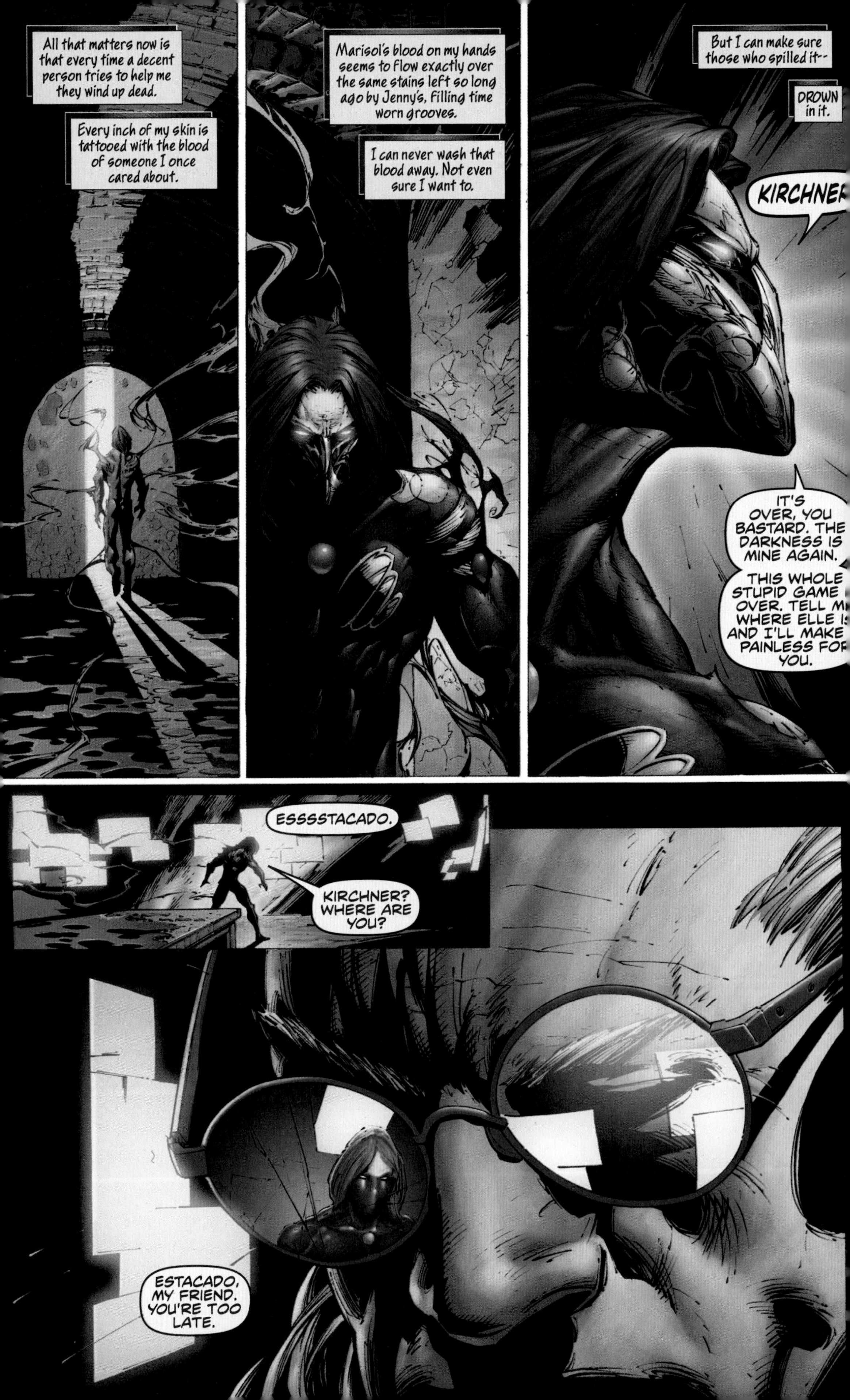
All that matters now is that every time a decent person tries to help me they wind up dead.
Every inch of my skin is tattooed with the blood of someone I once cared about.
Marisol's blood on my hands seems to flow exactly over the same stains left so long ago by Jenny's, filling time worn grooves.
I can never wash that blood away. Not even sure I want to.
But I can make sure those who spilled it--
DROWN in it.
KIRCHNER
IT'S OVER, YOU BASTARD. THE DARKNESS IS MINE AGAIN.
THIS WHOLE STUPID GAME OVER. TELL M WHERE ELLE I AND I'LL MAKE PAINLESS FOR YOU.
ESSSSTACADO.
KIRCHNER? WHERE ARE YOU?
ESTACADO, MY FRIEND. YOU'RE TOO LATE.

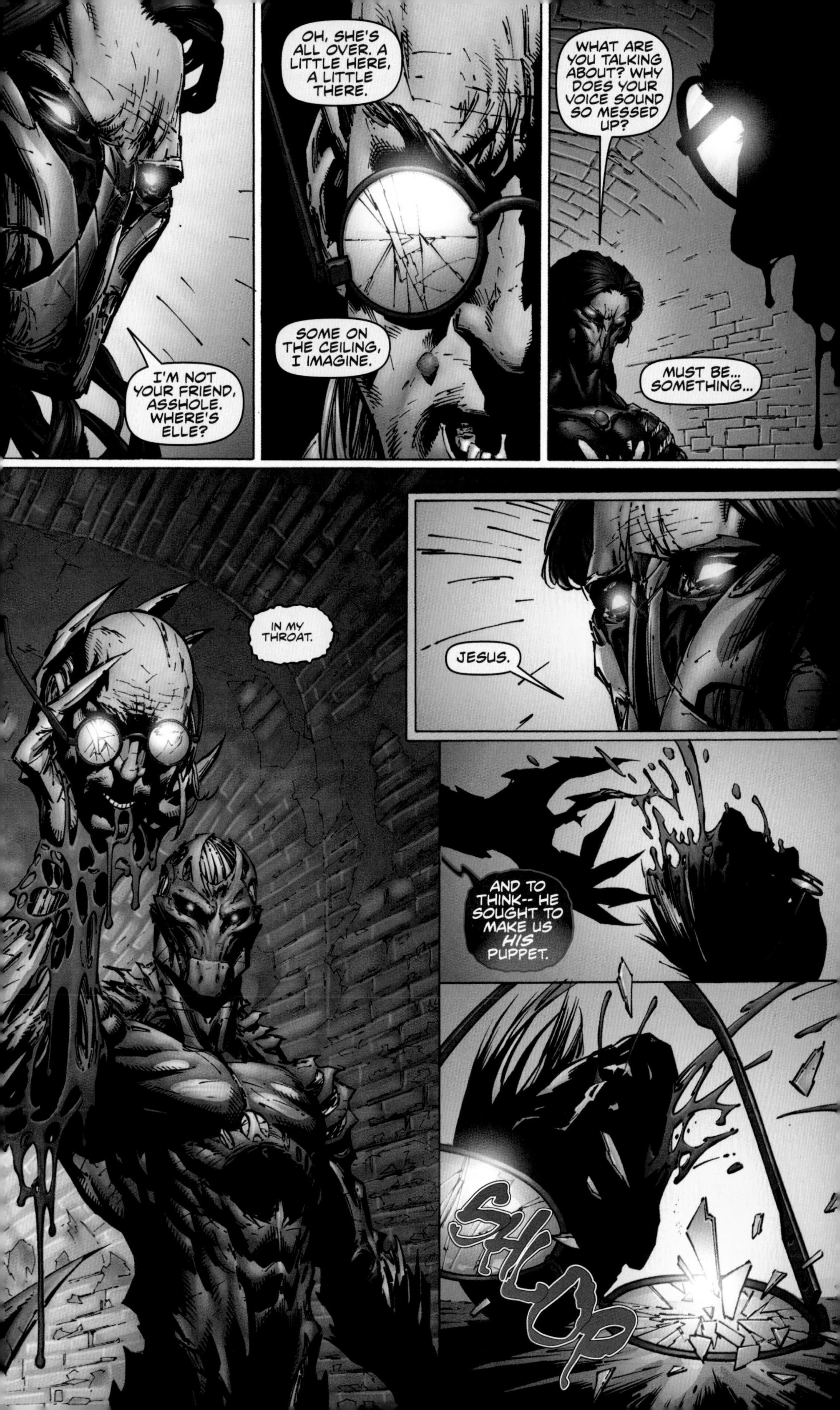
I'M NOT YOUR FRIEND, ASSHOLE. WHERE'S ELLE?
OH, SHE'S ALL OVER. A LITTLE HERE, A LITTLE THERE.
SOME ON THE CEILING, I IMAGINE.
WHAT ARE YOU TALKING ABOUT? WHY DOES YOUR VOICE SOUND SO MESSED UP?
MUST BE... SOMETHING...
IN MY THROAT.
JESUS.
AND TO THINK-- HE SOUGHT TO MAKE US HIS PUPPET.
SHLOP

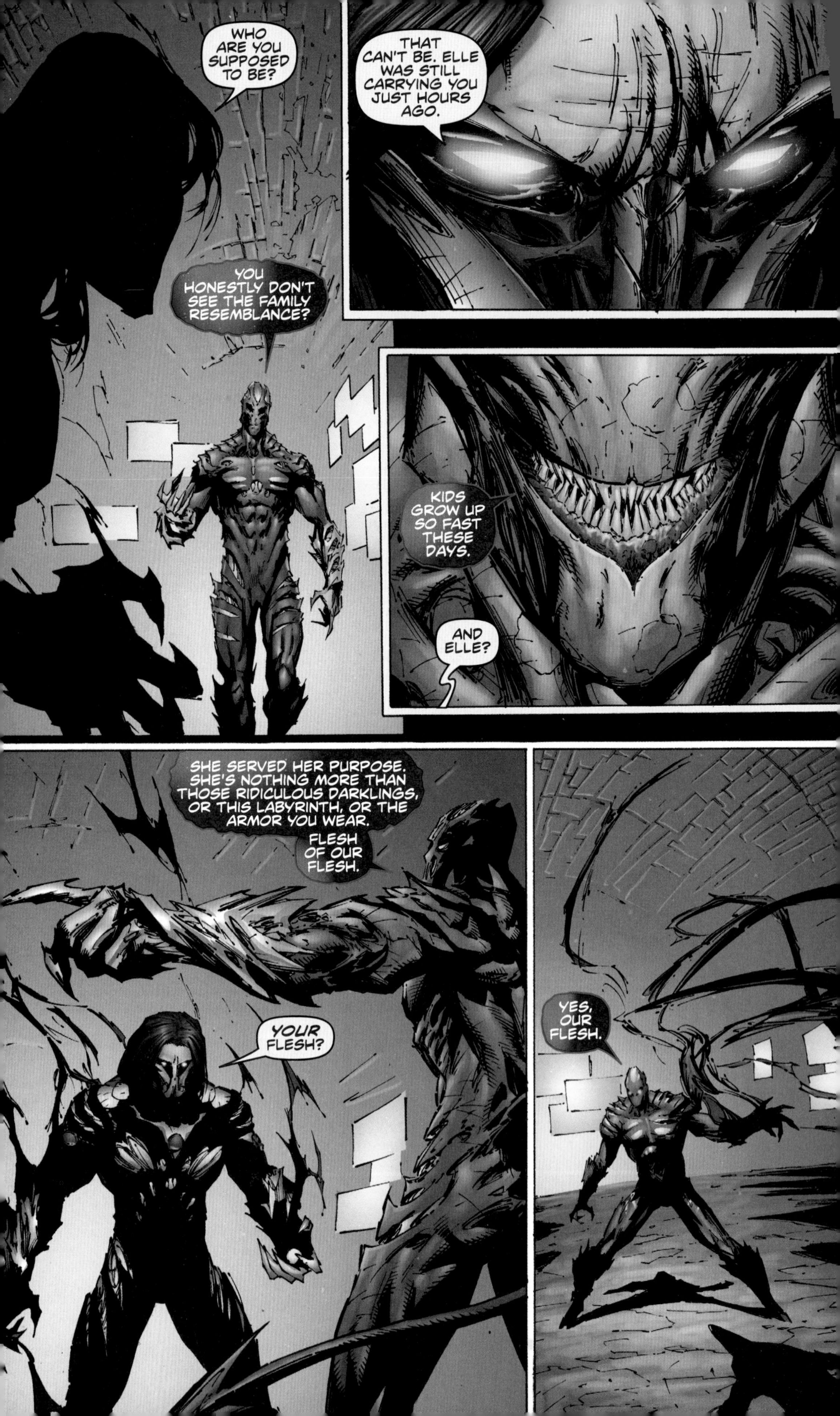
WHO ARE YOU SUPPOSED TO BE?
THAT CAN'T BE. ELLE WAS STILL CARRYING YOU JUST HOURS AGO.
YOU HONESTLY DON'T SEE THE FAMILY RESEMBLANCE?
KIDS GROW UP SO FAST THESE DAYS.
AND ELLE?
SHE SERVED HER PURPOSE. SHE'S NOTHING MORE THAN THOSE RIDICULOUS DARKLINGS, OR THIS LABYRINTH, OR THE ARMOR YOU WEAR.
FLESH OF OUR FLESH.
YOUR FLESH?
YES, OUR FLESH.

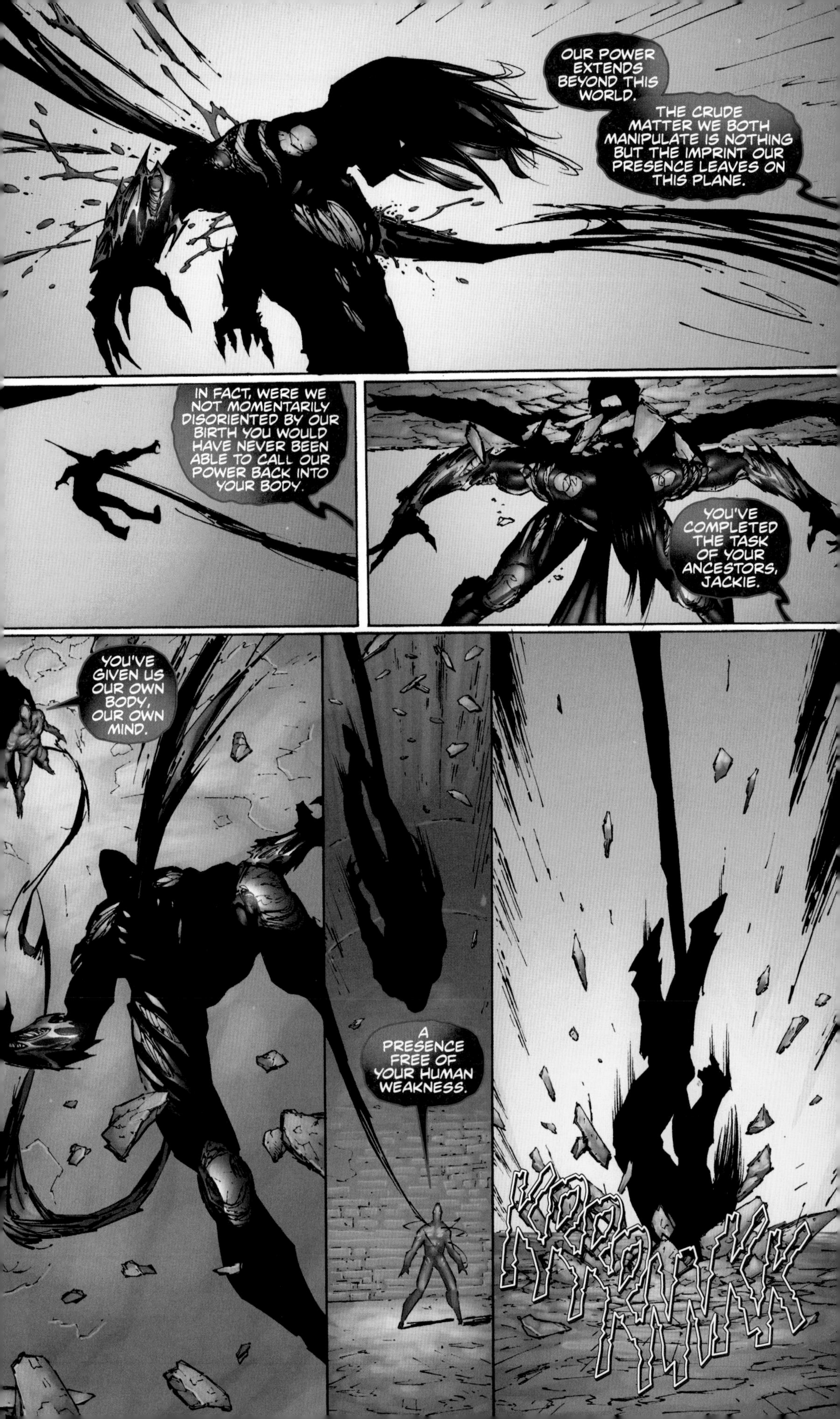
OUR POWER EXTENDS BEYOND THIS WORLD.
THE CRUDE MATTER WE BOTH MANIPULATE IS NOTHING BUT THE IMPRINT OUR PRESENCE LEAVES ON THIS PLANE.
IN FACT, WERE WE NOT MOMENTARILY DISORIENTED BY OUR BIRTH YOU WOULD HAVE NEVER BEEN ABLE TO CALL OUR POWER BACK INTO YOUR BODY.
YOU'VE COMPLETED THE TASK OF YOUR ANCESTORS, JACKIE.
YOU'VE GIVEN US OUR OWN BODY, OUR OWN MIND.
A PRESENCE FREE OF YOUR HUMAN WEAKNESS.

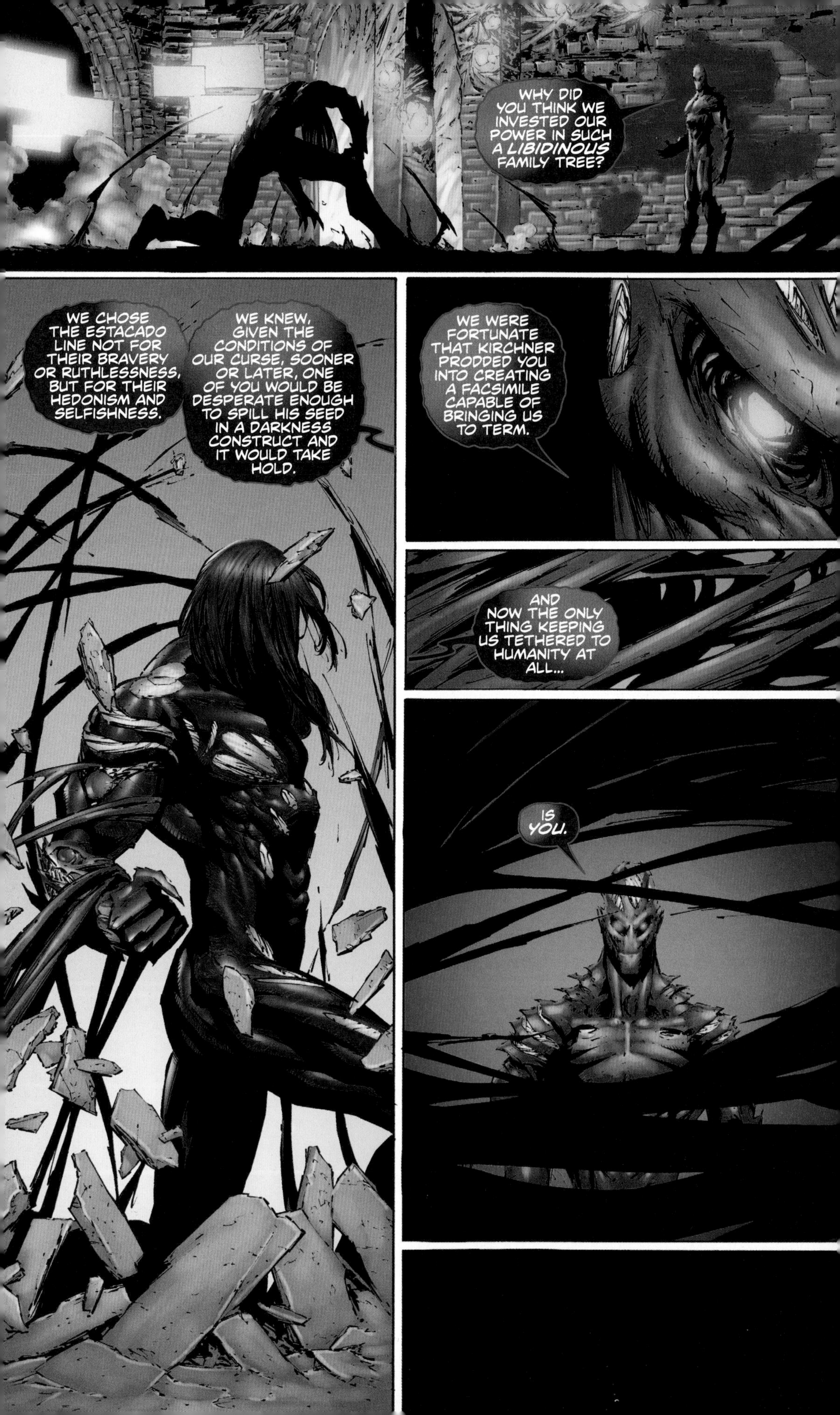
WHY DID YOU THINK WE INVESTED OUR POWER IN SUCH A *LIBIDINOUS* FAMILY TREE?
WE CHOSE THE ESTACADO LINE NOT FOR THEIR BRAVERY OR RUTHLESSNESS, BUT FOR THEIR HEDONISM AND SELFISHNESS.
WE KNEW, GIVEN THE CONDITIONS OF OUR CURSE, SOONER OR LATER, ONE OF YOU WOULD BE DESPERATE ENOUGH TO SPILL HIS SEED IN A DARKNESS CONSTRUCT AND IT WOULD TAKE HOLD.
WE WERE FORTUNATE THAT KIRCHNER PRODDED YOU INTO CREATING A FACSIMILE CAPABLE OF BRINGING US TO TERM.
AND NOW THE ONLY THING KEEPING US TETHERED TO HUMANITY AT ALL...
IS *YOU.*

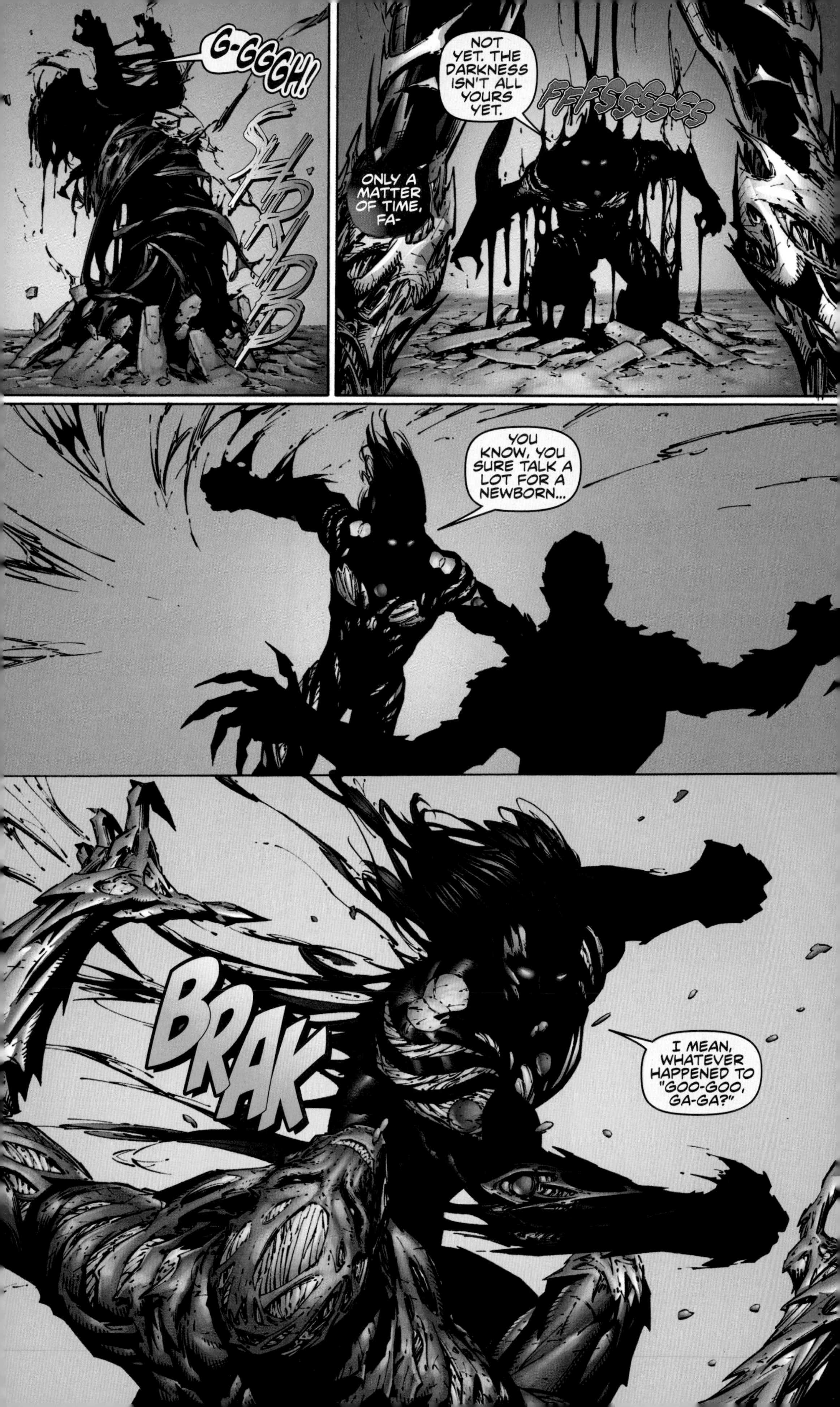
G-GGGH!
SHRIPPP
NOT YET. THE DARKNESS ISN'T ALL YOURS YET.
FFFSSSSSSS
ONLY A MATTER OF TIME, FA-
YOU KNOW, YOU SURE TALK A LOT FOR A NEWBORN...
BRAK
I MEAN, WHATEVER HAPPENED TO "GOO-GOO, GA-GA?"

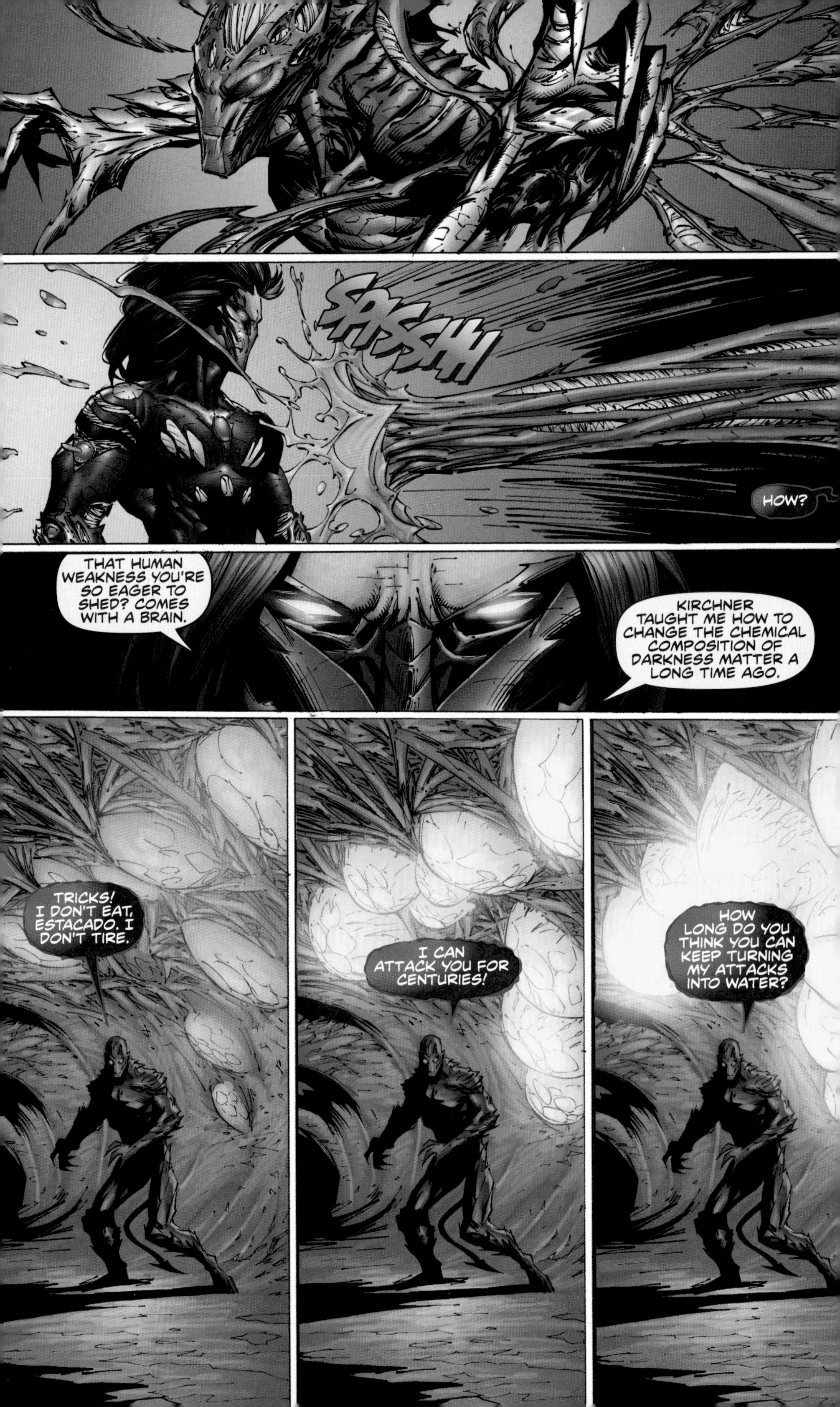
SPSSH
HOW?
THAT HUMAN WEAKNESS YOU'RE SO EAGER TO SHED? COMES WITH A BRAIN.
KIRCHNER TAUGHT ME HOW TO CHANGE THE CHEMICAL COMPOSITION OF DARKNESS MATTER A LONG TIME AGO.
TRICKS! I DON'T EAT, ESTACADO. I DON'T TIRE.
I CAN ATTACK YOU FOR CENTURIES!
HOW LONG DO YOU THINK YOU CAN KEEP TURNING MY ATTACKS INTO WATER?

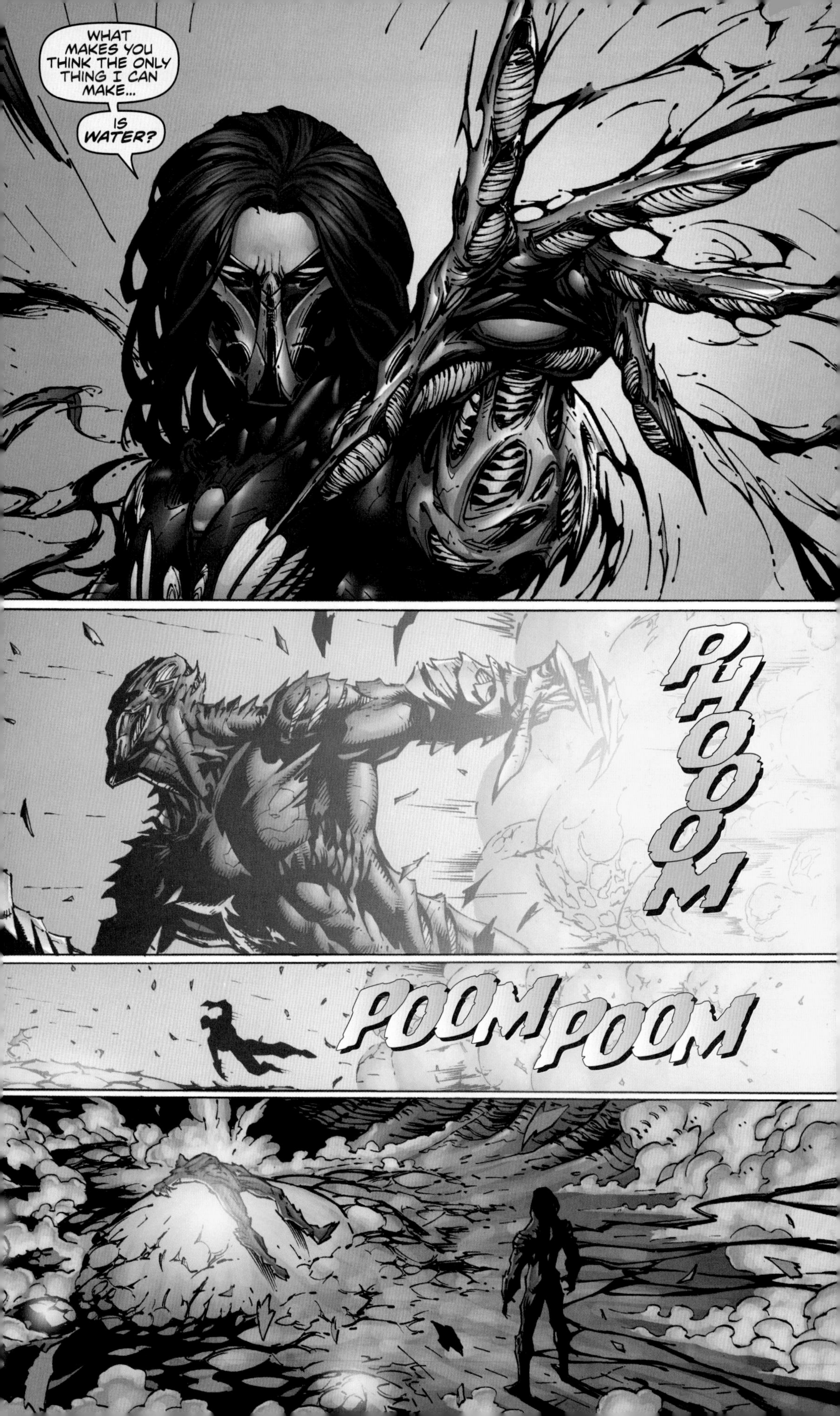
WHAT MAKES YOU THINK THE ONLY THING I CAN MAKE...
IS WATER?
PHOOOM
POOM POOM

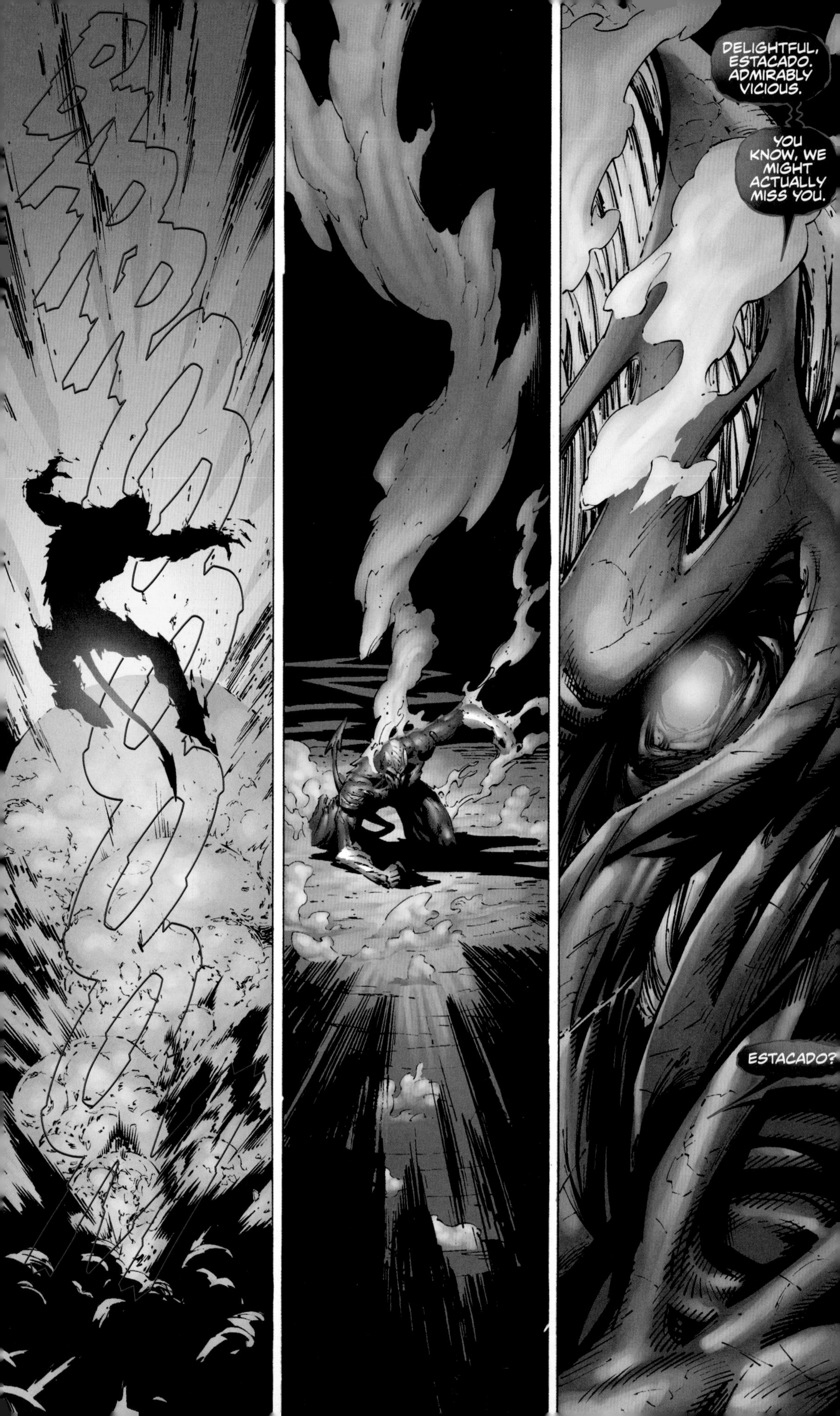
DELIGHTFUL, ESTACADO. ADMIRABLY VICIOUS.
YOU KNOW, WE MIGHT ACTUALLY MISS YOU.
ESTACADO?

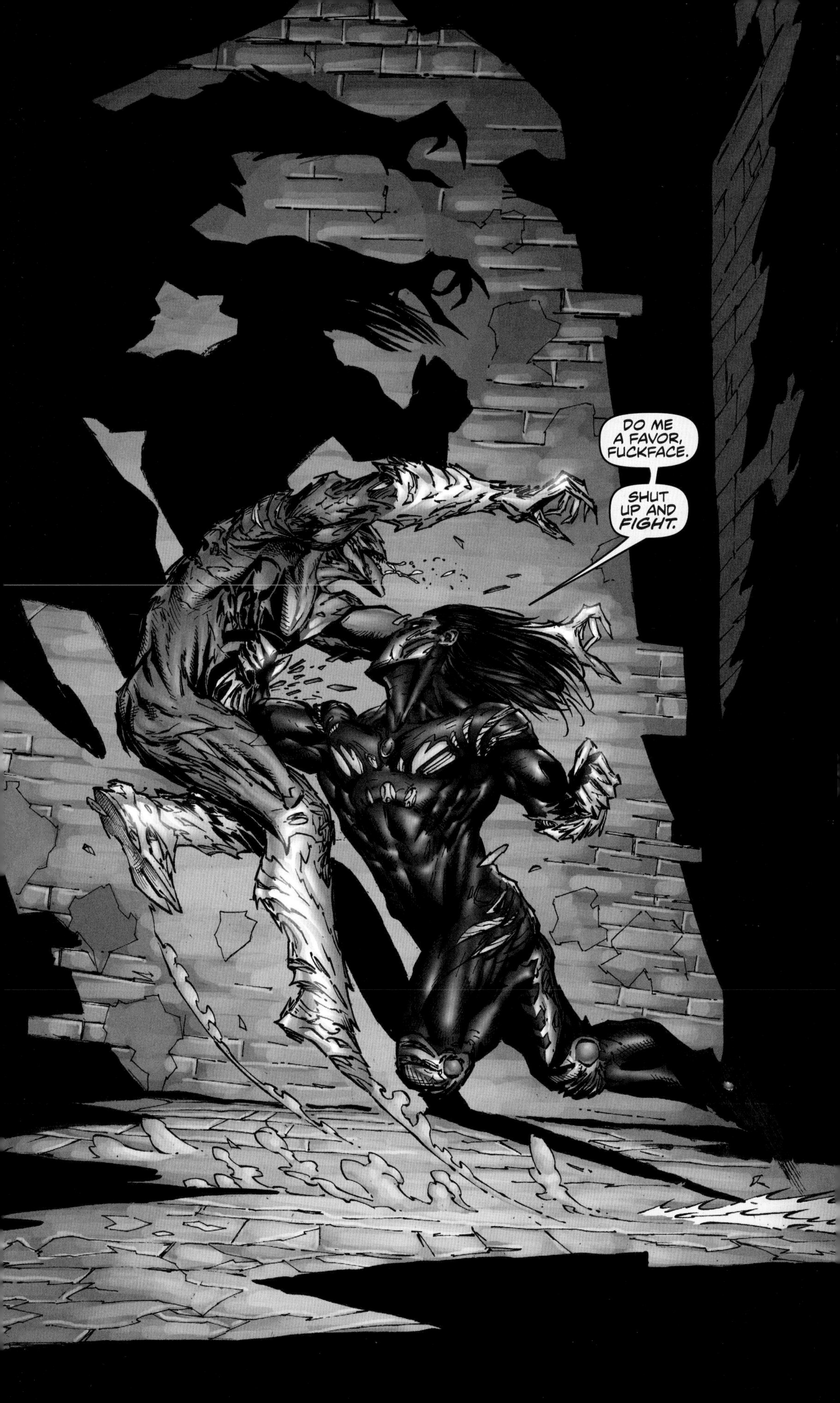
DO ME A FAVOR, FUCKFACE.
SHUT UP AND FIGHT.

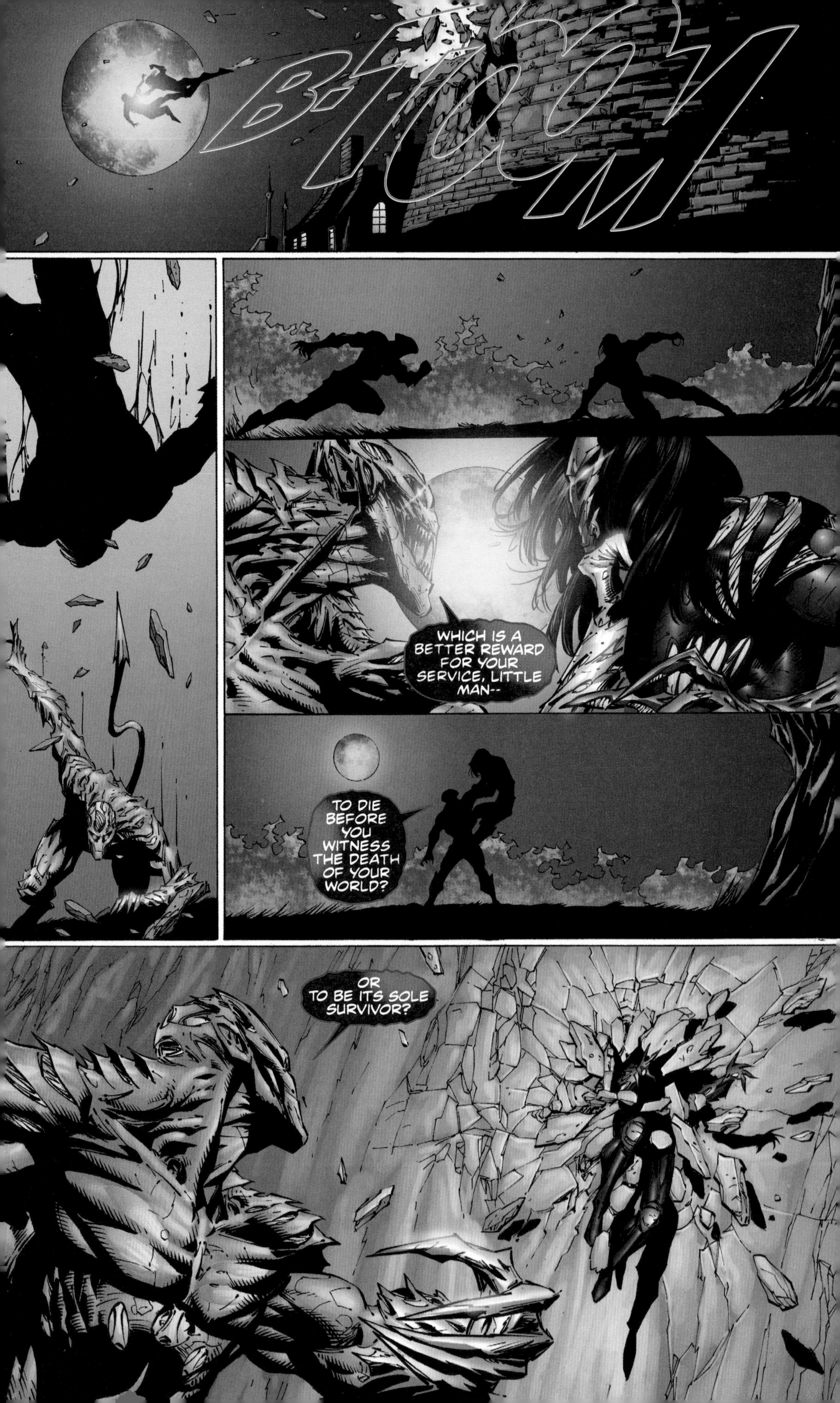

BTHOOM
WHICH IS A BETTER REWARD FOR YOUR SERVICE, LITTLE MAN--
TO DIE BEFORE YOU WITNESS THE DEATH OF YOUR WORLD?
OR TO BE ITS SOLE SURVIVOR?

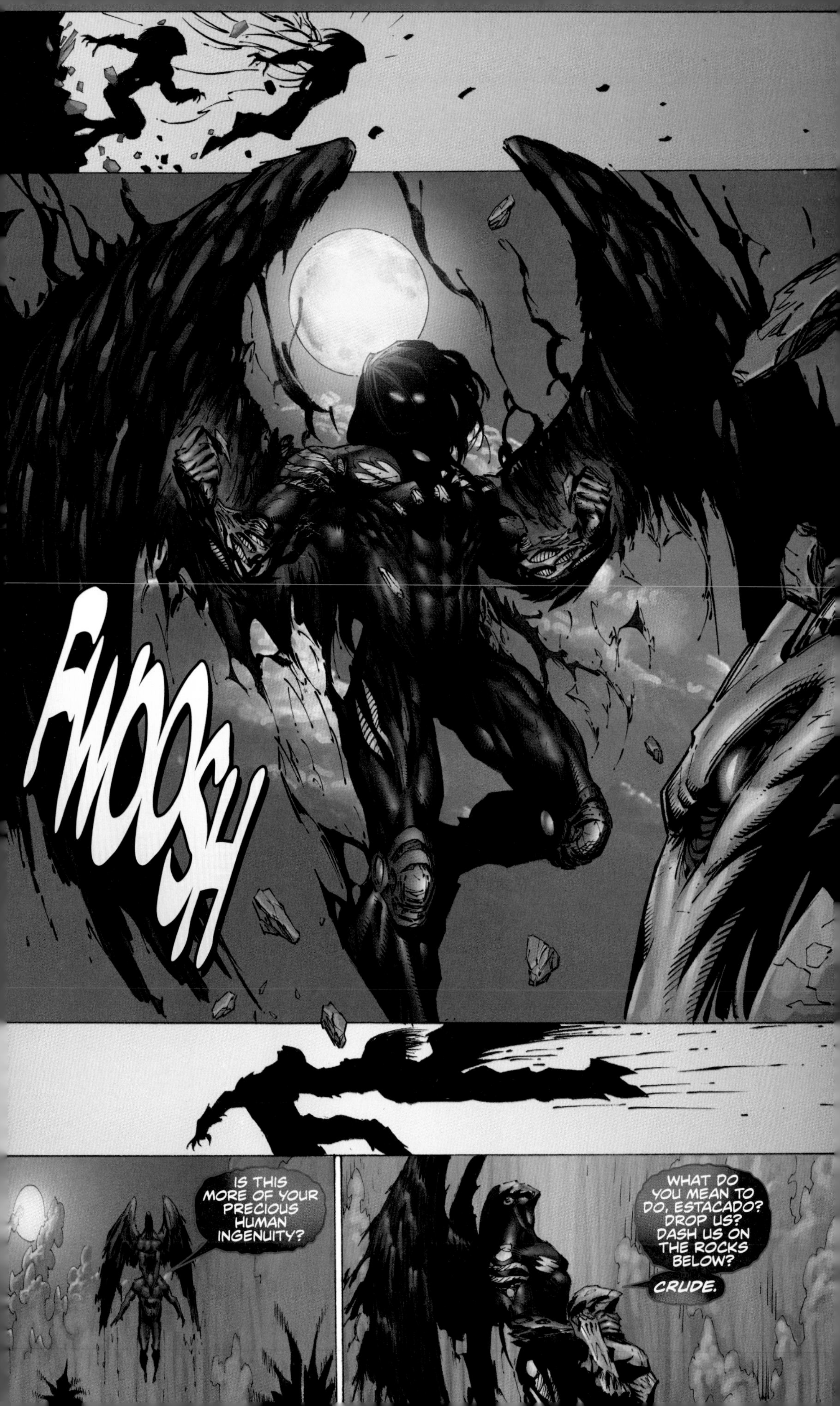
FWOOSH
IS THIS MORE OF YOUR PRECIOUS HUMAN INGENUITY?
WHAT DO YOU MEAN TO DO, ESTACADO? DROP US? DASH US ON THE ROCKS BELOW?
CRUDE.

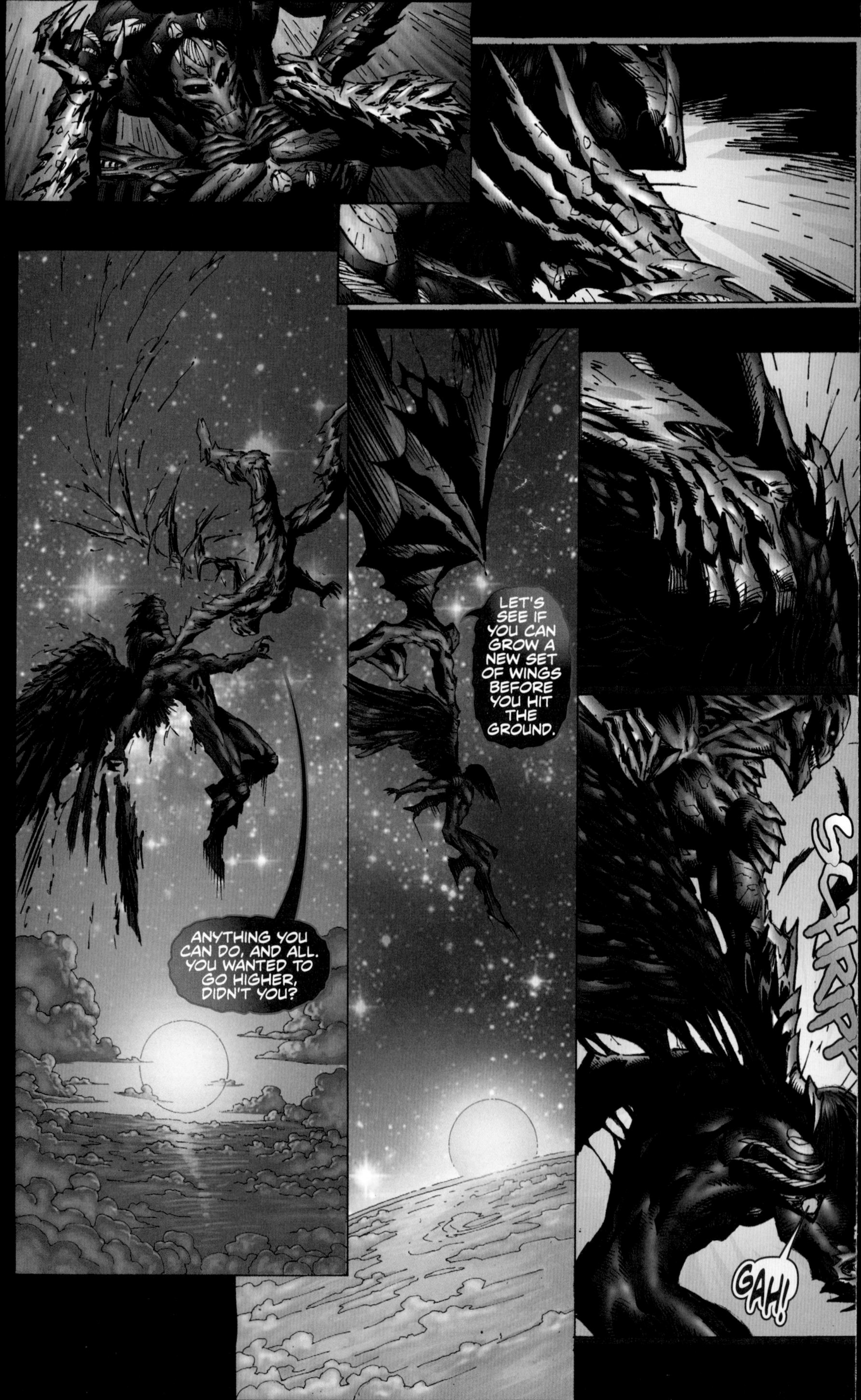
ANYTHING YOU CAN DO, AND ALL. YOU WANTED TO GO HIGHER, DIDN'T YOU?
LET'S SEE IF YOU CAN GROW A NEW SET OF WINGS BEFORE YOU HIT THE GROUND.
SCHRRFF
GAH!

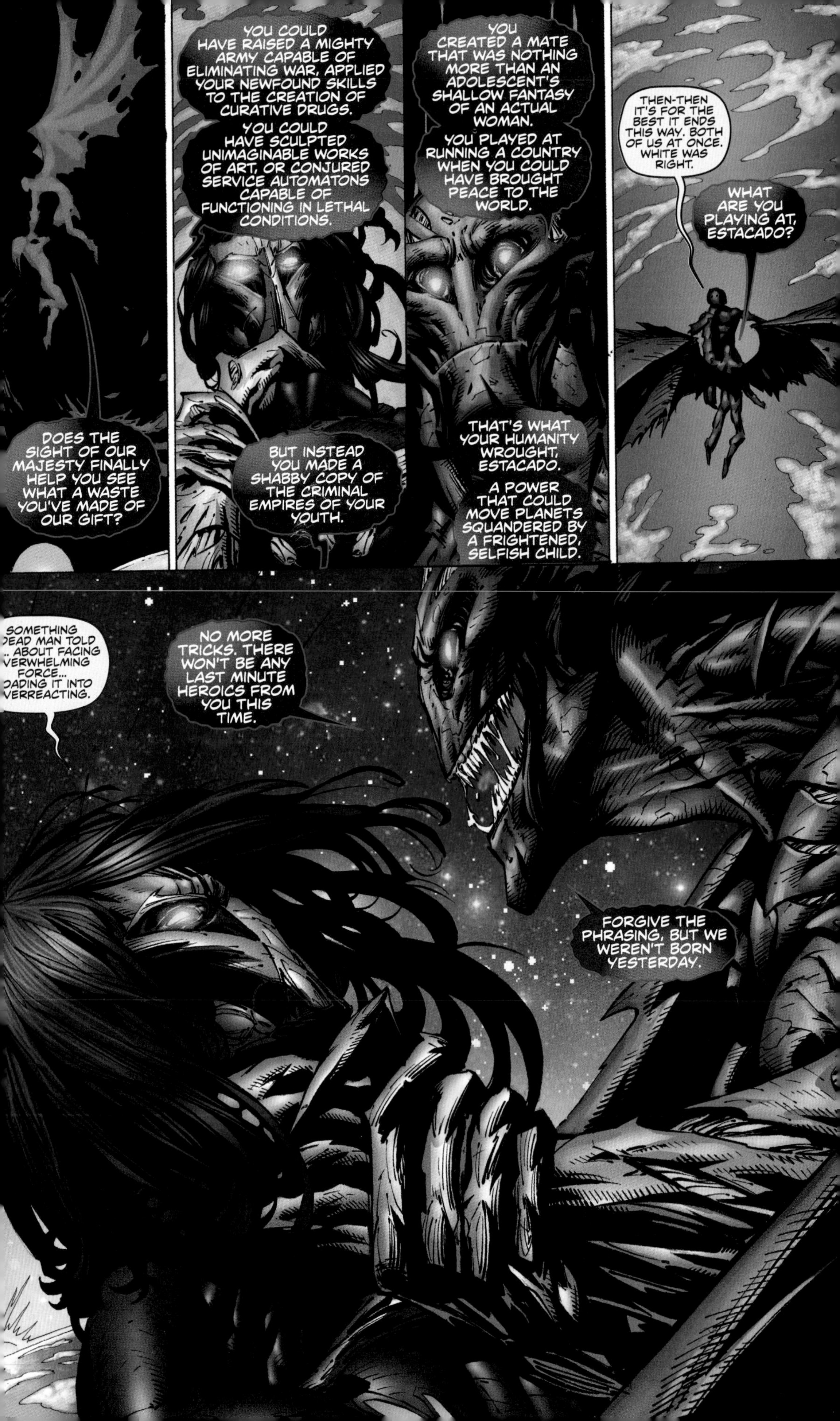
DOES THE SIGHT OF OUR MAJESTY FINALLY HELP YOU SEE WHAT A WASTE YOU'VE MADE OF OUR GIFT?
YOU COULD HAVE RAISED A MIGHTY ARMY CAPABLE OF ELIMINATING WAR, APPLIED YOUR NEWFOUND SKILLS TO THE CREATION OF CURATIVE DRUGS.
YOU COULD HAVE SCULPTED UNIMAGINABLE WORKS OF ART, OR CONJURED SERVICE AUTOMATONS CAPABLE OF FUNCTIONING IN LETHAL CONDITIONS.
BUT INSTEAD YOU MADE A SHABBY COPY OF THE CRIMINAL EMPIRES OF YOUR YOUTH.
YOU CREATED A MATE THAT WAS NOTHING MORE THAN AN ADOLESCENT'S SHALLOW FANTASY OF AN ACTUAL WOMAN.
YOU PLAYED AT RUNNING A COUNTRY WHEN YOU COULD HAVE BROUGHT PEACE TO THE WORLD.
THAT'S WHAT YOUR HUMANITY WROUGHT, ESTACADO.
A POWER THAT COULD MOVE PLANETS SQUANDERED BY A FRIGHTENED, SELFISH CHILD.
THEN-THEN IT'S FOR THE BEST IT ENDS THIS WAY. BOTH OF US AT ONCE. WHITE WAS RIGHT.
WHAT ARE YOU PLAYING AT, ESTACADO?
SOMETHING DEAD MAN TOLD .. ABOUT FACING VERWHELMING FORCE... OADING IT INTO VERREACTING.
NO MORE TRICKS. THERE WON'T BE ANY LAST MINUTE HEROICS FROM YOU THIS TIME.
FORGIVE THE PHRASING, BUT WE WEREN'T BORN YESTERDAY.

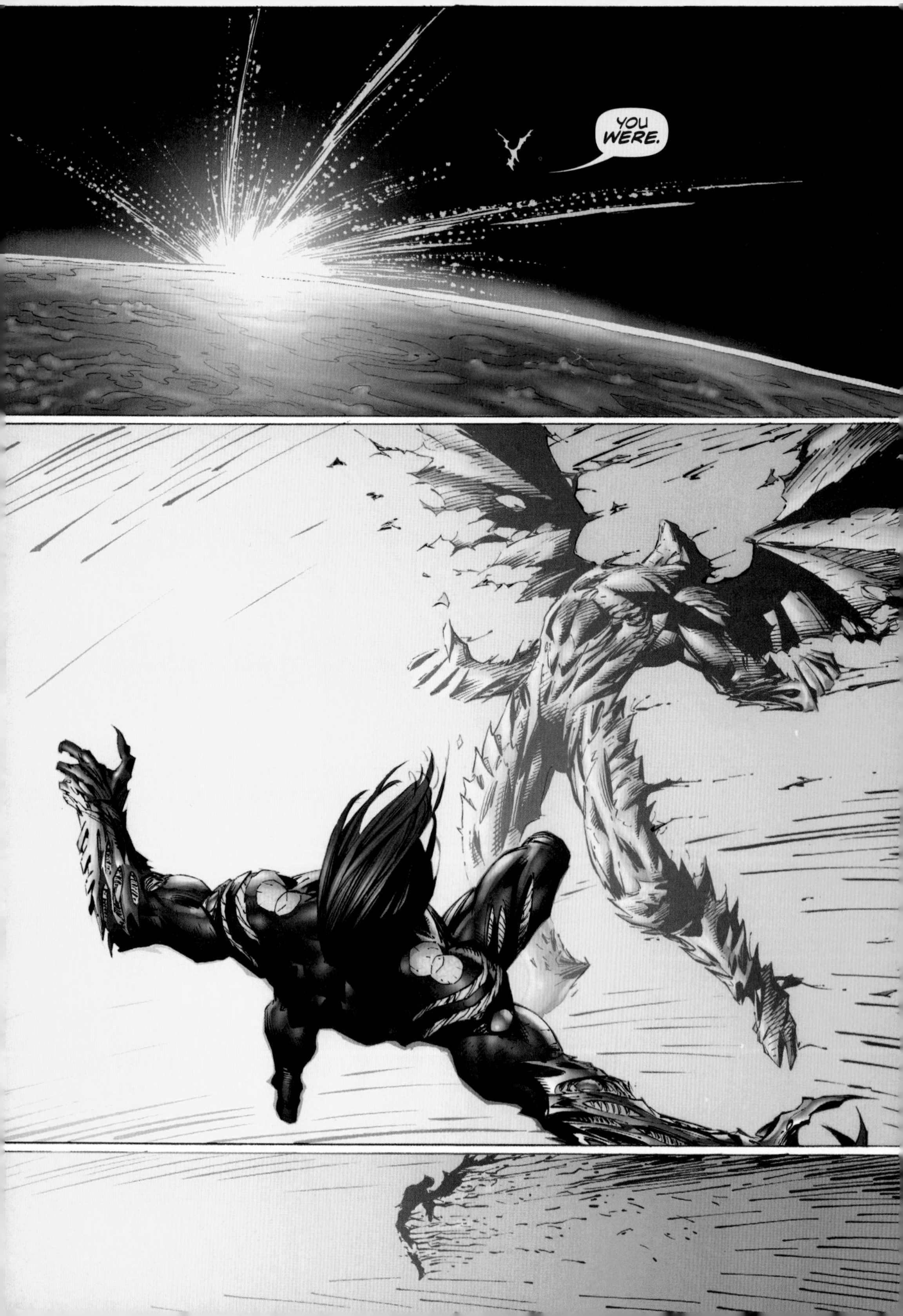
YOU WERE.

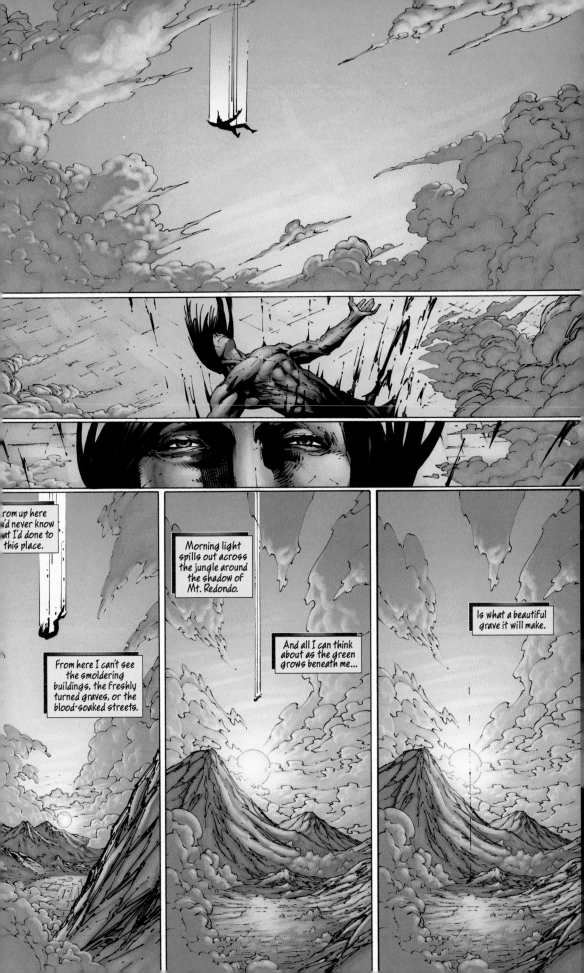

From up here I'd never know what I'd done to this place.

From here I can't see the smoldering buildings, the freshly turned graves, or the blood-soaked streets.

Morning light spills out across the jungle around the shadow of Mt. Redondo.

And all I can think about as the green grows beneath me...

Is what a beautiful grave it will make.

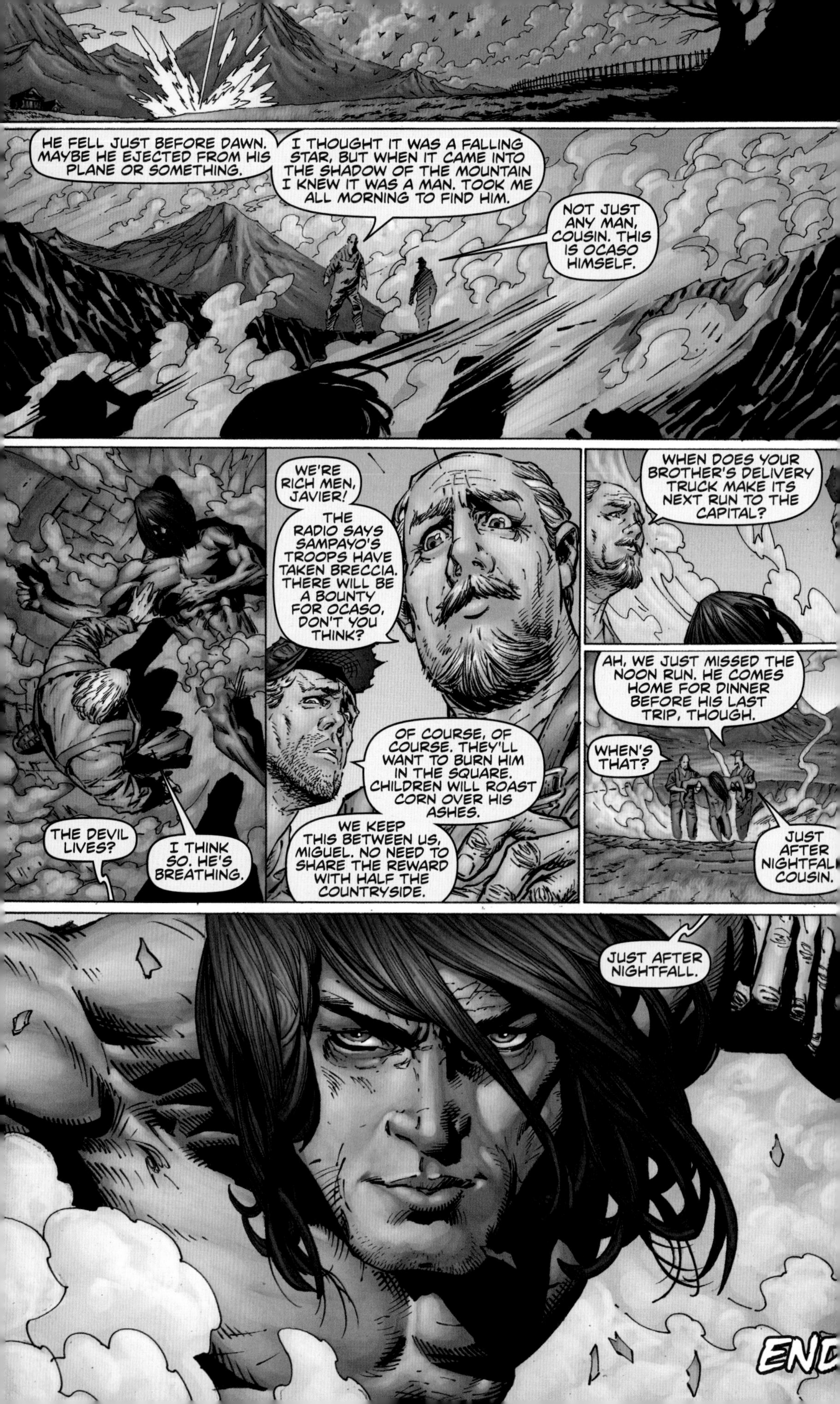
HE FELL JUST BEFORE DAWN. MAYBE HE EJECTED FROM HIS PLANE OR SOMETHING.
I THOUGHT IT WAS A FALLING STAR, BUT WHEN IT CAME INTO THE SHADOW OF THE MOUNTAIN I KNEW IT WAS A MAN. TOOK ME ALL MORNING TO FIND HIM.
NOT JUST ANY MAN, COUSIN. THIS IS OCASO HIMSELF.
THE DEVIL LIVES?
I THINK SO. HE'S BREATHING.
WE'RE RICH MEN, JAVIER!
THE RADIO SAYS SAMPAYO'S TROOPS HAVE TAKEN BRECCIA. THERE WILL BE A BOUNTY FOR OCASO, DON'T YOU THINK?
OF COURSE, OF COURSE. THEY'LL WANT TO BURN HIM IN THE SQUARE. CHILDREN WILL ROAST CORN OVER HIS ASHES.
WE KEEP THIS BETWEEN US, MIGUEL. NO NEED TO SHARE THE REWARD WITH HALF THE COUNTRYSIDE.
WHEN DOES YOUR BROTHER'S DELIVERY TRUCK MAKE ITS NEXT RUN TO THE CAPITAL?
AH, WE JUST MISSED THE NOON RUN. HE COMES HOME FOR DINNER BEFORE HIS LAST TRIP, THOUGH.
WHEN'S THAT?
JUST AFTER NIGHTFAL COUSIN.
JUST AFTER NIGHTFALL.
END

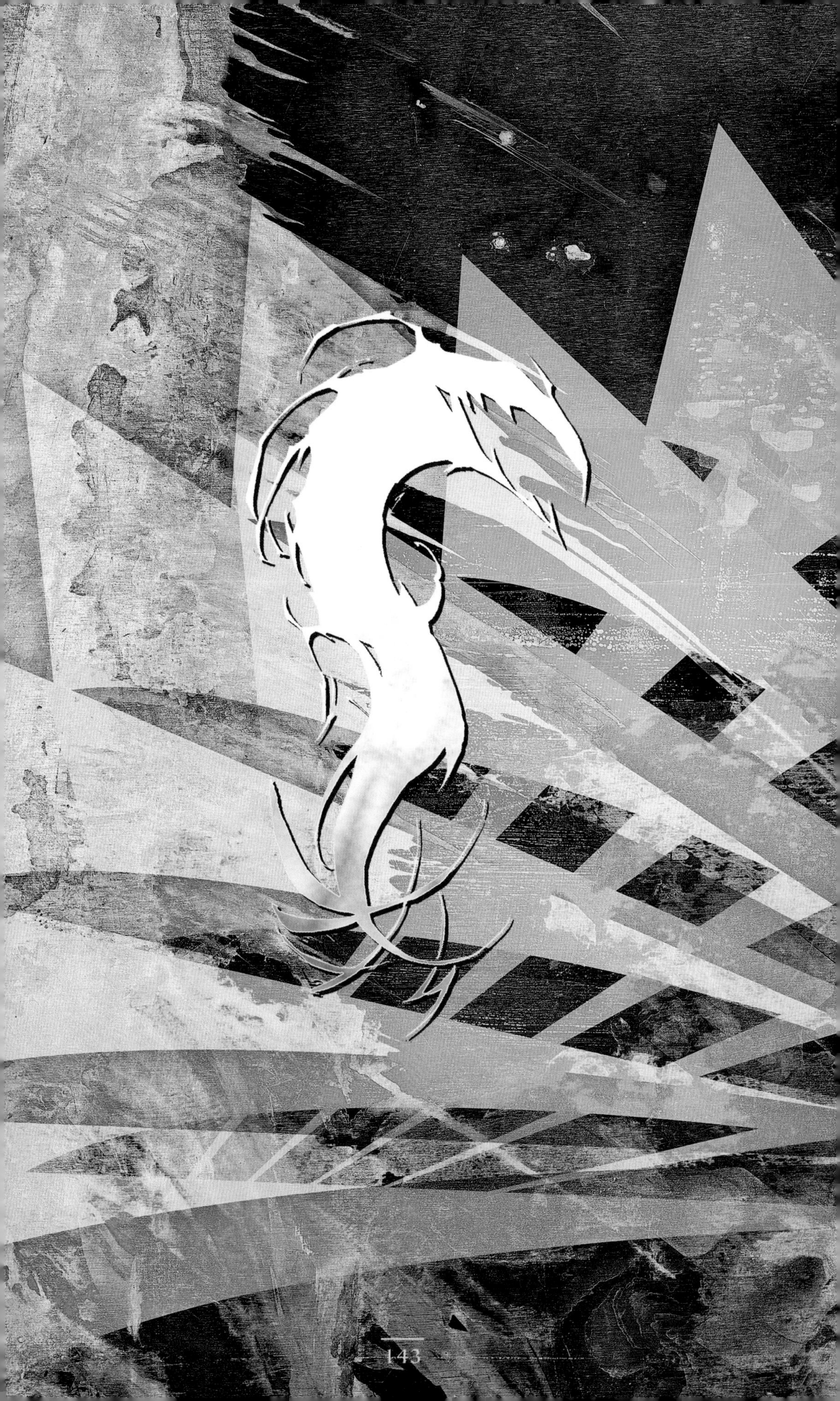

THE DARKNESS®
ACCURSED
VOLUME 1

COVER GALLERY

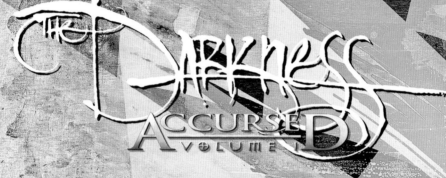

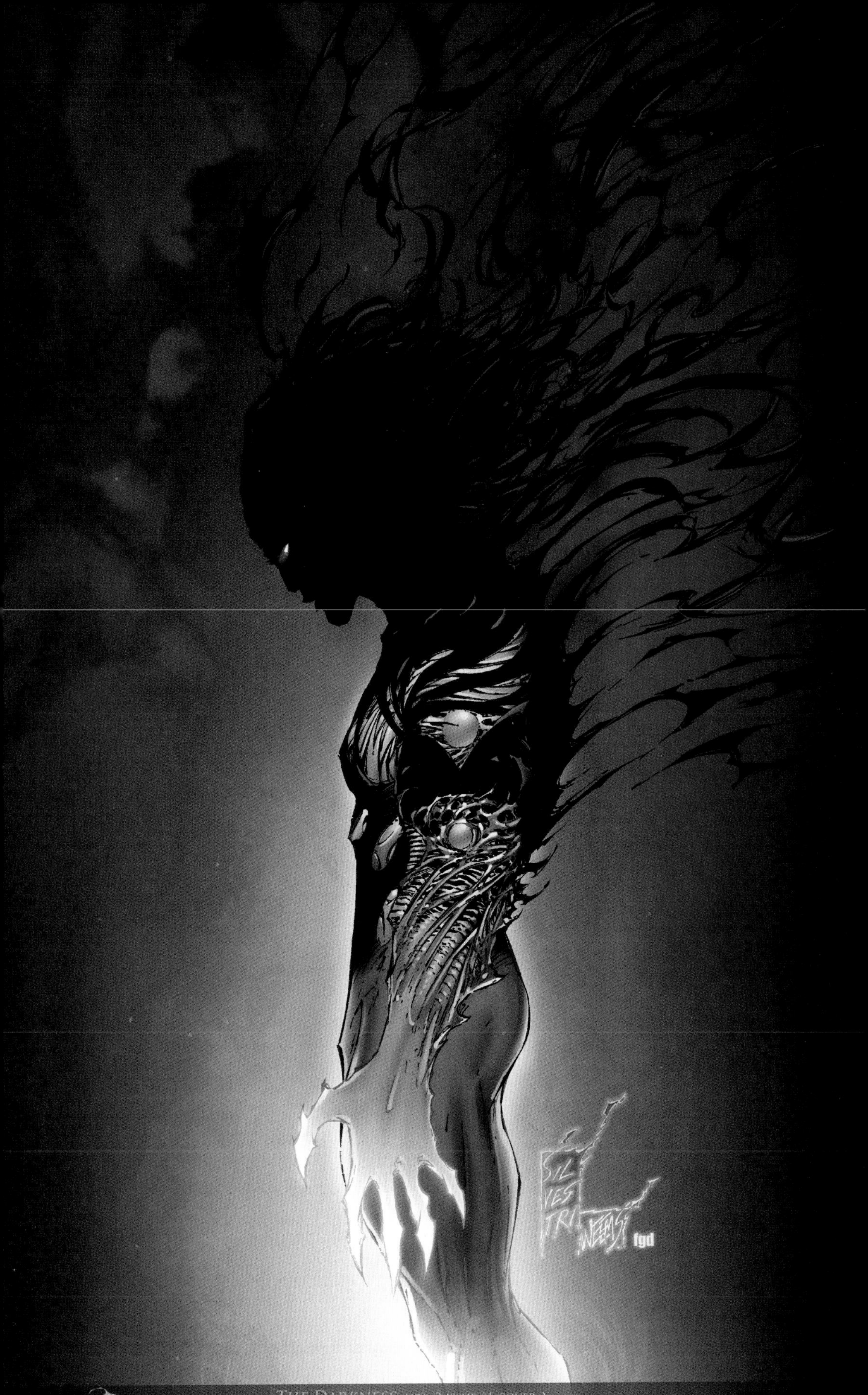

THE DARKNESS, VOL. 3 ISSUE #1 COVER A
ART BY: MARC SILVESTRI, JOE WEEMS V AND FRANK D'ARMATA

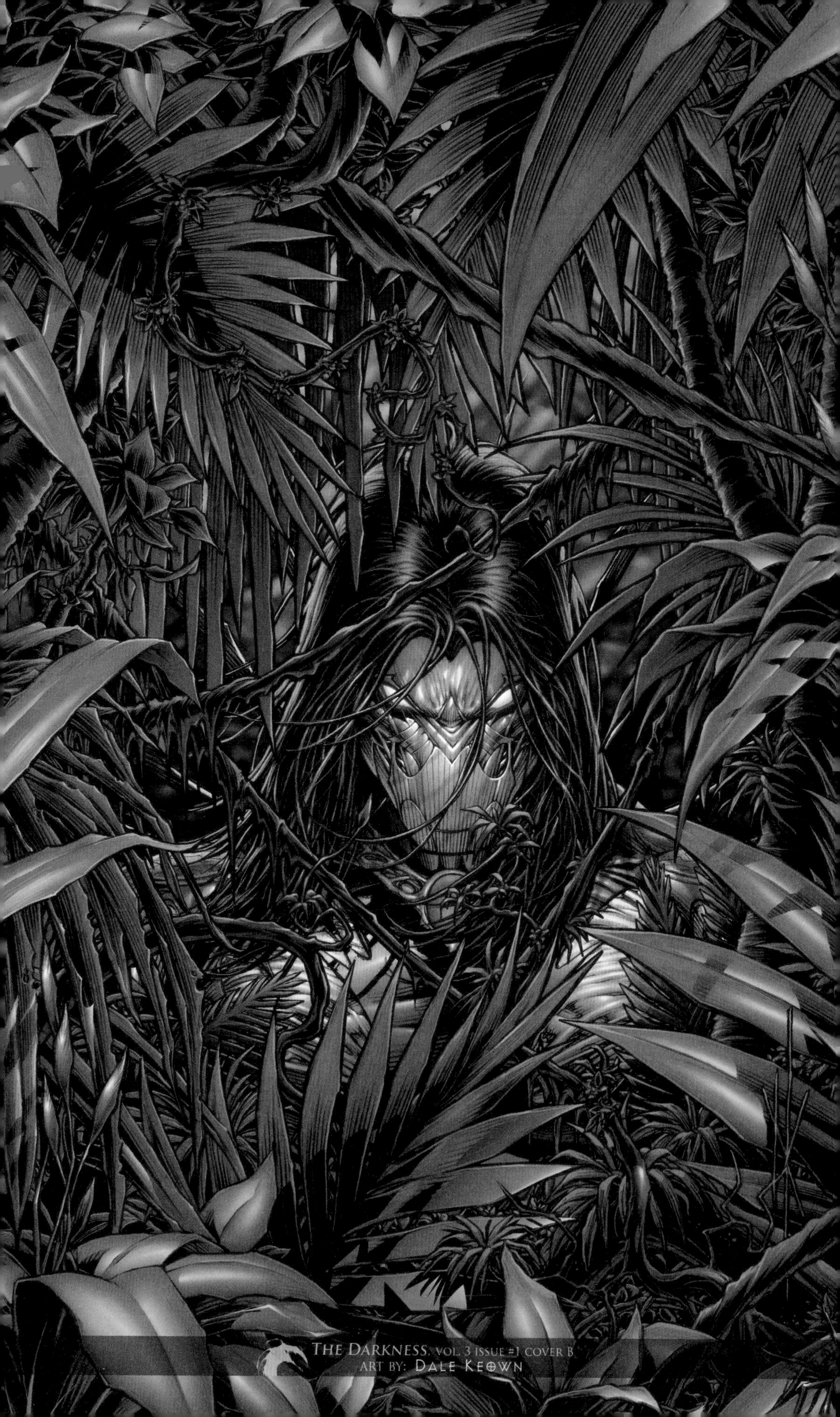

THE DARKNESS, VOL. 3 ISSUE #1 COVER B
ART BY: DALE KEOWN

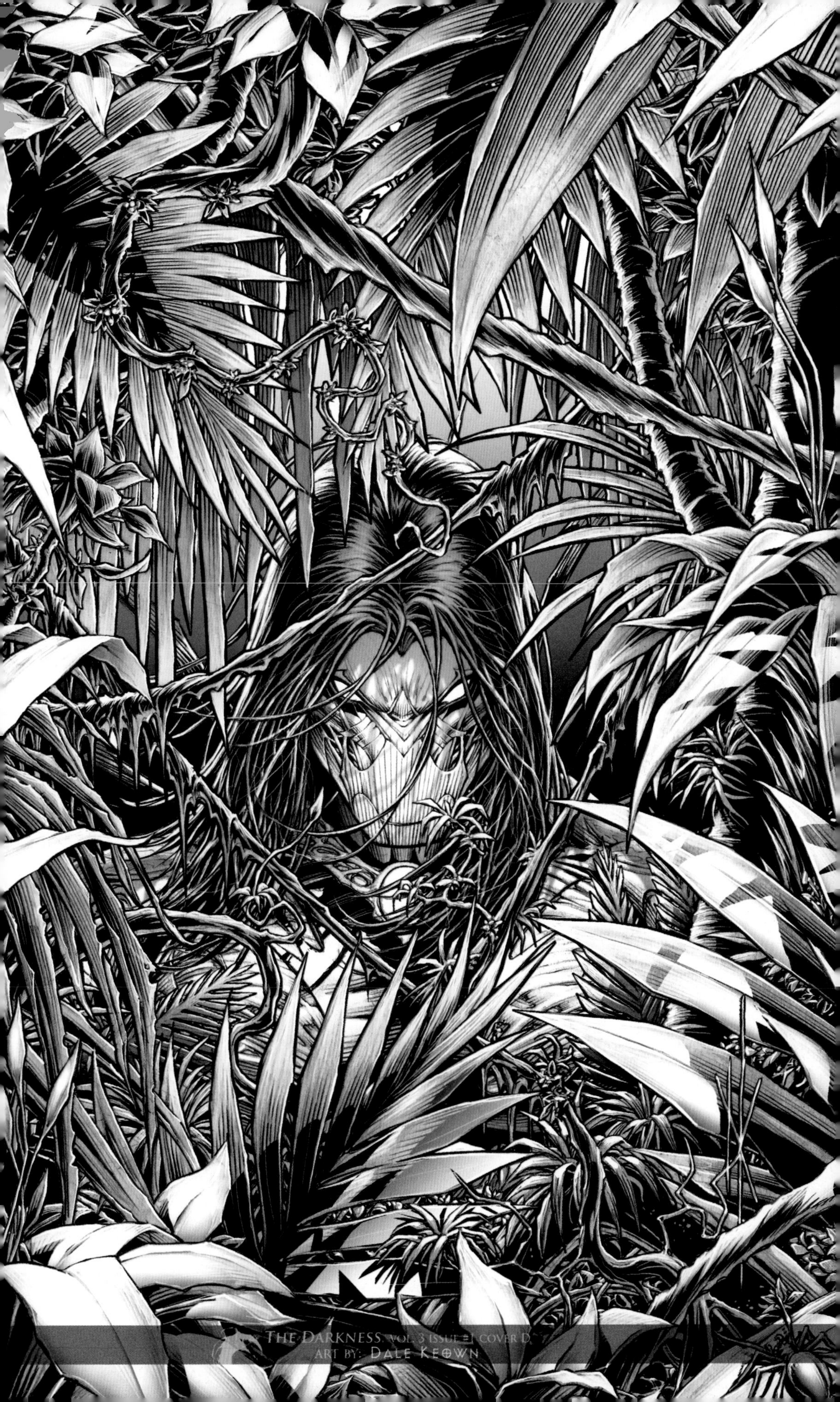
The Darkness, vol. 3 issue #1 cover D
Art by: Dale Keown

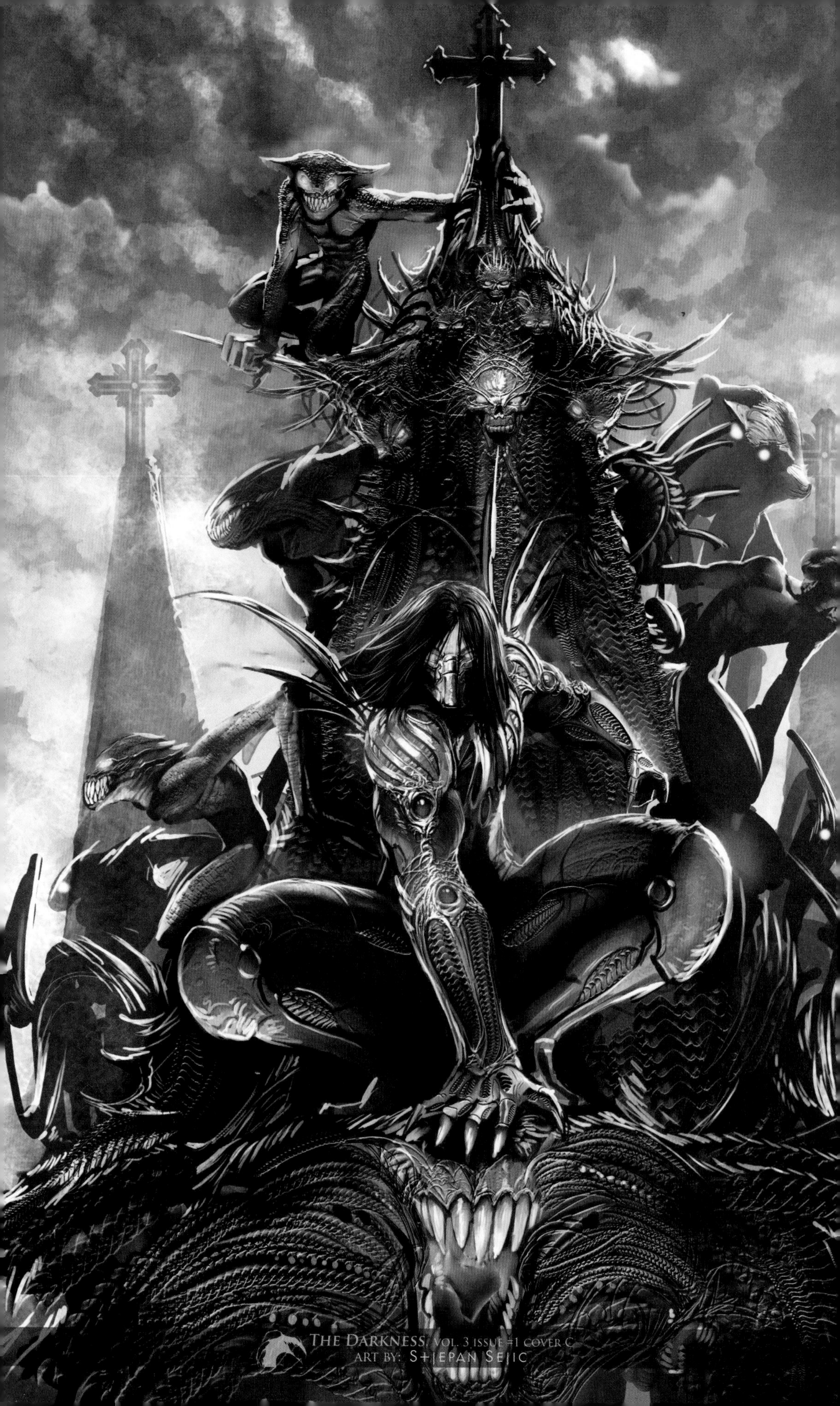

THE DARKNESS: VOL. 3 ISSUE #1 COVER C
ART BY: STJEPAN SEJIC

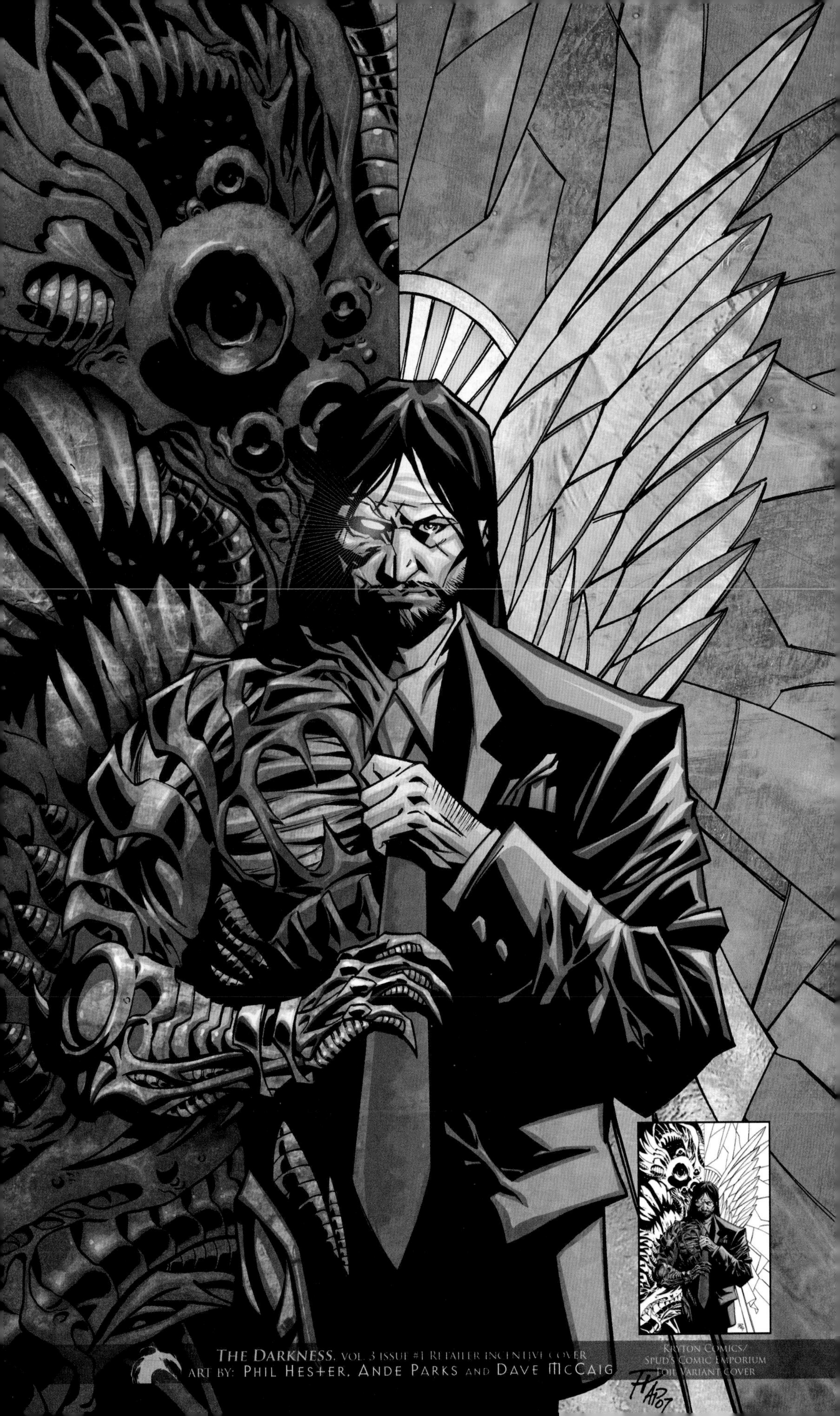

THE DARKNESS, VOL. 3 ISSUE #1 RETAILER INCENTIVE COVER
ART BY: PHIL HESTER, ANDE PARKS AND DAVE MCCAIG

KRYTON COMICS/
SPUD'S COMIC EMPORIUM
FOIL VARIANT COVER

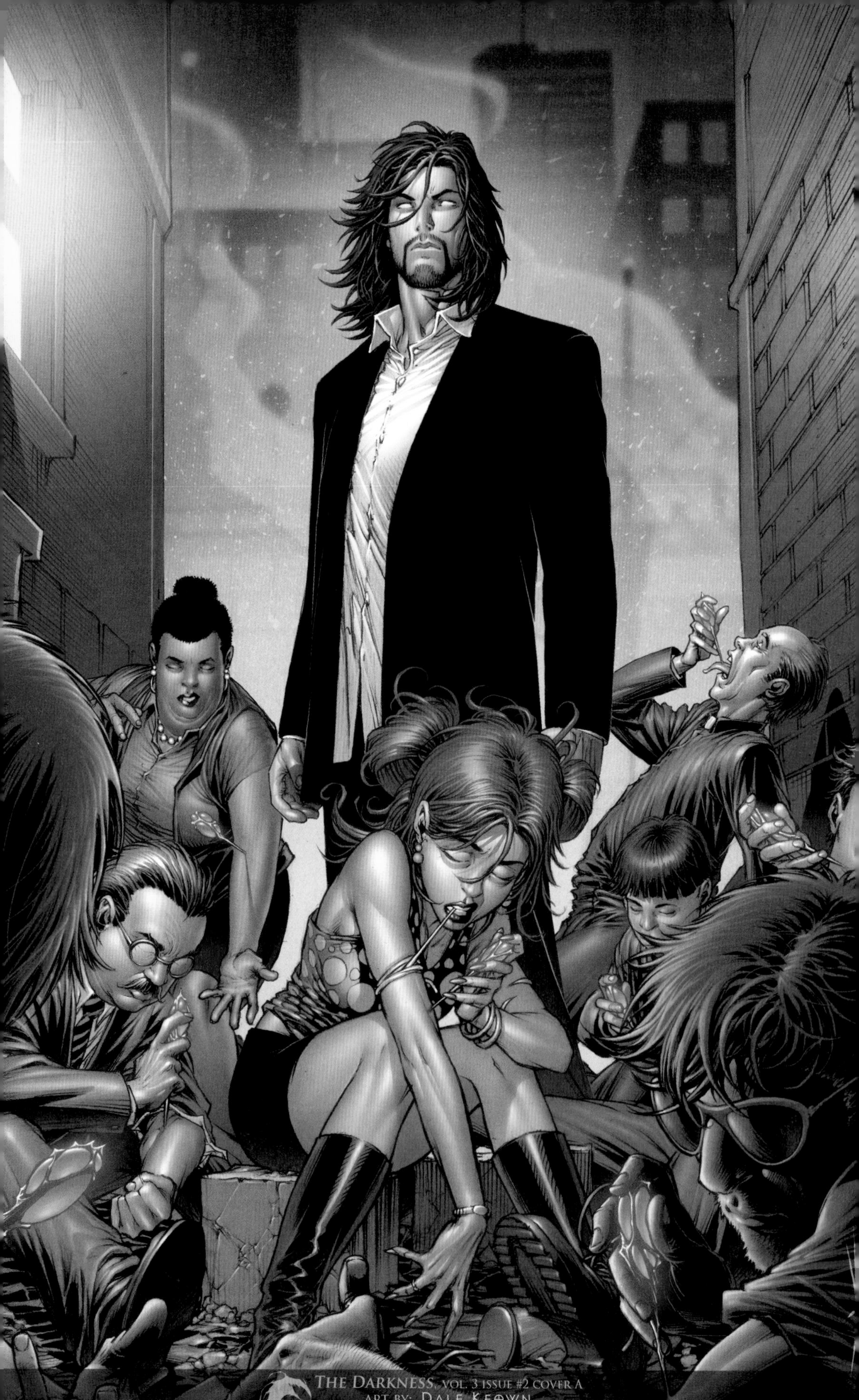

THE DARKNESS, VOL. 3 ISSUE #2 COVER A
ART BY: DALE KEOWN

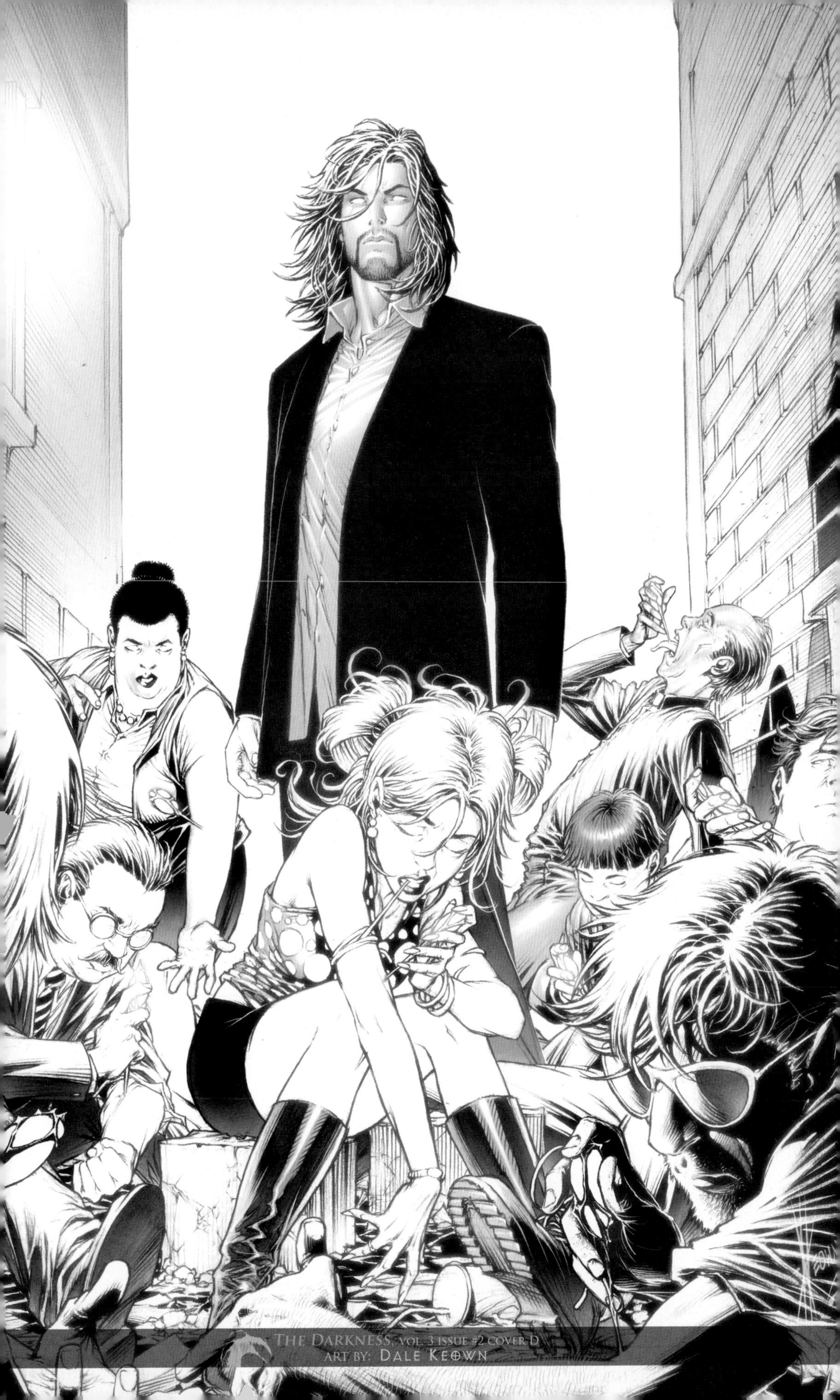

THE DARKNESS, VOL. 3 ISSUE #2 COVER D
ART BY: DALE KEOWN

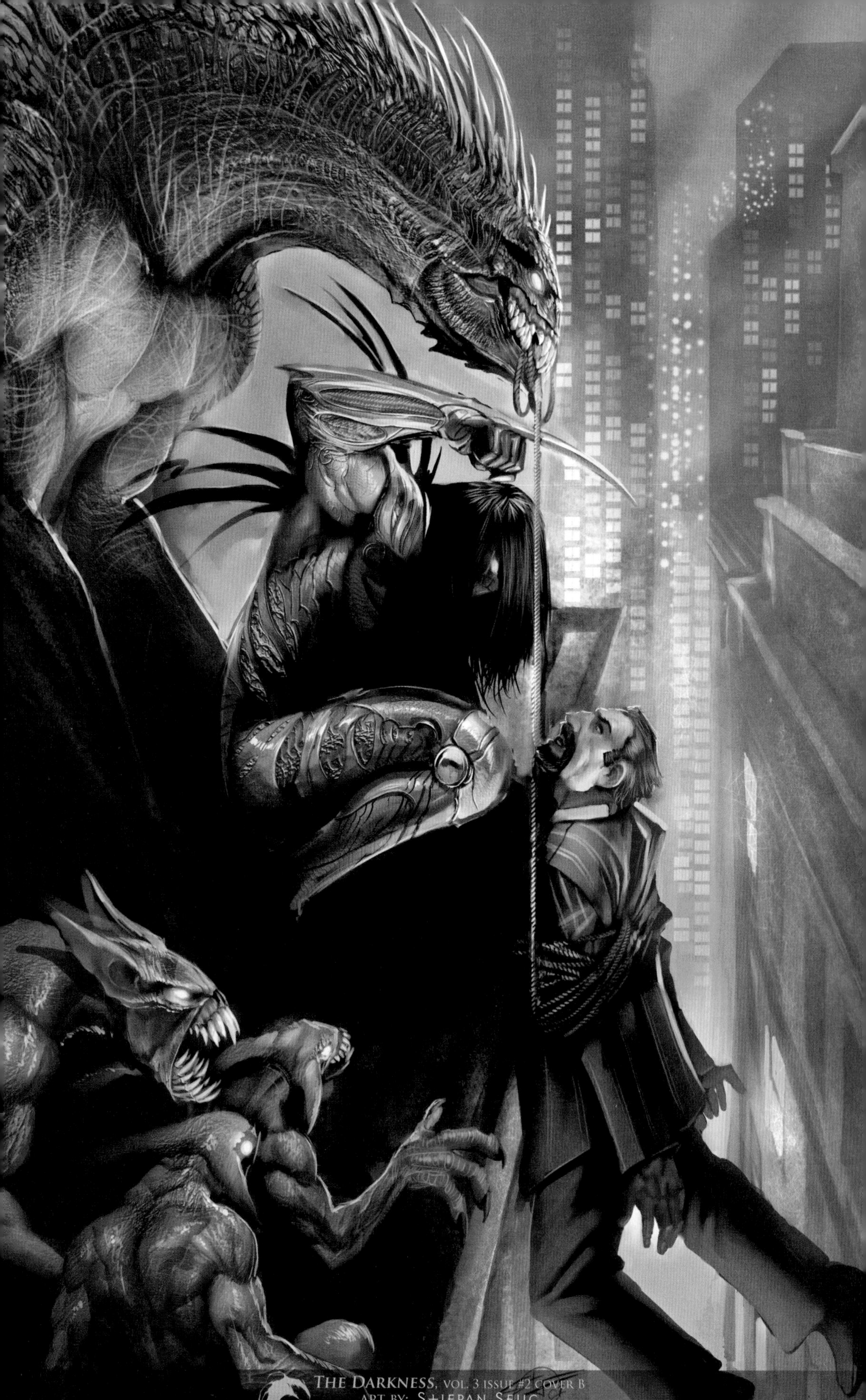

THE DARKNESS, VOL. 3 ISSUE #2 COVER B
ART BY: STJEPAN SEJIC

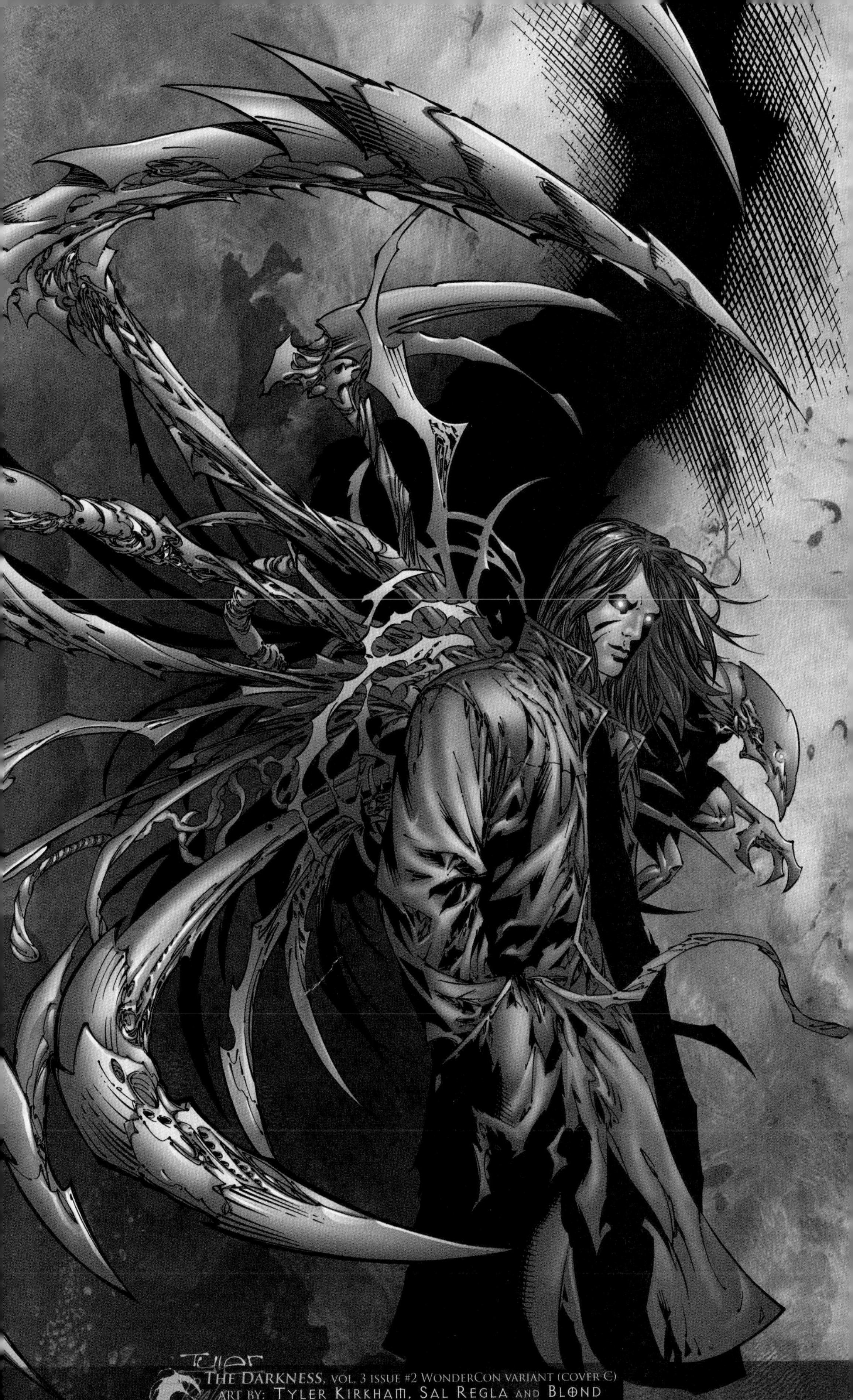
Tyler
BLOND

THE DARKNESS, VOL. 3 ISSUE #2 WONDERCON VARIANT (COVER C)
ART BY: TYLER KIRKHAM, SAL REGLA AND BLOND

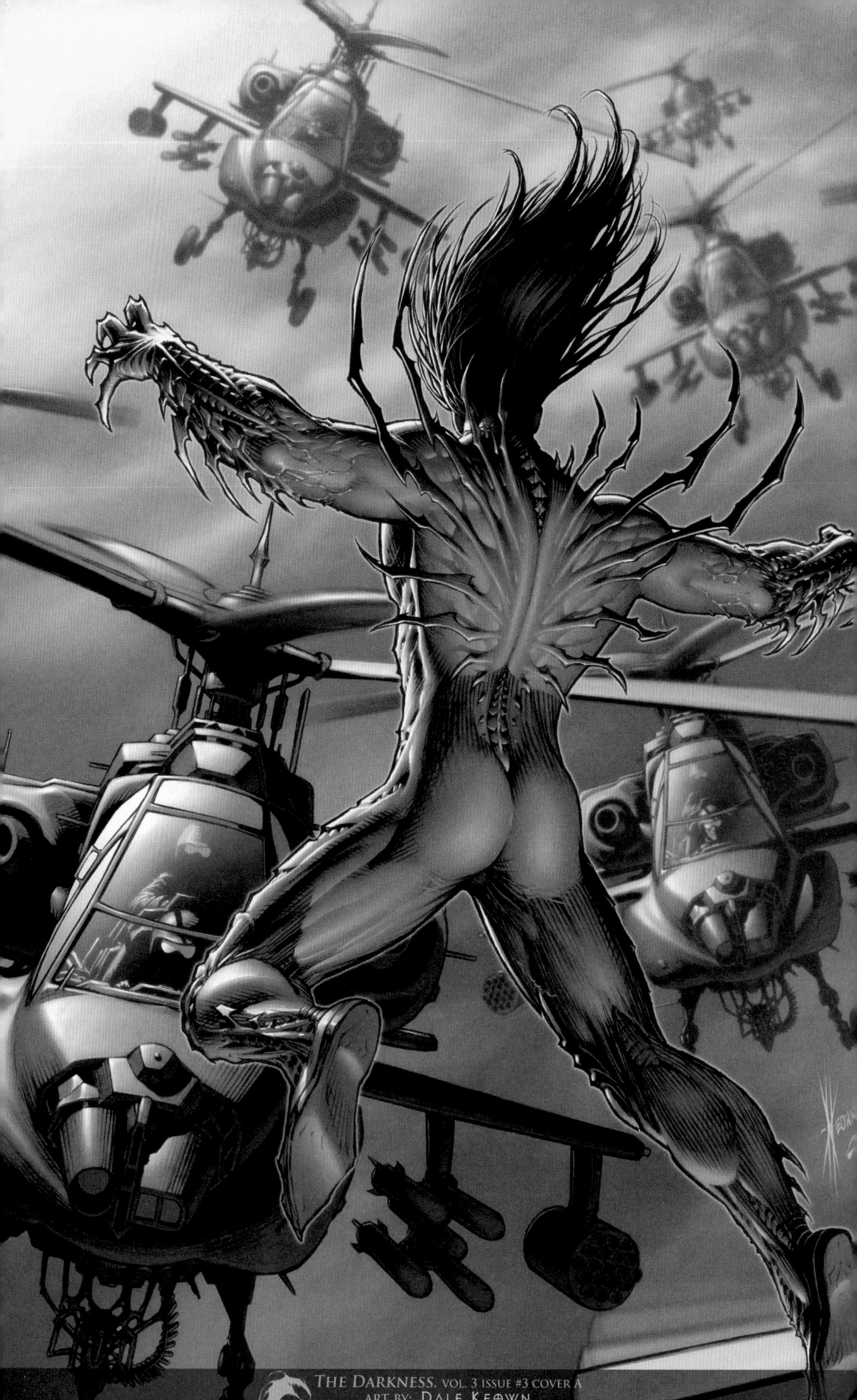

THE DARKNESS, VOL. 3 ISSUE #3 COVER A
ART BY: DALE KEOWN

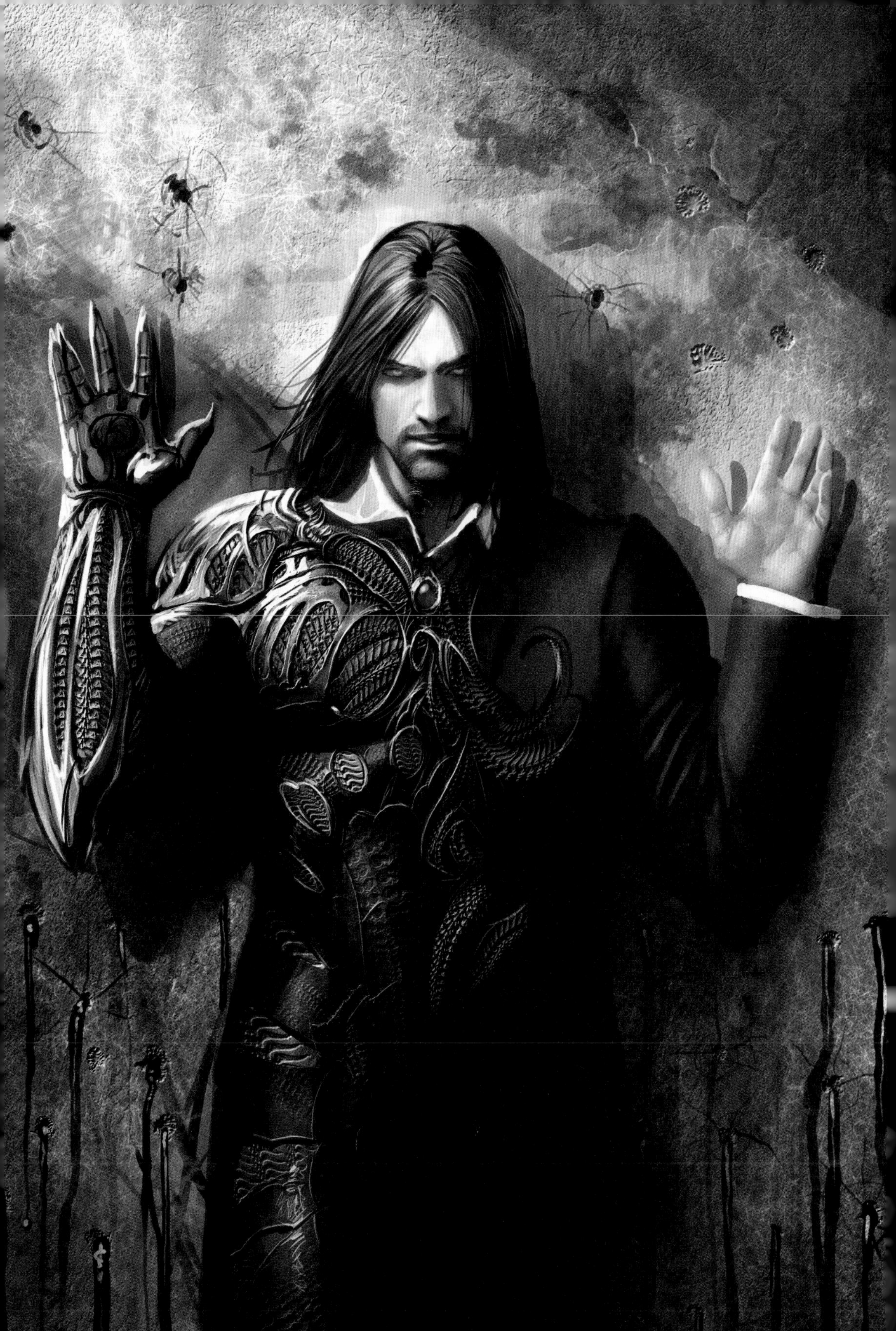

THE DARKNESS, VOL. 3 ISSUE #3 COVER B
ART BY: S+|EPAN SE|IC

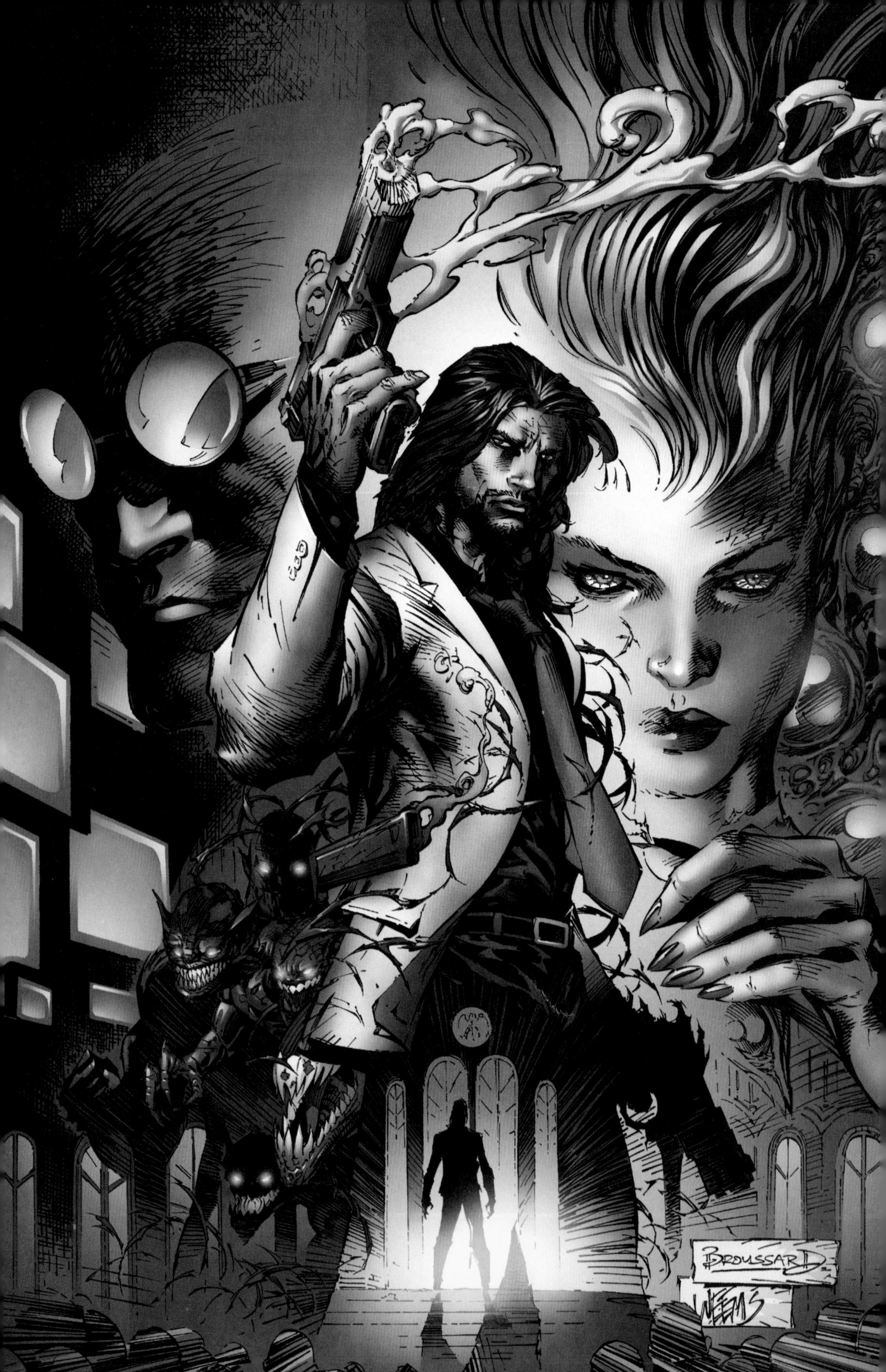

BROUSSARD
WEEMS

THE DARKNESS, VOL. 3 ISSUE #3 NEW YORK COMIC CON VARIANT (COVER C)
ART BY: MICHAEL BROUSSARD, JOE WEEMS V AND MATT MILLA

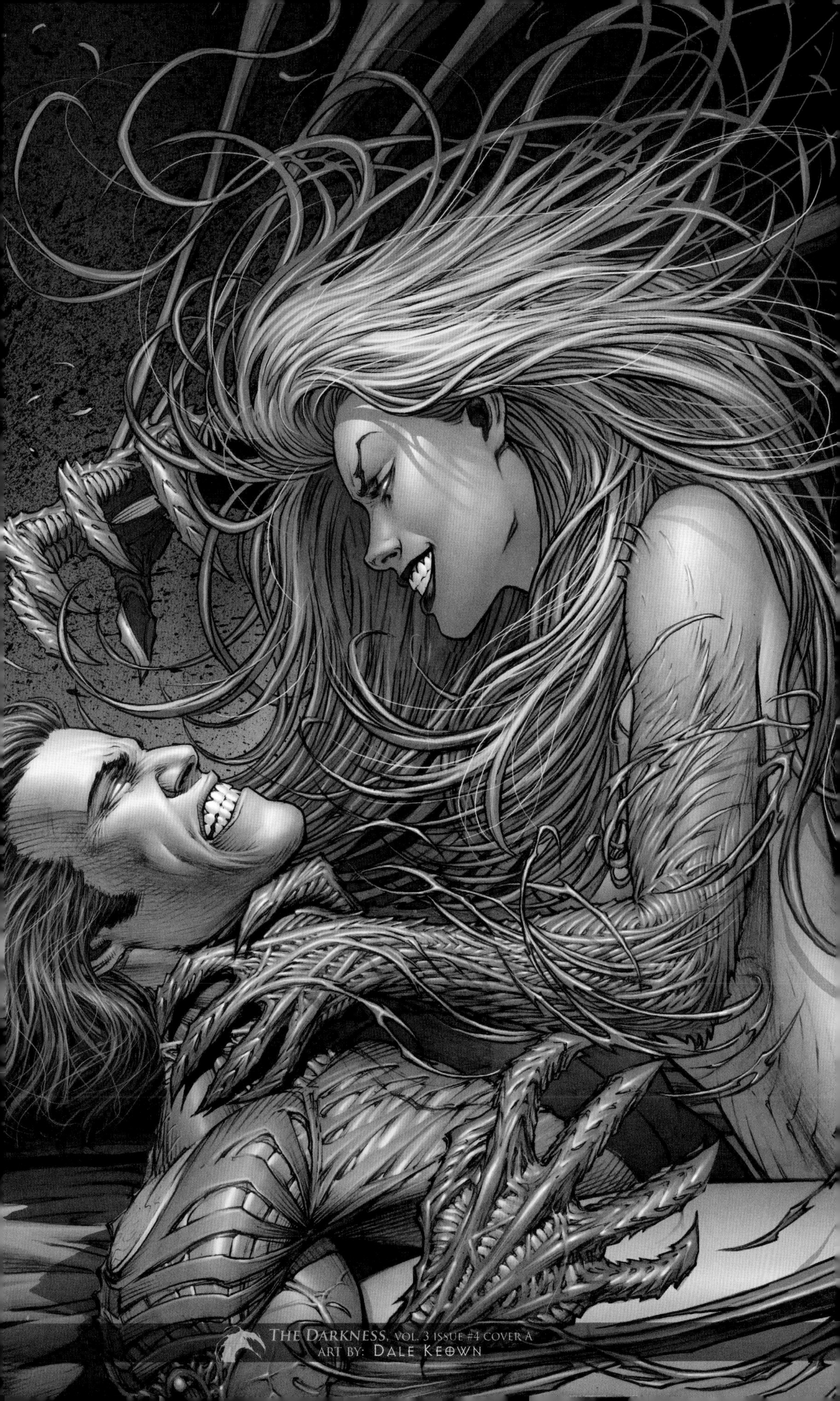

THE DARKNESS, VOL. 3 ISSUE #4 COVER A
ART BY: DALE KEOWN

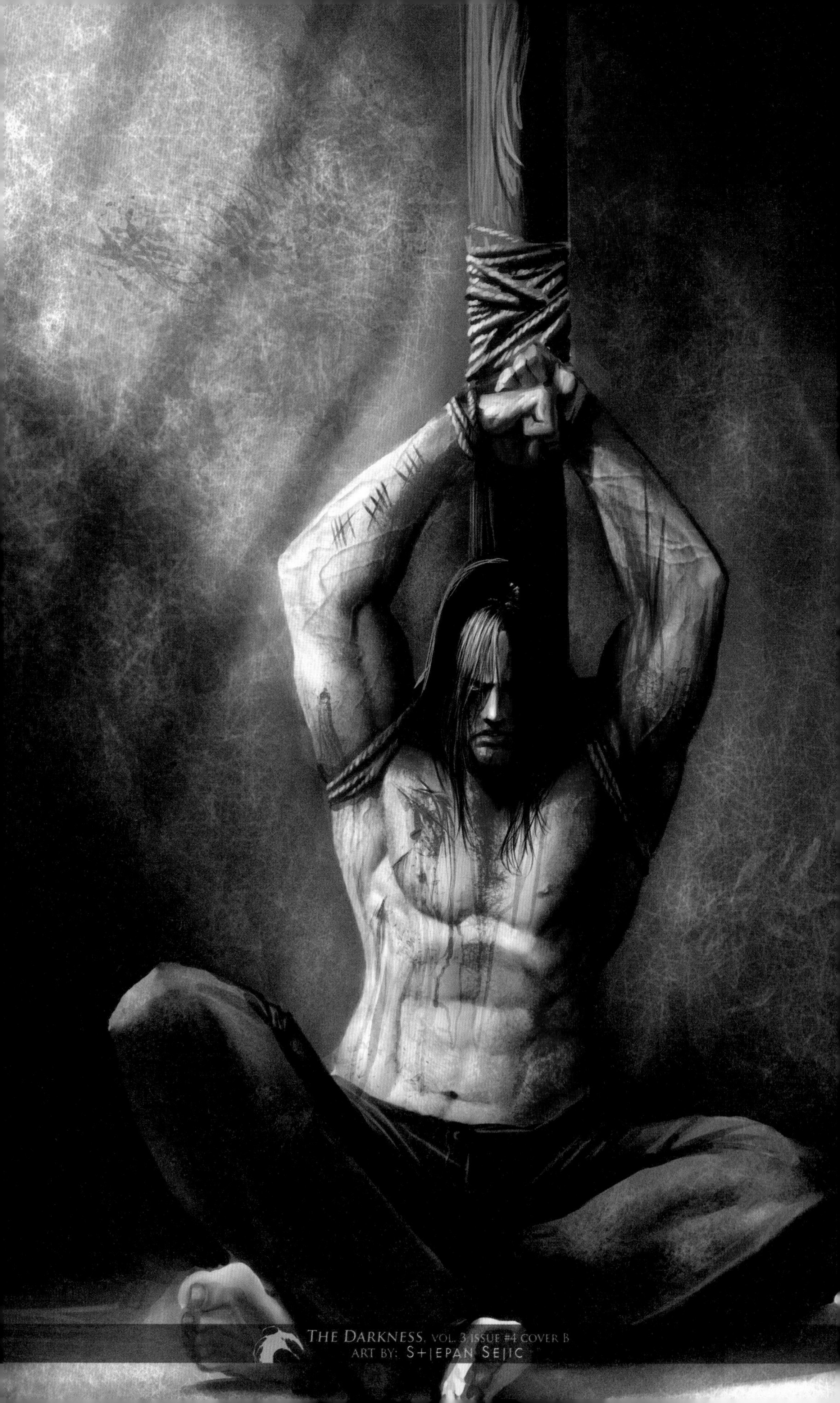

THE DARKNESS, VOL. 3 ISSUE #4 COVER B
ART BY: STJEPAN SEJIC

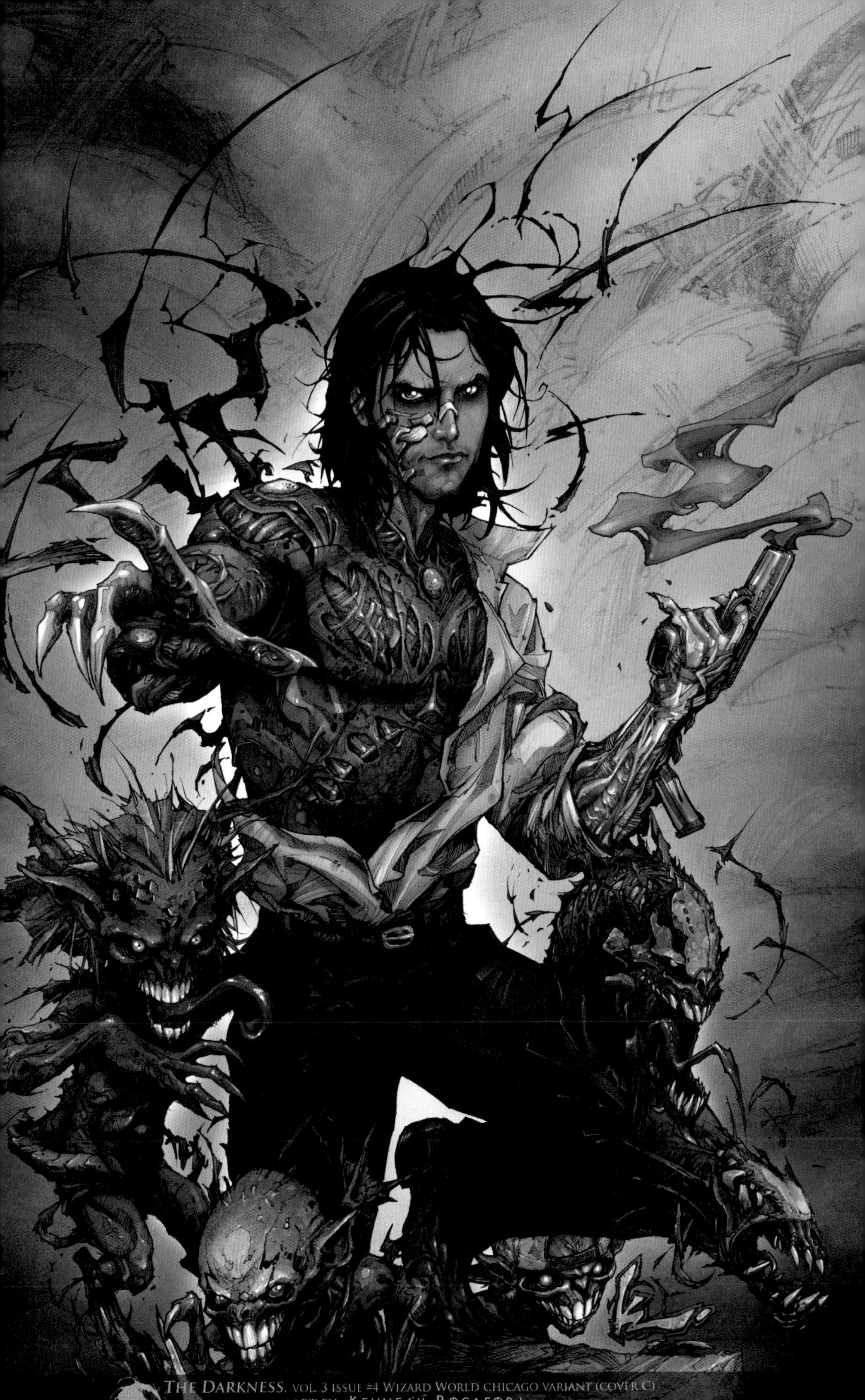

THE DARKNESS. VOL. 3 ISSUE #4 WIZARD WORLD CHICAGO VARIANT (COVER C)
ART BY: KENNETH ROCAFORT

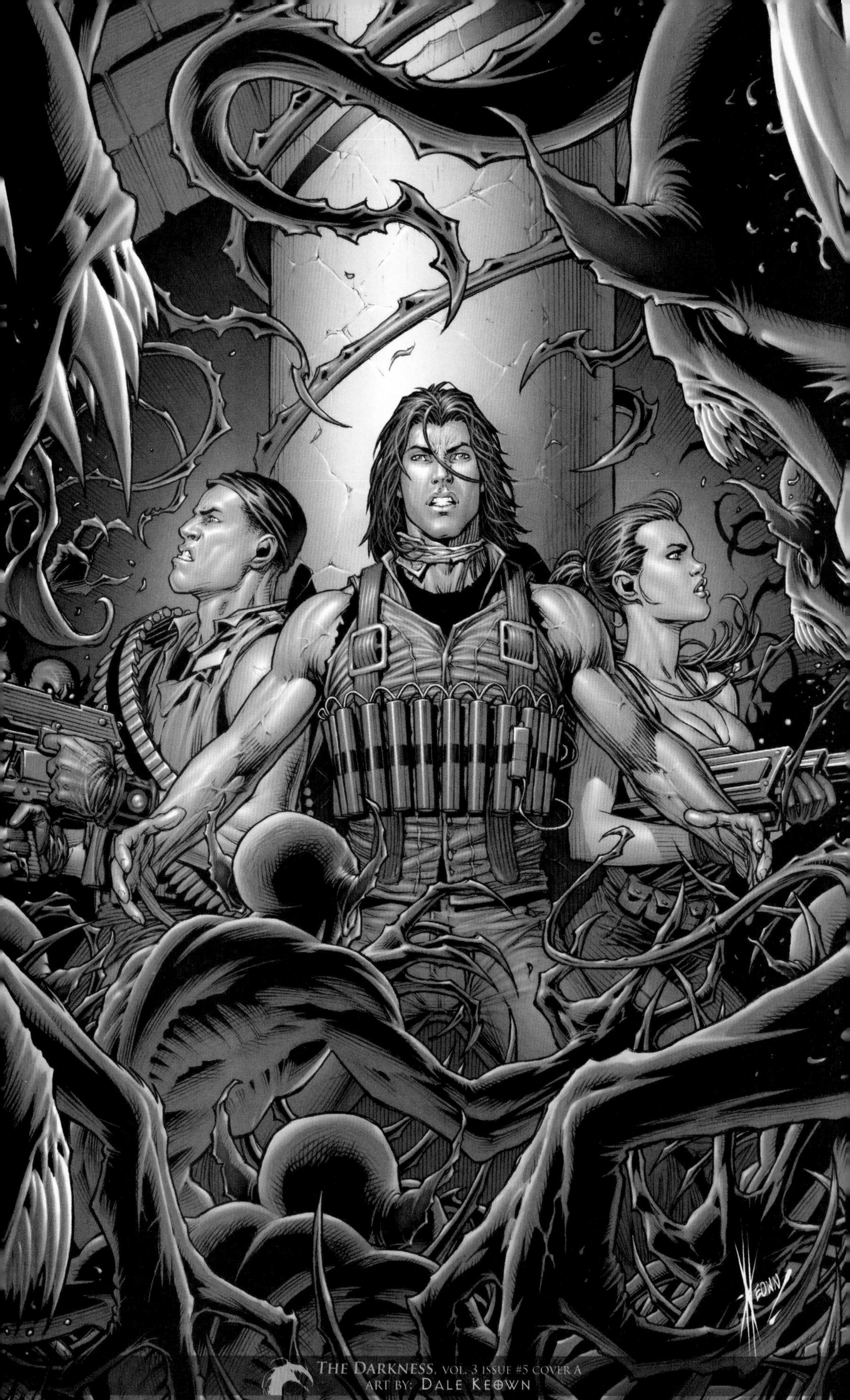
KEOWN

THE DARKNESS, VOL. 3 ISSUE #5 COVER A
ART BY: DALE KEOWN

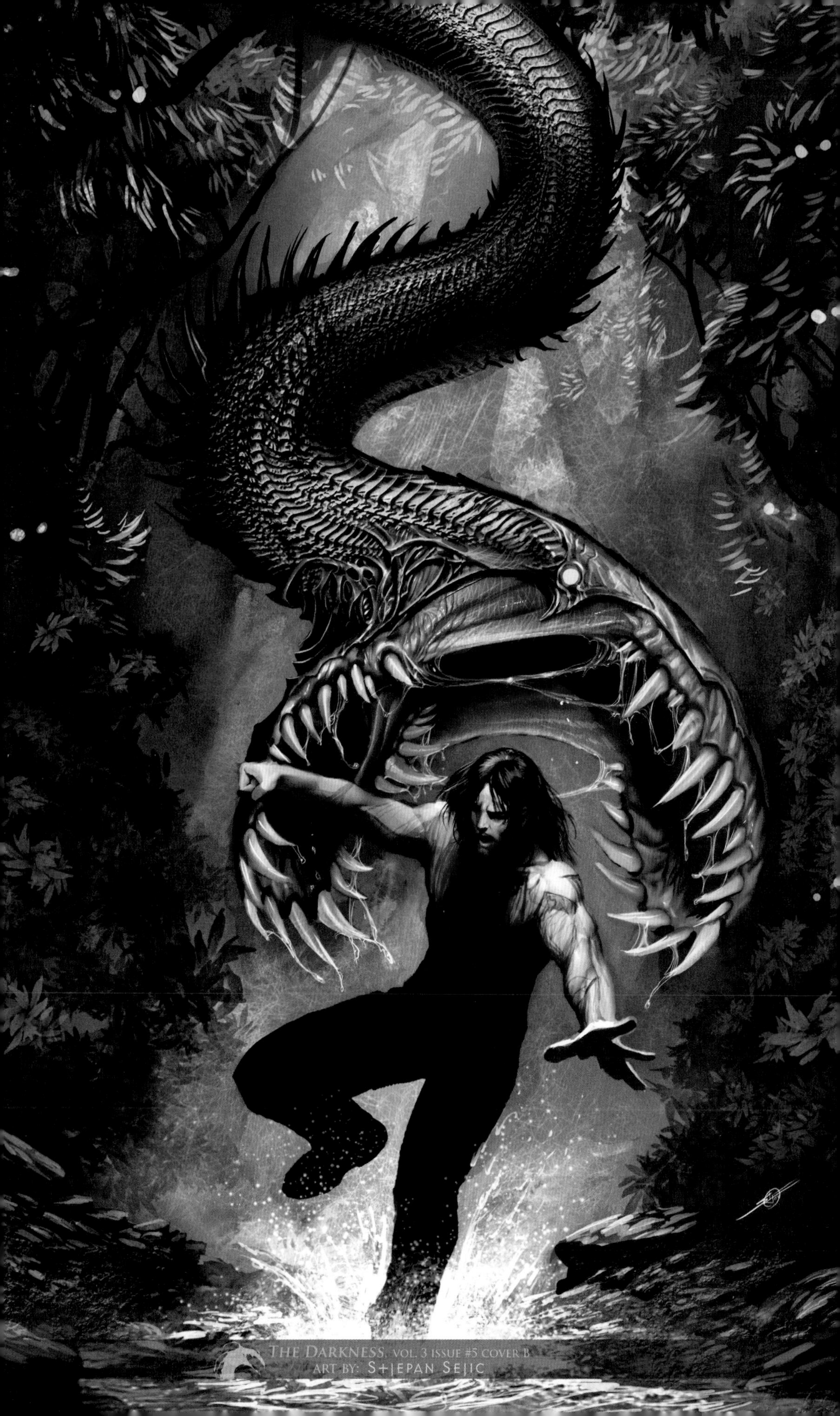

THE DARKNESS, VOL. 3 ISSUE #5 COVER B
ART BY: STJEPAN SEJIC

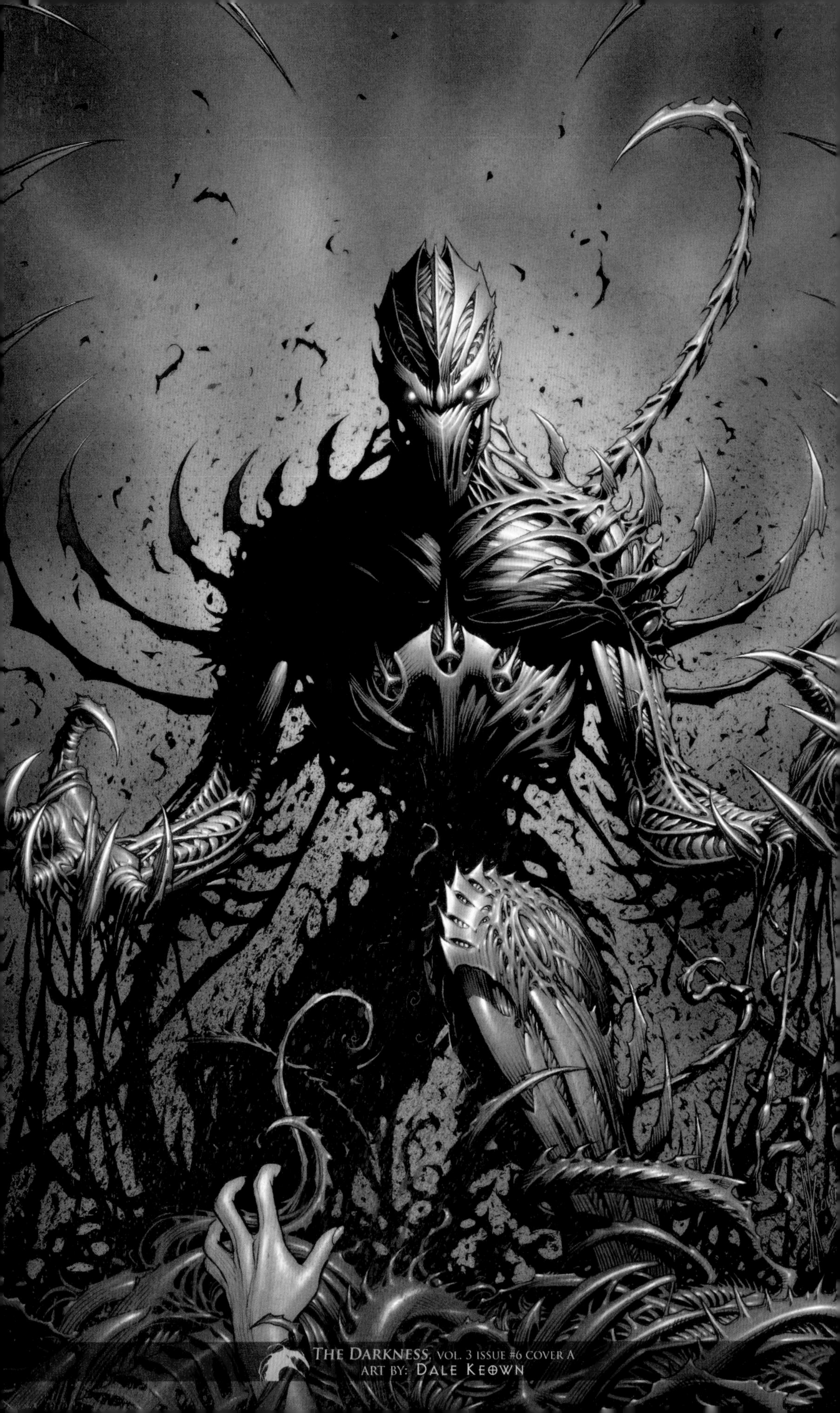

THE DARKNESS, VOL. 3 ISSUE #6 COVER A
ART BY: DALE KEOWN

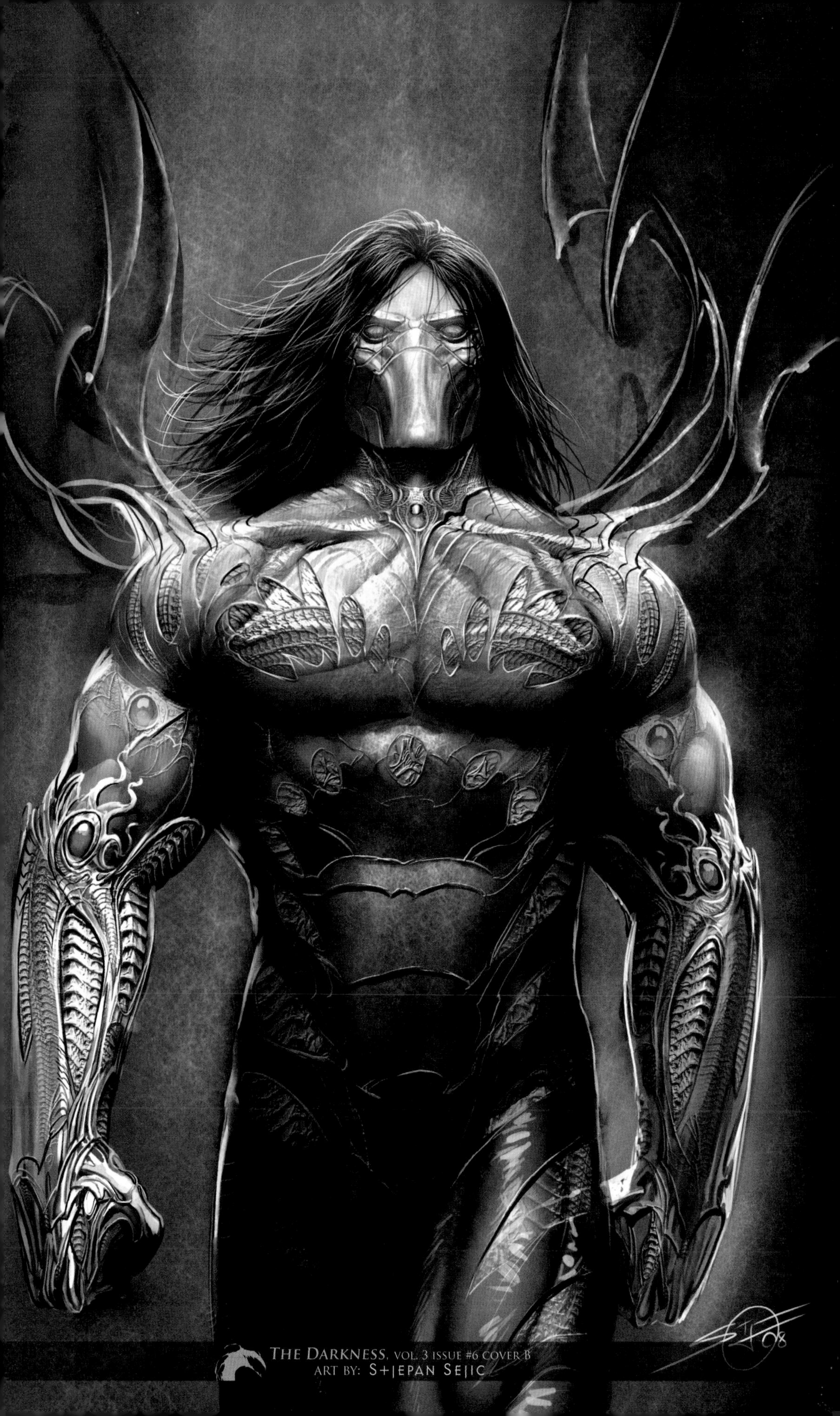

THE DARKNESS, VOL. 3 ISSUE #6 COVER B
ART BY: STJEPAN SEJIC

BONUS MATERIALS

On the following pages take a tour of the making of *The Darkness: Accursed* vol. 1 with sketches, cover progression and a behind the scenes look with Michael Broussard on how the story and the art came together.

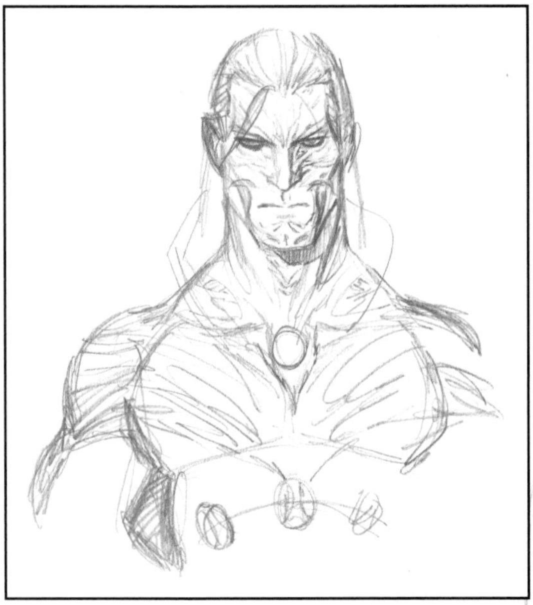

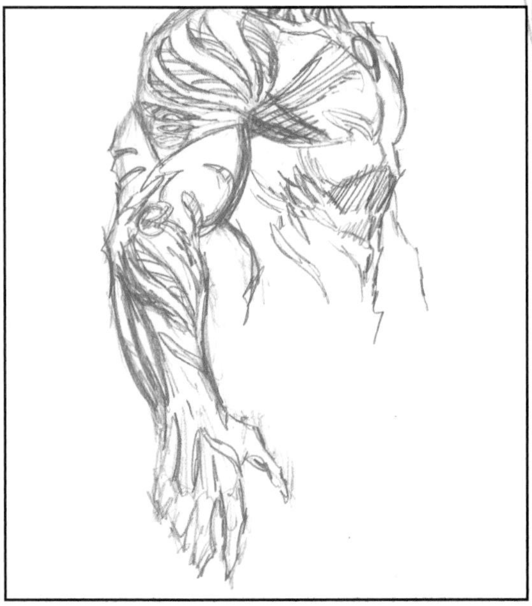

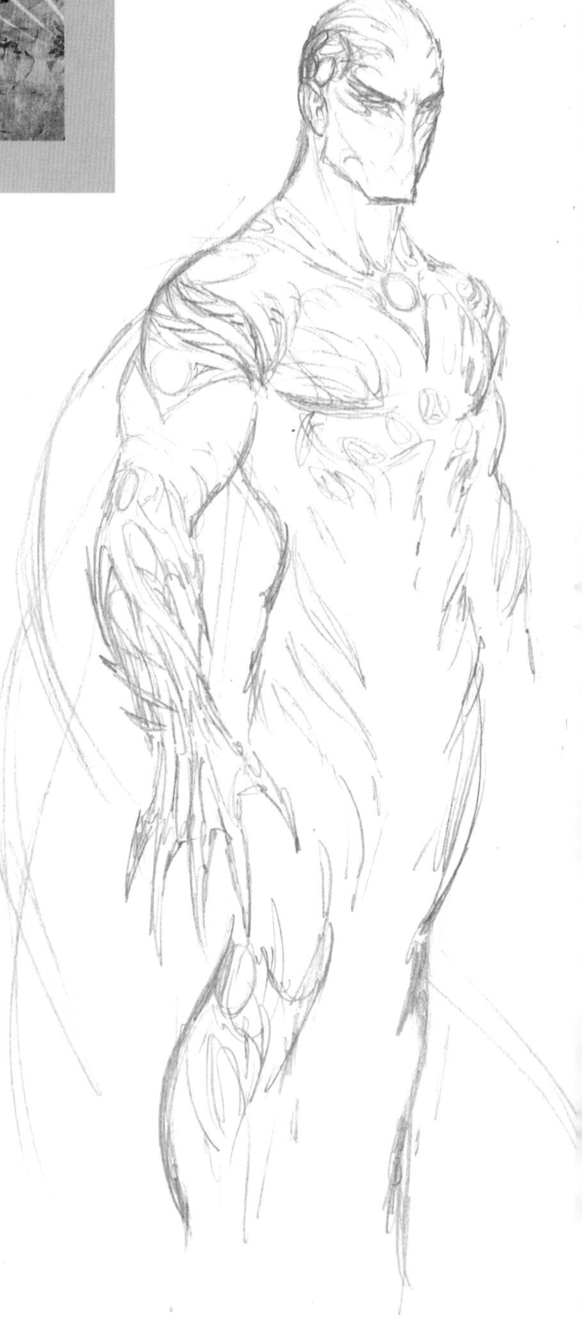

Character designs by **Michael Broussard**

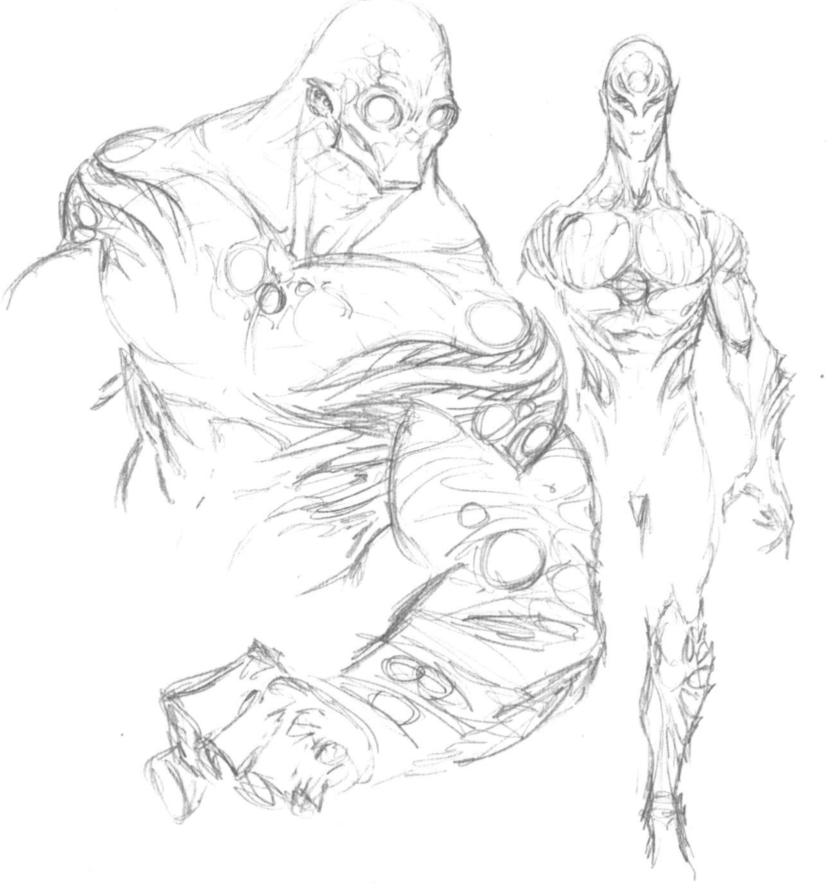

Character designs by
Michael Broussard

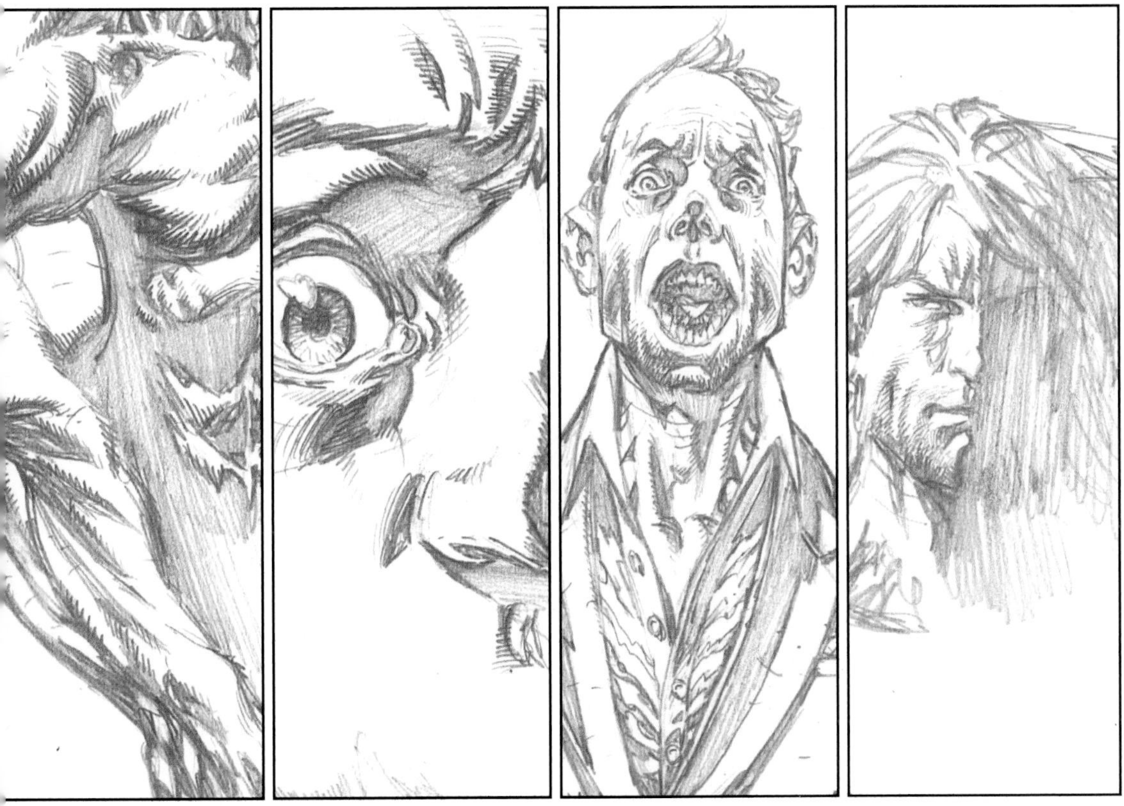

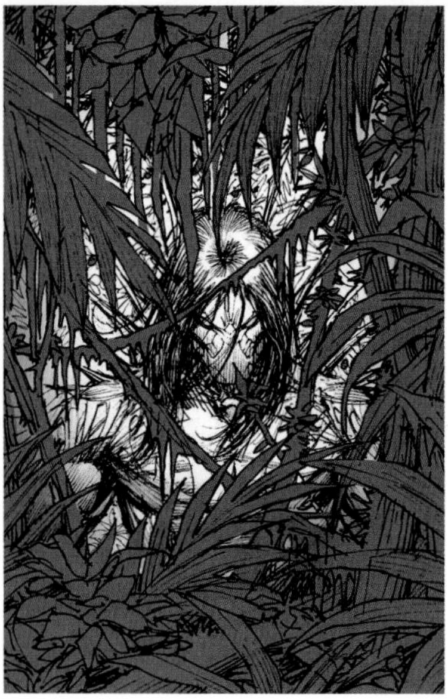

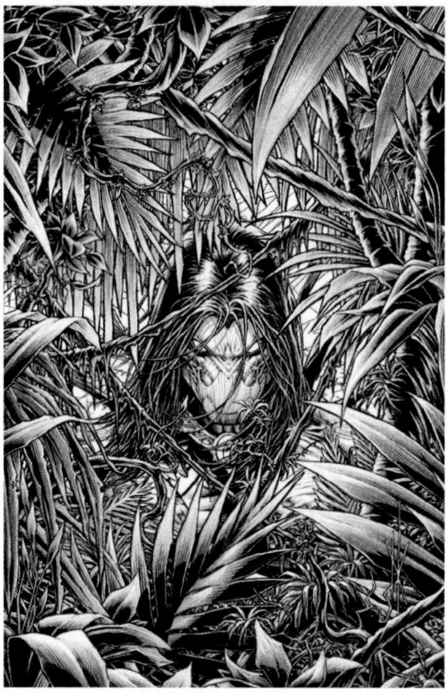

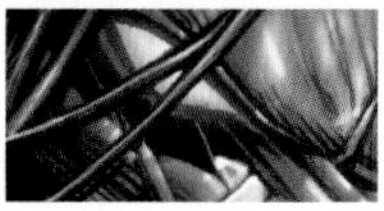

issue #1 cover B

sketch/value rough
inks/value render
final

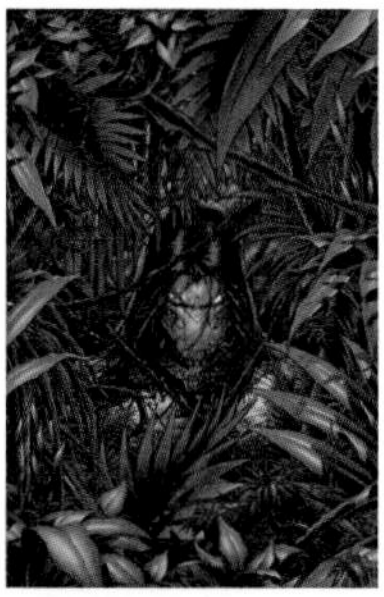

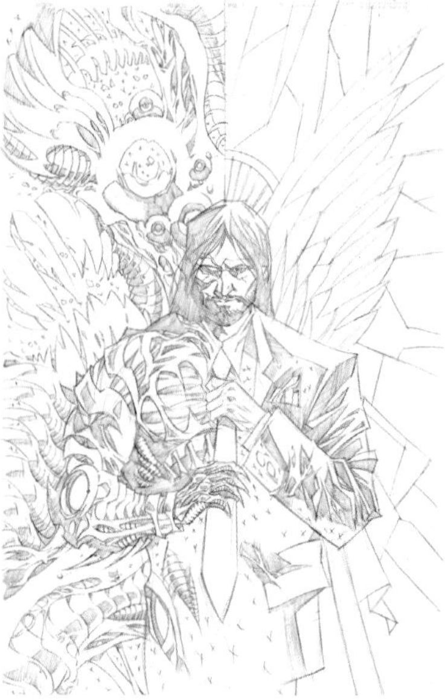

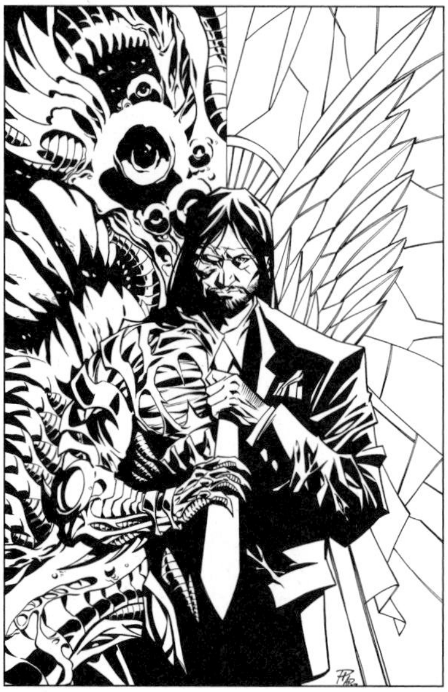

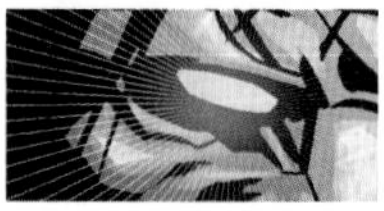

issue #1 variant

pencils
inks
final

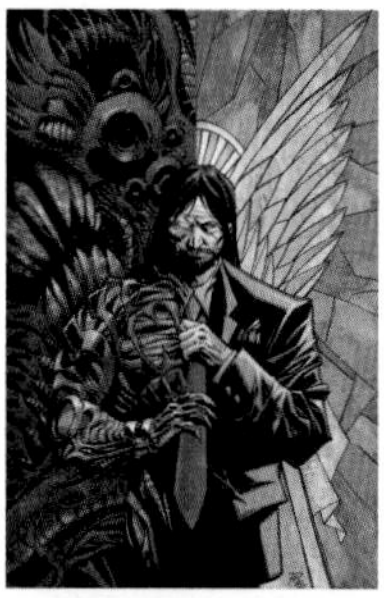

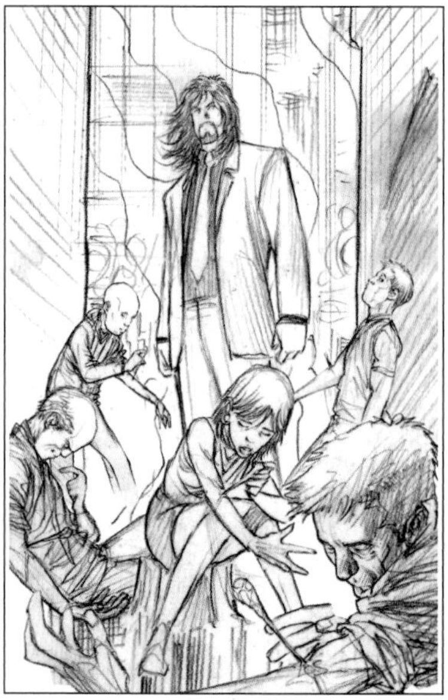

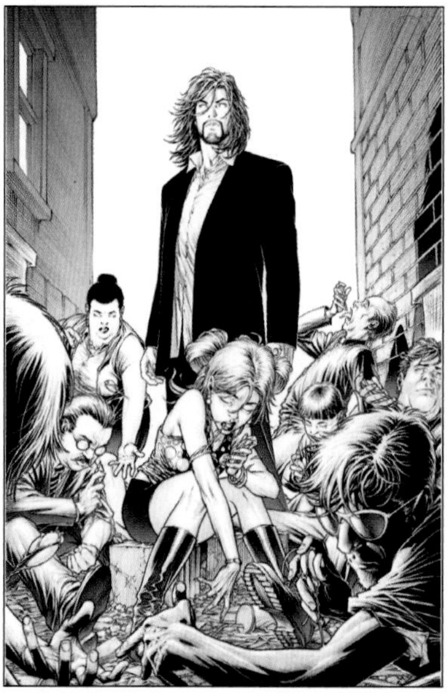

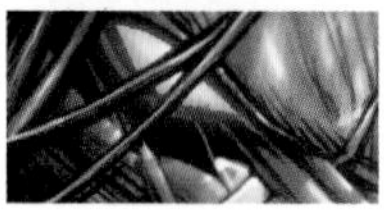

issue #2 cover A

sketch rough
inks/value render
final

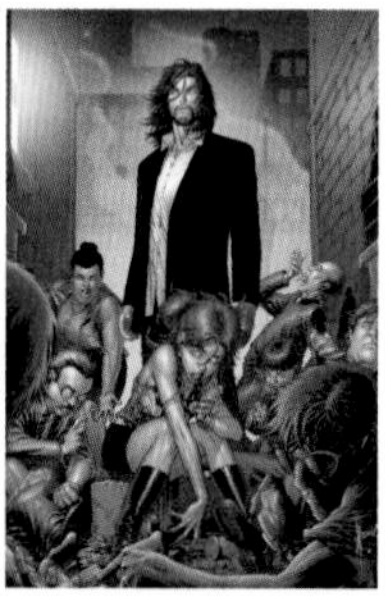

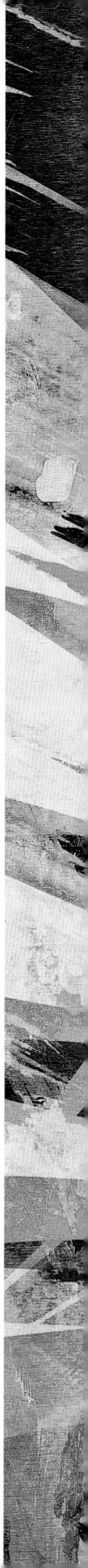

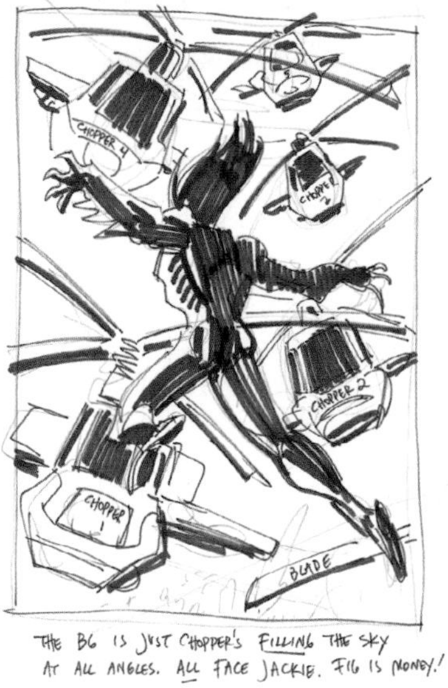
CHOPPER 4
CHOPPER 2
CHOPPER 1
BLADE
THE B6 IS JUST CHOPPER'S FILLING THE SKY AT ALL ANGLES. ALL FACE JACKIE. FIG IS MONEY!

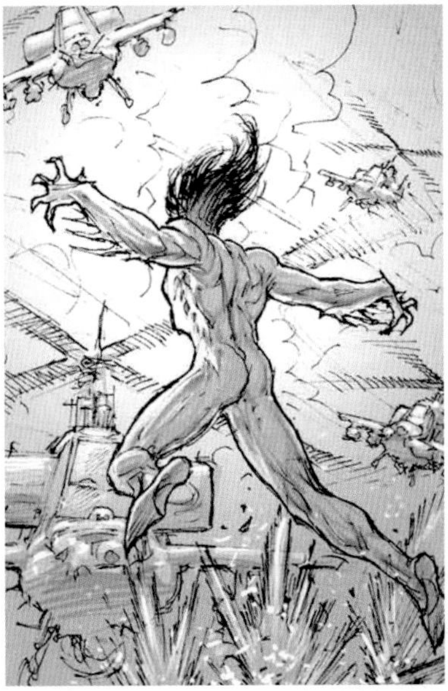

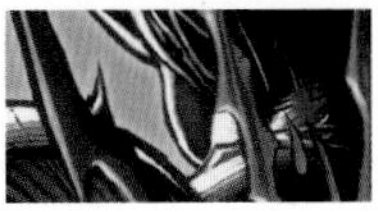

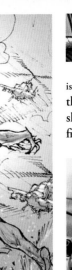

issue #3 cover A
thumbnail rough
sketch rough
final

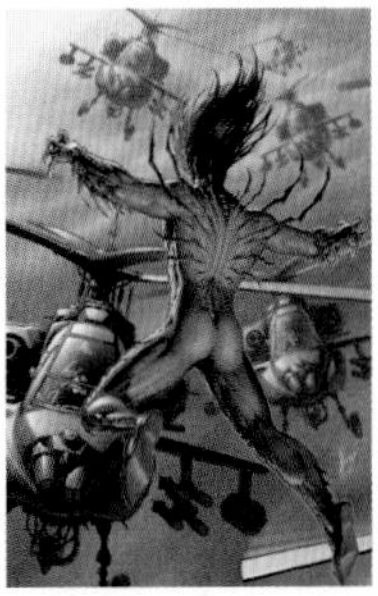

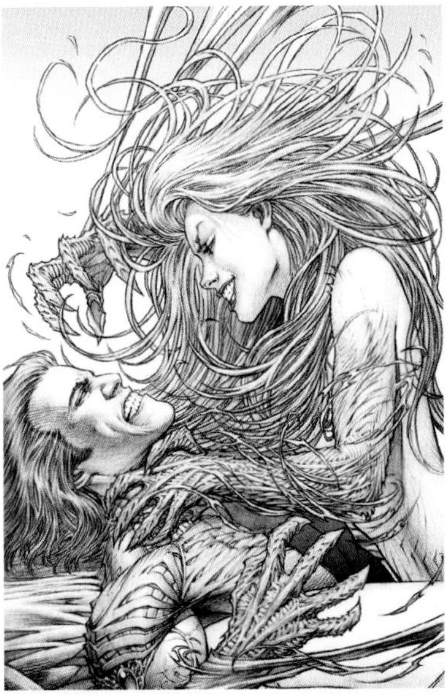

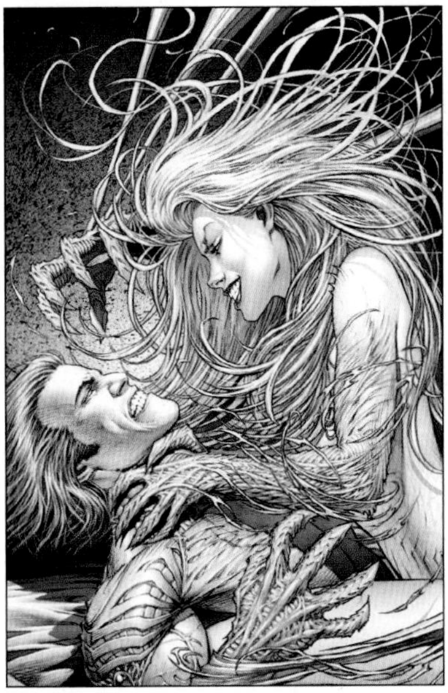

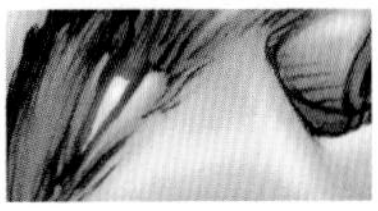

issue #4 variant
tone render
value render
final

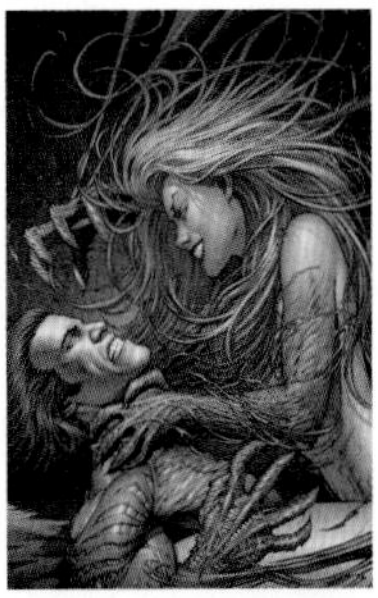

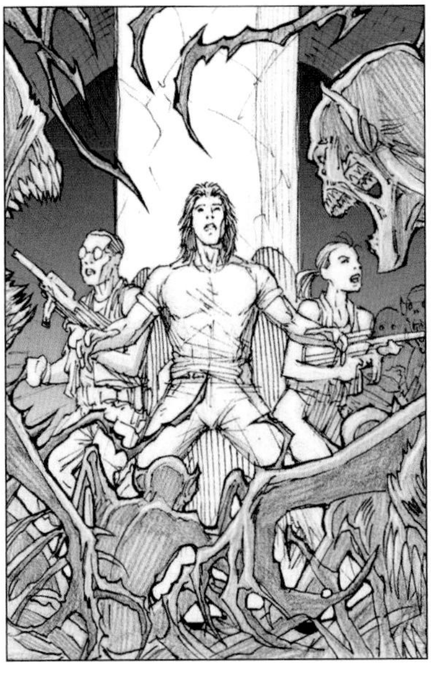

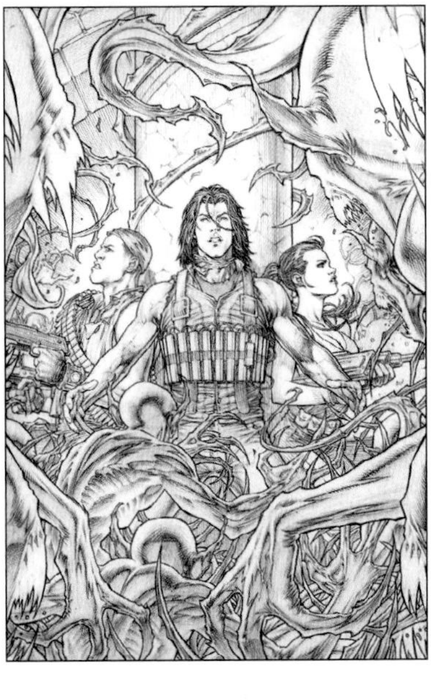

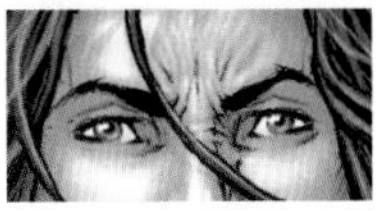

issue #5 cover A
sketch rough
pencils
final

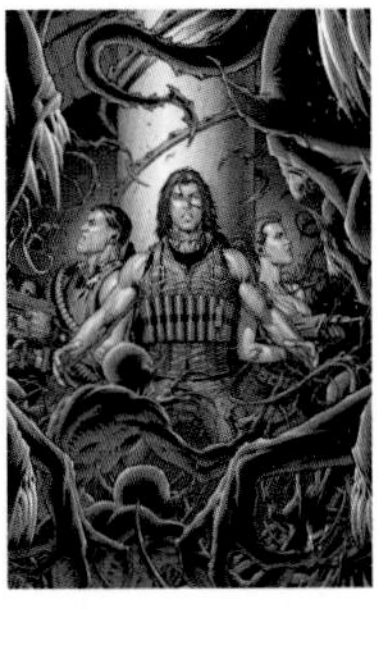

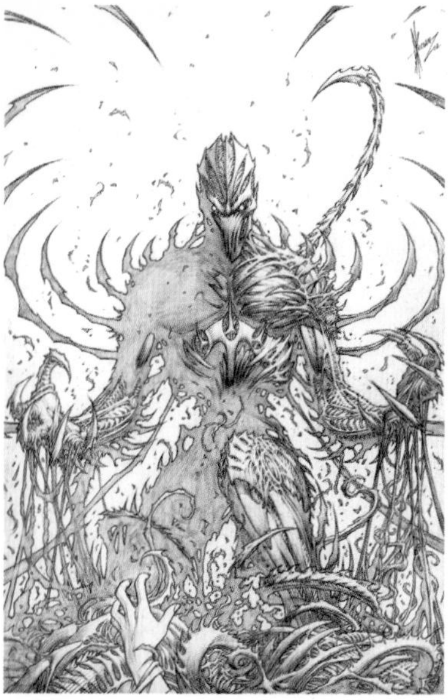

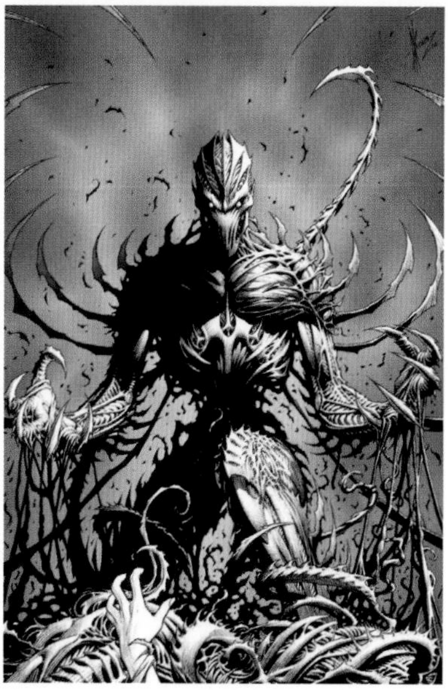

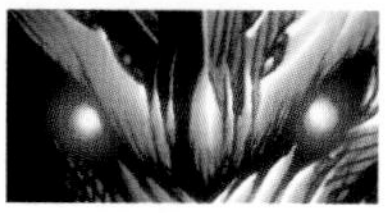

issue #6 cover A

pencils
inks/value render
final

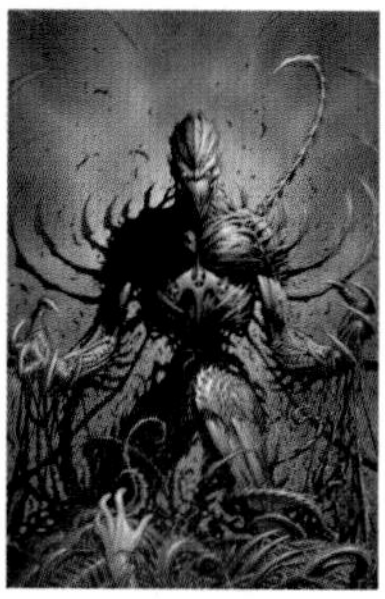

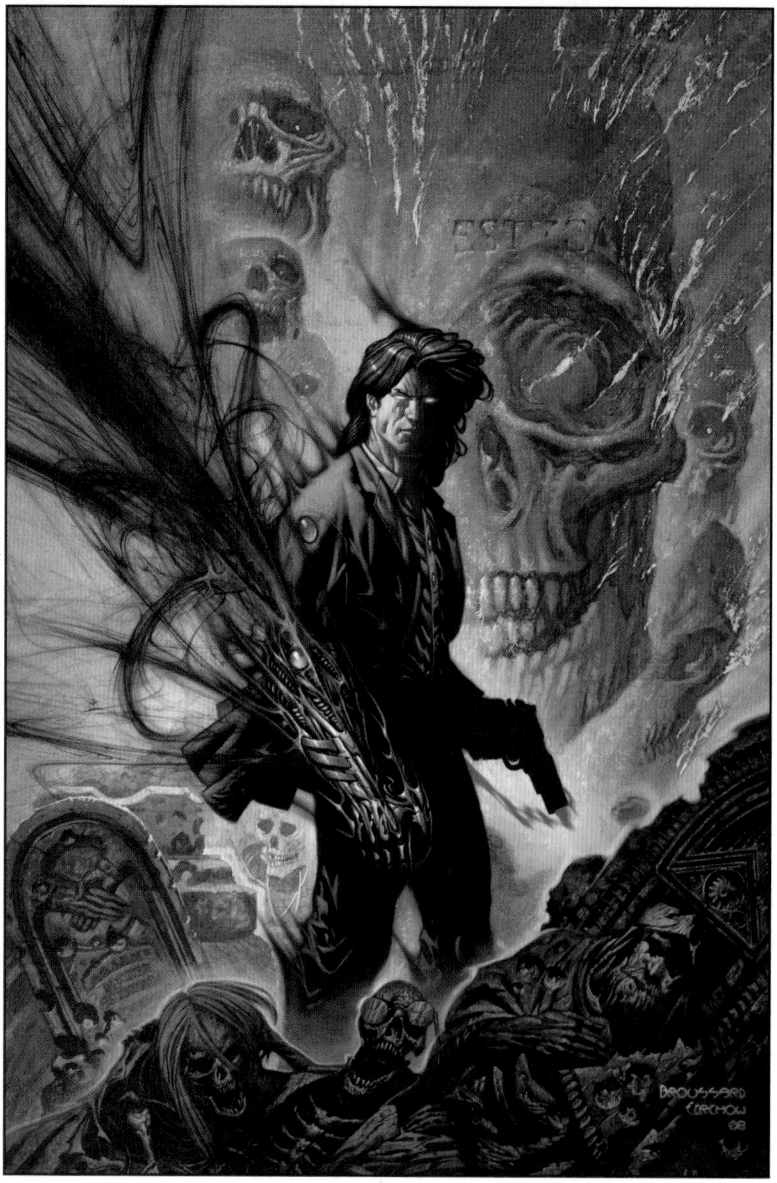

"Accursed" vol. 1 cover

left
final

facing page
pencils

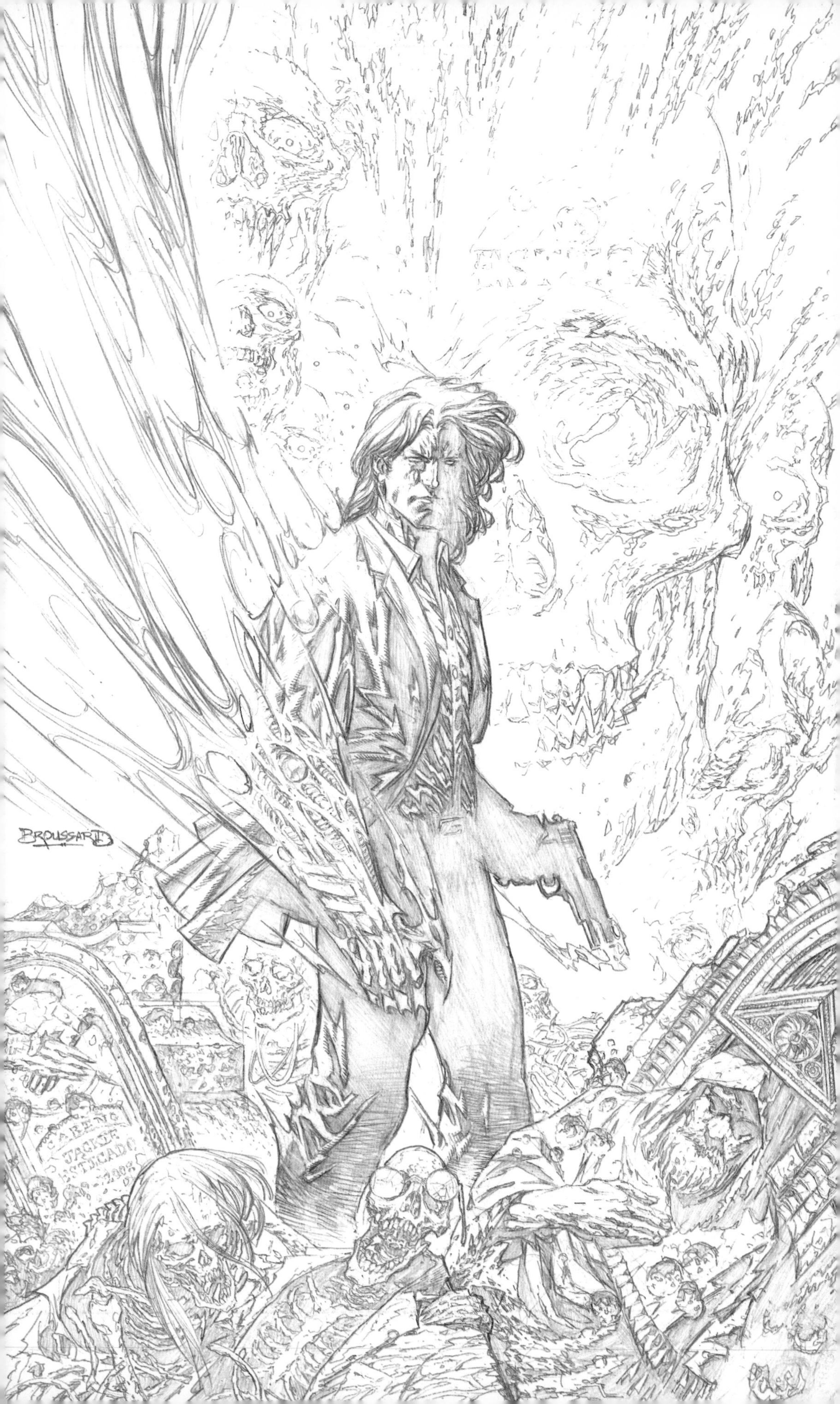
BROUSSARD
JACKIE

SCRIPT TO PAGE

On the followiung pages take a walk through a few of the panels from *The Darkness: Accursed* vol. 1 with writer Phil Hester and artist Michael Broussard

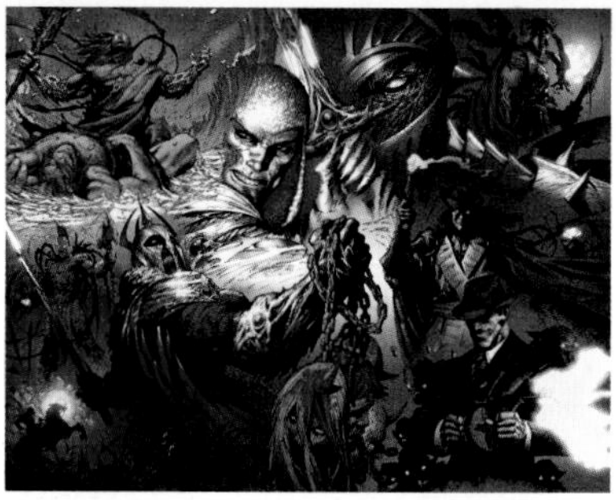

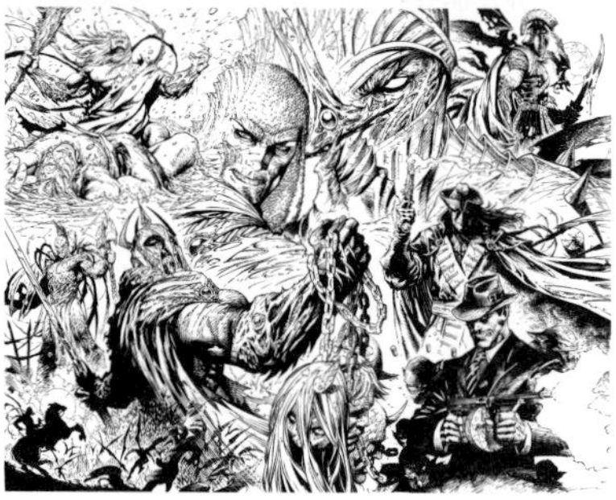

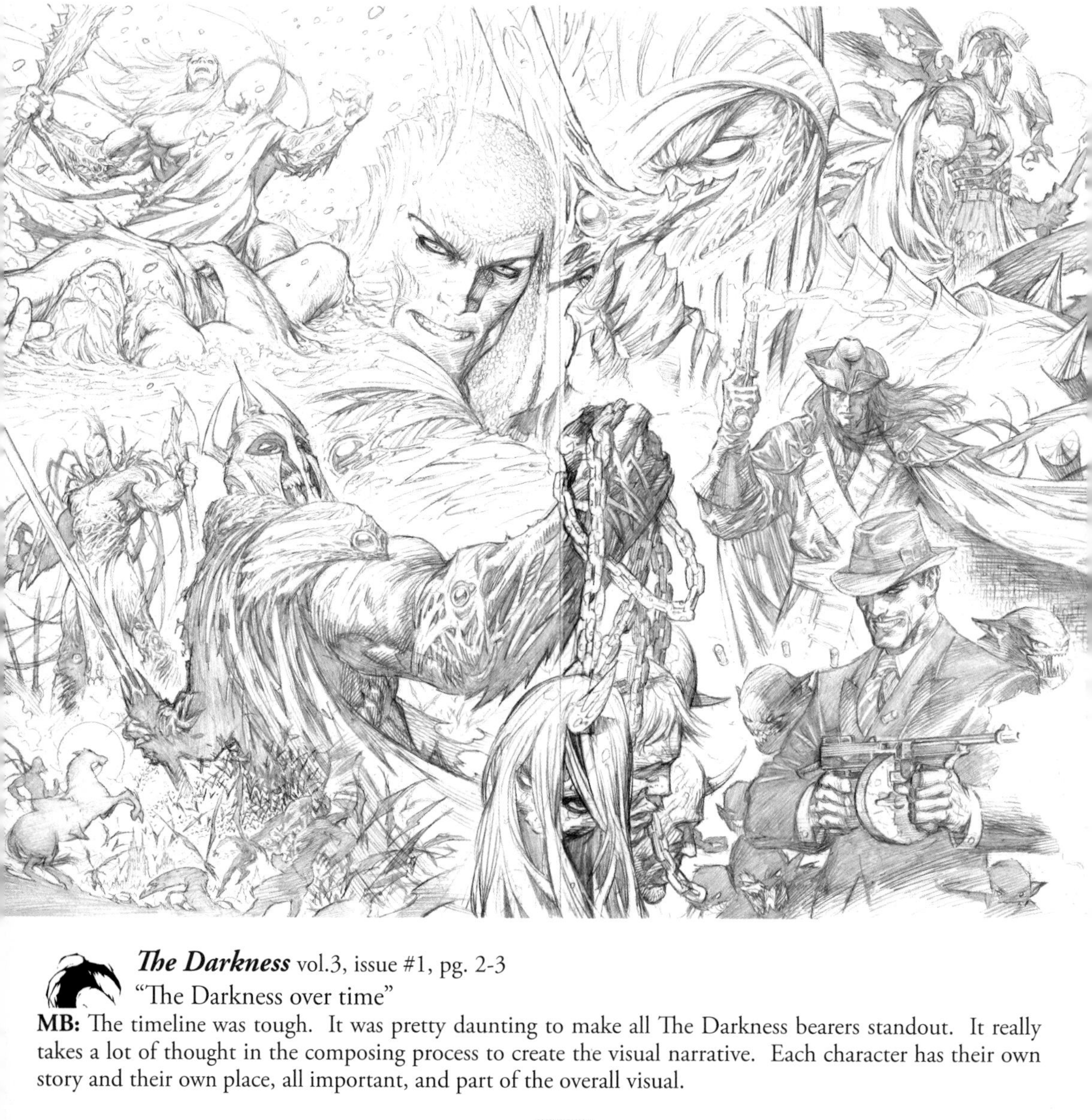

The Darkness vol.3, issue #1, pg. 2-3
"The Darkness over time"

MB: The timeline was tough. It was pretty daunting to make all The Darkness bearers standout. It really takes a lot of thought in the composing process to create the visual narrative. Each character has their own story and their own place, all important, and part of the overall visual.

DARKNESS #1 PAGE TWENTY-FOUR
Caprio finds himself trapped in a Darkness labyrinth. He is attacked and killed by the frightening new Darklings.

PAN 1
1 OFF PANEL CAPTION KIRCHNER: "There's been an opening."

2 CAPRIO: The hell?

PAN 2
3 CAPRIO: Joke's over, Kirchner!

4 ATT CAPRIO: Kirchner, open up!

PAN 3
5 CAPRIO: Oh, God. Is that you, Estacado?

6 DARKLING 1: You should be so lucky.

PAN 4
7 CAPRIO: Stay back!

8 SFX: BLAM! BLAM! BLAM!

PAN 5
9 DARKLING 1: That's not very hospitable. The slugs do make a nice appetizer, though.

10 DARKLING 2: Would you look at that pinky ring? The sight of those things always makes me hungry.

PAN 6
11 DARKLING 2: It's been so long...

PAN 7
12 DARKLING 2: ... since I've had decent Italian.

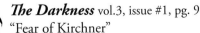

The Darkness vol.3, issue #1, pg. 24, panel 5
"The Money Shot"

MB: Here I choose to blow the image up although it was not in the script to give the page a focus or "money shot." The idea is similar to a splash page, not every page can be a splash, but each page should have its own flow with highs and lows. Having the money shot also helps to establish turning points in story or action. Phil Hester in addition to being a great writer is also a great artist and leaves you the room you need to deliver an exciting page.

PH: I felt very guilty trying to cram so much action into one scene, but in #1 is was so important to get to that last page in the space allowed that I had to compress some stuff. Michael did such a flawless job with it that I'm pretty sure no one noticed the cramped quarters.

The Darkness vol.3, issue #1, pg. 9
"Fear of Kirchner"

MB: Here I tried to express the menace that Kirchner projects and the fear he instills in the people around him. I enjoy drawing people's emotions; it helps the storytelling and adds the subtext to the story.

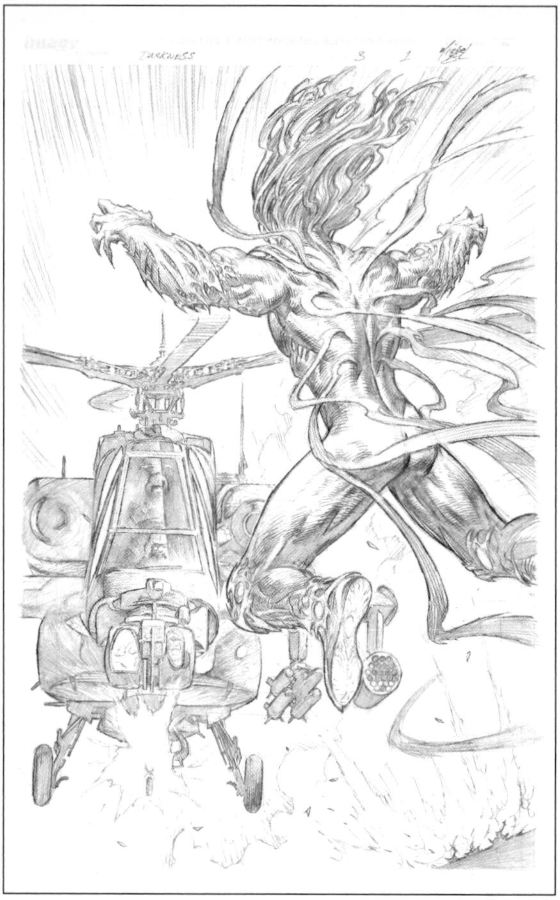

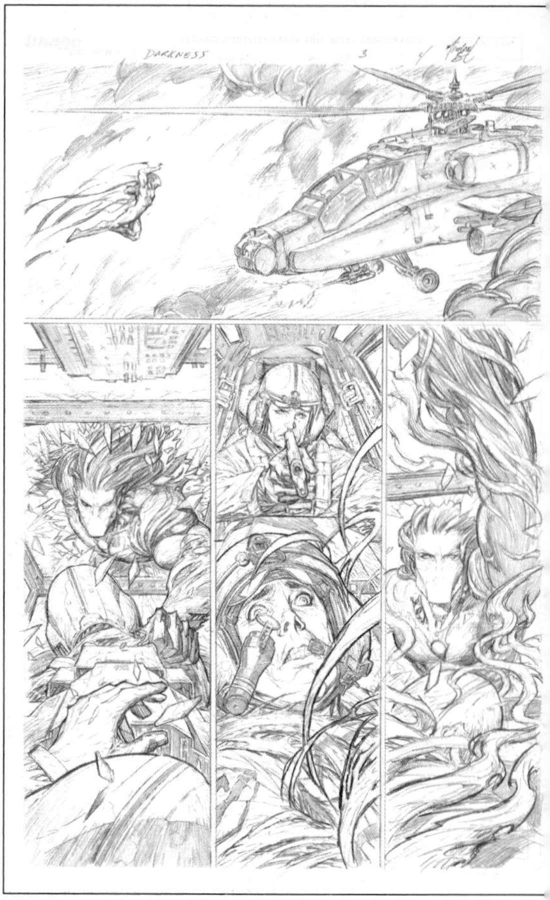

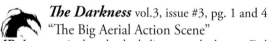

The Darkness vol.3, issue #3, pg. 1 and 4
"The Big Aerial Action Scene"

MB: I was excited to do the helicopter takedown. Dale did pages 2-3. I thought about how powerful the character really is, how he would use his power to take down the chopper. He uses his tentacles to jam the controls. As the character evolves we see new insights into his potential, more than just killing other human beings etc..

PH: This splash is actually one of the first images that came to me when I started the process of imagining my take on The Darkness. I felt we had never seen Jackie's powers on display on such a large, real world scale, and the image of him just leaping into the jaws of a bunch of attack helicopters had so much inherent power. It spoke to my inner twelve year old, that's for sure. And to see both Dale and Michael riff on that image and refine it was really gratifying.

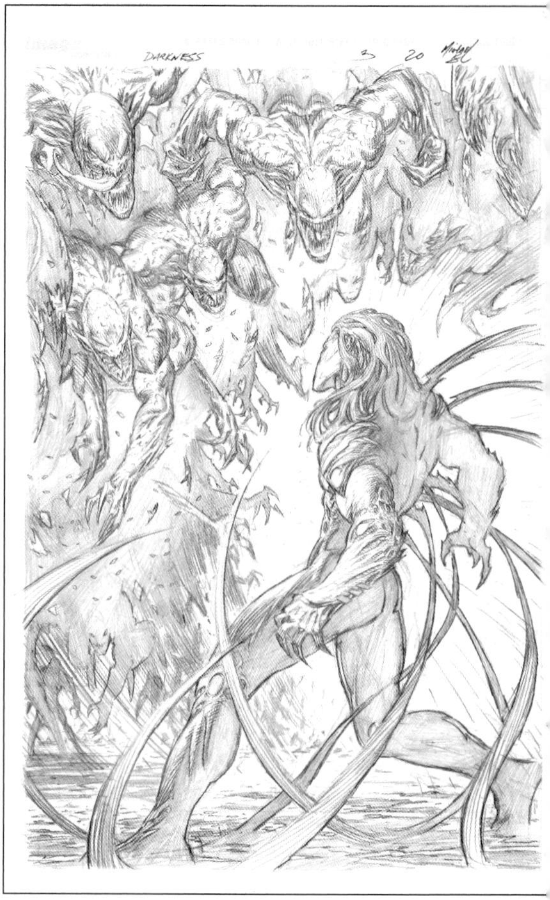

The Darkness vol.3, issue #3, pg. 20
"Body Language"

MB: One thing I had to be careful of was the composition on this page, this one was tricky, I had to make sure he read as being attacked. The retreating stance and shoulder posture help sell it.